DISPLACEMENT, IMPOVERISHMENT AND EXCLUSION
Political Economy of Development in India

Edited by
Sujit Kumar Mishra
R Siva Prasad

LONDON AND NEW YORK

AAKAR

In the Memory of
Late Prof. R S Rao
Sambalpur University, Odisha

First published 2021
by Routledge
2 Park Square, Milton Park, Abingdon, Oxon OX14 4RN

and by Routledge
52 Vanderbilt Avenue, New York, NY 10017

Routledge is an imprint of the Taylor & Francis Group, an informa business

Co-published with Aakar Books, New Delhi. Print edition not for sale in South Asia (India, Sri Lanka, Nepal, Bangladesh, Pakistan or Bhutan)

British Library Cataloguing-in-Publication Data
A catalogue record for this book is available from the British Library

Library of Congress Cataloging-in-Publication Data
A catalog record for this book has been requested

ISBN: 978-0-367-61885-8 (hbk)
ISBN: 978-1-003-10699-9 (ebk)

Typeset in Palatino
by Arpit Printographers, New Delhi 110092

AAKAR

Contents

Foreword

This book edited by Dr. Sujit Kumar Mishra and Prof. R Siva Prasad deals with contemporary issues relating to the political economy of development in India. The foremost among them is the very meaning, purpose and objective of development. Questions being asked today are what development ultimately amounts to? Who are its beneficiaries? And what is the position of the state as a stakeholder in the process of development? Another issue being debated today is the institutional instruments devised by the state to mediate in the process of development. The chapters on this topic deal with the principles and objectives which should guide the state machinery entrusted with the task of development. Another construct which has acquired salience recently and is discussed in the book, is the importance and role of 'development community' in the process of development. How should this construct be defined? What legitimacy it has? And how it can be enabled to play its due role as an agent and beneficiary of development?

The above issues have been examined in this book with the help of a number of case studies from across the nation, of problems faced by the people displaced by development projects. It emerges from case after case that the development community defined as those adversely affected by development projects, are neglected in the process of the negotiation for the projects. Besides, in these negotiations, the wider purposes of development, as defined by Professor Amartya Sen, i.e. development as freedom and as the creation of capabilities, are totally ignored. Finally, the book advances suggestions on how the re-settlement of people displaced from projects can be done in a just, fair and effective manner. The main recommendation is that the regulatory mechanism and institution should consciously involve the development community in the negotiations for the project and take into cognizance its perception on the consequences of intervention for development.

Development has been defined in the Oxford Dictionary as "a change in conditions" or "a stage of advancement" or "the realization of full potential". From this it appears that development is a continuing process. It is happening all the time. What is important is its pace and the extent to which it brings about changes in conditions. Development to be worthwhile cannot be business as usual. It cannot proceed on the basis of the state or society getting reconciled to the status quo. It is for this reason that concepts such as "big push", "all around transformation" and "stages of development" were introduced in the literature on development.

Industrialization plays a key role in the process of transformation of an economy and has, therefore, been regarded as the next important stage of development for an economy which is basically agricultural or depends on a single or a few primary commodities for deriving national income. India's Second Development Plan conceived by Jawaharlal Nehru and Professor P.C. Mahalanobis was predicated on the India economy making a transition to the stage of industrialization. The celebrated Argentinean economist Raul Prebisch regarded transition to industrialization as inevitable for the realization of the full potentials of the Latin American economies. Like Nehru and Mahalanobis, Prebisch believed in import substitution as an important strategy for making a transition to the stage of industrialization. According to him, for smaller Latin America economies, import substitution was possible only by the enlargement of market through regional or sub-regional integration. Thus, one of the major contributions of Prebisch in the realism of development, was the role assigned in it to sub-regional and regional integration. Prebisch played a pioneering role in translating this concept into reality in Latin America.

W.W. Rostow introduced the concept of "stages" of development through which developing countries have to transit in order to reach what he called "the take off" stage or the stage after which development sustains itself by its own momentum without the infusion of massive capital or other factors of production. After the "take off", the economy becomes self-sustained. We will see later that in the late 1980s, sustainability acquired a somewhat different connotation.

In the first decade and a half of the post-Second World War period, development was identified with growth, that is, rate of increase in national and the per capita incomes. Wider purposes of development, such as all round structural changes in the economy and the building of human capability mainly through progress in health and education, did not come into play during this period. It was also not appreciated that the participation by the people in the process of development was as important as the deployment of inputs for development. Theodore Schultz played the pioneering role by his research in underlining the importance of the human factor for development. Amartya Sen was mainly responsible for highlighting 'expansion of human capability', 'exercise of freedom' and 'widening of choices' as important objectives of development. He regarded them as having both intrinsic and instrumental values, that is, both as an end result of as well as contributory factors for development.

The United Nations became pre-occupied with the issue of development right from its inception. One of the principal objectives of the U.N., as stated in its Preamble, is "to promote social progress and better standards of life in larger freedom". This has been elaborated in Article 55 as the promotion of "higher standards of living, full employment and conditions of economic and social progress and development".

It soon became clear to the membership of the United Nations that in the pursuit of these objectives, the top priority had to be attached to the development of developing countries. The objective of development that the U.N. pursued till the mid-1960s was in terms of accretion to the national incomes of member nation, particularly the less developed among them. When wider objectives of development acquired salience starting from the mid-60s, the United Nations was the first to embrace it. It was from the pulpit of the United Nations that for the first time the call was given for the effective participation of the people in the process of development. Then the U.N. made meeting the basic needs of the people and alleviating poverty as its primary concern. A direct link between amelioration of poverty and the U.N.'s core objective of promoting peace and prosperity was promptly perceived. The phrase, "poverty anywhere is a threat to prosperity everywhere" acquired currency. It was at that time that Pope John came out with the aphorism that 'development is another name of peace'. In spite of these welcome shifts, growth remained at the centre of U.N.'s pre-occupation with development. The 1960s was declared the First U.N. Development Decade and at average growth target of five percent per annum for developing countries, was agreed upon as the objective to be realized during the decade. In the International Development Strategy for the second U.N. Development Decade (i.e. the 1970s) a higher average overall growth rate for the decade was agreed upon and a whole set of measures were negotiated in the fields of trade, domestic mobilization of resources and flow of finances to developing countries, to realize these goals.

By the end of the decade, it became clear that the pursuit of an annual average growth rate for the developing world as a whole was both elusive and not of much operational significance. As a result, the objective of achieving higher rates of growth in national incomes was virtually jettisoned and attention came to be focused mainly on the elimination of poverty. The Millennium Development Goals (MDGs) represented a high point in the diversion of U.N.'s focus from development as a process of change and as accretion in national and per capita incomes to achieving goals like the elimination of poverty and quantifiable targets in the social fields.

By the end of the first decade of the new millennium, negotiations started on the replacement of the MDGs. This gave rise to the hope that in this process the U.N. would revert to its original pursuit of development in the sense of structural transformation, without which goals like those put in the MDGs made little sense. However, by the end of this exercise, the member states could not agree on the logical approach of reviving the broad development agenda, and instead launched upon a new set of goals under the title "Sustainable Development Goals" (SDGs). No doubt, some important conceptual advances were made in the negotiations for the SDG's. Firstly, bringing in the element of sustainability to the concept of development itself was of considerable significance. This related development to climate change and future management of resources. Sustainability was defined as "meeting the needs of the present generation without compromising the ability of the future generations to meet their needs". Secondly, this time, the goals in different sectors were defined in an inter-related and holistic manner and the measures recommended were of both for the medium and long term. Taken to its logical extent, the best outcome would have been to prescribe the Gandhian precept of meeting the need and not the greed of every one. This aspect of sustainability, however, did not command acceptance. Developed member countries resolutely objected to any mention of bringing about a change in the life styles of their peoples in order to meet the needs of the future generation.

Development as originally conceived meant the development of the nation or of the people as a whole. That is why it was denominated in terms of growth in national income. From this was derived the notion of average per capita income, after taking into account the growth in population. No dichotomy was seen at that time between state-centric and people-centric development. Moreover, development was not seen as a source of revenue for the government. Government was involved as an agency to promote development of the nation or the people, and not as a beneficiary of its products. It is true that as development accelerated, the state benefitted from the opportunity it created for collecting larger revenue through taxation and other devices. But these revenues were supposed to be invested for achieving still higher rate of growth or for direct disbursement for welfare and social security purposes.

Recently there is a tendency on the part of governments, very much in evidence in India, to make investment in social sectors and provision of resources for welfare measures, dependent on higher rate of growth which is supposed to result in enhancement of government revenues. This is nothing but an attempt by the government to evade their primary responsibility for investing in these sectors. This logic acquires a more sinister dimension when one finds that lack of resources is used as an excuse by the government to hand over the responsibility of delivering social services which are in the nature of public goods, to the private sector. Knowing that the private sector has no incentive for delivering such services directly or creating institutions to do so, the net result is the commercialization of these services to the detriment of goal of sustainable development and the interest of the marginalized sections of society. This is done by various means including direct privatization, resort to public-private-partnership (PPP) mode, disinvestment of public sector enterprises and acquisition by the government of natural resources for transfer to the private sector. Acquisition of land for this purpose has far-reaching consequences. A number of chapters in this book are devoted to dealing with this dimension of development projects.

Finally a word on the concept of development community brought in the analysis in several chapters of the book. The development community is defined in the book in negative terms i.e. those who are at the wrong end of development projects which result in displacement or those who are adversely affected by development projects. It will make greater sense from the point of view of clarity of analysis and policy perspective if the term development community is defined in a broader context, embracing people who are benefitting from development projects as well as those who are adversely affected by them. The development community will acquire bona fide if it is so recognized statutorily by established authorities like the *Gram Sabha*, according to a well laid down criteria and transparent procedure.

The real issue in contemporary debate on this subject is how to reconcile the wider national purpose served by development projects with the impact they have on the development community. The consensus that seems to have emerged on this matter is that the professed wider national interest should not be allowed to be pursued at the cost of the interest of the affected community. This is firstly because it is simply unjust and hence unethical; and secondly, it will not work because neglect of or damaging the interest of the affected people will sooner or later emerge as the biggest constraint to the implementation of the project. Evidence shows that it may even lead to conflict and violence, having much wider implications for society as a whole. It is, therefore, not surprising that a major provision in the Right to Fair Compensation and Transparency in Land Acquisition, Rehabilitation and Resettlement Act 2013., is to make a social impact assessment before a project involving displacement of people is taken up for implementation. The Act was duly notified but before its implementation could start, the new government at the Centre passed an Ordinance incorporating drastic revisions in the Act. One of the casualties in the revision made in the Ordinance was the obligation to conduct social impact assessment before the implementation of any project involving displacement of people. As the replacement of the Ordinance by a new Act did not command the support of the Parliament, the Ordinance was allowed to lapse. However, the Central Government allowed States to amend their own land acquisition, rehabilitation and resettlement laws taking into account the provisions of the Ordinance as guidelines. Accordingly, several states have amended their laws and in the process substantially diluted and departed from the Act of the Parliament, thus, in effect scuttling it. In any case, this Act remains unimplemented.

Given the importance of the subject, the Council for Social Development has remained pre-occupied with various aspects of it for a long time. I led a team of three experts to enquire into the procedure followed by the Government of Orissa for acquiring land for companies with which it had signed Memoranda of Understanding or Contracts, for bauxite mining. We particularly looked into the excesses committed by the state law and order authorities against the project affected people who resisted the acquisition of their land, and the NGOs who mobilized and supported them for claiming their legitimate rights. The Report that we submitted after our field visit was one of the earliest reports on the subject. It attracted widespread attention and was cited in the report of commission of enquiry on this case. The Council also painstakingly analyzed the different versions of the bill on acquisition of land and the resettlement of project displaced persons, under consideration by the Central Government at different stages, and made the outcome of its analysis available to the public. One of the issues of the flagship publication of the Council, namely, *India: Social Development Report* was devoted to Land Acquisition and Resettlement. Since the publication of this Report, the Council has been conducting an annual training workshop on the subject every year. One of the projects recently undertaken and completed by the Council on behalf of the Ministry of Rural Development, Government of India, was the preparation of guidelines for social impact assessment of projects involving land acquisition and displacement. This book is a part of our continuing involvement with this crucial issue.

With my observations in the above paragraphs on some of the issues raised in the book, I commend it to policy makers, researchers and other experts in the subject, civil society organizations working in this area and general readers. I have reasons to believe that they will find the book interesting and derive much benefit from it.

Muchkund Dubey
President
Council for Social Development
New Delhi
July 12, 2017

Acknowledgements

We are grateful to Prof. Muchkund Dubey, President, Council for Social Development (CSD), New Delhi for the foreword written to this book. Prof Kalpana Kannabiran, Director, CSD, Hyderabad has been a constant source of encouragement without whose support the publication of this book would not have been possible. Our special thanks to Indian Council for Social Science Research, New Delhi for the financial help to conduct the seminar from where the book is an outcome. The present book contains 13 papers, selected from the national seminar titled 'Impoverishment vs. Reconstruction in Development Induced Displacement: Approaches and Issues' organized by CSD, Hyderabad. We are equally thankful to Prof. D Narasimha Reddy, Professor of Economics (Rtd) from University of Hyderabad and Shri B P Acharya, IAS, Special Chief Secretary, Government of Telangana for the comments made on the book. We wish to thank all the co-authors for their contributions.

Prof. B N Yugandhar has been very supportive of our work and in bringing out this volume. Our very special thanks to Prof. K B Saxena and Prof. Hari Mohan Mathur for their valuable feedback and suggestions at different stages. Late Dr. Vasudha Dhagamwar meticulously went through all the papers and offered her comments. We thank Mr. M V Kannan for the comments on each and every chapter of the book. Our thanks to Dr. Jafar K for designing cover page of the book. Special mention need to be made of each and every members of CSD, Hyderabad especially Mr. K Sanjiva Rao, Mr. Y S S Prasad, Ms.

K Mahalakshmi, Mr. P S Nagesh and Mr. P Kumar for their support for compiling the book. Our publisher Mr. K K Saxena of Aakar Books, Delhi needs a special mention for his consistent support with patience and good humour.

Sujit Kumar Mishra
R Siva Prasad

Introduction

Sujit Kumar Mishra
R Siva Prasad

When we deal with the idea of 'Political Economy of Development' in the context of displacement, the immediate concern that requires one's attention is a conceptual clarity on the issue of 'development'. Does it refer to increase in income or is it an improvement in the socio-economic condition or what else? There are several views on this debate. Amartya Sen in his work 'Development as Freedom' introduced the word 'freedom' as both means and ends in development (Sen, 1999). His focus was largely in terms of 'choices', 'capabilities' and 'freedom'. The rise in the social and spatial disparities within the society as experienced during the recent decades highlights the importance of these terms in redefining the concept of 'development'. With the inclusion of 'choices', 'capabilities' and 'freedom', the impact of development will be shared homogeneously across the entire group, which we call them the 'development communities'. Otherwise, it will be a simple depiction of arithmetic mean for the entire mass. Development Community refers to the community who always pay the cost of development. For example, most of the time, these are the people thrown from their habitats when the development projects are land based (largely irrigation projects); in case of mining projects, they are the ones who pay the cost in the form of externalities—agriculture, health and livelihood (Mishra, 2008; Mishra and Pujari, 2010; Mishra, 2012). Veiga, Scoble and McAllister (2001: 191-192) call them as Mining Community and define them 'as a community where the population is significantly affected by a nearby mining operation'.

A 'state-centric' view of development always tries to maximize its profit (be it a dam, mine, park, sanctuary, etc.). This view of development generally involves the nexus of 'state, development intervention and the development community' where the main objective of the development intervention is to add large revenue to the State's economy. For instance, the two mineral rich districts of Odisha (namely Sundargarh and Jharsuguda) contribute to the State's exchequer, as can be seen from the figures of 2010-11 (Government of Odisha, 2015). The institutional parameters are instrumental in this success. However, these mechanisms are limited to few stages of development, giving very little space to the development communities.

Much has been talked and debated about the impact of the so called 'development' on local communities in India, and rightly so, as the impact of development (in terms of large dams, mine, roads, infrastructure projects, etc.) on socio-economic, cultural and ecological aspects of local community over the years are getting increasingly disturbed. Globally, 'development communities' all over share several common characteristics in terms of the environmental, social, economic, or other impacts, and the impact sharing mechanisms.

One such impact is displacement and India is the best case study for this as large number of States in it, truly depicted the displacement scenario of the country. According to Mathur (2008), 'displacement is not uncommon in the development process, but it is its expanding size and adverse impacts that are now a cause for serious concern'. Displacement, until recently, remained not only a non-issue in the public policy discourse (Saxena, 2008) but also hindered the achievement of millennium development goals and compromised the future of our country. It is largely connected with land as it is one of the most important indicators that impact the outcome of development. In this context, land acquisition has emerged as the biggest hindrance to this so called development (Chakravorty, 2013). The problem arising out of land acquisition is not new. It has been there since last so many decades, for instance, Hirakud Dam, Narmada Dam, Rengali Dam, Posco, Tata Nano, Rourkela Steel Plant, Yamuna Express Way, Singur, etc. However, it gained momentum very recently, thanks to the civil society organizations and the media, due to which several interventions got cancelled at the land acquisition stage. A lucid picture on the classification of agitations related to land acquisition has been made in a study by Chakravorty (2013). He broadly categorized them into two – (i) price-based, and (ii) over land use. Some people want more prices to their land and allow acquisition, whereas for some their land is priceless and do not wish to part with it. According to him, the seller of the land should be 'willing' and 'informed'. The entire game of land acquisition centres on these two words. In a different form, Government of India (2007) uses the word 'consultation' for a sustainable resettlement. Mishra (2016) and Kannabiran and Mishra (2016) differentiated 'consultation' and 'consent' as two different concepts, since the victims own no right to say 'no' when the project site is identified.

Whenever India talks about development through some interventions - whether it is construction of large dams or recent demonetization, it is usually stated that it is 'for the nation' or 'for the country'. Who does it intended for when it talks of 'nation' or 'country'? Who are the ones at the receiving end? A simple answer to these questions is the 'marginalized communities'. The famous statement of Pandit Jawaharlal Nehru, the first Prime Minister of India, during the construction of the longest earthen dam of the world, Hirakud Dam in Odisha, is quite apt to cite here. He stated that 'if you are to suffer, you should suffer in the interest of the country' (*The Bombay Chronicle*, April 12, 1948 quoted by Kothari, 1996). Here a question can be raised—why the marginalized communities always and why not the others? Examples are aplenty. For example, a large number of households became wage labourers in the case of Rengali Multipurpose Dam Project in Odisha (Mishra, 2002). Even after the passage of a long time some Hirakud Dam affected households are still struggling for their pending compensation (*The New Indian Express*, December 8,

2016). Capital penetration for 'development' has not included the marginalized sections of society into a capitalistic framework, rather has alienated them from it (Nath, 1998).

There are some who have better knowledge and resources always gain in the process of development. As Arundhati Roy (1999) rightly says, 'those who know, know a lot. Most know nothing at all'. It is observed in few cases where some of the households approached courts and demanded higher compensation for their land, trees and even for the business environment that they lost. Many of them won the cases and received enhanced compensation (Mishra 2002). If we look at their background, these are the few knowledgeable and land-owning people who derived the fruits of development in many different ways. There is another group, consisting of a larger number of 'livelihood losers' and they are intentionally ignored from the ambit of development. They generally depend on others' land for their sustenance. It was observed that many of them end up in scavenging in the mining areas or other demeaning occupations (Rao, 2005; Mishra and Mishra, 2014). The State depicts them as illegal miner and hence, are not eligible for availing any benefit included in the institutional mechanisms.

Two major issues emerge from the above discussions: (i) asymmetry of information between the project authority and the development communities; and (ii) skewed participation of the development communities in the bargaining process. Many of the following issues puzzle the development communities: (i) what is the nature of compensation? (ii) who will receive the compensation? (iii) who will decide the amount or quantum of compensation? (iv) how much will be the quantum of compensation?

As Lahiri-Dutt (2007: 60) rightly observes, 'the legal instruments are colonial vintage, anti-poor and are unable to deal with contemporary realities'. From the different studies on the impact of development projects, we can notice a vast majority of the people are rendered totally vulnerable as they could not restore any semblance of their previous quality of life (Mishra, 2016). In this context another issue which needs discussion here is financing resettlement and rehabilitation (R & R). According to Reddy (2011), financing in settlement and rehabilitation involves not only financial but also other institutional financial elements. He further argued that financial compensation is not the only way of settlement as there are issues which need to be equally prioritized. According to him, legally empowered independent institutional mechanism need to be put in place in order to address an array of issues pertaining to R & R. In his opinion, a comprehensive view, which is democratic and sensitive, should be taken. To assess the cost of displacement, an independent cost assessment, both direct and indirect, independent of the project, should be taken. One has to think beyond the conventional way of R & R practised in India by incorporating models of certain practises elsewhere (In China, there exists a system of direct transfer of returns to people displaced, in Japan there exists a practise of leasing the land in place of land acquisition where in rent to the displaced is reviewed periodically and in Canada, there is a system of equity participation in projects). In sum, he pointed out that only a legally empowered structure can address sustainable financing of resettlement. Thrust of the argument was that lack of resources is not the problem but the lack of agency is.

In this context, this book is based on the following research questions:

- What are the existing institutional mechanisms that attempt to regulate development induced displacement in India?
- What is the impact of regulatory institutions and mechanisms on the communities in India?

Organization of the Book

This book is intended to present the contemporary research work and the related outcomes on the cross-cutting theme of development induced displacement. The contributors to this volume represent a wide background: government, research institutions, universities, civil society, NGOs and international development agencies. They take a pluri-displinary perspective, seeking to draw on concepts and arguments relevant to R & R that come from diverse disciplines. This book consists of 13 chapters organised in to two distinct thematic sections. They are (i) legal instruments; and (ii) impact of regulatory institutions on communities.

Part I: Legal Instruments

This section starts with a broader discussion on development and subsequently the different legal instruments designed by the State to achieve development. Using interesting and relevant case studies, the first four chapters address these issues theoretically and practically. While Vasudha Dhagamwar argued about a narrow and short sighted understanding of the phenomenon called development in the first chapter, R Siva Prasad in the second chapter emphasized that piecemeal approach to development is more dangerous than no development. Vasudha cited many examples from her own experience of different types of projects in India – Narmada, Durgapur Steel, Steel Authority of India Limited, Rourkela, Koel Karo Basin, Posco, etc., and examines not only the scenario of displacement but also the relevance of R & R. She focused on different issues like the Land Acquisition Act 1894 and their impact. On the other hand, R Siva Prasad analyzed the major development initiatives in the tribal and backward areas, and the way in which development is being viewed by the policy makers, academics and civil society organizations and its consequences for the betterments of tribal and poor.

Beginning with the classical economists to the modern welfare economists, various views on distributive aspects are critically analyzed and compared with contemporary situation of development by Sanatan Nayak in the third chapter. Sanatan Nayak attempted to find out some of the observations on displacement and development through the established theories of classical, neo-classical and modern economists.

K B Saxena, in the fourth chapter, argued that land acquisition affects all the prominent indicators of vibrant society, such as equity, democracy and governance, which in turn influence the overall economic development. He observed that India had a poor track record when it comes to resettlement, though India had a greater success with resettlement of people affected with partition. He argued that India did not have a Land Acquisition Policy for a long time. He argues that land acquisition should be minimum and through consensus of the displaced and confined to the Sovereign (the Government). The reduced land acquisition brings about small scale displacement and thereby reduces conflict. While throwing light on existing laws on land acquisition, Saxena called for a single law in the place of existing multiple laws. He also argued that the recently introduced policy on land acquisition should be modified in order to make it sensitive to fragile communities and rehabilitation should be addressing the community rather than the individual.

While recognize the fact that Government of India had introduced many institutional mechanisms in terms of activities like act, policies and schemes for development induced displaced population, the present book can be considered as an attempt to see their effectiveness in the ground and use the experience of Indian States to explore how they work locally. The experience in various regions of India suggests that the engagement of civil society organizations with development projects and displacement issues had some positive effects on identifying the weakness of the existing mechanisms and greater attention to its importance from the policy makers and general public alike. In several contexts, it has led to conflict situations following agitations and resistance with wider participation at grass root level participation and awareness. Thus, it has reduced the information asymmetry exist in the field and made the concerned authorities to rethink about the existing mechanisms and introduce new strategies. For instance, it led to the introduction of Social Impact Assessment (SIA) to identify risks, develop counter strategies against the identified risk factors which in turn become helpful in developing a sound rehabilitation action plan. By implementing the National Resettlement and Rehabilitation Policy (NRRP) 2007, the Government made it mandatory for all project authorities to conduct a proper SIA before undertaking any projects. The fifth chapter by Rudra Prasad Sahu is a depiction of the conceptual and methodological framework undertaken for conducting SIA. While acknowledging the benefits of SIA as a tool for social development by measuring and analyzing the social cost of an ongoing project in the particular human settlement, the presents a critical analysis of NRRP 2007 in the light of new innovation in social and cultural thinking and SIA and makes the book more interesting.

Felix Padel in chapter six, and Charu Singh and Sujit Kumar Mishra in chapter seven present a detailed critique of the present institutional mechanisms. They also provide useful suggestions on how rehabilitation of involuntarily displaced people might be more effective and fair. Felix Padel presented an anthropological view of development induced displacement. He pointed that it is impossible to define projects displacing large number of people from their natural habitat as 'development', since these projects lead to massive impoverishment, neglect and injustice to those displaced. He also criticised the NRRP 2007 for not recommending full land for land compensation, the ambiguity in cash compensation and job offer packages, lack of recognition for self-employment, defining cultivators as unskilled. He also criticized the lack of adequate training programmes for the displaced in any of the R & R packages so far implemented. Padel lamented that none of the R & R policies account for people's voices nor takes the fate of 'communities'. Community gets divided or uprooted by projects, their economies are completely delinked from ecology and the entire social structure is destroyed. This is compounded by the vast amount of corruption, violence and anti-social activities in the process of implementation of R & R policies. Thus, displacement often leads to cultural genocide and ecocide —the fragile balance between economy and ecology nurtured and built over generations by communities are destroyed. In addition, none of the promises of land, water, electricity, health and education for the displaced are met with. The displaced, especially the tribals, remain dispossessed and are the worst affected.

Based on their research work Charu Singh and Sujit Kumar Mishra[1] have implied at better functioning of the institutional parameters like additions of new components like SIA, the process of consultation and etc in the rehabilitation policy, amendments in the Land Acquisition Act, conducting training for the people on the issue of R & R, inclusion of compulsory *gram sabha* and good infrastructure facilities in some of the rehabilitation centres. They also identified quite a lot of indicators which led to the institutional incapacities in the entire system. In this context, weak extension services, poor coordination across administrative bodies, dysfunctional relationship between the planner and the affected groups, poor implementation and skewed government intervention have emerged as the foremost impediment to the rehabilitation process. Hence, they suggested that in order to improve the status of rehabilitation, it is necessary that a system be created for increasing preparedness at all levels, i.e., government, civil society and community, to effectively reactivate these institutions in performing the roles they are intended for.

One of the striking features inherent in the present book is the examination of relationship between local level institutions and the outcome of development in India. It problematizes the ambiguous role that local authorities play in supporting the rights of displaced people on certain contexts while opposing their resistance to displacement on other. Satyapriya Rout and Pratyunsa Patnaik, in the chapter eight on 'Neo-liberal Development, Displacement and Exclusion: Tribal Resistance to Vedanta', explore the roots of tribal resistance to the process of neo-liberal development and resulting displacement. Taking the struggle against Vedanta Alumina in the State of Odisha as a case in point, they argue that resource capture by the State and its allies, justified in the name of national development, have always resulted in livelihood insecurity, marginalization and exclusion of Scheduled Tribes; and have challenged their cultural integrity. Such a process of exclusion has become more severe in the wake of globalization and liberalization, when the private capitalist interests have joined hand with the nation-state to carry forwards their neo-liberal mandate. This chapter explains that the neo-liberal development initiatives in the tribal regions have not only resulted in displacement of tribal communities, but have proved to be an onslaught on their cultural traditions and customary practices. Further, it indicates that transformation in agrarian relations and changes in feudal modes of production had several adverse implications for the tribal communities.

Part II: Impact of Regulatory Institutions on Communities

This section of the book explores the relationship between the regulatory institutions and mechanisms and its impact through interesting and relevant case studies from across the country by Bhaskar Majumder on Uttar Pradesh (ninth chapter), K Anil Kumar on Andhra Pradesh (chapter ten), D C Sah and Subhra Singh Tomar on Narmada (chapter eleven), Richa Minocha on Himachal Pradesh (chapter twelve) and Suresh Reddy on Telangana (chapter thirteen). The thread that connects these five chapters in different geographical locations of India is the concept called 'exclusion' of the development communities from the development process.

Bhaskar Majumder focuses on recent experiences on displacement by acquisition of agricultural land for setting up and expansion of industries both in public and private sectors in Uttar Pradesh as a case of delayed industrialization. This chapter examines critically the role of the State in this context and suggests safeguards. D C Sah and Subhra Singh Tomar in their chapter documented some of the controversies associated with Sardar Sarovar Project, like the sharing the benefits and cost of the project between Gujarat, Madhya Pradesh and Maharashtra; agitation for relocation and rehabilitation policy; estimation of social and environmental costs and economic benefits. This paper tried to find out important lessons from the project, so that mistakes committed in SSP can be avoided in future development projects. K Anil Kumar's chapter titled 'Displacement of Tribal People in the Name of Development: A Case Study of Indira Sagar Project in Andhra Pradesh' sheds light on the problems of dam-induced displacement in the State of Andhra Pradesh. This chapter attempts to understand the problems of dam-induced displacement and impoverishment risks from an empirical study in the State of Andhra Pradesh. It discusses about reconstruction plans and policy issues on dam-induced displacement. The chapter by Richa Minocha titled 'Development at what Cost? A Study of Migration, Loss of Livelihood Security and Development-Induced Displacement in Himachal Pradesh' has been an overview of major development projects in Himachal Pradesh and the pattern in which they have reinforced caste and gender bias. In Himachal Pradesh, the resists led by the project affected people in many places and the criticism around the Government's policy followed while implementing some of the recent projects highlights the importance of reviewing their impacts on local people, local economy and ecology and possible alternatives. Apart from this the development paradigm is undermining the basis of the equilibrium (ecological and social) which had evolved over generations leading to much loss of indigenous knowledge, effective conservation methods and the language in which local values and cultures are communicated.

Apart from development projects, growth of new cities in India also is cause of rapid displacement of people. Creation of cities are the central factors involved in the variation of geography, production and finance (Naerssen, 2001). Rao (2010) considers it as 'emerging objects of theory, debate and policy intervention'. In his chapter titled 'Emergence of Megacity: Impact on Poor – An Analysis based on the Field Study in the Peri-Urban Areas of Hyderabad' in the present book Suresh Reddy also argued that the urban poor are unable to understand the change (land alienation – loss of livelihood) that is taking place given the boom of real estate and influence of middle men and realtors. The urban poor have sold their lands at cheap rates and the basic facilities in the event of displacement in relocated areas are found to be inadequate. The paper argued for protection of assigned lands to Dalits who are often misled and threatened by real estate agents to sell their lands. The author in his suggestions put forth the need for an advocacy cell to guide the urban poor and Dalits and called for uniformity of land records and people friendly revenue system.

Concluding Remark

This book has attempted to draw attention to a multiplicity of issues related to the side effects of development projects, though, in fact, development is intended for growth of a nation. These issues have been addressed through a collection of thirteen papers. Development community is the only thread that connects all the issues as they feature in the entire discussion. All these examples reflect the failure of the classic thought of 'Development as Freedom' propounded by Amartya Sen, where 'choices', capabilities' and 'freedom' are the three main pillars of development. However, in all the examples cited in the book, the roles of these three indicators are found to be almost nil. The most important point is lack of proper dissemination of information. In this crucial process, where obtaining consent plays an imperative responsibility in the resettlement process, the analysis of the thirteen essays in the book finds the absence of negotiation element from the entire regulatory mechanism. Therefore, our regulatory institutions and mechanisms should emerge after exploring the development communities' perceptions on the intervention so that the development will be called as development with 'choices', capabilities' and 'freedom'.

NOTE

1. Earlier version of this chapter has been presented at the International Conference on Development induced Displacement and Resettlement by Refugee Studies Centre, University of Oxford on 22-23 March, 2013.

REFERENCES

Chakravorty, Sanjoy. 2013. *The Price of Land Acquisition Conflict Consequence.* New Delhi: Oxford University Press.

Government of India. 2007. *National Rehabilitation and Resettlement Policy, 2007.* Ministry of Rural Development, Department of Land Resources, Land Reforms Division, New Delhi.

Government of Odisha. 2015. *Odisha Economic Survey 2014-15.* Planning and Coordination Department, Directorate of Economics and Statistics, Government of Odisha

Kannabiran, K. and S K Mishra. 2016. *Measuring Institutionalized Capacities for Development Projects in India*. New Delhi: Indian Council of Social Science Research.

Kothari, S. 1996. 'Whose Nation? The Displaced as Victims of Development,' *Economic and Political Weekly* 31, No. 24: 1476-1485.

Lahilri- Dutt, K. 2007. 'Illegal Coal Mining in Eastern India: Rethinking Legitimacy and Limits of Justice,' *Economic and Political Weekly* 42, No. 49: 57-66.

Mathur, H M. 2008. 'Introduction and Overview'. In *India Social Development Report 2008 Development and Displacement*, edited by H M Mathur. New Delhi: Oxford University Press.

Mishra, P P. 2010. 'Economic Valuation of Health Impacts in a Coal Mining Region.' *Review of Development and Change* 15, No. 02: 183-200.

Mishra, P P. and A K Pujari. 2008. 'Impact of Mining on Agricultural Productivity: A Case Study of the Indian State of Orissa.' *South Asia Economic Journal* 09, No. 02: 337-350.

Mishra, P P. and S K Mishra. 2014. 'Coal Mining and Local Livelihoods.' *Economic and Political Weekly* 49, No. 08: 25-26.

Mishra, S K. 2002. *Development and Displacement: A Case Study of Rengali Dam in Orissa, India*. PhD Thesis, University of Hyderabad, Hyderabad.

Mishra, S K. 2012. *Coal Mining Externalities: A Study in Basundhara Coalfield, India*. New Delhi: Indian Council of Social Science Research.

Mishra, S K. 2016. 'Dispossessed by Development: Mining, Habitations, Lives and Livelihoods'. In *India Social Development Report 2016 Disability Rights Perspectives*, edited by K Kannabiran and A Hans. New Delhi: Oxford University Press.

Naerssen, T V. 2001. 'Cities and the Globalization of Urban Development Policy.' In *Globalization and Development Studies: Challenges for the 21st Century*, edited by F Schuuman. New Delhi: Vistar Publications.

Nath, G B. 1998. *Socio-Economic Re-Survey of a Village Submerged under Rengali Dam Project*. New Delhi: Indian Council of Social Science Research.

Rao, N. 2005. 'Displacement from Land: Case of Santhal Praganas.' *Economic and Political Weekly* 40, No. 41: 4439-42.

Rao, V. 2010. 'Slum as Theory', *Editoriale Lotus*, 143.

Reddy, D N. 2011. 'Financing Resettlement and Rehabilitation.' Paper presented in the National Seminar Impoverishment vs Reconstruction in Development induced Displacement:

Approaches and Issues.' February 18-19, 2011, Council for Social Development, Hyderabad.

Roy, Arundhati. 1999. 'The Greater Common Good', *Outlook,* May 24, 1999.

Saxena, K B. 2008. *Rehabilitation and Resettlement of Displaced Persons- A Critique of the Policy and the Bill.* New Delhi: Council for Social Development.

Sen, A. 1999. *Development as Freedom.* New Delhi: Oxford University Press.

The Bombay Chronicle. 1948. April 12, 1948.

The New Indian Express. 2016. 'Hirakud Oustees Demand Promised Land.' *The New Indian Express,* December 8, 2016.

Veiga, M M., M Scoble and M L McAllister. 2001. 'Mining with Communities.' *Natural Resources Forum,* 25: 191- 202.

1

The Development Debate: Listening to People First

Vasudha Dhagamwar

At the outset I must make a disclaimer. This is not a learned article; it is not replete with references, data, statistics or tables and chart. In the thirty years that I have been involved with the issue of rehabilitation, we have seen it all and it has got us nowhere. Other numbers can be produced and the battle loses focus. I am inclined to look at the overall or panoramic picture as has developed over the last half a century and make my deductions from what I can see.

My starting point is this: the development debate is no longer about displacement alone. It is also about resettlement and rehabilitation. This is why taking the views of affected people has become so crucial. What is it that they want? *Who are the people? Who are the PAPs* (Project Affected Person)?

My first premise is this: the affected people are not only the elderly. People are not only the landholders. They include the young and not so young. We must listen to all categories of affected people. And we must look at what they are doing. They may not want the same thing. What I notice is this: there are two sides to the debate on development and neither seems to pay attention to the people in the above sense. We are mesmerized by the landholders.

Roughly speaking, we can divide the debaters on displacement caused by development into pro and anti development lobbyists. Their stands have not changed over the years; rather, they have hardened. Both are equally passionate, and equally convinced that theirs is the only way. It reminds one of the Greek tale about two men standing on either side of a giant medallion, the two sides of which are made of two metals. One insists it is made of copper and the other that it is of silver. They nearly come to blows until a passerby makes them change sides. The Indian story of five blind men who decide what an elephant looks like by touching one part of the pachyderm bears a similar moral. Except their own selves there is no one here to make them see the other side of the coin and certainly they do not consider themselves to be blind.

Neither side is talking to the affected people. This is frequently true even of NGOs which claim to speak on behalf of the people threatened by displacement.

Let us look briefly at what the two sides say. Development is a good word for some and a very bad one for others. Those in favor of development are absolutely certain that a rosy future lies ahead of the country, if we go in for industry, urbanization, and infrastructure. They do not pay much heed to the people who must be displaced if the land is to be put to other uses. Those against it see it as leading to destruction and death of the helpless and hapless people who lie in the path of the juggernaut called development. Interestingly, both sides have an ambivalent view on environment and ecology. Spokespersons for forest dwellers hate wildlife being preserved at the cost of the villagers. The development lobby also steals land from national parks, marshes and riverbeds.

Either side has much in their own favour. Those who speak on behalf of the people have built up a strong case for their side. The problems they see can be divided into four or five points:

- Bad or inadequate laws and rules
- Inadequate provision for rehabilitation
- Poor administration
- Paucity of land for rehabilitation.
- Litany of broken promises.
- History of disastrous displacement and impoverishment.

These criticisms are based on experience although they do not always contain the whole truth. They overlook the history of the Land Acquisition Act and deny that a project can lead to satisfactory rehabilitation.

The much maligned Land Acquisition Act of 1894 was perfectly adequate for the limited needs of British Indian Government. They needed land for their army for urbanization, roads, and railways, schools and hospitals, even a few parks, zoological gardens, or a museum or two. The British were not into developing local industry. They were in the business of taking away raw material cheaply, converting it into finished products in Britain and then reselling it to India at a huge profit. Naturally they did not need land for factories or steel plants. or even textile mills. Most of them came up *Swadeshi* or nationalist endeavours. Secondly, land was plentiful and population relatively sparse. The people who were deprived of their land could move away a little, set up their village and clear some land for tillage. Life went on. Even in 1961, when Rihand Dam was constructed on the **UP-Bihar** border, the villagers were told to do just that. They moved up into the forest, felled trees and set themselves up on the old pattern. In 1980s when the UP Government needed to fill the quota for afforestation the twenty-years-old-villages were suddenly asked to produce papers or quit.

In short, the old Land Acquisition Act (LAA or LA Act or LA Bill) was quite adequate for its purposes. As we shall see, it no longer serves our changed socio-economic goals.

In independent India, we wanted to make our own finished goods; so we needed land for many more purposes. Industry needed power, that is, coal or electricity; we also wanted more water for irrigation in order to have better agricultural yields. Both irrigation and electricity called for dams. Pandit Nehru, our first Prime Minister, famously called them the new temples of India. At the same time, the old requirements remained; land was also needed for the Army, urbanization, roads, schools, hospitals, and so on. The economy of an independent, socialist India inevitably made more claims on resources, including land.

At the same time, the population was rising. If we remember

our Malthus, population rises geometrically. Let me give one of my few figures. In 1901, the population of British India was 200 million. This figure included princely states. In 1947, on the eve of partition the population was said to be 400 million. After correcting the land mass left in independent India for the gain of the princely states and was loss of Pakistan, clearly we have less land. In 2011 our population was over one billion or 1000 million. It is still rising and the land mass is not stretching away from either coast.

Until 1984, only the Government could acquire land. Everyone else had to buy it directly from the farmers. That put certain limits. But by 1950s we were in the era of public sector; thus, the Government began to acquire vast areas of land for public sector companies like the steel plants of Durgapur, Bhilai, Bokaro and Rourkela. By the 1980s we were also into private enterprise. The Land Acquisition Amendment Act, 1984 Act allowed public sector companies to acquire land directly and private sector companies to acquire through the Government. Acquisition is a process of compulsion. The farmer cannot refuse. He can only negotiate the price, but that too within limits. This leaves the farmer utterly at the mercy of the Government, making it a bad law.

In the original Land Acquisition Act, provision was made for cash compensation. There was no mention of resettlement and/or rehabilitation (R and R). Resettlement is literally resettling that is giving land for housing. Rehabilitation is to provide alternative livelihood, a more complex concept. As people and NGOs who led them became more aware of the implications, demand for both grew. Government began to pay lip service to this aspect. The Sardar Sarovar project plan document is four inches thick. Four lines are set aside for resettlement and rehabilitation. This was the extent to which the oustees—as they were called—were remembered. Because acquisition and rehabilitation were paired together, only landholders were considered as persons entitled to R and R and the landless were brushed away.

The rules under the LA Act laid down that once the first notice of impending acquisition was issued, no repairs could be made without Government permission. Anyone can see how long that would take. The idea was to prevent householders and farmers from improving the property to claim more compensation. It was a penny pinching rule. New construction is quite different from repair.

• **Poor administration**. The rules did not require officials to be slow. But they were. The lofty officials—they are all lofty by definition—would not deign to examine a lowly farmer's application for permission to repair a wall. It would remain pending. So a well which was caving in or a house wall in imminent danger of collapsing on those sleeping inside were left insecure. No bank would advance a loan. No department would mend a road or any other civic facility. And this went on for years. Compensation was not paid for decades. In 1974, in Akkalkua, (then in Dhule district now Nandurbar district in north west Maharashtra) the farmers who had lost their land to road widening had been waiting for twenty years for the compensation. There were other problems; as one of the Rihand farmers said, it was impossible to get a son married. The in laws were not sure of the groom's future circumstances. The bad rules were implemented even worse.

I have no access to records of acquisition before independence, or even till the Sardar Sarovar Dam (SSP) on the River Narmada. The administration may have been just as hostile to the peasants. But given that they could move just a little, sideways, perhaps the impact was not so terrifying. But from my experience in SSP, I can say that the Indian bureaucracy especially below the district level, puts one to shame. They threaten, they bully, and they misinform. They underestimate and undercount. They take pride in giving as little compensation as possible. For example, the price of a tree was calculated as it stood, without considering its future yield. But the petty official who looked at it up and down reduced its price as much as possible, as though he was going to pay out of his own pocket. As we saw, the rules were bad enough; their implementation was mindlessly brutal.

• **Paucity of land**. With the increasing demands for land and increase in population, it is not surprising that there was and is simply not enough land for satisfactory resettlement or rehabilitation. Over and above that the demands from NGOs were escalating. They demanded that the whole village should be not only resettled, but rehabilitated together as one unit. Resettlement was still possible but not rehabilitation, especially with the Government promising land to every major son.

NGOs notably the Narmada Bachao Andolan working for tribals as in the case of SSP demanded forest land so that their life style would not change drastically. But the forest laws were strict on that point. The forest cover had already depleted at an alarming rate. The number of people considered as Project Affected Persons (PAP) had been rightly increased to include the landless inhabitants of the affected region, as well as major sons and now daughters are being included. All of them are seen as entitled to not only resettlement but also to cultivable land.

• **Poor notions of R and R**. The earliest and largest land consuming projects were of dams. The oustees from them asked a single question-'Why do you want our land?' When the answer was 'To convert dry agricultural lands downstream into irrigated land', they demanded a share in those lands. But the demand was not an absolute one for land. It was a demand for a share in whatever their lands would create. It was by chance that the first major projects were for irrigation. But in the industrial projects like steel plants, the affected farmers did demand and get jobs. Unfortunately, we have forgotten that and our notions of rehabilitation flutter around land as the desired rehabilitation. The Maharashtra Resettlement and Rehabilitation Act 1976 specifies that every PAP should get irrigable land downstream of some dam. That may be far away from his original place; but when I asked the framer of the Act, Dr Adhav, he said 'In Maharashtra people will not want land. About 45 per cent of our population is already in urban settlements'. It goes without saying that this assumption cannot form the basis of a central law. In agrarian states in northern and eastern India, land is highly desirable not just for occupation but for the status it confers.

Nevertheless, the demand for jobs has been slowly making

itself felt; planners are now promising one job per family for the loss of a certain amount of land. In coal projects, the loss of three acres entitles one to a surface job. If the farmer loses only two acres then his son will get an underground job. It seems that the lives of poor may be put at risk. But now it transpires there are not enough unskilled jobs, not even in labour intensive coalmines. We now are in a situation where the Government would like to give cash compensation and land only for housing.

Currently, when acquiring land, the Government offers land for village resettlement unconditionally. But there is a caveat on rehabilitation: land for rehabilitation and jobs will be provided if available. The situation is fraught with uncertainty. It is a universal belief that the Government does not mean to keep its promises. It will deceive people and take away whatever they have and leave them destitute. That belief is grounded in experience. The net result has been a huge and potentially explosive trust deficit.

Most of the criticisms of the current model of development are valid. But they offer no satisfactory answer. Those against acquisition seem to have a simple solution. Stop acquisition. One can never cease to marvel at the anomaly of travelling by air to distant parts of the world to voice such demands, which requires using scarce resources in a profligate fashion. But hold on! If by some magic we do stop at absolutely this very moment, will it stop change? These are political and economic questions. Already, we have seen that the persons displaced by industrial projects are demanding jobs and not land. This is particularly true of the younger generation which sees no future in cultivation. The inviting prospects of a regular job with a salary that comes every month have to be seen to be believed. No more uncertainty about the next meal!

When the industrial sector promised one job per family of landholders, they did not realize what they were doing. The land was owned jointly by the family. All men and women worked on it and shared the produce. But the job was for one person. He alone worked at it and he got the wages. The joint family became a nuclear family in no time. We found this in Korba where men bluntly said they would try to support their parents but the brothers had no claim on them. So one job per family is not a solution either.

The professional middle class expects every grown member of the family to get a good job. Yet we expect the farmer to be satisfied with one job in the family! As we found in Korba, the son with the job refuses to share his money and the other sons will not look after their father as he favoured the other son.

Strangely, a potential PAP in Odisha—from the POSCO site—pointed out other solutions to me. He was a taxi driver, already unable to live in his village. He could drive a vehicle back home, he said. They would need so many services, from the corner and tea shop and the pan shop to cyber cafes for instance. Carpenters, cobblers and smiths would all find work. I found that he could think of so many opportunities. Getting a job would be lucky, he said, but there were other ways to earn a living in a new township. He gave me his mobile number, thinking I could actually do something for him.

As mentioned earlier, most of the criticisms of the current development model are valid. But none of them makes a case for stopping all development. None of them makes a case for preventing change in land use. They do make a case for better planning, of land resources and for people.

Even as there is opposition to land acquisition, the young men and women are flooding into cities. They do any job that comes their way, learning skills as they go along. Many are in the domestic service. This is especially true of young tribal women. But they get neither appreciation nor respect. There may be one Raj Thackeray mocking immigrants; but there is also one Rajiv Gandhi challenging the men from Uttar Pradesh, and demanding to know how long they will beg in Mumbai. Migrants who come out to survive and to send money home to farmer parents are despised. Skilled and professional migrants who come out to do better are welcomed. It is as simple as that. Even as there is a dearth of skilled labour, there is an excess of unskilled workforce. The factories that open on acquired land import their skilled staff from places far and near. The untrained locals cannot fill those vacancies.

The answer of course is to give better direction, and do better planning. The demand for non-land-based work is not going away, but it is increasing day by day. Not only that, the youth coming in search of work to urban centres are mostly from the agrarian states. They send money home and live miserable lives themselves. Many of them say that if they could get jobs at half the salary back home they would go back rather than maintain two establishments. This is even true of professionals. The director of a Cancer Foundation in West Bengal told me not so long ago, that they were able to hire part time doctors at a salary of five thousand rupees a month to work from their villages. If they have that much assured ready cash then they can risk living at home. It is cheaper and more comfortable. They are allowed private practice and that is a tidy extra.

I am a great believer in talking to people and listening to them. Samples of what I have heard may sound anecdotal, but they are not. Over thirty years they have added up.

Way back in 1965, when I was moving around with Acharya Vinoba's Bhoodaan team members, I learnt my first lesson. They were showering praises on the wonderful life in the villages; fresh air, healthy food, clean water, friendly community and a life lived close to nature.

I was sitting with the women. They giggled as they expressed their envy of my lifestyle. 'No hard work in the fields and the house' they chuckled 'all you have to do is to dress up and make a cup of tea on a kerosene stove which lights ever so quickly. Every month your man brings home a pay packet and there are no in laws around. You can talk to your husband any time'.

A few years later the woman who pressed clothes round the corner from me in Delhi expressed the same sentiment. *Dilli ki beti, Mathura ki gaai, Karam phute to bahar jaai'*. Only when the luck turns will the daughter from Delhi and the cow from Mathura go away from that place. Not for them the romance of the rustic life.

Again in 1980, two of us city women were trekking in Narmada valley, trying to understand the depth of the problem the as yet oblivious region would face when the dam was constructed. Despite the grimness of the task before us, we had a grand time, inhaling the fresh air and reveling in the open spaces and gasping our way up the steep slopes. We were escorted by two boys who were barely in their teens and who were all ready ploughing their own fields. They were very bright and smart; they were also more independent than city kids their age. They were with us for a day and a night. And they observed us. They heard us talking to each other, to our bilingual Bhil guide and to the travelling pilgrims. Finally one of them spoke to his companion. 'These women speak many languages; they travel far. They know a lot. If we had been educated we would have done the same'. Yes indeed!

In 1985, Lawrence Ho from Ranchi, in the Koel Karo Basin said much the same thing more forcefully. He was in the first year of college. The elders were asking for their cultural-religious sites to be kept above water. As every village has a burial ground and has the stone that was laid by the founder, clearly a dam was not a possibility. The dam would bring much needed electricity and drinking water, and perhaps irrigation. The elders wanted none of it. With great courage, Lawrence, the only youth in that meeting stood up. 'You are all setting suns,' he told the old men. 'We are the rising suns. How long will you keep us back? We don't want to scratch the land with a wooden hoe. We want to be doctors, nurses, engineers, and teachers. We want to go ahead.' No one heeded him. They went on exactly as though he had not spoken.

That dam is yet to be constructed. A couple of years ago participants from the dam submergence zone came to a meeting. The activist with them was all for hanging the officials. The two tribal young men with him were of a different opinion. One of them said, the Government needs to prove it will keep its word. The Government had promised to resettle us. We said, Construct two model villages. They have not done it. 'The Government said they would start an Industrial Training Institute (acronym ITI) to train us to become fitters, electricians etc which would help us to avail of the new type of jobs in industry. But the ITI wound up after six months. We will give up our land if another door opens. Let the Government do it.' Who can deny that they were eminently sensible words?

The youth want out. They want more than and different from what they see their parents having. They no longer want the precarious lives of their fathers working small holdings which will become ever smaller with every generation and make them even more dependent on the capricious monsoon. It is a tragic mistake to listen only to the elders. They may want land but their children aspire to something else.

Some people certainly move away because they aspire to a better life. Others are forced to do it because the land back home cannot sustain the entire family. If the father is able-bodied all the sons migrate. Otherwise one brother stays back permanently unless they take turns. Their families live in the village because they cannot afford housing in the city. They migrate so that their cash strapped parents can survive. When West Bengal's Nandigram and Singur were occupying the central space in the media because of forcible acquisition, in Delhi, I had the opportunity to meet some migrant young men from West Bengal from that very region. According to them, the maximum out-migration was from West Midnapore District. Those men had a different take. Their land had lost its productivity due to over cultivation. It no longer sustained the farmers. The sons had to do it. They were saving every paisa to send back home. They were asked to send money to buy seeds or an ox; to mend the roof, for mother's medicines and sister's clothes. They had no life in the city. They would prefer it if an industry came up in their own backyard. Then it struck me: there were many speaking on behalf of the PAPs. But they themselves were invisible. May be the odd old man was asked for a byte; but the young were missing. What the Bengali young men said was echoed by Jaggannth, who drove a taxi for a transport company. For some reason best known to himself he thought I could help him get a job in Ranchi. His wife and children were back home. There he had a small house and a small plot. If he could get a job driving there he would go for half the salary.. I advised him to go back for a holiday and try his luck with the officers of the many companies coming up. With his experience of driving in Delhi and his local knowledge he stood a good chance of getting a job; six months later he went back.

The PAPs want to know why their land is being taken from them. If it is for a dam then they want watered land. But if it is for industry then they want a share in it. They do not want land as an absolute good. That was what the young men from the multi-industrial complex of Korba in Chhattisgarh wanted. They wanted jobs, not land. Even more important, their parents wanted jobs for their sons.

When no one listens to them they tell us with their actions. The young men and women they simply start migrating to towns and cities. The states opposing land acquisition, and opposing industrialization are the very states sending more unskilled workers to industrial towns and cities. They are desperate for work. Recently two men died of noxious fumes in a public drain. The name of one was Jha; he was a Brahmin and the other was Verma, a Kayastha; they were upper caste men from eastern India. Neither would have touched such work back home. But it was all they could get so they took it and died far from home.

There are other signs of the imminent changes. The aggressively militant demand for more and more castes to be included in reserved categories must tell us something if we are willing to listen. It is not for seats in legislatures. It is into benefit from reservation in education and Government posts. The cities are growing faster because the countryside cannot sustain the population. It is no good saying 'stop acquisition.' Instead we must demand intelligent planning; for intelligent read farsighted. Only saying a categorical 'No' to all change is going to get us nowhere. Demanding land for all R and R of PAPs is also a non starter. It inflates the demand for land, possibly to create the impression that the project is not viable. Remove the absentee landlords from the list. Remove those family members who live elsewhere. Keep only the actual, the real tillers in the list of those to be given land for rehabilitation. Keep only the actual residents in the list for resettlement. Again, remove the family members who live elsewhere. By all means give them cash compensation, but not land. Thus the amount of land needed for rehabilitation and even resettlement will be reduced.

At the same time, planners must insist on minimum

acquisition. The LA Bill 2007 came into force on May 7, 2007. It requires the overburdened collector to decide how much land a project needs. Not allowing acquisition for housing will reduce the quantum of land sharply. It will also not stretch the poor collector to devise his own parameters.

Acquisition for housing colonies must be forbidden. The townships created for the Damodar Valley Corporation's four dams in South Bihar are now ghost towns, barely occupied. At the same time, as far as possible, residential areas of villages must not be acquired. In urbanization projects, it is possible to omit them. Delhi's *Lal dora* villages have proved this. They have become part of the growing city and have found multiple opportunities for livelihood there. They received only cash compensation for their agricultural lands. They rebuilt their own lives. This policy may even be practicable in industrial and infrastructure projects.

The new projects must involve the villages in development. Invite them to provide housing for rent. It is most important to leave the villages their residential space in the new townships. These are the *lal dora* villages in Delhi which are prospering like never before because they are virtually in the centre of things. From being landlords of land they have become landlords with houses and offices. Even the landless could rent out a room, built with the tenant's advances. They have rebuilt their lives (MARG, 1998).

At one meeting in Korba of affected villagers, Government servants and project authorities- getting all three together itself was a miracle- I suggested that the company's staff should live in the village. The company should get flats constructed to their specifications and rent them. Secondly, they should not go for presidential size accommodation. But the officers and staff should mingle with the villagers. They should not distance themselves from the villagers. Rather, they should, share transport, schools, hospitals and other civic facilities with them after charging them. It is unnecessarily embittering to be denied access to a hospital or a school built on the village land or to wait for state buses while the project buses whizz past.

The general manager of a big project would have none of it.

He explained why very graphically. 'Look at my well pressed clean white shirt.' He said, 'Supposing one sleeve was torn and muddy. I would not wear it. You are like the dirty sleeve. I am like the clean sleeve. How can I live with you?'

It says a great deal about the suppression of the Indian villager that they heard him without reacting. That was left to me and I was quite sharp about it. He was offended, but he was not convinced. Ten years later, the staff of the various thermal power corporations at an all India meeting reacted similarly. Living next to a villager was a big no even though your home would be separate. But this one change would reduce acquisition by a wide margin.

Acquiring land for future expansion has to be spelt out. For example, a primary school should, indeed aim to become a high school. Otherwise, children drop out, especially the girls, who do not travel afar. But to acquire land in order to expand into a university at a future date is not acceptable.

The LA Bill 2007 makes it punitive to purchase more than 100 acres of land. The would-be purchaser must rehabilitate all PAPs. The buyer may resettle; he cannot rehabilitate. That is the state's responsibility. By all means make it difficult to acquire excess land; penalize if the land is not used in the approved time frame. But do not stop or try to stop all change.

The farmers may be overjoyed, but again we are not listening; we are not looking at what is happening on the ground. Cities are growing rapidly while villages are going the other way. The increasing demand for reservation in education and jobs carries a message for us. A look at the Supreme Court's business over the decades tells us something. In the early decades, the petitions were mostly about land. Then they were about service matters. Now they will be about reservations, or fake certificates. This is a good topic for research for a M Phil thesis or the work assigned to a student working as a clerk of a Supreme Court judge.

Lastly, we need to collect data on issues which relate broadly to migration. They should include answers to questions such as this:

From which states is there high out-migration?
Are the migrants rural or urban dwellers?

Where do they go?
What work do they do once they get there? Skilled? Semiskilled?
What is their contribution to their families?
What is their contribution to their home state's economy and to its GDP?

Given that the home state is basically agrarian, what is its record in food sufficiency and other parameters of development?

We may find that land use is changing, economy and aspirations are changing and people are on the move. The planners and thinkers must at least stay with them, if they cannot lead the way. Not just me but many others -academics, scholars, demographers- who have a better command over hard data are seeing the oncoming change. They see the ever burgeoning urban population, the demand for urban employment and the hard truth that many do not wish to acknowledge: that more and more people will live in the cities in the future, in non land based occupations. Even so, if our findings are different, then we can continue the way we are going, with no infrastructure, no industry, no civic facilities, and no trained workforce.

Let us just recollect that the price innocence is the same as the price of ignorance. The price of the ageless Shangri-La is the inability to protect oneself. We may erect walls but we cannot stop the winds from blowing where they please. That is how Chernobyl affected the world Thousands of kilometers away. Pollution upstream will have its effect downstream even though the hamlets keep their cultures intact and refuse to let in the outside world. Either we learn to direct the forces of change or they will control us. But change has been coming. Indeed that was in motion from the time zero was invented, and not just since the first ship set out to sail.

BIBLIOGRAPHY

Enakshi, G Thukral. 1992. *Big Dams Displaced People*. New Delhi: Sage Publications.
MARG (Multiple Action Research Group). 1998. *Shahpur Jat A Village Displaced: A Study in Self Rehabilitation*. New Delhi: Multiple Action Research Group.
Dhagamwar, V., Subrata De. and N Verma. 2003. *Industrial Development and Displacement: The People of Korba*. New Delhi: Sage Publications.

2

Development: The Nemesis of the Poor and the Weak

R Siva Prasad

Introduction

A society and a people always struggle to surge ahead against all odds and would aim to improve their living conditions, be it in terms of regulating or controlling surrounding environment or nature, harnessing the existing resources sustainably, gaining knowledge to manage and prudently use the available resources, etc. In the process, a number of institutions, regulations, arrangements, accommodations, etc., are devised to oversee the distribution of benefits of progress and involved in this is also a principle of inclusion of the excluded.

The word development is always viewed with a positive connotation. It is usually meant a forward movement, a movement towards progress. Development is considered as an effective tool to deal with reduction of disparities and inequalities and to tackle the problem of poverty among a large section of the deprived populace, be they tribal, rural or urban. These largely include Dalit and backward communities and minorities. In a way, it is regarded as an effective tool of social engineering to achieve equity with social justice and social development. It is also an important tool for the progress of a nation to build infrastructure, to enhance the resource base, to achieve economic growth, and to promote overall enhancement of living standards of people. Looked at from this perspective, it appears as if development has only positive consequences. In fact, on the contrary, the negative consequences are more to the detriment of the poor and the deprived.

It is essential to note that development has both intended and unintended consequences as well as anticipated and unanticipated outcomes that have a bearing on the lives and livelihood of the poor. Therefore, there is the need to take cognizance of these outcomes in estimating their impacts. Any development planning that does not take the cost and benefits of the programmes to the poor are not worth its name; they always become its first victims and also are the ones who sacrifice everything for the larger benefit. The question arises as to who benefits more from development and for whom it is meant? Why should the poor always get only the spillover benefits and why not the major benefits in tune with their sacrifices of their resources? Who decides the benefit sharing and why are they not involved in the process of decision making as these development initiatives always affect their lives and livelihood, most of the time negatively?

It is apt to remember that 'In India around fifty million people have been displaced due to development projects over fifty years. Around 21.3 million development induced IDPs include those displaced by dams (16.4 million), mines (2.55 million), industrial development (1.25 million) and wild life and national parks (0.6 million)' (Negi and Ganguly, 2011: 6). Given this, Negi and Ganguly observe further that, 'Their quality of life and potential for physical and emotional growth is dormant, family and community life is almost totally destroyed; the opportunity for cultural activity hardly exists and the right of movement is highly restricted. Those living in camps, especially women, have to endure outrageous invasions of their privacy. Basic health care for all and education of all children are virtually non-existent. Their right to participate and contest in the political processes is difficult' (2011:7). Is the notion of participatory development, participatory planning only a rhetoric and confined to official gimmickry or a facade to impress upon the funders (Siva Prasad, 2006). No wonder development is a wonderful business for all planners, politicians, contractors, consultants, professionals, and what have you.

I

All our approaches to development are piecemeal and we experiment on the people as if they are guinea pigs. We refuse to draw any lessons from our past mistakes and continue to practise the trial and error method, learning the least from errors. All our policies and programmes, right from the time of our national independence, are piecemeal, whether it is forest policy, tribal policy (if there is one), rural or urban policies, land policy, agriculture policy, credit policy, industrial policy, or for that matter any policy adopted and implemented by the Union of India and the state governments. We have to bear in mind that a piecemeal approach to development is more dangerous than no development.

We have a tendency to project groups of people if they are opposed to any 'development' programme as regressive and backward-looking. We don't even hesitate to use force to silence those who raise their voices against it. Development at any cost is not development, as it is the poor who bear the brunt. It is important to always remember that shifts in the policies and programmes should be based on the lessons learnt from the past experiences or mistakes. But what is painful to note is that instead of the old ones we make new mistakes, thereby not learning any lessons from the past experiences because the consequences of these are felt always by the poor only, be they tribal, rural or urban. Negi and Ganguly rightly observe that, 'New mega-projects displace already resettled communities; in some districts the population has been displaced several times in just a few decades. The utter casualness with which oustees are sometimes subjected to multiple displacements is described in the Bargi Tribunal report... To impose the trauma of forced relocation on any population once is grave enough. To do it again and again merely because of casualness or slipshod advance planning or lack of coordination by engineers and project officials reflects bureaucratic insensitivity and callousness at its nadir' (2011: 11-12). Why does this always have to be so?

There is a great need to introspect about our models of

development. These are highly skewed against the poor and their resources. There is a tendency in the bureaucracy with regard to looking at cases of success as if they can be replicable. We always look for one or two successful cases and try to use them as models for replication all over, ignoring the fact that the people, the regions, and many other diversities are not controllable like the chemicals or other elements in a laboratory where we conduct the experiments under given temperature and pressure levels. As the people are diverse, their cultures are diverse, their knowledge levels are diverse, their experiences are diverse, their micro-natures are diverse, their climatic conditions and adaptation to them are diverse, and one can go on and on to identify the diversities. Given such a complex nature, can we really replicate a few successes all over the country? It must be kept in mind that nothing can be replicated, as diverse conditions are responsible for the success and the same conditions cannot be replicated even in the same place after passage of time. Success is also many a time a short-lived phase. In fact, it is always essential to analyze the failure cases that can teach us much more than success stories, which keep us under an illusion of utopian progress.

The import of the above argument is that our development as well as policy needs to recognize these diversities, as our solutions to the problems of development have also to be diverse and not uniform. Traditional knowledge about management of resources, livelihoods and environment provides us excellent inputs and ideas to emulate. In the past, benefit to the community, rather than individual, was the main outlook and when the community gains, the individual automatically benefits. Today, our philosophy is the reverse and also short-sighted. Our focus is more on the individual (we call them 'beneficiaries') than on the community. Our development plans and programmes benefit a few individuals while the large majority remains at the bottom of the scale of development always. Why does this happen? Is it deliberate? Why are we adamant about the misplaced models of development?

II

Our models of development are Western and alien to our socio-cultural milieu, which is more diversified and pluralistic. We must understand that the Western models of development are based on their socio-cultural, economic and geographical realities. Their experiences are quite contrary to ours. In fact, many of the theories evolved in a Western context are not even applicable to us and if we do so, we end up with misleading findings that lead us to draw wrong conclusions. This does not mean we wish away the Western experiences (Beteille, 1974: 58-59; Siva Prasad, 1987: 48). Instead, we also take them along with the experiences of the other developing and underdeveloped countries, such as those in Asia, Africa and Latin America and other regions that have experienced the same colonial exploitations and appropriations. The systems of all these countries came under severe influence of the Western conquest and hegemony, including its concepts of bureaucracy, governance, planning, treating resources of people as that of the 'State', and what have you. We have replaced our colonial masters with the new ones without much change in outlook and approaches (Agrawal, 1997). This is the root cause for the ills of governance or lack of it.

Our schemes of governance by and large continue to be the same. Our laws are largely the same; our outlook continues to be still colonial, except that we work in our 'independent' regimes controlled by the international aid agencies, donors and dominant nation states. Our development policies and programmes are dictated by the dominant sections as these benefit largely a select few dominant power elites and contractors. People who are poor and landless benefit from the temporary labour, but lose out on the resources and livelihood that they have already lost. Our development initiatives do not deprive the better off, rather they benefit them more, and it is always the poor who sacrifice for the 'larger good'. We always experiment on the poor and their resources, while we don't dare touch the rich and their resources. It is the rich and the better off whose interests are protected by the politicians, as both reap the benefits of development.

We are a bundle of contradictions. We talk of decentralization whereas our policies and programmes are highly centralized, including the judiciary. The governments and the powers to be, or those who aspire for it, behave as if they are the givers and the people (which really means the poor) are the receivers, as if they are doing a favour, forgetting the fact that it is their labour, and also votes, which have given them the means to do things, both in terms of material and power.

The real assessment of our policies and programmes is to see who gains and who loses. It is essential to see whether the gains outweigh losses in both in the short and long runs. Whether the gainers are more in number should be the moot point rather than the economic advancement of a few at the cost of the majority. Development and economic growth does not mean a few Indians becoming multinational corporations and a few urban technical or other professionals gaining more income and the boom in the real estate industry. The stark reality of our development has always outweighed against the poor and the marginal communities (Cernea, 1999, 2003a and 2003b; Dwivedi, 1999 and 2002; Fernandes, 1991, 1994 and 2007; Negi and Ganguly, 2011; Siva Prasad, 2001; Siva Prasad and Eswarappa, 2007; Siva Prasad and Alok Pandey, 2008; Siva Prasad and Vinay Tripathi, 2010).

The question we have to ask is what is in it for the losers in the development game? Universally, we know that the majority of the losers are the poor. We also know that it is always the poor who sacrifice their livelihood earning resources, homes and hearths in the 'larger interest' and 'public good'. The usually stated logic is that the spin-off effects will benefit the poor in the long run! The immediate and long run effects of development are displacement and distress migration of the poor. The policies that address development and evacuation do not show the same interest in making the people who sacrifice everything feel comfortable and assured. They always live under trauma and tension and become refugees or denizens in their own territories. Isn't it the irony of miscued 'development'?

Another stated dictum of development is that it is expected

to bridge the gap between the haves and have-nots. Instead, what we have witnessed uninterruptedly is the gap between the rich and poor is increasing and getting widened. Negi and Ganguly (2011: 10-11) observe aptly that the tribals are the major losers of development and displacement, while the non-tribals are the major gainers. Landless among them do not even receive any compensation. There are increased protests, rebellions and agitations against the demands for development of the resources of the poor (Negi and Ganguly, 2011: 8-9; Saxena, n.d). The widespread unrest is only symptomatic of the deeper malaise.

III

What has development done to the poor, whether they are tribal, rural or urban? Right from the time of independence, the initiatives of development have resulted in the displacement of the tribals and the rural as well as urban poor, leave aside the nomadic and semi-nomadic (pastoral) communities whose plight has not even touched the conscience of our development planners and political mandarins (Siva Prasad and Alok Pandey, 2008).

It has not only caused them misery, but denied them access to their traditional livelihood earning resources. The British made the tribals and other forest dwellers outsiders and illegal occupants in their own habitats. It is like the story of the Arab and the Camel. All the common properties have become 'public' properties, as if the tribal and rural folk are not the public. All the traditional institutions of resource management and governance were denounced as archaic and even barbaric. They have taken on the job of 'civilizing' these 'primitive' and 'barbaric' communities on themselves, forgetting the fact that these communities are more civil and democratic than the so-called 'civilized'. After taking the cudgels of power from the colonial rulers, our Indian masters have only continued the 'civilizing' policies of their colonial masters. In fact, they have become more draconian than the colonialists, while the colonialists themselves have reformed many of their institutions.

The paradox of development is that it is governed and designed by the better off. The belief is that the better off think better about what is good for the poor and they, therefore, usurp the right to 'develop' the poor. They cannot accept the role reversal in this regard and they can't put themselves in the position of the poor and refuse to accept if they have to forego their claim over their properties and privileges. The better off can knock on the doors of all powers, including the judiciary, which obliges them in delivering justice in a quick manner as they have the resources to invest in engaging the costliest advocates/lawyers. If it is for the poor, justice has to wait. If any activists take up the cases of the poor, then they get branded and hounded (Vinayak Sen is only one example). Since development is defined and governed by the better off, the rich benefit from it immensely.

As is well known, the major outcome of development is displacement. The pace of this has increased especially after 1991 economic liberalization on account of Special Economic Zones (SEZs). Whatever may be the cause of displacement, its end results are similar. They lead to disruption in the production system, loss of assets and jobs, disruption of local markets and relations between producers and consumers, dismantling of social and food security, credit and labour exchange networks, and deterioration of public health among the displaced (Kothari, 1996: 1477; Cernea, 1996; World Bank, 1994 cited in Dwivedi, 1999: 43). In other words, like twin brothers, development and displacement are corollary to each other.

Displacement was observed to be quite high during the colonial rule due to its policies related to forest land, land revenue, and exploitation of natural wealth, etc. What is noteworthy is the post-independent India has only accelerated this process further due to the continuation of the moribund legal and policy structures of colonial rule. It is now well established that large dams all over the world have displaced forty to eighty million people (Parasuraman and Sengupta, 2001). In India alone twenty million people have been displaced due to development projects and about 65 per cent of it of them due to construction of large river-valley dams (Kothari, 1996: 1476; Negi and Ganguly, 2011: 8).

John Madeley in his book on 'Food for All: The Need for a

New Agriculture', while writing on the big dams cites both the former Prime Minister of India, Rajiv Gandhi and the World Commission of Dams (WCD). He points out that, 'Despite the millions of dollars sunk into them, these dams have often proved disastrous. Costs have been far higher than expected, environmental side-effects have been severe, millions of people have been dislocated, and the schemes have proved unsustainable. In a damning comment on such schemes in India, the country's former Prime Minister, Rajiv Gandhi pointed out that of 246 large surface-irrigation projects that had started in India since 1951, only 65 were completed by 1986, and that little benefit had come from projects begun after 1970. 'For sixteen years we have poured money out', He said, 'the people have got nothing back, no irrigation, no water, no increase in production, no help in their daily life.' This seems typical of the performance of large dams overall. In November 2000, the World Commission on Dams ... published its findings. It said that large dams designed to deliver irrigation systems have typically fallen short of physical targets. In human terms, perhaps the powerful statistic is that large dams have uprooted between 40 and 80 million people. Their homes and their lands were flooded to make way for the new schemes and they were moved to other areas, often many miles away. The benefits of large dam schemes also tend to bypass the poor, who gain neither irrigation nor electricity' (2002: 68). While development programmes cause displacement of people directly, those who are displaced indirectly also constitute a substantial population. Citing WCD, Madeley points out that, 'Millions of people living downstream from dams ... have also suffered serious harm to their livelihoods and the future productivity of their resources have been put at risk' (ibid: 68). In most of the social impact assessments of development projects, the indirectly displaced have not been taken note of for appropriate rehabilitation and resettlement.

IV

It is widely noticed in many development programmes that they invariably lead to degradation due to the multiple effects of development. Usually, care is not taken with regard to the spillover effects of development that have negative impacts on the surrounding environment. Many a time, even the main programme does not take care of the environmental aspects of degradation and efforts to restore the ecological balance. While development has its impacts on the surrounding environment, it also directly impacts the poor by depriving them of the value of their traditional resources and knowledge. It is quite significant to note that it breaks the nexus of people with their habitat, resources, livelihoods and knowledge system. This very process has led the people to break away from their traditional livelihoods causing serious livelihood crises. Apart from this, the traditional knowledge about the resources, its utilization and livelihoods were some sort of insurance against all odds and crises. Once this knowledge is delinked from the resources and livelihoods, it becomes not only non-usable in the newer context but even becomes deficient. The dispossessed have to seek new livelihoods and resources to continue their living. This requires new knowledge and people need to rely for this on the others, thereby making them dependent and subservient to the others. In a way, it is widely observed that the people who once lived in harmony with nature are alienated from their resources, thereby leading to wanton destruction of the very resources that once they revered and protected (Guha, 1989; Siva Prasad, 1990 and 2001). Thus, development and other policies of the governments have set in motion the negative trend of development by not involving the direct stakeholders in the entire process, right from the stage of planning to the stage of its implementation. In a way, it has led to degradation of resources, caused environmental disasters, and denied livelihoods to the hitherto resource dependent communities. The top down approach has virtually placed or pitted people against the so called 'development' programmes.

It is now largely accepted that development has induced displacement of large sections of the poor from their habitat, be it forest dwellers, rural residents or urban poor living in the fringes or slums. The common pool resources (CPRs) that supported the tribal and rural poor have now nearly vanished

(Jodha, 1986; Thukral, 1996; Fernandes and Thukral, 1989; Fernandes and Paranjpye, 1997; Fernandes, 1991, 1994 and 2007; Parasuraman and Sengupta, 2001). Further, the customary rights of the people in their resources and CPRs have been given a complete go by (Siva Prasad, 2005). PESA (Panchayat Extension to Scheduled Areas) that was enacted by the Parliament and is supposed to ensure the customary rights of tribals in their resources as well as their customary judicial institutions has not only been substantially diluted by different state governments (the Central Act itself was a dilution from the Bhuria Committee's recommendations) but also they are not even adhered to. We do not find that the Tribal Advisory Councils are in place in the states where Schedule V Areas are located. None of the officials working in Schedule V Areas are even aware of the PESA and its adoption, for instance the tribal administration in Andhra Pradesh.

Schedule V Areas are not any way distinct from the Non-Scheduled Areas in terms of administration and appropriation of natural resources. In fact, large amounts of money invested in the Scheduled Areas in the name of development since national independence have only widened the disparities and increased the appropriation of resources by the non-tribal usurpers. Have we learnt any lessons from such developments? The rise of the left extremism is due to the economic backwardness and exploitation of the tribals and their resources by the greedy outsiders. The solution to tackle the left extremism is by changing our models of top down development to development from below with complete involvement of the main stakeholders (the poor – the tribal, the rural and the urban poor) in planning and execution of the programmes. They should be the decision makers as they are the main people who get directly impacted by any development programme. We must remember that the welfare programmes for the poor are only a small compensation for denial of their rights over the vast resources that they actually sit on but are not regarded as their owners, though they actually are.

Certain environmental disasters have been the results of our 'development' policy. There is enough evidence to show that the benefits of major development projects are much lower in proportion than their costs (Hoadley, 2004; Mehta, 2002; Saxena, n.d:13), including environmental, leave aside the loss of traditional knowledge, skills and resources. In fact, what our policy makers were looking for were short term gains and solutions and not the long term benefits and costs. For instance, our traditional agriculture has been completely, more or less, replaced by chemical fertilisers, pesticides and seed supply driven agriculture where the farmers are totally dependent on the companies that produce them. Thus, the traditional farmers are not only driven by these companies but also by the markets The chemical fertilizers have killed the soils and also polluted the ground water. The pesticides have also many more harmful effects. The negative effects of the industrial chemical fertilizer-pesticide agriculture are clearly visible today. There is increased realization about the benefits of organic agriculture. The Green Revolution, PDS and other policies have altered the food habits of the people due to the market forces. Most of the dry land crops have lost their market value and are almost disappearing from the menus of many of the rural and tribal poor, thus threatening their food security. There is a craving now for organic food among the better off and they are showcased in the markets with a big price differential. Today, organic farming is more expensive than the chemical fertilizer-pesticide agriculture. In a way, our policies were successful in killing a healthier and environment friendly agriculture, thereby making the tribals and rural poor more vulnerable.

The ruling sections that make the policies have constantly been changing their goalposts of development. We have moved from the pretentions of being a socialist republic to become capitalist republic. What is relevant to note is that our shifts in policy have always had a negative bearing on the poor. In fact, our development is driven by political and other considerations or interests rather than socio-cultural and economic considerations. Even when the economic considerations are taken into account, they are more to the advantage of the better off sections. As observed earlier, poor are never a part of decision making in development. While the better off decide the agenda of development, the poor are made to bear the brunt of the negative consequences of development. The returns for their sacrifices in the cause of national development are misery, loss of identity and self-esteem, livelihood and independent existence.

V

The watershed for the shift in Indian economy was the policy on economic liberalization in 1991. This has opened the floodgates to foreign capital and investment. This has also led to policy changes that have a bearing on the exploitation of natural resources. The policy on Special Economic Zones (SEZs), etc., have unleashed new types of displacement. SEZs are created in several parts of the country to encourage major players in the industry to start their ventures by way of giving special concessions to them, like land at low cost, free water, providing electricity, incentives like tax concessions and tax holidays, etc. Interestingly, the states have been competing among themselves to attract capital with the least concern about the people who are being displaced. The land and other resources are acquired and earmarked for this purpose at the cost of the poor tribals and other rural marginal communities. This has caused large scale displacement, deprivation and misery to the people. Interestingly, the burden of resettlement and rehabilitation has now shifted to these new players of 'development' from the government, which has now shirked its responsibility. Paradoxically, it is the government that is involved in the acquisition of vast tracts of land belonging to small and marginal farmers at low costs and giving the same to the players of industry at much higher costs, thus turning into a broker in land transfer. The argument put forth by some of the economists that economic development will have a trickle-down effect (the spillover effect) on the poor and thereby they will indirectly gain from the larger economic development and growth, is a specious argument with changed catchwords in catchy words – merely old wine in new bottles. This new policy of the SEZs has only further deepened the livelihood crisis of the poor.

The irony of the development is that the poor are always considered as the receivers, while the rich regard themselves as the givers. Therefore, the rich decide what is 'good' for the poor, though they benefit substantially from the development programmes, while the poor substantially lose out in the entire process. In a real sense, the poor are not really poor but are made poor by snatching away their resources in the name of development. Thus, the poor are always made to remain at the bottom of the growth curve, while the rich continue to remain at the top of the curve. Theoretically speaking, the top of the curve can never compromise its position with the bottom of the curve.

The paradox of development, thus, is that the majority of the affected population are the poor and the weak. It is also paradoxical that most of the poor live in resource-rich areas while they continue to remain poor. Eviction of the poor from the resource rich areas is inevitable for 'development' of the 'nation'. However, the 'nation' never recognizes the poor to be the owners (or even trustees) of these rich resources. It is in a way an irony, that while a 'nation' and its economy surge ahead, the tribal, rural and urban poor, who sacrifice everything, grow poorer. They are given some sops and allurements in the name of anti-poverty welfare programmes to vacate these resource rich areas, if they listen to those in power. Otherwise, the State stretches its muscle to evict them by force and in such an event they may not get what they were 'promised' otherwise. Today, development and welfare programmes have become a kind of anaesthesia to keep the tribals, rural and urban poor under check.

VI

In a way, development has become the nemesis of the poor and the weak. The tribals, Dalits and other marginal sections of the people are always the victims of the development initiatives of the State. What is important to recognize is that the victims of development need to be adequately compensated for their loss of livelihoods, resources and knowledge, as these are their rights. What is important also to remember is that there is the need to protect the wholeness of their identity and dignity.

The need of the hour is to move towards people-centric development which can only lead to sustainable development, economic growth and equity. This will also provide sustainable solutions to many of our social tensions and ensure peace, prosperity and harmony among the majority of the citizens of the country, who are largely poor. In a sense, there is the need for us to get out of development, displacement and resettlement/rehabilitation triangle.

REFERENCES

Agrawal, Arun. 1997. 'The Politics of Development and Conservation: Legacies of Colonialism.' *Peace and Change* 22, No. 4: 463-482.

Beteille, Andre. 1974. *The Agrarian Social Structure*. New Delhi: Oxford University Press.

Cernea, Michael M. 1996. *The Risks and Reconstruction Model for Resettling Displaced Populations*. Oxford: University of Oxford University Refugee Studies Programme.

Cernea, Michael M. 1999. 'Why Economic Analysis in Essential to Resettlement: A Sociologist's View.' In *The Economics of Involuntary Displacement*, edited by M M Cernea. Washington, DC: The World Bank.

Cernea, Michael M. 2003a. 'For a New Economics of Resettlement: A Sociological Critique of the Compensation Principle.' *International Social Science Journal*, nr 175 (UNESCO, Paris: Blackwell). http://web.mit.edu/cls/www/migration/dec05workshop/presenta tions/cernea_NewEconomics_of_Resettlement_ISSJ_2003.pdf.

Cernea, Michael M. 2003b. 'Impoverishment Risks, Risk Management and Reconstruction: A Model of Population Development and Resettlement.' *International Social Science Journal*, nr 175 (UNESCO, Paris: Blackwell). http://commdev.org/wp-content/uploads/2015/06/Impoverishment-Risk-Risk-Management-and-Reconstruction.pdf.

Dwivedi, Ranjit. 1999. 'Displacement, Risks and Resistance: Local Perceptions and Actions in the Sardar Sarovar.' *Development and Change* 30, No. 1: 43-78.

Dwivedi, Ranjit. 2002. 'Models and Methods in Development-Induced Displacement (Review Article).' *Development and Change* 33, No. 4: 709-732.

Fernandes, W. and E G Thukral, eds. 1989. *Development, Displacement and Rehabilitation.* New Delhi: Indian Social Institute.

Fernandes, Walter. 1991. 'Power and Powerlessness: Development Projects and Displacement of Tribals.' *Social Action* 41, No. 3: 243-270.

Fernandes, Walter. and V Paranjpye. 1997. *Rehabilitation Policy and Law in India: A Right to Livelihood.* New Delhi: Indian Social Institute.

Fernandes, Walter. 1994. *Development-Induced Displacement: Tribal Areas of Eastern India.* Indian Social Institute. New Delhi: Indian Social Institute.

Fernandes, Walter. 2007. 'Singur and Displacement Scenario.' *Economic and Political Weekly* 42, No. 3: 203-2006.

Guha, Ramachandra. 1989. *The Unquiet Woods.* New Delhi: Oxford University Press.

Hoadley, Marie 2004. 'Development-Induced Displacement and Resettlement – Impoverishment or Sustainable Development?' http://www.csmi.co.za/1/papers/Displacement_resettlement-Feb04.pdf.

Jodha, N S. 1986. 'Common Property Resources and Rural Poverty in Dry Regions of India.' *Economic and Political Weekly* 21, No. 27: 45-47.

Kothari, Smitu. 1996. 'Whose Nation? The Displaced as Victims of Development.' *Economic and Political Weekly* 31, No. 24: 1476-1485.

Madeley, John. 2002. *Food for All: The Need for a New Agriculture.* London and New York: Zed Books.

Mehta, Shalina. 2002. 'Detailed Development: Review of Development and Rehabilitation Models for Tribal India.' In *Anthropology: Trends and Applications,* edited by M K Bhasin and S L Malik. New Delhi: Kamala-Raj.

Negi, Nalini Singh. and Sujata Ganguly. 2011. 'Development Projects vs. Internally Displaced Populations in India: A Literature Based Appraisal.' *COMCAD Arbeitspapiere – Working Papers No. 103.* Series on Environmental Degradation and Migration. Editors: Jeanette Schade and Thomas Faist. www.uni-bielefeld.de/tdre/ag_comcad/downloads/workingpaper_103_negi-ganguly.pdf.

Parasuraman, S. and Sohini Sengupta. 2001. 'World Commission on Dams: Means for Sustainable Ends.' *Economic and Political Weekly* 36, No. 21: 1881-1891.

Saxena, Naresh C. nd. *Policies for Tribal Development, Analysis and Suggestions.* https://www.google.co.in/url?sa=t&rct=j&q=&esrc=s&source=web&cd=22&cad=rja&ved=0CDkQFjABOBQ&url=http%3A%2F%2Fwww.esocialsciences.org%2FDownload%2FrepecDownload.aspx%3Ffname%3DDocument1 1292005180.26

93292.pdf%26f category%3DArticles%26AId%3D205%26fref%3
Drepec&ei=xZg1 UvacNoKQrQeBpYGIDA&u sg=AFQjCNHQ3
pzKnem12POBQXRFxIqzgaE59A&bvm=bv.52164340, d.bmk.

Siva Prasad, R. 1987. *Social Mobility in Bangalore City.* PhD Thesis,
University of Mysore through ISEC, Bangalore.

Siva Prasad, R. 1990. 'Displacement and Rehabilitation: Issues for
Policy Planning.' In *The Uprooted: Development, Displacement and
Resettlement*, edited by V Sudarsen and M A Kalam. New Delhi:
Gyan Publishing House.

Siva Prasad, R. 2001 'Changing Frontiers and Resource Depletion in
South Asia.' In *Intra and Inter-State Conflicts in South Asia*, edited
by Sudhir Jacob George. New Delhi: South Asian Publishers.

Siva Prasad, R. 2005. 'Customary Modes of Dispute Resolution in
Schedule V Areas of Andhra Pradesh, Orissa and Madhya
Pradesh.' In *Self Governance for Tribals*, edited by S K Singh. MoRD-
UNDP sub-programme on Peoples' Empowerment through
Panchayati Raj Institutions in Scheduled V Areas and studies on
Laws affecting the poor, Vol. II Dispute Resolution, Tribal Customs
and Forest Laws, Hyderabad: National Institute of Rural
Development (NIRD), pp 43-180.

Siva Prasad, R. 2006. 'The Myth of People's Participation in Tribal
Development.' *Man and Life* 32, Nos. 3-4: 39-48.

Siva Prasad, R. and Alok Pandey. 2008. 'Changing Livelihoods: The
Burden of Pastoralists Shifting to Agriculture.' In *Sustainable
Solutions: A Spotlight on South Asian Research*, edited by SDPI and
SAMA. Islamabad and Karachi, Pakistan: SDPI and Sama Editorial
and Publishing Services.

Siva Prasad, R. and Kasi Eswarappa. 2007. 'Tribal Livelihoods in a
Limbo: Changing Tribe-Nature Relationships in South Asia.' In
*At the Crossroads: Research, Policy and Development in a Globalised
World*, edited by SDPI. Islamabad and Karachi, Pakistan: SDPI
and SAMA Publications.

Siva Prasad, R. and Vinay Tripathi. 2010. "Revisiting Development
and Environment: Case Study of Two Watershed Management
Programs in Bundelkhand Region, India." In *Peace and Sustainable
Development in South Asia: Issues and Challenges of Globalisation,*
edited by SDPI and Sang-Meel Publications. Islamabad and
Lahore, Pakistan: SDPI and Sang-Meel Publications.

Thukral, E G. 1996. 'Development, Displacement and Rehabilitation:
Locating Gender.' *Economic and Political Weekly* 31, No. 24: 1500-
03.

3

Welfare Economy and Land Acquisition: Theoretical Underpinnings

Sanatan Nayak

I. Introduction

Welfare of an economy involves various ultimate economic activities and the best polices to promote human well-being in a society. Such polices provide numerous tools for estimating the benefits of economic activity, valuing environmental features and determining the criteria for its sustainability. Hence, depending on the underlying welfare economic model, policy makers use tools such as Cost Benefit Analysis (CBA)[1], Total Factor Productivity[2] and Pareto Efficiency[3]. In the beginning, almost for a half century, economic theory and polices were mostly dominated by *Walrasian Welfare Economic Idea* of Leon Walras (1834-1910). The economic thought, i.e., optimal allocation of scarce resources for alternative ends dominated till World War II, which was further corroborated with the introduction of Pareto Efficiency. This establishes one of the key ideas of modern economics, i.e., welfare benefits of trade. This was further dependent on the correct market price and a situation of perfect competitive market force. In the absence of such an ideal situation, the market failed, various forms of externalities emerged, and subsequently market power and public good came to prevail in the economy. In addition, the well known Keynesian paradigm in the aftermath of great depression in 1930's also recommended large number of monetary and fiscal policies for attainment of highest degree of welfare, i.e., full employment by rejecting the classical paradigm of supply creates its own demand. He had proposed that the Government must intervene through appropriate monetary, fiscal and public spending policies to generate the aggregate demand necessary to reverse the recessionary state, until private investment would resume and reach levels near full employment and production capacity (Keynes, 1997). Therefore, Governments had the ultimate role for correcting market failure in order to establish proper value (Gowdy, 2011).

CBA is one of the cornerstones of modern policy analysis. It assesses the financial, economic, social and environmental impacts taking into consideration both the long term and the broad views. Further, it takes significant steps to assess deeply the effects of investment, change in pattern and extent of output, generation of employment, inter-generational distribution of income, decline in poverty and reduction in regional disparities, the dislocations and sufferings of the people, proper rehabilitation of the displaced people and measuring the sustainability of the development projects. It originated from welfare economics, which deals with maximizing the social welfare due to various programmes and development projects (Anderson et al., 1977). Welfare economics emphasizes the maximization of social welfare further deeply elaborating the efficiency, distribution and sustainability of scarce resources invested on development projects and their impacts in the society.

The economic efficiency of welfare economics was acknowledged long back, as numerous welfare economists opined that it focuses on the allocation of those scarce resources (land, labour and capital), which increases social welfare (Piguo, 1952; Anderson, et al., 1977), whereas, distributive aspect of social welfare allows the decision makers to distinguish among those activities or programme or projects that would make the society better off. The major theories concerned with the distributive aspect of the CBA are the theory of Pareto Optimality, Compensation Criterion of Hicks and Kaldor, Scitovsky Paradox, Bergson's Social Welfare Function and Arrow's Impossibility Theorem. The noted welfare economists provided various ways of distributive aspects for maximization of social welfare and suggested for the possible efficient agents to participate in the ethical value judgment of scarce resources, which are used for maximization of social welfare. Furthermore, the recent emerging ideas deal with the integration of environmental factors into the CBA, which predicts sustainability of the benefits of the projects.

The conventional CBA assumes that income is a reasonable measure of welfare (utility or well being). Subsequently, in the pioneering works of numerous welfare economists it was observed that income was not good a proxy for happiness (Easterlin, 1974; Spash, 2007). In other words, increasing income does not lead to any permanent increase in well-being. Further, this kind of observation has changed the idea of economists to find a much more robust approach for public policy that merely modifying the existing income based measure of social welfare (Layard, 2005). However, welfare economics has undergone a revolutionary change in due course of time. The conventional Walrasian thought of welfare economics has been greatly challenged by the new economics grounded in behavioural science, which recognized the social and biological contexts of decision making and the complexity of human behaviour (Gowdy, 2011).

While attempting to link some theoretical underpinnings of ethical value judgment of welfare distribution with land acquisition (land as scarce resources), this paper consists of four sections. The first section deals with introducing the changing scenario of measuring various approaches for Government projects and policies, whereas section two focuses on determining the distributive criteria of welfare maximization vis-à-vis identifying correct agents for value judgment on welfare distribution in an economy. Section three highlights macro-level developments of various agents since independence for determining the value of land, which are acquired for development of the economy. Section four deals with concluding the sustainability issue on the existing debate.

II. Important Developments in Increment in Welfare

Numerous thoughts were generated on prescribing various principles for compensating the project-affected people along with who should be the efficient agents for an ethical value judgment of welfare. The theory of social preference and consumer surplus deals with individualistic ethics, i.e., individual preferences. On the basis of this theory, the CBA adopts certain policies for a project, which are the most preferred in the society. This has been explained in the context of Pareto Optimality, which is popularly known as *First Fundamental Theorem of Welfare Economics in the neo-classical framework* of consumption, production and general equilibrium (Gowdy, 2011). However, the most important limitation of Pareto optimality is that it never says in case of a social project, whether the benefits made by the gainers are more than the losses made by the losers. In a restatement, it can be queried whether the benefits made by the gainers are able to compensate the losses made by the losers. This type of limitation was solved with the development of the Hicks-Kaldor (H-K) compensation principle.

H-K criterion justifies moving from one state of the economy to another identifying a Potential Pareto Improvement (PPI). It is because the magnitude of the gains of moving from one state of the economy to another is greater than the magnitude of the losers, then the social welfare is increased by making the move even if no actual compensation is made (Gowdy, 2011). This further justifies that The H-K criterion is the fundamental foundation, the normative justification for identifying policies that maximise the positive differences between benefits and costs (Stavins, Wagners and Wagner, 2002). In general, economists follow Kaldor's view that economic policy recommendations should be determined by efficiency; however distribution is a problem for politicians. Therefore, the efficiency improvement imposed by H-K criterion suggests avoiding interpersonal comparison of utilities. This was considered to be impossible. This kind of problem is basically due to drawing general equilibrium conclusions from partial equilibrium situations.

Theoretical difficulties were raised immediately after H-K

in 1939 that identifying PPI should be the goal of economics. If a movement from one point to another in utility space can be shown to be Pareto improvement based on H-K principle, then it may also show that a movement back to the original point is also Pareto Improvement (Scitovsky, 1941). To eliminate this cyclic problem, Scitovsky proposed a double criteria for the PPI. Furthermore, when we compare different projects or policies, the superior project is judged based on the largest net gain according to H-K principle. However, Boadway (1974) observes that one with highest net gain is not necessarily the best one. This is popularly known as Boadway paradox and it arises from the estimation of income compensated variations or welfare gains at constant prices are partial equilibrium measures. Subsequently and earlier also, many other theoretical dilemmas and paradoxes with the help of PPI approach have been identified (Samuelson, 1950; Bromley, 1990; Brekke, 1997). Hence, there is no theoretically justifiable way to make welfare judgments without invoking value judgments and interpersonal comparison of utilities, yet this is not permissible under the stringent requirements of neoclassical welfare economics. Therefore, economic efficiency can no longer claim to be an objective policy criterion (Gowdy, 2011). Further, it was also been earlier stated that the claim for efficiency as a policy goal is based on ideology, not science (Bromley, 1990). He observes that efficiency is not an objective goal but rather an opinion based on the system of beliefs embodied in the worldview of the Walrasian system.

The first Fundamental Theorem of Welfare Economics failed to maximize distributing social welfare due to distortion of prices, failing nature of market and entry of market forces. Therefore, the emergence of the *Second Fundamental Theorem of Welfare Economics* got its importance and most of the Governments had legitimacy to intervene and correct the market (Gowdy, 2011). In this regard, the emergence of two classic solutions against market failure emerged. First, the use of taxes and subsidies (Pigou, 1962) and second, complete property rights either to private individuals or to the public entity to control the tragedy of commons (Coase, 1960). It basically focuses that if a move from one particular state of economy to another is judged to be desirable, this move may be achieved through transferring resources from one person or activity to another through assigning property rights or imposition of lumpsum taxes or providing subsidies or comparing interpersonal utilities (Gowdy, 2011).

Furthermore, the emergence of a Social Welfare Function (SWF) under the neoclassical frame directed distribution of scarce resources to maximize social welfare. It is regarded as a social decision process for development of any social project by the Government and any private entrepreneur. It is a method, a collective choice rule for deriving social ordering from individual preferences. Bergson first suggested the implication of social welfare under two broad categories, i.e., economic and non-economic (Bergson, 1948).[4] The social welfare function determines the relative weights given in the utility indices of different individuals in arriving at an aggregate index. It focuses on interpersonal comparison of utilities among individuals. The major limitation of the Bergson welfare function is that it never specifies who provides the decision on ends.

Arrow's Social Welfare Function (SWF) is based on certain assumptions such as the criteria of Completeness, Unanimity, Universality, Non-dictatorship, Transitivity and Independence. Specifically, it is a method of collective choice rule for deriving social orders from individual preferences (Arrow, 1951). The logic behind the development of SWF by Arrow was the introduction into the theoretical economics of the concept for expanding the range of welfare economics beyond the Pareto optimality criterion. Hence, this alternative approach developed by Arrow explored the possibility of constructing a social ordering from individual preferences subject to satisfying a number of conditions as mentioned above. Arrow's SWF is closely differentiated from that of Bergson. Arrow's SWF is a collective choice rule for deriving a social ordering from individual orderings. Bergson's SWF (of the individualistic type) is a more general concept, where the social ordering may be derived from the individual ordering, i.e., by a specified ethical judgement (Dasgupta and Pearce, 1978). Bergson's SWF is regarded as an ethical judgment. It means, it is not a tool of personal likes or dislikes but it relates mostly to welfare economics, for counselling individual citizens to make choices. Arrow's version of the SWF is designed to counsel not the citizen generally but the public official who may be regarded as standing for society as a whole. Various possible agents are suggested for participation in the ethical value judgment of welfare distribution in the economy. Economists, sociologists and other professionals along with the community representatives are the best suitable agents for ethical judgments instead of deciding the SWF. However, the social choice theory of Arrow's is practically known as Arrow's Impossibility Theorem, which is popularly known as *Third Fundamental Theorem of Welfare Economics* (Gowdy, 2011). Therefore, the above discussed social choice theories on distribution for betterment of overall welfare of economies cannot be possible without making interpersonal comparisons of utility as the many paradoxes and impossibilities are embedded in the Walrasian welfare economics arise from the attempt to avoid interpersonal comparisons.

The Neoclassical frame of CBA for mainly public policy mostly deals with opportunity cost, efficiency and consumer sovereignty. However, due to the development of diversified perspective and techniques involved in various issues on environment for sustainability, and the recent growth of economic theories the public started distrusting CBA. Large scale precautionary measures are developed to take the loss aversion principle for environmental protection against uncertainty and irreversibility to respect human preferences. Therefore, conventional CBA is used to discount the future value of goods and services in order to avoid inappropriate estimation of future value. Subsequently, different discount rates were applied based on time and goods and services. Gradually, behavioural economics elements such as the game theory, neurological experiments, reciprocity, and inequality aversion are included in the climate change on various natural resources. These incorporations were made in order to improve the conventional CBA to overcome the problems of commensurability, irreversibility, and uncertainly to achieve sustainable welfare goods. The first such kind of sustainable goal was the origin of Hartwick–Solow rule, which provided the idea of converting natural capital into manufactured capital. This is popularly known as the weak sustainable principle. Further, the standard welfare approach assumes commensurability, biodiversity, climate stability and all other features of the biophysical world as ordinary market goods (Gowdy, 2011). Therefore, the strong sustainability approach emerged, which asserted sustainability of natural capital (natural resources and earth's life support system) to maintain human activity. The strong sustainability approach of CBA recognizes the need for public policy to regulate the ultimate sources of economic inputs and the flow of waste that are inevitable results of economic activity (Daly, 1977).

Further, the publication of Stern Review on the economics of climate change (Stern, 2007) debated over a proper discount rate to apply future costs and benefits of climate change mitigation. The debate summarized that higher the discount rate, the less value is allocated for spending on climate mitigation in the future. However, there is no scientific and objective way to determine the discount rate. Therefore, there is a requirement of collecting and evaluating evidence and making explicit value judgements for sound economic analysis. The debate on climate change on discounting the future value of assets for mitigation purpose is basically an ethical issue (Stern, 2007) and one can look at how much of insurance is provided to avoid the small chance of a ruinous catastrophe (Weitzman, 2007). Further, the researchers and policy analysts call for redefining and applying various conventional concepts to CBA such as rational behaviour, social welfare, and opportunity cost using empirical evidence, ethical judgments and sound scientific methods (Ackerman and Heinzerling, 2004; Knetsch, 2005; Revesz and Livermore, 2008).

III. A Macro Overview of Value Judgments on Land Acquisition in India

Conventionally, the buyers and sellers determine the value of land in the market. In general, land owners and representatives of the state are involved as agents in the land acquisition market in India. Specifically, the price is fixed by district level officials or the land acquisition officer (*Tehsildar*) based on recent prices or proximate land sales after negotiations with land owners (Chakravorty, 2013). However, in due course in the process of economic development, not only the number of agents for determination of price of land have increased but also the diversities within the existing categories have increased. Significantly, two important agents, viz., political parties and civil society (apart from landowners and state representatives) are the prominent agents for determining the value of land in the acquisition process.

Buyers of land are either the public or private sector. However, land acquisition is done by the Government on a formal basis for both the sectors in India. The land is acquired based on formal laws and acts, which are formulated by the Central Government and implemented in the country.[5] Further, the State Governments have their own rules and acts for land acquisitions. The important public sectors, who have acquired land for public utilities, viz., Indian Railways, National Highway Authority of India (NHAI), Irrigation department, National Thermal Power Corporation (NTPC), Electricity Board etc. Similarly, land acquired for private sector needs formal process either by the private sector itself or by the Central Government (State Government in the State projects). However, in the liberalized era, the Governments (both Central and States) take responsibility in many ways to provide land to the private sector on easy terms and conditions (Chakravorty, 2013).

On the other hand, no doubt sellers are the owners of land. However, there have been large scale diversities observed across the owners and dependents of land (those who do not own land). In India, mean sizes of land of the land owners are different, and the proportions of marginal and small landholdings are also different. Therefore, the interests of the States for acquisition of land obviously differs. As per Agricultural Census, the mean size of land in country as well as across the States since 1970s has been declining. Nearly, 60 per cent of total landholders, who are called marginal farmers occupy hardly 20 per cent of the total land size in the country along with large scale variations across the States. Furthermore, there is another group of people in the country who do not own land but their livelihood is largely dependent on the land. Tenants (11 per cent of the farmers), wage labourers, self-employed workers, artisan, are adversely affected if their work places get affected. Similarly, communities such as *Dalits, tribals, minorities* get hugely affected, when their common property resources (CPR) are lost through sale or due to development of various projects. Therefore, larger the land acquisition projects, larger are the numbers of affected stakeholders (Chakravorty, 2013). The recently published data of the Socio-Economic Caste Census (SECC), 2011 observed that nearly 50 per cent of the households in rural India are landless, dependent on casual manual labour and live in deprivation. Now, poverty in India is worse than previously estimated. Therefore, landlessness has become more widespread over the last sixty-seven years after independence. Therefore, the obvious question arises; will the Government (the NDA led by BJP) reverse its stand on dispossessing more farmers of their land through its land bill amendments in 2015?

The history of involvement of political parties and civil society in the land acquisition speaks volumes on the subject. Though the involvement of various political parties in the process of land acquisition is a recent phenomenon, yet the involvement of the Left and Congress parties in land reforms, land distribution, consolidation has a long and significant history (Conning and Robinson, 2007; Hanstad et al. 2009; Bardhan et al., 2011). However, land acquisition is taken as a thought process in the reverse direction of land distribution. Surplus land was taken from the rich and landlords (surplus over ceiling) and given to poor and landless under the land reforms process, whereas land from marginal and small holders has been acquired in the name of development in the process of land acquisition in the recent decades. In this regard, Chakravorty felt as 'Truth to tell: much of their (political parties) actions are purely opportunistic; generally a party is in favour of land acquisition where it is in power and against it where it is not.' It has been observed that political parties in most of the cases show large scale inconsistencies in the issues of land acquisition in the recent decades.

The emergence of civil society in the land acquisition market is a recent phenomenon but very widespread (nearly 3.3 million non-profit organisations were involved in land acquisition by mid-2000), though their role is not uniform like the activist type. However, mostly civil society serves as a carrier of information and organizer at the grass root level. Their role is significant as they help in spreading and exchanging information within specific project affected communities, between affected people in different projects and communities, and between affected people and the general citizenry and State institutions (Chakravorty, 2013). The activities of civil society are felt important at four levels such as the ground, regional, national and international levels. The organization and their movements are mostly project specific (ground level) and due to the lack of skills and resources, their activities are restricted to project areas only.[6] Civil societies at regional level mostly took shape with deviations from the mainstream party position to form local resistance movements and their activities are spread within the State or regions of the State.

In addition, The National Alliance of People's Movements is a popular national level civil society, which is an umbrella organization for a number of regional organizations and their leaders. They promote more knowledge production and network activities. A few of the well known civil societies are Narmada Bachao Andolan by Medha Patkar in Gujrat, Madhya Pradesh and Maharastra; Sarvahara Jan Andolan by Ulka Mahajan in Maharastra; Jan Sangharsh Vahini by Bhupendra Singh Rawat in Delhi; Mazdoor Kisan Shakti Sangathan by Aruna Roy in Rajasthan. In case of Sardar Sarovar Project (SSP), the principal leadership was of Medha Patkar (NBA) alongside another social activist Baba Amte who provided moral leadership to the cause to preserve the river. Though it is perceived that the Narmada movement faces defeat as the new India confronts it with indifference, silence and nonchalance, it reflects a journey, a pilgrimage and a recollection of thirty years of resistance (Visvanathan, 2015). This struggle is about a collective history of a nation State. It is symbolic of all marginal struggles of the displaced, the landless and that which is tribal. Therefore, numbers alone cannot make sense of it because it demands a different kind of storytelling.

The involvement of international civil societies has been very important in land acquisition in India over the recent decades. Some of the international organizations, viz., Survival International, Action Aid, and Amnesty International have remained very vocal for settlement of land issues, while public and private sectors grab land in the name of development projects in the country. However, the big question arises about these civil societies for remaining clean, when big amounts of money are flowing in the name of development projects. Can they be far away from corruption while involving themselves and making value judgements relating to land acquisition in the country?

The Land Acquisition Act (LAA) of 1894 got amended in 2013 after 119 years of its existence during the UPA-II rule, which is popularly known as Land Acquisition, Rehabilitation and Resettlement (LARR) Act, 2013. The basic purpose of the act was to reduce the forcible acquisition of land, offer fair prices to the landowners and maintain transparency in the process of delivering information. The important requirements of LARR Act, 2013 are as follows. It requires prior consent of 80 per cent of the owners for land acquisition for private projects; while in case of public private partnership, consent of 70 per cent is required. Furthermore, it mandates for Social Impact Assessment (SIA) to assess the costs and benefits of the projects and therefore based on SIA, the project shall be judged whether it is in favour of the public or not. Besides, the Act restricts the acquisition of irrigated and multi-crop land. Additionally, the NDA Government put up a bill in 2014 (still it is in impasse as in August, 2015) and the legislation under consideration aims to amend the Act with the same title, i.e., LARR, 2013. However, in contrast the bill proposes to scrap these provisions for defence projects and those belonging to vaguely defined categories like affordable housing, industrial corridors and infrastructure including Special Economic Zone, PPPs and urban development projects (Singh and Panwar, 2015).

The LAA of 1894 was implemented during the post-independence period, under which the State played a paternalistic role keeping the citizens ill informed or asymmetrically informed in the land acquisition market. As a result of that, the country faced large scale resistance, many times violence, and unjust and unequal situations over the last six decades. The method of land acquisition resulted in large scale devastation mostly to the marginalized communities especially Dalits, tribals and the minorities in different parts of the country. Based on the past experience and the present reality, the process of land acquisition can be divided into three approaches as portrayed by Maitresh Ghatak and Parikshit Ghos (Chakravorty, 2015). First, let the market decide the land acquisition process. Under this process, price determination is purely based on demand and supply in the market. Second, let the farmers decide on land acquisition and a process of referendum among the project affected people shall be persisted with. Third, let the bureaucrats and experts speak on land acquisition. They argued basically there should be a single method; however, the recently enacted LAAR, 2013 adopted a 'kitchen sink' approach where all the approaches complement one another. As a result of that, the law carries within it the seeds of its own destruction. On the other hand, the recently proposed bill by the NDA Government for amendment of the existing Act of LAAR, 2013 seeks by removing the 'farmers speak' and 'experts speak' components in the vaguely defined areas of affordable housing, industrial corridors and infrastructure. Besides the recent Act and the proposed bill, the country has been implementing an Act for land acquisition since independence for its development process, where the Act did not allow farmers to speak on public sector projects. This is very significant to understand because nearly 90 per cent of the total land acquired in the country has been for the public sector.

Summary and Conclusions

The Western thought on ethical value judgment for distributing the social welfare has undergone various development processes such as optimization of scarce resources (Walrasian vis-à-vis Classical thought); Pareto Optimality (no one can be better off without making others worse off) as also determination of Social Welfare Function based on unanimity, completeness, democracy and transitivity by involving various agents in the process of development (Arrow's Impossibility theory). Eventually sustainability of economic development has been brought into existence by integrating environmental impacts. Based on these ideas (many of them are not mentioned here), refinement of the theory of cost benefit analysis has been accomplished for determining the social welfare across the globe over the past nearly 200 years of economic development processes. Furthermore, a sustainable economic development model has been integrated with CBA by developing both the weak and strong sustainable approaches. Considering land as one of the most precious natural resources, the ethical value judgment of land for distribution of social welfare is one of the most critical areas. Therefore, this paper tries to provide some thoughts on the process of value judgment of land in the course of economic development in India.

Land acquisition (for both public and private purposes) is an important process for economic development in India. The determination of price of land is mostly done by the seller (owners of land) and a representative of State. However, various political parties and civil society's involvement in the process of price determination and dissemination of information is a recent phenomenon. When the critical assessment of value judgment of land is done, it portrays that land acquisition for various projects (public as well as private) has devastated the livelihood of many citizens in the country mostly belonging to the marginalized communities. The LAA of 1894 was mostly State and bureaucracy-centric and denied the farmers in right to speak on land acquisition in the country. The LAAR of 2013 is of the kitchen sink variety in nature, where the NDA led Government is trying to delink the perception of farmers and experts to speak on land acquisition in the recently proposed bill of LAAR, 2015 (not yet finalized). Therefore, there is serious concern about considering the ethics of democracy (farmers and experts' views) and the sustainability aspects (SIA for each project).

Therefore, in order to avoid past injustice and present legal follies in land acquisition process, the asymmetries in the information system have to be rectified and made a very powerful and transparent system; some of the measures are as follows. First, all the land records are to be digitalized and some of the States are in the progressive stage. Second, all the land transaction records (all private sales and all Government acquisitions) are to be placed in the public domain. Third, the nominal price of every land transaction is to be determined in the public domain. Four, the lists of buyers and the sellers are to made in the public domain. Five, all the selling deals including the price, lists of buyers and sellers are to be discussed in Gram Sabha in case of small projects in the rural areas. Furthermore, the recently developed land pooling method in Andhra Pradesh suggested by the Chief Minister Chandra Babu Naidu, which mandates involving the farmers and donating land voluntarily in the process of development. This is an alternative method of land acquisition and we are yet to judge its practical authenticity. Eventually, the ethical value judgment of land is solely dependent on the ethics of democracy and politics.

NOTES

1. The Cost Benefit Analysis (CBA) deals with assessment of financial, economic, social and environmental impacts of various developmental projects in the world (Sinha and Bhatia, 1989).
2. Total factor productivity (TFP) is an attempt to measure the effects of pure technological change on output growth (Gowdy, 2011).
3. The end result of free and voluntary exchange is that no further trading will make one person better off without making someone else worse off.
4. Subsequently, it was developed by Graff and Arrow.
5. Land Acquisition Act, SEZ Act and Resettlement and Rehabilitation Act etc.
6. The ground level civil societies were worked at Singur in West

Bengal, POSCO in Odisha, Kalinganar in Odisha, Nandigram in West Bengal, Vedanta in Odisha etc.

REFERENCES

Ackerman, F. and L. Heinzerling. 2004. *Priceless: On Knowing the Price of Everything and the Value of Nothing*. New York: The New Press.

Anderson, L G and R F Settle. 1977. *Benefit-Cost Analysis: A Practical Guide*. Lexington: Lexington Books.

Arrow, K J. 1951. *Social Choices and Individual Values*. New Haven: Yale University Press.

Bardhan, P., M Luca., D Mookherjee. and F Pino. 2011. 'Evolution of Land Distribution in West Bengal 1967-2004: Role of Land Reforms and Demographic Changes'. Paper presented at the WIDER Conference on Land Inequality, Hanoi.

Bergson, A. 1948. 'Socialistic Economics.' In *A Survey of Contemporary Economics*, edited by H S Ellis. Vol.1, Philadelphia.

Boadway, R. 1974. 'The Welfare foundations of Cost Benefit Analysis.' *Economic Journal* 47: 926-39.

Brekke, K. 1997. 'The Numeraire Matters in Cost Benefit Analysis.' *Journal of Public Economics* 64, No. 1: 117-123.

Bromely, D. 1990. 'The Ideology of Efficiency: Searching for a Theory of Policy Analysis.' *Journal of Environmental Economics and Management* 19: 86-107.

Chakravorty, S. 2013. *The Price of Land: Acquisition, Conflict, Consequence*. New Delhi: Oxford University Press.

Chakravorty, S. 2015. 'How to Get Ourselves a Better Land Law.' *The Business Line* 7 April: 8.

Coase, R. 1960. 'The Problems of Social Cost.' *The Journal of Law and Economics* 3: 1-44.

Conning, J H. and J A Robinson. 2007. 'Property Rights and the Political Organisation of Agriculture.' *Journal of Development Economics* 82, No. 2: 416-47.

Daly, H E. 1977. *Steady State Economics*. San Francisco, CA: W.H. Freeman Co.

Dasgupta, A K. and D W Pearce. 1978. *Cost Benefit Analysis: Theory and Practice*. London: English Language Book Society and Mac Millan.

Easterlin, R. 1974. 'Does Economic Growth Improve the Human Lot? Some Empirical Evidence.' In *Nations and Happiness in Economic Growth: Essays in Honour of Moses Abramowitz*, edited by P David and M Reder. New York: Academic Press.

Government of India. 1975. *The Land Acquisition Act of 1894*. New Delhi:

Ministry of Law, Justice and Company Affairs.

Gowdy, J M. 2011. *Micro Economic Theory: Old and New*. New Delhi: Orient Black Swan.

Hanstad, R T., R Nielsen., D Vhugen. and T Haque. 2009. 'Learning from Old and New Approaches to Land Reforms in India.' In *Agricultural Land Redistribution: Towards Greater Consensus*, edited by H P Binswanger Mkhize, C. Bourguignon and Rogier van den Brink. Washington DC: The World Bank.

Keynes, J M. 1997. *The General Theory of Employment, Interest and Money*. New York: Prometheus Books.

Knetsch, J. 2005. 'Gain, Losses and the US-EPA Economic Analysis Guidelines: A Hazardous Product.' *Environmental and Resources Economics* 32: 91 112.

Layard, R. 2005. *Happiness Lessons from a New Science*. New Work: Penguin Publication.

Pigou, A C. 1962. *The Economics of Welfare* (1920 Reprint). London: The English Language Book Society and Macmillan.

Revesz, R. and M Livemore. 2008. *Rethinking Rationality: How Cost-Benefit Analysis Can Better Protect the Environment and Our Health*. New York, Oxford University Press.

Samuelson, P. 1950. *Evolution of Real National Income*. Oxford Economic Paper, New Series, Vol.2.

Scitovsky, T. 1941. 'A Note on Welfare Proposition in Economics.' *Review of Economic Studies* 9, No. 1: 77-88.

Singh, R. and D A Panwar. 2015. 'Subverting a Progressive Law.' *The Hindu*, 9 July: 11.

Sinha, B. and R Bhatia. 1989. *Economic Appraisal of Irrigation Project in India*. New Delhi: Ashish Publication.

Spash, C. 2007. 'Deliberative Monetary Valuation (DMV): Issues in Combining Economic and Political Process to value Environmental Change.' *Ecological Economics* 63: 690-99.

Stavins, R., A Wagner. and G Wagner. 2002. 'Interpreting Sustainability in Economic Terms: Dynamic Efficiency plus Intergenerational Equity.' *Discussion Paper 02-29*, Washington D.C: Resources for the Future.

Stern, N. 2007. *The Economics of Climate Change: The Stern Review*. Cambridge: Cambridge University Press.

Visvanathan, S. 2015. 'Chronicle of a Struggle Retold.' *The Hindu* 6 August: 10.

Weitzman, M. 2007. 'A Review of the Stern Review on the Economics of Climate Change.' *Journal of the Economic Literature* 45: 703-724.

4

Development, Displacement and Impoverishment Centrality of Land Acquisition Law and Policy: The Enterchanged Colonial Legacy

K B Saxena

Magnitude of Displacement

The Development paradigm pursued since independence has induced considerable involuntary displacement of people from their land, habitat, livelihood and social environment. This has resulted from forced acquisition of their land and settlements for execution of various projects. The magnitude of such displacement has not even been accurately mapped. State agencies have shown no interest in collection of information on the subject, its analysis and dissemination. The few estimates that have been compiled by non-official agencies place the number of displaced persons up to the year 2000 at 6.0 crore (Fernandes, 2006)[a]. The official figures, however, acknowledge only 2.13 crore – which is a gross under estimate. There is a consensus that the tribal communities have borne the brunt of this onslaught as more than 40 per cent of the displaced belong to these communities. Dalits constitute another 20 per cent of such persons. It is estimated that about 5 lakh persons get displaced each year as a direct consequence of land acquisition for development plan projects. This does not include displacement caused by non-plan projects, changes in land use induced by development projects and acquisition of land for urban growth. But the scale of displacement which is now taking place from mega mining, industrial, infrastructural and urban development projects would far exceed the pace and spread witnessed since independence. This is because development in the earlier phase was constrained by the State's financial capacity to invest and the overall paradigm of the economy it had committed itself to which did not assign the lead role to private capital for growth. This barrier has been broken by policy reforms oriented towards neo-liberal transformation of economy and its integration with the global economic order. This shift has led to private (national and international) capital centric growth and export-oriented liberalized economy which has attracted large FDI projects. These investments involve acquisition of huge areas of land across the country but largely in the central tribal region which has concentration of resources-minerals, forest areas and water. With the enactment of SEZ Act, 2005, the land acquisition has extended to agriculturally rich areas (multi-cropped) with developed infrastructural facilities as well. Faced with stiff opposition from peasantry against this acquisition spree, the State agencies are now promoting acquisition of land by private companies through voluntary market transactions for setting up such zones in what is termed as a mode of Public-Private Partnership. Around 267 such zones were approved during UPA regime which involved acquisition of 1,34,000 hectares of land. The land has been acquired for 67 such SEZs. The affected peasantry and other agrarian social groups are seething with unprecedented anger and localized movements of resistance and protests have sprung up against this mode of acquisition as well.

Multi Dimensionality of Displacement

Involuntary displacement is a traumatic phenomenon. It involves more than physical dispossession from the place of residence and termination of their livelihood. It results in dislocation of social, moral and economic life from networks and support structures built over generations. This process triggers a chain of impoverishments landlessness, homelessness, joblessness, marginalization, food insecurity, increased morbidity, loss of access to CPRs and social disarticulation (Cernea, 1998). To this list has been added discontinuation of schooling of children (Mahapatra, 1999) and deprivation of access to basic services and development programmes ahead of displacement (Mathur, 1997). The poor among the displaced persons, particularly the Tribals and Dalits, emerge from this process as 'victims' of development. The affected Tribals perceive this pattern of development as a declaration of 'war' against them and would consider their existing underdevelopment as 'benign' in comparison. This forced displacement is violative of the Constitutional protection to the sanctity of human life under Article 21 which Supreme Court has interpreted as right to life with dignity. Yet, the legal dispensation of land acquisition (until 2013) i.e., Land Acquisition Act, 1894 and conceptual articulation of development enshrined in State policy permit the State to displace people without their consent and with no obligation to rehabilitate them honourably to smoothen their transition to a new life in an altered environment. This retrogressive character of the legal and policy regime was pursued ignoring the obligation of the State to refrain from and protect against forced eviction from home(s) and land rooted in several international instruments to which India is a party.

Lack of Concern for Rehabilitation

The lack of concern for the displaced in acquisition of land is exacerbated by dismal performance in respect of their re-settlement and rehabilitation. In the context of the tribals who constitute the single largest group among the displaced, the Tenth Five Year Plan document honestly concedes that only 25 per cent of the displaced have received even a modicum of rehabilitation, (Planning Commission, 2003) though the ground realities would convey a pretty dismal picture of even those officially claimed to have been rehabilitated. It is evident that the 75 per cent of the displaced persons have been left to fend for themselves. Most of such persons would have moved into the urban destitute labour market with uncertain livelihood options, low wages, hazardous working conditions and low quality of life. Ironically, this outcome had emerged even when most projects were State- funded and project implementing agencies were Public Sector units controlled by the State. The apathy, therefore, can only be attributed to the reluctance of State to accept a clear obligation to rehabilitate the displaced persons since the law/laws under which land is acquired for development projects do not carry such a provision. This insensitivity to human suffering was compounded by indifference to put in place even a policy on rehabilitation of displaced persons until 2003. Though individual project agencies had formulated adhoc 'rehabilitation' packages, these were neither uniform nor need-based and much less enforceable. Even these packages were substantially diluted over time. The State virtually assumes that payment of cash compensation to land losers, and house-site with some financial assistance for construction of their houses to all those displaced from their habitat, satisfy the requirements of rehabilitation. In the early years of independence, some projects did provide land for cultivation to land losers, where land was acquired for dams, though of a poor quality and with no provision for its improvement by the project agency. But even this arrangement has not continued. The replacement of assets, the most effective form of rehabilitation, was never accepted as a policy or even a feasible option. As for durable and dignified employment, some PSUs (like coal companies) did have in the earlier years a provision for giving employment to a member of the displaced family losing a specified area of land. But this provision was subsequently removed based on TN Singh Committee Report (Parasuraman, 1999). The displaced persons have also failed to get any support from the judiciary in enforcing even limited assurances contained in diverse packages which the Central/ State Governments announced for different projects. The situation in respect of creating infrastructural facilities and social amenities in the resettlement colonies was equally bad. The displaced persons were shifted to the resettlement sites without such facilities having been provided. In any case, there was no Central law matching the Land Acquisition Act, 1894 which obligated the Government to undertake a specified package of resettlement and rehabilitation measures. Some States, for example, Maharashtra, Karnataka and Madhya Pradesh (later Punjab also joined them) did enact a law providing for such a package applicable only to sector specific projects. This, however, did not constitute a uniform policy. But even this package was not sincerely implemented. The lack of adequate sensitivity and political will to enforce provisions of such laws inspires no confidence that a legal entitlement of this sort for all the displaced persons uniformly throughout the country would necessarily translate into desirable outcomes.

Displacement and Impoverishment

It is widely accepted that the people affected by displacement suffer multiple types of impoverishment. This happens for the following reasons:

- The displacement from Land takes away a (usually the only) productive asset, a source of assumed livelihood, and makes the affected household asset less. This loss not only deprives the loser of the most assured source of livelihood and, for many, the only source of livelihood but also insurance against adversity, a collateral for getting credit. The landlessness in a rural society also symbolizes the loss of status, identity and visibility and therefore translates into total powerlessness.
- With the loss of a 'source of livelihood' the affected person/persons is/are forced to seek employment as wage labour. Here they are exposed to uncertainty of work, low wages, long hours of work, hazardous working conditions and indignities besides a drastic fall in family income and standard of living and lowering of status from being a self-employed to a wage labourer.
- The inadequate/uncertain purchasing power leads to food insecurity and malnutrition which make the members of affected household vulnerable to ill health which diminishes the toiling capacity and productivity of the bread winners. This in turn aggravates impoverishment.

- The meager compensation obtained from loss of land is spent on meeting subsistence needs after forced eviction till such time the affected person manages to get work. It is also used in construction of house as, usually, the shelter provided at the resettlement site is unfit for occupation. This prevents the use of meager financial compensation for rebuilding the asset base. The quantum of compensation, in any case, is insufficient to replace the asset. The non-payment of compensation or payment of compensation with delay or in instalments pushes the affected family into destitution.
- The disintegration of social networks –a source of mutual help and social and moral support against adversity resulting from displacement deprives the affected person with informal credit and other forms of material assistance to take up income generating activities or meeting contingent needs. This exposes the person/family to rapacious moneylenders and causes indebtedness and inter generational bondage from which the victim is unable to extricate itself.
- As the work suited to the skill base of the affected persons is usually not available near the new settlement, the displaced persons have to migrate in search of it wherever available and get exposed to multiple forms of exploitation which accentuate their poverty, vulnerability and misery.
- At the place of migration, they not merely face poor quality of life in terms of shelter and access to social amenities but also are deprived of all State provided development benefits admissible to them in their settlement at home. The migrants are also denied by the local host communities access to basic social amenities near the temporary (shelter) they make. This further contributes to their impoverishment as they end up by paying for free public goods like drinking water, sanitation facilities, health care, ration card etc.
- Due to the loss of assured income and faced with uncertainty of work and low wages, the family is forced

to withdraw their children from school and push them also in the labour market in order that they also contribute to the family income for sheer physical survival.

- The women suffer worse than men in the family. In the absence of opportunities for work as agricultural labourers in the new settlement, they lose their status as workers and get reduced to the position of housewives. The loss of access to CPRs not only deprives them fuel wood, fodder, and other benefits but also the share in the household economy as an equal partner. Deprived of work on farms and access to CPRs, they are forced to seek work in the labour market where they face acute discrimination and end up getting informal/ degrading work with extremely low wages. Additionally, they face extreme vulnerability to social (sexual) exploitation (Parasuraman, 1999). They also lose assertiveness, share in decision making and consequent reduction in status in the family (Fernandes, 2006).

- The family members facing these adversities suffer from extreme mal-nutrition and therefore fall easy preys to illness with diminished capacity to purchase health care resulting in prolonged morbidity and early mortality.

- The trauma caused by adversities faced in life resulting from displacement and the hostility of the new environment in which they are settled also leads to social abnormalities like alcoholism, violence within and outside the family and mental illness which only aggravate the poverty of the displaced and reduce their capacity to recover.

- The land acquisition impoverishes not merely those who lose land but also those who lose livelihood based on land owned by others or land pertaining to the common pool. Their plight is worse than those who lose land because they get no compensation even for transitional subsistence let alone rehabilitation. They lose alternative work opportunities in the emerging labour market and therefore leave the area in search of work with nothing to fall back upon. The resultant destitution threatens even physical survival.

Instrumentality of the Law in Displacement

The most striking part of the development-induced displacement is the instrumentality of law in its legitimization. The law provides the rationale for use of State power to displace and lays down contours within which affected citizens can challenge its propriety and/or seek relief against its arbitrary or unjust use in a designated judicial fora. It creates an arrangement that seeks to strike a balance between exercise of State power and citizen entitlements. It is therefore important to see what the law entails in terms of its provisions, why its application causes so much hostility among the affected persons and how it impoverishes people and restricts their options to seek justice and prevent catastrophic consequences from taking place.

Colonial Legacy

The most distinctive change introduced by the colonial rule in India was the centrality of law in the governance of the country. This implied that the conduct of both the State and its citizens would be determined within the limits set by it and thus prevents any arbitrary or absolute use of power. A judicial system was put in place to enforce sanctity of this arrangement. This required State to justify its action in terms of law. The need for enactment of a law on acquisition of land thus emerges from this imperative, more so because acquisition of land entailed dispossession of the existing occupant user of land. We have no authentic information on how such acquisition was undertaken by the pre-colonial State and on what terms and what its magnitude were. Presumably oral or written order issued by the local ruler would have constituted its basis. The Colonial Government's attempt to legislate on the subject shows the complexity involved in this exercise which entailed several revisions of the first enactment in 1824 before attaining finality in the Land Acquisition Act, 1894. The 1894 Law was preceded by seven attempts, starting from Regulation I of 1824 of Bengal

Code, followed by extension of its operation to the town of Calcutta and later to the city of Bombay. The First Law enacted and made applicable to the whole of British India was Act VI of 1857, amended by Act II of 1861, Act XXII of 1863 and all three replaced by Act X of 1870. A separate law XVII of 1885 was enacted for mines and minerals. The Act I of 1894 replaced by all previous versions. The crucial thing that emerged from this exercise in law making was progressive expansion of State power of acquisition not only in terms of territories to which it was applicable but also the ambit of its purposes. While a Regulation I of 1824 was operative throughout the provinces coming under the jurisdiction of Bengal Presidency, it applicability was extended to Calcutta and acquisition for railway (1850) and whole of India (1857). In terms of ambit, the Act of 1861 extended acquisition to temporary occupation and 1863 Act expanded State power to acquire law for private companies for works of public utility. The 1885 Law entirely dealt with acquisition relating to mines & minerals. Even 1894 Act was subjected to amendments on various minor matters in 1914, 1919, 1920, 1921, 1923 and 1933 during the colonial period itself. (Shanmukham, 2001).

The power of the Government under the Land Acquisition Act 1894 is absolute. It establishes total control of State over land as an attribute of State sovereignty. The landowner has no choice to opt out or refuse to part with land. This is the reason why people who are dependent on land for their subsistence are so agitated about the prospects of its acquisition. The Land Acquisition Act, 1894, however, requires that land can be acquired only for a 'public purpose' or for a company after observing the prescribed procedure. Compensation must be paid for such acquisition on the basis of market value of land so acquired. The procedure prescribed in the Act requires a preliminary notice to be issued informing the prospective land losers about the intention of the Government to acquire land for an identified public purpose with details of the village/area, plot numbers of land followed by measurement and assessment of land. This notice is required to be published in two newspapers and displayed at important places in the locality to ensure reach of information to the persons concerned. The persons who are interested in the land so notified can object to the proposal within a period of thirty days of such notification. After looking into these objections, the Government conveys its decision to finally acquire the land and proceeds to fix compensation for it. A notice is issued to the persons who had shown interest in land seeking their views on the nature of their interests and amount of compensation admissible under the law. After scrutinizing the validity of claims, the amount of compensation, called the award, is announced. Thereafter, the compensation is paid to the claimant and the land is taken possession of. Any person, interested in the notified land and aggrieved by the amount of compensation awarded, can require his/her case to be referred to the designated court for adjudication. The decision of the court or the appellate court, if an appeal has been preferred on the amount of award, is final and has to be implemented .

Land Acquisition Law and Impoverishment

- The 1894 law of land acquisition was heavily tilted in favour of the State, investing it with absolute power to acquire private land with virtually no checks against its indiscriminate use. This left the affected persons with no space to prevent the increasing intensity of land acquisition and their consequent displacement and impoverishment. The opportunity provided under the Act for raising objections to the notification conveying the intention to acquire land was of no value since it provided no option to prevent forcible acquisition and created no pressure on the land acquiring authority to accommodate the viewpoint of the affected person or consultation with them through a meaningful dialogue.
- The law created no corresponding obligation on the State to undertake requisite rehabilitation and resettlement of the affected persons which ensured a dignified survival and restoration, if not betterment, of the standard of living from which they were displaced. Therefore, impoverishment and social degradation became integral

features of the operation of law which failed to recognize or reflect it. This made the law expropriatory, undemocratic, unjust and inhuman.

- The law had a strong class bias in favour of the propertied persons. The framework of law entirely ignored affected persons without property rights in land from any entitlement whether in terms of participation in proceedings for land acquisition or accrual of compensation for loss of access to land. It did not take into account loss of interest in land other than ownership such as those of tenants and sharecroppers as well as loss of opportunities for wage employment, self-employment, fishing, trade and craft-related activities etc. which arise from use of land owned by others as also land of common pool used by all residents of the village. As a result such persons got left out from the ambit of compensation schemes as well as appropriate rehabilitation package which impoverished them even more than those losing their land.
- The orientation of law was entirety individual-centric. It ignored the existence of 'community' as a stakeholder with its rights and interests distinct from those of the individuals constituting it. This disregard for the existence of 'community' resulted in failure to recognize it as an interested party and consequently to enlist its participation in the proceedings and provide it with compensation for loss of its rights. Additionally, it caused social disarticulation of affected persons, disintegration of their social networks and loss of social force to help affected persons cope with trauma of displacement and resulting impoverishment. It also deprived the resettled displaced persons of an agency to manage common property resources and exert pressure on the Government to provide for its replacement in the scheme of resettlement.
- The conceptualization of rights and interests in land in the law was embedded in colonial legality which restricted them to parcels of land in individual possession validated by land records. This left out rights and interests in forests and other common property resources which people

intensively accessed on a customary basis. The loss of this access in the absence of a legally validated right of use was not compensated. For the loss of common property resources resulting from acquisition, the compensation accrued to the Government which is usually recorded as their 'owner' in land records. The Government did not pass on this compensation to the users of land due to this flawed legality. This made the displaced persons even more vulnerable as the poor among them derived a sizable part of their income from such resources besides other benefits. The women among the displaced persons suffered the most on account of this loss as, in the domestic division of labour in the family, they are the ones who access these resources. The disempowering effect of this deprivation on them was therefore more pronounced as they were forced to seek wage employment in the market where they were exposed to least paid and low status work. This changed situation also led to loss of status and decision making power within the family and intensified deterioration of their condition.

- The law took no notice of wide ranging inequalities arising from access to land and social structure, and benefits accruing from them. As a result, differential economic and social conditions of groups in society made some groups more vulnerable due to their lack of skills and cultural resources to take to another vocation for livelihood. It created no space for exempting them from acquisition of land or providing for a differential treatment to them in the scheme of compensation. It ignored, in this context, the most vulnerable pre-agricultural tribes like hunters and food gatherers who after displacement suffered early mortality or even extinction due to excessive stress caused by pressures to adjust to a new environment for survival alien to their traditional living spaces and resource base. Their physical constitution was not conditioned to undertake hard manual labour or sedantry work which was forced upon them in the absence of a resettlement appropriate to their situation.
- The law fails to take into account the plight of persons

exposed to multiple displacement and provided no mitigating or compensating mechanism to overcome the traumatic experience.

- The compensation scheme embedded in law contributed to impoverishment in many ways:
  - ➢ It was restricted to financial compensation with no provision for alternatives like land which particularly suited certain groups such as the tribals.
  - ➢ It provided no mechanism for assessing market value and addressing distortions that arise in assessing this value from sale and purchase transactions, and, therefore, led to assessment of compensation which was totally inadequate to replace the land lost or acquire other assets for livelihood.
  - ➢ It did not take into account the restrictions governing sale and purchase of tribal land and the perception of the value of land in the psyche of the tribes which goes far beyond its instrumentality as an income generating asset. The 'market value', conceptually, was a wholly inadequate parameter for computing its loss in their case.
  - ➢ The payment of compensation was conceived in terms of cash disbursement which rendered tribal communities most vulnerable due to their lack of adequate exposure to cash economy and ability to handle large amount of cash. As a result, they were unable to protect themselves against varied attempts by non-tribals such as traders, middlemen liqour vendors and other vested interests to squeeze this money from them.
  - ➢ It was restricted to loss of land with valid rights and excluded loss of employment/income generation from its use, access to CPRs, fishing rights, and forests besides economic and social suffering and trauma. The persons so affected received no assistance to alleviate impoverishment caused by this loss.
- The law took no notice of laws against alienation of tribal land and protection provided by the Schedule V of the

Constitution which prohibited transfer of tribal land to non-tribals and therefore had the effect of nullifying these protective and beneficial arrangements. As a result, it caused irreparable damage to the interests of the tribal communities.

- The law did not provide for any pre-acquisition scrutiny of the reasonableness of the quantum of land sought for a specific project or a 'public purpose'. It therefore failed to regulate the quantum of acquisition leading to acquisition of land far in excess of the present and future requirements, resultant misuse of land and enlarged displacement on this account. It neither made provision for punitive measures against land requiring agencies for seeking acquisition of excessive land or for misusing the acquired land nor for return of land to the erstwhile owners after acquisition if it remained unutilized.

- The Law created an open-ended space for acquisition of land through its definitions of 'public purpose'. This enabled the ever increasing acquisition of land thereby causing increasing displacement and impoverishment. No regulatory checks were provided for against indiscriminate and injudicious application of 'public purpose' and no space was provided to challenge the rational of its purported use.

- The Law did not take into account the social reality that
  - ➤ Land records were not updated and therefore failed to accurately reflect all rights and interests in land. The law provided for no obligation on the part of the Government to update land records and check motivated transfers of land prior to initiation of land acquisition proceedings.
  - ➤ Land transactions were taking place just prior to the start of acquisition proceedings. This enabled certain interested groups to purchase cheaply poor people's land by spreading disinformation. The persons affected by these phenomena belonged to poorer sections of the displaced persons and therefore suffered further impoverishment as they were deprived of even the

meager entitlements admissible under the law and the policy.

- The law empowered the Government to take possession of land, if necessary, by use of force without ensuring payment of full compensation and necessary amenities and infrastructure at the resettlement site. This left the affected persons utterly miserable with not even a habitable shelter. They failed to recover from this trauma.
- The law did not take into account the consequences of acquisition on environment and the differential impacts on the affected social groups. It, therefore failed to place before the land acquiring authority an accurate assessment of the adverse impact and its social cost as against the benefits claimed before proceeding with the acquisition of land. As a result no provisions were made for preventive measures to check damage to the environment and the ameliorative measures to neutralize the adverse social impact and to ensure that their cost was taken into account to assess the viability of the project as against the benefits that were projected to accrue. These negative externalities accentuated the impoverishment of the affected persons and reduced the potential for their satisfactory resettlement.
- The law placed no regulatory checks on the application of 'urgency' provision to prevent its misuse. This increased the vulnerability of the affected persons as their land and employment were taken away without even observing necessary procedural formalities and complying with the minimum level of their participation. The shock caused to them in such circumstances was greater as they were unable to adjust to the social reality of sudden displacement. This further limited their capacity to alleviate their poverty.

Complicity of the Land Acquisition Policy

The policy and law are intertwined. Public Policy making is an essential function of Government. A public policy is an expression of the social goals which a Government wishes to achieve in a particular arena of activities. The law is an instrument enacted by the Government to translate policy into operable action and lays down the processes through which this would be realized. The law provides transparency and legitimacy to a policy to ward off any challenge to its rationale. The design of law therefore reflects the framework and contents of the policy. The law, once enacted, becomes an empowering instrument for the Government which it uses to expand and deepen the ambit of policy. The two are interdependent and reinforce each other. Therefore, if certain consequences emerge from the operation of law, they are directly attributable to the policy in the furtherance of which the law has been used. The phenomenon of displacement and the spiral of impoverishment it causes is a direct offshoot of the land acquisition policy of the Government. The law of acquisition is instrumental in enabling the Government to proceed in this direction.

Until 2003, Government formulated no formal land acquisition policy as such and perhaps never felt the need for one. This does not imply that it had no policy on the subject. Such a policy even if not expressly outlined can be deduced from the actions of the Government and the practices of its agencies observed in the acquisition of land.

Post Colonial State: Colonial Legacy Intensifies

The policy is, however, more crucial than the law as a factor in causing impoverishment. This is because a policy determines the contours of law with a view to facilitating its fructification. The 1894 Law on Land Acquisition was enacted by the Colonial Government to achieve its economic and the political goals focused on maximization of revenue extraction and creation of infrastructure for enabling collection of raw material for industries for the metropolitan country and penetration of markets for goods produced there. The political goal related to creation of infrastructure for governance and provision of a minimum of social amenities for a small group of governing elites. It did not have any developmental goals for welfare of the subject population. The policy of acquisition centered on these limited objectives and therefore entailed acquisition of a small area of land. As a result, it was able to contain the resentment and negative impact resulting from such acquisition to a relatively smaller number of persons and areas. The authoritarian nature of the regime did not permit such resentment to spread. But the post-colonial State was a democratic State wedded to a wide ranging social and economic goals emerging from the provisions contained in the Constitution and those evolved during the course of national movement in the deliberations of the congress party. Therefore, State in India embarked upon a wide ranging development programmes which entailed acquisition of large areas of land, particularly for irrigation, industrialization and mining. This affected a larger number of people across the country but particularly the tribals in whose areas many such projects were located. The Democratic State also endowed people with essential human rights which enabled articulation of their misery resulting from such acquisition. This enabled civil society groups to document the adverse impact of such acquisition on the affected people and exert pressure on the Government to make changes in the law and policy to address them. The Government, however, ignored such voices. It considered acquisition of land a necessary sacrifice for the progress of the nation and benefit of the larger society. It therefore, never considered it desirable to change the law or democratize and humanize it. Rather, it chose to expand the ambit of its application and speed up the process of acquisition. This was done though a major change in law in 1984, though the Land Acquisition Act 1894 underwent several minor changes preceding it. The objective of 1984 amendment to the Act was to plug some loopholes, accommodate some grievances of the affected persons but more importantly to undertake acquisition of land for private companies. The changes introduced through this amendment included (1) Payment of interest with effect from the first notification under section 4 till the date of award, (2) Increase of solarium from 15 per cent to 30 per cent, (3) shortening the period within which a declaration under section 6 had to be made from three years to one year, (4) Fixing a two year limit within which an award had to issue and (5) Mandatory publication of Section 4 Notice in two local papers one of which should be a regional language paper (Ramesh &

Khan, 2015). There was nothing in this amendment to neutralize the detrimental consequences of acquisition on the affected persons outlined above. The Post colonial States policy was also entirely responsible for the extent to which law was applied, its injudicious use and abuse. This was evident from the indiscriminate acquisition of land in terms of the purposes for which it was resorted to. It was the policy which refrained from defining the expression 'public purpose' tightly to limit its application. Rather, it kept it on adding to the list of purposes defined as 'public purpose' which made it virtually open ended so as to stretch its coverage and extend it to any purpose the Government considered necessary. Similarly, the policy also failed to regulate the quantum of land acquired by rigorous scrutiny of the demand placed by the requiring agencies. As a result, land acquired was far in excess of the immediate and future requirement and remains unutilized. Consequently, it is encroached upon, transferred for purposes other than those for which it was acquired and lavishly used for certain purposes well beyond the reasonable needs. No private agency ever does that when it plans and executes a project with its own resources. That the Government has not taken any measures so far to check this tendency shows lack of concern not only for public resources but more important, for the people who are displaced. The policy is also instrumental in interpreting the provision of law in a manner that hurts the interests of the affected persons. This is exemplified by restricting the definition of land only to validly owned private land. This conservative view is conveyed not by a plain reading of the law but by practice of the acquiring authorities. The expression 'Land' could have been liberally interpreted to cover forests, CPRs and Government owned land customarily used by the people for drawing various benefits. Similar was the case with the application of law with regard to the expression 'person interested'. The Government could have adopted a policy to interpret the provision liberally with a view to addressing the concerns of persons who were dependent upon the land acquired but did not own it. In fact, the Government had the freedom to go even beyond the provisions of law to mitigate the suffering of different categories of the affected persons. For example, the Government was not prevented from compensating informal tenants, agricultural labourers, fisherpersons, artisans and such other displaced persons using the acquired land by interpreting the word 'Person interested' to inclusively cover all of them. Similarly, it could provide additional compensation to the land losers over and above the amount calculated as market values so as to enable them to replace their asset. This practice is often resorted to in the form of ex-gratia payment when people opposed acquisition of their land. It could also devise a methodology of assessing 'market value' in ways other than through sale/purchase transactions as the law did not lay down any method for its assessment. Various alternatives proposed by the civil society for assessing market value more realistically were available with the Government. But the Government has chosen not to consider these alternatives to reduce the injustice to the displaced persons. The policy was also responsible for deciding how much information about the project should be provided the affected persons which enabled to them raise objections against the proposal to acquire land. Here too the Government chose the most conservative approach and the least information was included in the in the notification and that too through modes which failed to reach the most vulnerable among the affected persons. The Government did not go beyond the modes prescribed in the law in making adequate information available to the affected persons though it was quite aware about their inadequacy. It was not prevented by law from going beyond these modes to ensure that sufficient and timely information is reached to the persons likely to be affected and their apprehensions and doubts were allayed. The Government response to the pressures exerted on it both for and against acquisition proposals also conveyed the tilt in its approach to decision making. These pressures usually emerged from the affected persons opposing acquisition of their land on the one hand and from the agency requiring land and dominant sections of society not affected by acquisition pressing for acquisition. From within the affected persons, the pressures may also be conflicting in some cases (a) from land owners (absentees as well as rich) who may be interested in selling land for material gains or to get rid of tenants and other interests subsisting on it, (b) from the poorer sections who are keen to protect their only source of livelihood. The policy has all along tilted in favour of the agencies seeking acquisition of land, as also some sections of land owners and upwardly mobile middle class supporting it. The Government decision on whether to acquire land considering various objections raised, to leave some portion out of acquisition or denitrify it after the issue of declaration to acquire land almost invariably reflected a bias in favour of acquiring agencies and large land owners and other dominant sections of society who hoped to benefit from the project. As the law was heavily loaded in favour of the Government in making a decision on the issues, the objections of the affected persons opposing acquisition were ignored.

The practice of the Government also disregarded views of the affected persons even where it was mandatory in law for it to take them into account. This happened in complying with the provisions of PESA, 1996. The law requires that gram sabha should be consulted before acquiring the land in the scheduled Area. The local officials producing subverted this requirement by producing 'manufactured consent'. This was done by suppressing dissenting opinion of a large section of people in the Gram Sabha meeting as they feared that it might go against acquisition. The Government encouraged this conduct of local officials because it was so committed to the proposal of the land requiring agency. The affected persons were perceived as adversaries by the Government because they opposed land acquisition. The nexus between corporates and the Government officials on the issue of land acquisition is so strong that the affected people have lost faith in the compliance of the legal provisions. The Government could also dovetail in its policy divergent modes of compensation so that the affected persons could choose from them depending upon the suitability to their situation. The policy has, however, confined the payment of compensation to cash disbursement only. Even in the matter of cash compensation, the Government could interpret the provision of 'market value' of land in the law to imply 'replacement' cost of the land acquired in order that the affected persons could purchase alternative land from the market. Such a replacement value would in any case constitute the genuine 'market value'. The policy could go even beyond the 'market value' to legitimately take into account the 'appreciation in value' of the land which occurred from anticipation of development of the area with the incoming project so as to give the benefit of upgraded market value to the losers of land. As per the prevailing situation, the benefit of appreciation of the market value of land exclusively accrued to the project agency to which the land was transferred after acquisition. The Government could also decide on the alternative modes of making land available to the requiring agency other than by transfer of ownership which resulted in dispossession of land owners and build it in to the design of the policy. This could include long term lease which would provide annual rent to the land losers the quantum of which could be revised periodically. These are only a few examples which showed that the policy was the moving force in using the law in a manner that caused impoverishment of the displaced persons since the policy was entirely determined by the Government, the responsibility for the precarious situation of the people resulting from displacement exclusively lay with the Government. The law was merely an instrument of its will.

Policy on Land Acquisition

The first attempt at articulating a policy on land acquisition, albeit implicitly in the form of rehabilitation and resettlement of displaced persons was made in 2003, and that too under the pressure of World Bank without any consultation with the civil society. But the policy remained on paper and was never enforced. The civil society was extremely critical of it. A revised policy on rehabilitation and resettlement of displaced persons was formulated and notified in 2007. This policy throws some light on the policy of land acquisition. In the preamble to the National Rehabilitation and Resettlement Policy, 2007, it was stated that the land acquisition through exercise of legal powers of 'Eminent Domain' was considered necessary for provision of public facilities and infrastructure. Therefore, involuntary displacement of persons depriving them of their land, livelihood, and shelter, restricting their access to traditional resource base and uprooting them from their socio-cultural environment as a result of it was inevitable. The policy however, stressed on minimizing large scale displacement as far as possible. It is also advised that waste land, degraded land or un-irrigated land should be acquired and acquisition of agricultural land may be kept to the minimum. The acquisition of multi-cropped land may be avoided to the extent possible and acquisition of irrigated land if unavoidable, may be kept to the minimum. Alternatives that may minimize displacement, minimize acquisition of agricultural land and minimize total area of land for the project may be taken into consideration. This should be done by setting up suitable institutional mechanism in a transparent manner. Three features of the policy emerged from this statement (a) inevitability of displacement, (b) the need to minimize it, (c) avoidance of acquisition of irrigated multi-cropped agriculture land. It is evident that the pious wish in respect of (b) and (c) above, articulated for the first time since independence, was hedged by so many *ifs* that acquisition of land sought by a project agency could be easily justified as unavoidable. The post policy experience of land acquisition undertaken showed that these caveats did not work in regulating the acquisition proposals. The institutional mechanism proposed for pursuing these objectives in future, as indicated in subsequent documents (for example) the Rehabilitation and Resettlement Bill, 2009, consisted of a committee of officials who were required to undertake such a scrutiny (MORD, 2009)[a]. This structure of scrutiny did not have a participatory character since there was no representation of the affected persons in it as its members. This raised question marks on the objectivity and genuineness of this exercise. Besides, this arrangement was not inserted in the Land Acquisition (Amendment). Bill, 2007 in the absence of which the exercise, even if it had been carried out in pursuance of this provision, would have made little difference to the affected persons as their views were unlikely to influence the decision on acquisition of land, its quantum and nature. In any case, the following features of the policy would indicate that the declaration made in the National Rehabilitation and Resettlement Policy (2007) could not be taken very seriously.

Features of the Policy Contributing to Impoverishment

Progressive Enlargement of the Ambit of Acquisition

When the policy to compulsorily acquire privately owned land for a public purpose was conceived originally during the colonial period, it was intended to use this drastic measure sparingly for the limited purpose of executing works of public utility by the Government. Its enforcement therefore, affected a negligible number of people. But this ambit of acquisition in the post colonial period increased enormously due to the enlargement of development activities requiring land for their implementation. With the amendments carried out in the land acquisition law post independence, the power of land acquisition by the State was extended to the needs of public sector corporations and in 1984, to the requirements of private companies registered under the Companies' Act, Societies registered under the Societies' Registration Act and cooperatives registered under the law relating to cooperative societies. Post 1990, the acquisition for the latter activities has grown manifold. With the onset of economic reforms, even development activities earlier executed by Government agencies are undertaken now largely by private companies for profit. In addition, conservation of biodiversity (particularly the protection of wildlife) also emerged centre stage in the public policy profile which has further expanded the scope of compulsory acquisition of land. The pressure to achieve faster growth extended acquisition to the requirement of land for setting up of Special Economic Zones.

Insensitivity to the Quantum of Acquisition

The failure to make any effort to effect pre-acquisition scrutiny of the proposal of acquisition and the quantum of land required for a project, and to establish a credible institutional mechanism for this purpose led to excessive acquisition of land quite disproportionate to the present and future needs of the project. As a result, huge areas of land remained unutilized leading to encroachment wrongful transfer and misuse of the acquired land.

Unwillingness to Seek Non-Displacing and Least Displacing Alternatives

No exercise was undertaken if the acquisition of land as proposed by the requiring agency could be avoided or at least reduced and the extent of displacement minimized by considering the option of utilization of land acquired earlier for some other project but are lying vacant and exploring alternative sites for the project.

Refusal to Recognize the Obligation of Rehabilitation and Resettlement of Displaced Persons

The emphasis in the earlier policies had all along been on acquisition of land with no corresponding obligation, urgency and anxiety to rehabilitate and resettle affected persons displaced by such acquisition. The ad-hoc arrangements for relocating the displaced families pursued were confined to shifting them to a new site with minimal housing arrangement/ infrastructure and social amenities, leaving the rest to the affected persons to manage. The 2007 Policy incorporated in a limited way this need but remained unenforced.

Imposed No Obligation on Land Using Agencies to Provide Benefits to the Displaced Persons

While the project agencies provide their staff a high standard of modern living, not even a tiny fraction of it was extended to the displaced persons in the colonies established for them. The policy pursued in the matter incorporated no such direction to them.

Ignored the Social Reality of Outdated Land Records and Unenforced Legal Entitlements

A very large number of affected displaced persons were deprived of even the inadequate entitlements of financial compensation and other concessions, if any, in the course of resettlement. This was because the policy of the Government did not recognize the validity of the following categories of displaced persons for such entitlement.

1. Unrecorded tenants, sharecroppers and interest holders on the acquired land
2. Customary users of common property resources including forest and Government land
3. Occupants of Government/public land waiting for settlement of their claim for regularization as per existing government policy law
4. Agricultural labourers, artisans, fisher folk etc., dependent on the acquired land for livelihood
5. New interest holders emerging from land transactions, land allotments and intra-family transfers of land not entered in land records.

The problems arise from the inaction of the concerned Government Agencies to update land records in the case of 1, 2, 3 and 5 and the property-centric approach in the case of the 4 above.

Disregarded Protective Laws for Preventing Alienation of Tribal Land

The policy ignored the legally embedded rights of the tribals in their land despite the Constitutional protection admissible to them. This was due to refusal to harmonize the land acquisition law with protective laws prohibiting tribal land alienation and the Samtha judgment of the Supreme Court which provided for non-transferability of tribal land in any Scheduled Area. This had the effect of nullifying these protective provisions. The tribal interests were also disregarded by not making adequate provisions for correcting distortions arising from non-marketability of land in the assessment of 'market value' for acquired tribal land. This led to the amount of compensation payable to the tribals which was even lower than what was admissible to the other affected persons. The policy also failed to design mechanism of compensation assessment for lands acquired in the area of shifting cultivation. It showed no appreciation for the fragility of pre-agricultural communities and most vulnerable tribal groups by leaving their land out of acquisition proceedings. It also declined to design any special compensation packages for the displaced tribals so as to provide land for the land lost by either giving available Government land or purchasing land from the market or acquiring additional land from the on-tribals to address their extreme vulnerability to handle cash compensation.

Did not Spare even Prime Agricultural Land from the Ambit of Acquisition

No effort was made nor was any mechanism put in place to avoid acquisition of the rich agricultural multi cropped land so as not to jeopardize food security. There was no insistence until 2007 that uncultivable land should be prioritized for acquisition to meet the requirement of projects.

Increased the Vulnerability of Poor and the Marginalized Groups by Promoting Direct Acquisition of Land by Private Companies

Unmindful of the unequal power relations between the parties undertaking land transactions in the market, Government encouraged direct acquisition of land by cooperates leading to pressure, fraud, intimidation, manipulation and even violence in the process of negotiation with a view to forcing the affected poor and particularly members of vulnerable groups to part with their land. This happened with the connivance of the local Government officials. The provision of this option in policy had consequences for the tribals far worse than those resulting from acquisition by the Government.

Stubborn Refusal to Seek a Consensual Mode of Acquisition

There was insistence in the policy on continued enjoyment of absolute power to acquire privately owned land derived from the notion of Eminent Domain. The determined refusal to democratize and humanize the process of land acquisition despite widespread resistance to it by the affected persons led to the intensification of conflict between the State and the people. No effort was made to seek a negotiated mode of acquisition. Rather, the resistance of affected persons against acquisition of land was dealt with by use of force causing, at times, death and injury to them, and destruction of their assets.

Increasing Use of Violence by Government to Expeditiously Accomplish Acquisition and Displace Affected Persons Disregarding Human Rights

The deployment of security forces to clear the land required by projects of existing possession and curb protests by affected persons by violence is not only violative of human rights and international covenants but also make land acquisition policy central to the destitution and marginalization of the affected persons. The approach reduced hope of resolving the conflict generated by the policy through dialogue and accommodation.

Took No Notice of Post Acquisition Loss of Land

The formal displacement caused by acquisition of land for a project over time leads to a much larger wave of informal displacement which takes place without direct acquisition of land by the Government. This is on account of the pressure of immigrants to the area attracted by project activities and their need for land for a variety of needs. This is called secondary displacement. The process of acquisition in this phase is invisible to the Government as it is carried out through a variety of transactions legal or illegal and, at times, pushing people out of land through fraud, manipulation, intimidation and force. This phenomenon did not figure in any policy frame and therefore continues apace without being recognized much less getting addressed.

Failed to Take into Account Adverse Impact of Acquisition on Environment and Social Conditions and Provide for a Regulatory Mechanism to Check it

The policy ignored the adverse externalities of land acquisition on environment, people, infrastructure and institutions resulting from change of land use after the land was acquired. It also failed to factor in this dimension in the proposal of acquisition and made no attempt to incorporate the monetized value of this externality in the cost of the project as against the benefit arising from the project while evaluating the cost-benefit ratio in decision making on the project. It made no provision to check or reverse it by appropriate interventions and imposed no obligation on the project agency to undertake corrective measures.

Declined to Exclude Persons Affected by Displacement Earlier from Acquisition

There were persons/households who had suffered displacement more than once – some even four to five times. Yet there was reluctance to spare them from this trauma despite the fact that they were resettled on the site by the Government itself. The policy totally ignored their plight and provided no mitigating action to check it.

Indifference to the Unjust Compensation Regime despite Full Knowledge of the Suffering It Caused to the Displaced Persons

The indifference of policy to the unjust compensation regime in assessment of compensations was reflected in inaction to correct distortions in the land market transactions which lowered the market value of land. It was also manifest in refusal to take into account appreciation of land as a result of changed land use and pass on its benefits to the land losers. The Government was also, disinclined to address the inadequacy of the assessed amount as market value to procure alternative land of the same productive potential near the project site and substitute it by replacement value. The policy also ignored the claim of the affected persons other than landowners who lost livelihood for compensation entitlement due to its property centric approach. In addition, the reluctance to provide land for land as compensation to the extremely vulnerable group such as the tribes, and the unwillingness to include the loss of access to CPRs in the ambit of compensation entitlement were instances of lack of concern in the policy for the suffering of the affected persons.

Created no Binding Instrument to Require Project Agencies to Provide Employment to Displaced Persons

There was a provision to provide employment to one member of the displaced family losing a specified area of land in the ad hoc policy of resettlement for some projects pursued by some PSUs in the earlier phase of land acquisition. This was scrapped without substituting it with an alternative provision to obligate the project agencies, whether public or private, to make durable and dignified employment available to the displaced persons and, pending this arrangement, provide financial assistance for subsistence to the affected displaced families. The absence of sustainable livelihood and a productive asset for income generation made it impossible for the affected families to recover from the spiral of impoverishment.

No Insistence on Provision of Reasonable Level of Housing, Infrastructure, Social Amenities

The project agencies were not charged with the responsibility of providing housing and other amenities to the displaced persons which were at least not inferior to those from which the affected persons were displaced. The policy neither imposed such an obligation on them nor on the Government. The extremely poor quality of life resulting from such callousness aggravates their impoverishment with no possibility of ever recovering from it. The 2007 policy made some advances in this direction which were inadequate and remained unenforced.

Provided no Framework to Protect Interests of Vulnerable Groups in the Resettlement Arrangement

Despite the special provisions in the Constitution requiring the Government to protect the interests of STs/SCs, the policy neither spared them from compulsory acquisition nor built adequate safeguards to prevent them from sinking further in poverty, degradation and disempowerment. Despite adequate documentary evidence, no efforts were made or binding instruments created to check the dehumanizing effects of displacement, particularly on the STs some of whose groups faced the prospects of early mortality or even extinction under excessive stress of adjustment to a new life.

Created Disharmony with its own Social Policies of Poverty Alleviation

By sliding the displaced families into acute poverty, the Land Acquisition Policy negated what the policy of rural development seeks to achieve i.e., to alleviate poverty through a package of measures. This exposed the incoherence and glaring contradictions in the public policy regime. No effort was made to resolve this incoherence and harmonize conflicting policies by integrating rehabilitation and resettlement policy with poverty alleviation measures.

Total Tilt in Favour of Land Requiring Agencies in Governance

The policy on land acquisition overwhelmingly focused its attention on pursuing the interests of the land requiring agencies to the neglect of the losers of land and livelihood. The latter were perceived as adversaries if they resisted land acquisition. Even any semblance of neutrality in governance was abandoned in dealing with the grievances of the affected persons which reflected a strong tilt in favour of the project agencies. The policy also created pressures which prioritized the task of acquisition and sought to accomplish it in the shortest time and at least cost. It placed no comparable emphasis on satisfactory and expeditious rehabilitation and resettlement of the displaced persons which got relegated to the background. This left the displaced persons helpless and powerless.

Absence of Judicial Oversight

The Supreme Court and the High Courts in India have the inherent powers of judicial review of laws and policies to ensure that they are in harmony with the basic principles enshrined in the Constitution and do not infringe the fundamental rights guaranteed therein. The consequences of displacement emerging from acquisition of land are in violations of human rights and negate social justice which the Constitution seeks to protect. In particular, the consequences of displacement violate literally the Right to Life (Article 21) as interpreted liberally by the Supreme Court in other contexts.

And yet, the judgments of these courts did not show requisite concern, for the plight of the displaced persons and made no decisive pronouncements to protect their interests. The courts consistently upheld the propriety of State action in such matters (Upadhyay and Raman, 1998). They also validated the colonial doctrine of 'Eminent Domain' as the legitimate source of State power in taking over privately owned land and therefore, declined to strike down the undemocratic nature of the law or to humanize it so as to balance its heavy tilt in favour of the State. This was despite the fact that the Constitution itself repudiates the notion of 'Eminent Domain' by carving out a special status and governance arrangement for the Scheduled and forest Areas which severely limit the absolute exercise of State power. Not only this, they steadfastly refused to look into the rationality of application of 'Public Purpose' in specific cases and upheld that the mere declaration by the Government that the purpose of acquisition was public is sufficient to justify it. This view is taken even in cases where the purpose of acquisition is declaredly for a private company and the land would be used for earning profit. Thus, the abuse of 'Public Purpose', and excessive acquisition of land quite disproportionate to the need, the future as well the present, remained outside the pale of judicial scrutiny. The courts also did not castigate the Government for non-payment of full compensation before eviction of the occupants from the acquired land. They also refrained from examining whether provisions of law were adhered to both in letter and spirit in the process of land acquisition. The State tried to adhere to the letter of the law irrespective of whether its spirit was achieved or not. This was, for example, so in the case of dissemination of information regarding the intention to acquire land contained in the preliminary notification. The specified procedure of publication in the newspapers was followed without giving adequate information to enable the affected persons to raise objections. It was ignored that there was limited circulation of newspapers in the rural areas and most of the affected people were illiterate. Gazette notifications were usually published with inordinate delay though they are technically issued in time. They were not easily accessible even to the educated and well-informed. The people affected by proposed acquisition had many doubts, apprehensions and questions which were not addressed to enable their informed participation in acquisition proceedings. The acquiring agency exercised excessive control over information with the intention of pre-empting objections to the acquisition proposal for ensuring its smooth completion. The objective therefore of reaching adequate and timely information and in the language that was intelligible to them for raising objections did not materialize. Similarly, objections raised after the issue of preliminary notification were routinely dismissed in a non-speaking order, thereby defeating the purpose of critical scrutiny of the acquisition proposal. None of these aspects invited courts' scrutiny or intervention generally. The courts also did not show any activism in critiquing the Government on the absence of a rehabilitation policy and issuing directions to formulate comprehensive policy which ensured a dignified life for the displaced persons in terms of its own understanding of Article 21. On the other hand, the courts even declined to enforce the assurances contained in various packages announced by the Government and intervene in the matter on the ground that a policy did not have the legal backing. In other words, the courts did not use the power of judicial review to render justice and provide relief to the displaced persons in their plight caused by land acquisition. The only arena where they used their interventionist role was the quantum of compensation and the correctness of assessment of market value – an option which was exercised only by the better off oustees who could muster resources to fight long legal battles. In the 2013 Act the Government has eroded even this space to prevent the contingency of enhanced compensation being awarded by constituting a quasi judicial body called the 'Compensation Settlement Authority' for this purpose. It is doubtful if the victims of land acquisition would get justice form this quasi-judicial forum.

Government Response

The critique of law and policy on land acquisition presented above is not new. People's organizations, social activists and sensitive professionals have raised these issues before and even submitted proposals of amendments to the LA Act and the rehabilitation and resettlement policy (CPCNR, 2001; Fernandes and Paranjpe, 1997). The Government policy, however, steadfastly focused on smooth and speedy acquisition of land rather than on changing the law and practice to accommodate people's concerns. The amendments to the Land Acquisition Act undertaken till 2000 were largely geared to reducing the time taken to complete acquisition proceedings and raising the cash compensation by way of solatium and provision of interest in the case of delay in its payment. Responding to the pressure of the civil society, Government did propose some amendments to the Land Acquisition Act in 2000. But this effort failed to materialize. The proposal was strongly critiqued by the civil society groups for ignoring the major points of concern voiced by them and, worse, rejected by the top bureaucracy on the ground that the changes would stall all acquisition proposals leading to time and cost overrun of development projects (MORD, 2004). Meanwhile, people's resistance to the ever increasing land acquisition had grown enormously. The Government used force to push land acquisition with huge social costs in terms of lives lost and injuries inflicted leading to the upsurges in civil society critiques and protests.

The Land Acquisition (Amendment) Bill, 2007

To tide over this strong opposition across the country against acquisition of huge areas of land, particularly for the corporate, under the SEZ Act, 2005 and those required for FDI projects in industry, mining and infrastructure, which led to delay in their execution, the Government introduced the Land Acquisition (Amendment) Bill, 2007 in the Lok Sabha with far more extensive changes than those proposed/undertaken in the past.

The changes proposed in the Land Acquisition (Amendment) Bill, 2007 (MORD, 2007)[a] sought to address some of these concerns. The Bill removed acquisition of land for companies from the scope of the Act. This implied that land could not be acquired for such companies. It also made a provision for resettlement and rehabilitation of persons affected by involuntary displacement including acquisition of land. For this purpose, the National Rehabilitation and Resettlement Policy, 2007 (MORD, 2007)[b] was notified. In order to make the provisions of the policy justiciable, the Resettlement and Rehabilitation Bill, 2007 was also introduced in the Lok Sabha (MORD, 2007)[c]. An obligation was cast in the Bill on the implementing agency to carry out a social impact assessment in respect of the project for which land was acquired for preparing the rehabilitation and resettlement scheme. The term 'public purpose' was also precisely defined to cover strategic purposes relating to defence forces or any work vital to the State and infrastructure projects. In addition, it also included 'any other purpose useful to the general public' for which 70 per cent of land had been procured directly from the landholders by the requiring private agency. The remaining 30 per cent was proposed be acquired by the Government as 'public purpose'. The tribals and other traditional forest dwellers and tenants were included in the definition of 'person interested' so as to entitle the former to compensation for loss of access to forest and agricultural land respectively and the latter for the loss of access of land for cultivation. For ensuring timely acquisition of land, a provision was made that the proceedings would lapse and no fresh notification could be made for a period of one year if the declaration to acquire land was not made within the specific period following issue of preliminary notification. Land records were required to be updated before the final decision on acquisition of land was taken so that eligible persons were not excluded from consideration for payment of compensation. Land transactions, after initiation of land acquisition proceedings, were disallowed to prevent motivated transfers of land immediately before its acquisition with a view to checking vested interests from cheating the poor landholders, particularly the tribals of their entitlements. The rules of compensation were elaborated and liberalized by laying down the method for its determination, specifically in respect of tribal land where sale/purchase transactions did not usually take place. The market value was proposed to be assessed taking into account the intended future use of land rather than its existing use at the time of acquisition. Higher compensation was payable in the case of urgent acquisition of land. This, along with enhanced solatium and interest, would increase the amount of compensation compared to what was admissible earlier. The compensation was required to be paid within a period of sixty days from the date of declaration of award. The possession of land could be taken thereafter only. A part of the compensation could also be taken in the form of shares, if acquisition was carried out for a company issuing such shares. A new Compensation Settlement Authority was proposed for expeditious disposal of reference cases and a time limit of six months was prescribed for disposal of a case. The acquired land, if not utilized within the specified period, would revert to the Government for its alternative use. Where the land, acquired by the Government, is transferred to another agency at a price higher than what was paid to the landholders, 80 per cent of such amount would be passed on to them. The process of reference for adjudication of compensation claim was also tightened so as to ensure time-bound endorsement to the Compensation Settlement Authority for disposal. The agency requiring land was being made liable to pay the entire cost of acquisition of land including that of the rehabilitation and resettlement of displaced persons.

Critique of 2007 Bill

While some concerns of the affected persons were responded to in this proposal, major issues raised by them and the civil society remained unaddressed. From the view point of the affected persons, the most serious flaw in the Bill was that the Government showed no willingness to give up or dilute its absolute power to acquire land without the consent of the landowners using the colonial notion of 'Eminent Domain'. The Bill, therefore, continued to retain the undemocratic character of the existing Act. There was little inclination to seek a less coercive and more consensual mechanism to acquire land for a 'public purpose'. No restriction was incorporated with regard to the acquisition of tribal land thereby nullifying the effect of laws relating to the alienation of tribal land and protection provided by the Fifth Schedule which prohibits transfer of tribal land to non-tribals and the ruling of the Supreme Court concerning it in the Samatha case. The Bill continued to ignore PESA, 1996 and did not incorporate the need for consultation with the *Gram Sabha* of the concerned village in the matter relating to acquisition of land as required by it. It thus repudiated the ethos of self governance and management of natural resources conferred on the tribal communities in the scheduled areas by PESA, 1996.

The overwhelming concern of the people facing acquisition of their land is to get some respite from acquisition by curtailing the scale of acquisition currently in process and likely to be taken up in future. The least that could be done was to incorporate a provision that the acquisition should be avoided wherever possible by exploring non-displacing options and, if unavoidable after exhausting this exercise, it should be minimized by working out the least displacing alternative. No such provision was built into the Bill to demonstrate some degree of sensitivity of persons likely to be displaced. The National Rehabilitation Policy, 2007 does require that the objective of exploring non-displacing and least displacing alternatives to be explored generally but this requirement was not inserted in the suggested amendments to the Land Acquisition Act.

Recommendations of the Standing Committee

The Bill after it introduction was referred to the Standing Committee of the Ministry of Rural Development for scrutiny before its discussion in the Lok Sabha. The Standing Committee considered the Bill and submitted its report in October, 2008 in which it made a number of recommendations (Lok Sabha, 2008)[a]. The Committee preferred to retain the definition of 'public purpose' in the original Act rather than that contained in the revised one proposed in the Bill. It laid down stringent conditions for acquisition of agricultural land which included a certificate from the collector that no waste/barren land was available and a requirement that an equivalent of waste/barren land would be developed at the cost of the project. The period for filing objections was enhanced to sixty days. The notice of acquisition was required to be published in at least three newspapers of which two should be in the vernacular. Social Impact Assessment was recommended to be carried out even where the number of families to be displaced is lower than what is stipulated in the Bill at the discretion of the Standing Committee on Rehabilitation and Resettlement.

Of the other recommendations made by the Parliamentary Committee, the most significant was to delete the provision which fixed the percentage of land to be acquired by a private agency directly from the market and the Government in the ratio of 70:30. The assessment of compensation was recommended at 50 per cent higher than the highest price reflected in the land transactions of the last three years. In the case of multiple displacements, the benefits to the displacees should be doubled each time the repeated displacement takes place. The issue of shares and debentures to the displaces as part of compensation was not favoured. The power of acquisition in an emergency was required to be restricted to a minimum area of land for the purpose of defense and national security only. The committee also laid down that no future acquisition of land would be taken up without the Government certifying that no unutilized land was available in the area. The optimum size of land for a project should be settled by an expert committee before notification for acquisition was issued. The rights of Tribals should be recognized and settled before taking up any acquisition of land in their area. The area where displaced tribals are settled should be declared a Scheduled Area.

The Land Acquisition, (Amendment) Bill, 2009

The Government accepted some recommendations of the Standing Committee and incorporated them in the Bill. These relate to the protection of agricultural land, constitution of an expert committee for scrutiny of projects, the enhancement of the period for filing objections, and acquisition of land in the case of urgency etc. Besides, the Government also added a provision that only the minimum area of land would be acquired and a project site which entails minimum displacement would be selected from the available options. The period for payment of compensation was enhanced from sixty to ninety days. The provision for payment of enhanced compensation in the unsettled cases was deleted. The revised Land Acquisition (Amendment) Bill, 2009 (MORD, 2009)[a] was introduced in the Lok Sabha and passed on February 25, 2009. But it could not be passed in the Rajya Sabha as the Lok Sabha was dissolved for parliamentary election. The Bill, therefore, lapsed and was required to be reintroduced in the new Lok Sabha. A similar situation existed in respect of the revised Rehabilitation and Resettlement Bill, 2009 (MORD, 2009)[b] which was introduced after taking into consideration the recommendations contained in the fortieth report of the Standing Committee on Rural Development (Lok Sabha, 2008)[b]

Critique of 2009 Bill

Notwithstanding some positive changes made in the Bill, 2007 and some improvements inserted in the Bill, 2009, the basic framework of the Land Acquisition Act, 1894 and contours of the Land Acquisition of Policy did not undergo any change. There was no indication that the Government was contemplating to enact a wholly new legislation on the subject as recommended by the Committee. Therefore, the major issues raised in this paper such as those relating to undemocratic nature of acquisition, restricted definition of land and persons interested, enlarged scope of using of 'public purpose', narrow ambit of compensation entitlement, disinclination to return unutilized land to the erstwhile owners, failure to concede 'replacement value' of land lost and the lack of commitment to provide either land and/or durable and dignified employment to each family of the displaced persons remained unchanged.

The Land Acquisition Policy of the Government too did not undergo any change. This was to be expected because without reversing or significantly limiting the existing neo-liberal paradigm of growth which focused on gobbling up natural resources and, therefore, fueled the ever increasing demand for land, the scale and ambit of acquisition would not reduce. The Government was not prepared for this policy shift at all. While the Government did include a provision in the Land Acquisition (Amendment) Bill, 2007/2009 deleting provision for acquisition of land for companies to placate critics of policy, this was, however, a cosmetic change. The acquisition for companies was brought in from the back door under 'infrastructure' included in the expanded definition of 'public purpose' as also in the provision 'any other purpose useful to the public'. As the bulk of the projects in the existing economy relate to infrastructure and are financed by private companies, their requirement of land would now qualify for 'public purpose'. Government also sought to externalize acquisition by encouraging companies to directly acquire land. This created havoc among the poor and marginalized sections of the affected persons because the corporates' goons used unethical practices and muscle power in collusion with the local administration to force people from these categories to sell their land. The latter got no protection from the local administration against these practices. Worse, they neither got a fair price for the land sold nor the assurance of rehabilitation in such transactions. The interests of tenants, sharecroppers and those who lose livelihood were totally ignored in this mode of land acquisition. This arrangement therefore turned out to be worse than compulsory acquisition by the Government. Even the Rehabilitation and Resettlement Policy, 2007 and the Bill to give legal backup to it offered no solace to the affected persons as they were neither assured of land in lieu of the land lost nor any dignified and durable employment. All that was offered was a little more cash compensation. The property-centric compensation regime also remained unaltered. There was persistent disinclination to protect tribals against alienation of their land through acquisition. Rather, some State Governments have even relaxed these protective laws for smoothening them. Government continued to use force and violence to take possession of land for transfer to the corporates where peaceful protest continued. There was thus no prospect for a peaceful resolution of this problem. An expanding area of conflict was on the horizon.

Overall, the thrust of changes proposed in the two versions (2007 and 2009) of the Bill brought out clearly that the Government was more interested in quicker acquisition and externalization of its mode so that land was quickly passed on to the project agencies than in meeting the single most important concern of the people which was to get respite from the ever increasing prospect of involuntary displacement. There was no basic change in the policy on acquisition of land for development projects in terms of the issues raised in this paper. As a result, there was going to be no let up in the deprivation of peasantry of its land and livelihood whether effected through compulsory acquisition or negotiated procurement. The changes proposed in the Bill (2009) did not reflect any rethinking on economic policies which induced such transfer of land from farmers to the Government and corporate agencies. Even on the issue of compensation and rehabilitation, there was little to generate hope in the affected persons for a better deal.

The foregoing analysis signified the narrow limits of the State's willingness to undertake legal and policy changes to render justice to them. In the circumstances, the bulk of peasantry was not enthused to part with its land willingly the local resistance to acquisition/procurement of land, therefore, continued in various parts of the country while the Government was planning to re-introduce the LA (Amendment) Bill 2009 with minor modifications

Developments leading to reconsideration of the Bill (2009)

Meanwhile, there were three significant developments which necessitated a review of the proposed amendments contained in the Bill (2009). The National Advisory Council headed by the chairperson of the ruling UPA (United Progressive Alliance) looked into the existing amendments and suggested major changes in it. Also, the Supreme Court and Allahabad High Court quashed land acquisition proceedings for some projects and made critical observations on undertaking land acquisition without addressing the grievances of the persons affected. Further, Mamta Banerjee of Trinamool Congress who as a

Minister in the Central Cabinet, had objected to forcible acquisition of land for development projects had become the Chief Minister, West Bengal and had to be consulted on the proposed changes in view of her party's strength in the Parliament for the smooth passage of the revised Bill. Taking into account these developments, the Ministry of Rural Development came out with a substantially revised draft of the Bill (2009) which was placed on the website for obtaining feedback from all those interested (MORD, 2011)[a]. State Governments were also consulted on this draft proposal. Based on the feedback received, the Land Acquisition and Rehabilitation and Resettlement Bill 2011 (Bill No 77 of MORD 2012)[b] was introduced in the Lok Sabha. In view of the substantial changes introduced in this Bill compared to the 2009 Bill, it was referred to the Parliamentary Standing Committee of the Ministry for detailed scrutiny.

The Land Acquisition and Rehabilitation and Resettlement Bill 2011

There were several departures in the Bill from the proposals contained in the Bills of 2007 and 2009. The LA and R&R Bill (2011) (henceforth, the Bill) combined land acquisition with rehabilitation and resettlement in the body of a single law and replaced two separate Bills on the subject in the proposals of 2007 and 2009 Bills. This met a long standing demand from civil society organizations for a single law on land acquisition and rehabilitation and resettlement so that the land acquisition authority was also made directly responsible for the rehabilitation and resettlement of displaced persons. A single law also removed distortions and discrepancies in certain common provisions of the two separate Bills. It also conveyed a clear intent that the rehabilitation and resettlement of displaced persons was an integral part of land acquisition process and the unified legislation represented two sides of the same coin. The Bill, for the first time, took cognizance of the prohibition on alienation of tribal land and laid down that no land shall be transferred by way of acquisition in contravention of the laws in scheduled areas and provided for consultation with the Gram

Sabha before the issue of preliminary notification in compliance of PESA 1996. It also protected the interests of persons displaced as a result of acquisition of land by Private Agencies through market transactions by mandating their rehabilitation and resettlement, if the quantum of such acquisition involved more than 100 acres of land in rural and fifty acres of land in urban areas or where the private company requested that part acquisition of their requirement should carried out by the Government. The rigour of exercise of Eminent Domain was also diluted by providing that the consent of 80 per cent of the affected persons would be necessary for acquisition of land where land to be acquired was required for private companies or public-private partnerships for production of goods for public or public services and even by the Government for public purpose other than those specified. Restrictions on acquisition of irrigated and multi-cropped land were tightened to protect food security of the country by disallowing acquisition of such land as a rule but, where unavoidable, limiting it to 5 per cent of the total area of the district, and where no irrigated multi cropped land is involved in acquisition of land, such acquisition in aggregate for all projects shall not exceed 10 per cent of the total net sown area of that district where the net sown area was less than 50 per cent. A provisions for pre-acquisition scrutiny of the proposal of land requiring agency was also introduced and the ambit of Social Impact Assessment was elaborated. The definition of 'Person interested' was expanded so as to include those whose livelihood was adversely affected which would enable them to file a claim for compensation. Among the persons entitled to claim compensation, occupiers of land were also included which would hopefully, entitle informal tenants also to claim a share. The amount of the assessed compensation package was increased by multiplying by two the market value assessed on the basis of the method prescribed and solatium amount by one. The application of provision for acquisition of land under urgency was restricted only to cases where it was required for meeting the needs of defence, national security and natural calamities and persons affected by such acquisition were required to be given the benefit of 75 per cent additional amount of the assessed compensation in such cases. The declaration of individual awards would permit effective enforcement of package in respect of each displaced person. Where the acquired land remained unutilized for a period of 10 years from the date of transfer to the project agency, it would revert to the Government and would be added to the land bank to be created for this purpose. Any change in the purpose for which the land had been acquired was disallowed. Where land after acquisition was transferred by the Government to another agency for a consideration, 20 per cent of the appreciated value of such land would be passed on to the erstwhile land losers.

In the rehabilitation and resettlement package, the provision for one acre of land to the landlosers in the irrigation projects and upto 2.5 acres to STs and SCs land losers in all projects was a major highlight of the revised Bill. In the urban areas, the land losers would get a share of the land developed from the project proportionate to the land lost for which 20 per cent was to be earmarked out of the total land acquired subject to its cost being deducted from the total package of financial compensation. There was a clearer provision for employment to all landlosers with three options being provided to choose from a) a job to one member of the affected family where jobs are created in the project or available elsewhere b) Rs. 5 lakh if a job was not provided c) annuity policy which would pay not less than Rs. 2,000 per month to the affected family. The definition of affected family was elaborated so as include an adult of either gender with or without spouse or children or dependents as a separate family. This removed gender discrimination in the earlier Bills (2007, 2009). The application of 'public purpose' for acquisition of land was split into two categories a) where Government acquires land for defence, national security, police and planned development of rural or urban area, infrastructure, rehabilitation of displaced persons, for use by Government and public sector companies, Government administered Institutions and private companies for provision of social amenities. b) where land is acquired the public private partnerships for production of goods or provision of public services as also for purposes other than those specified in (a) above where benefits largely accrue to the general public. For the first categories of purposes, 'Eminent Domain' would be used for acquisition of land without the consent of the land owners. For the second category of purposes, the informed consent of 80 per cent of the affected people would be necessary.

Critique of 2011 Bill

Notwithstanding certain improvements made in the Bill which addressed some concerns of the affected displaced persons, it was unlikely to neutralize the widespread discontent arising out of land acquisition and resistance to projects which involve large scale dispossession of people from their land, livelihood, habitat and environment. What people desired (barring a small section of rich/absentee land owners and those near the metropolitan centres) was a halt to the destabilization of their lives resulting from ever increasing acquisition of land. The Bill provided no assurance that the scale of acquisition would get drastically reduced not to speak of a halt to the acquisition spree currently in process and forthcoming. Though, the Bill provided for pre-acquisition scrutiny of land acquisition proposals to minimize displacement and acquisition of land, this exercise was designed to be carried out by a committee dominated by officials and was unlikely to inspire any confidence in its deliberations. Similarly, though some relief was provided by mandating informed consent of 80 per cent of the affected families for certain categories of land acquisition, such acquisition would indeed be very small and the land acquisition agencies were known to subvert even this process and produce manufactured consent by forcibly driving out dissenters from or preventing their entry into the meeting. But an overwhelmingly large part of acquisition by the Government was left out of this conditionality of prior consent for which the route of compulsory acquisition was used. Overall, the willing submission of the affected people to acquisition of their land was unlikely and use of force, specifically provided for in the Bill to take possession of the acquired land would continue to generate hostility and bitterness among them. The provision made for adherence to the laws prohibiting alienation of tribal land should ordinarily stop acquisition of land in the scheduled area. But this did not seem to be the case going by a general reading of the law and the location of projects. Besides, some State Governments were amending their laws for protection of tribal land from alienation and resorting to other subterfuges to facilitate acquisition of the tribal land in the scheduled areas. The prescription of a benchmark of 100 acres in rural areas and fifty acres in urban areas for acquisition by companies directly though market transactions to attract obligation of rehabilitation and resettlement of displaced persons had no rationale. It would induce the companies to split the requirement of their acquisition to avoid this liability. In any case, the industry was highly-critical of the Bill and particularly of this clause and lobbied for its removal/dilution. The dilution of the ban on acquisition of irrigated and multi cropped land which had been proposed in the earlier draft showed that these prescriptions would be difficult to enforce as the Government was far more committed to the execution of projects than to ensuring food security. As for the expansion of the definition of 'person interested', it was not clear whether land acquisition authorities would entertain the claims of informal tenants and sharecroppers for compensation since the landowners whose land they were cultivating would oppose it fiercely. The wording of the provision itself lacked sufficient clarity on whether the oral tenants are eligible to claim compensation.

The adequacy of increased compensation was required to be tested on the ability of a land loser to purchase equivalent land of the same productive potential in the vicinity. The concept of 'replacement value' which was not accepted would have rendered greater justice and would have reduced intensity of resistance to acquisition. But even in terms of cash entitlement offered, the proposal in the Bill was regressive when compared to the 'six times increase in market value' that had been promised in the draft Bill (MORD, 2011)[a] for circulation. It was also disappointing that the proposal of the National Advisory Council to distribute the unutilized land among the erstwhile land losers had been disregarded as such land as per the Bill would go to the land bank. The objective for inserting the provision had been defeated. The provision proposed would benefit the Government rather than the affected displaced persons. Also disappointing was the change in the rehabilitation package, where the provision relating to allotment of land to the displaced ST land losers had been reduced from 5 acres in the draft Bill (2011) to 2.5 acres in the proposed Bill which was too low an area to restore lost livelihood and dignity. Even more insensitive was the deletion from the Act the earlier proposal contained in the draft Bill (2011) regarding allotment of at least one acre of land to the displaced landless STs. The provision of mandatory employment in the draft Bill (2011) was also diluted by substituting it for cash if no employment was given. Through this monetary equivalent, an escape route was created for project agencies to comply with the requirement of giving employment by payment of financial compensation. As money equivalent, the promised amount of Rs. 5 lakh did not even represent the capitalized value of the wage of the lowest level of unskilled wage worker i.e., agricultural labourer over a period of 20-25 years. The option of annuity provided was too low an amount to assure even barest subsistence. The provision that in the acquisition of land relating to the Scheduled Tribes, alienation of their land shall be treated as null and void and benefits of compensation and rehabilitation and resettlement would accrue to the original ST land owner would be unenforceable as alienation of land in most cases got validated by revenue and judicial courts and alienators of tribal land would drag every such case to Courts. There was no provision in the Bill to negate such a possibility. Besides, in the absence of similar provision being inserted in the land alienation laws of the concerned States, this declaration was cosmetic and would generate unrealizable hope. The provision of ST development plan in the rehabilitation and resettlement policy and included in the Bill lacked conceptual clarity. It did not take into account diverse needs of different ST groups, their ecological situations, social and cultural traditions and the economy on which they subsist. The existing provision would fail to render any meaningful rehabilitation to them. This was specifically true of the Particularly Vulnerable Tribal Groups (PTGs)-hunters, food gatherers, shifting cultivators who are neither socialized in agriculture nor in sedentary activities and therefore would be ill suited to the homogenized model of rehabilitation and resettlement envisaged in the Act. Overall, what the present Bill offered was a little more cash, a more rigorous process of acquisition with some space for participation and accountability of those entrusted with the task of rehabilitation and resettlement. But the disrupted life resulting from displacement could not be rebuilt without assured and dignified employment and access to productive asset for this purpose. Even with provision of these inputs, continued development support and affirmative action would be required over a long period of time for stabilizing life at a new place. The Bill lacked the vision and inclination to provide such a support. The Bill was also totally silent on the backlog (75 per cent) of rehabilitation from earlier displacement. These victims of development virtually became invisible in policy discourse and were again left in the lurch in the Bill. The limited beneficial provisions of this Bill would not even apply to the future acquisition under 16 other central laws through which land is acquired and equal number of State specific laws of acquisition unless the Central Government issued a specific notification to this effect and no modifications or exceptions were made to such application.

The Standing Committee on Rural Development submitted its Thirty First Report (15th Lok Sabha) submitted on May 16, 2012. It made 13 recommendations and also advised that all the suggestions received from general public, industry, farmers, ngos, experts, Central Ministries, State Governments should be considered in consultations with Ministry of Law before bringing in a revised Bill. The Committee recommended that (1) land should not be acquired for use by private companies and the public private partnerships. Infrastructure projects may be included within the definition of 'public purpose', (2) the clause regarding definition of infrastructure should be deleted as it gives wide discretion to the Government in notifying a project as infrastructure project, (3) the threshold for Rehabilitation and Resettlement provisions should be fixed by States and not by the Central Government (4) no acquisition or alienation of land should be permitted in Scheduled Areas and, if unavoidable, land losers should be given increased compensation and R&R benefits, (5) a maximum of five percent of irrigated multi-cropped land may be acquired in a district, with certain conditions and this restriction should also apply to land under agricultural cultivation. The percentage restriction should be fixed by the State Governments, (6) no Central Act should be exempted from the applications of the new law and these laws should be amended to harmonize with it, (7) consultation with Gram Sabhas, wherever provided, should be replaced by consent and should be made applicable to all decision making points, (8) a multi-member land pricing commission or authority should determine cost of land acquisition State wise/Area wise and 12 per cent per annum interest should be paid in addition to compensation from the date of notification in the Award, (9) in urgency cases, extra compensation should be 75 per cent of the total compensation package and soalatuim, (10) unutilized land should be returned to land owners and not to land bank and it should be done after 5 years of acquisition and not 10 years, (11) the change in the Schedules of the Bill should be done only by amendment brought in Parliament and not by Government, (12) monetary components of R&R in Schedule II should be inflation indexed, (13) minimum infrastructure at R&R sites should be decided on a case by case basis (Lok Sabha Secretariat, 2012) .

Government accepted all but two recommendations and dovetailed them appropriately in the new Bill, the Right to Fair Compensation and Transparency in Land Acquisition. Rehabilitation and Resettlement Bill 2013. The Bill was introduced in the parliament, discussed and passed. After receiving Presidential assent, it was formally notified on September 26, 2013. Nearly 158 formal amendments of which 28 were substantial (main) amendments were introduced in the 2011 Bill which included 13 based on Standing Committee's recommendations, another 13 amendments were based on recommendations of Group of Ministers and two emerged from the leader of the opposition. The Act that finally emerged did not include two recommendations of Standing Committee. One was that land should not be acquired for use by private companies and PPPs. The other was that no Central Law on acquisition should be exempted and all such laws should be amended to harmonise with the new law. On the question of setting up of land prices determination commission, the Government assured that it would try to appropriately include it in the Rules after examining it (Ramesh and Khan, 2013).

As it emerges, may amendments that were incorporated in 2013 Bill and which got finally approved by the Parliament were regressive in nature. These amendments resulted from the demands and pressures of three powerful lobbies, besides the report of the Standing Committee, (1) Industry backed by the concerned Ministries of the Central Government, (2) State Governments, and (3) Political Parties. These demands particularly those from industry and State Governments and Central Ministries related to relaxing the crucial provisions to reduce the time and cost of acquisition and to make the process of acquisition easier and quicker and diminish responsibility for rehabilitation and resettlement of affected persons beyond payment of compensation. Some of the recommendations of Standing Committee also served to dilute the rigour of earlier provisions, as for example, giving discretion to State Governments to determine the thresh hold level regarding acquisition of multi cropped and other agricultural land, R&R provisions as also to permit them to acquire land in Scheduled Area, if unavoidable. Three crucial and progressive recommendations of the Committee which were not accepted by the Government related to (1) acquisition of land for private companies and for PPPs, (2) deletion of a provisions empowering Government to notify any project as infrastructure project, and (3) bringing all Central Land Acquisition Laws on par with the 2013 Act. Even where the Committee's progressive recommendations regarding return of unutilized land to land owners after a five years period was accepted, it was diluted by also retaining the provisions of its transfer to the land bank and leaving it to the State Governments to decide on the matter. Overall, the 2013 Act had no improvement over 2011 Bill in terms of protecting the interests of the land losers and dependents in respect of acquired land. In the process of balancing various stakeholders - requiring agencies, State Governments and land dependent people, the latter had to give way.

2013 Act was hailed by the Government as a very progressive law which would substantially meet demands of land losers and therefore put an end to the agrarian discontent. But a critical reading of its would belie this optimism. The ambit of acquisition has not been curtailed. The structures put in place to scrutinize the rationale of acquisition, its inevitability, quantum and site on the basis of Social Impact Assessment are ineffective as these bodies are dominated by bureaucrats or nominated experts and, in any case, the final decision about acquisition and its quantum would still be determined by the Government. The ambit of 'public purpose' has been so widened and kept open ended that it would fail to exclude any project that the Government is keen on taking up. The dilution of 'Eminent Domain' is cosmetic. The consent of landlosers prior to acquisition merely applies to a miniscule number of cases. Around 90 per cent of acquisition would be covered by 'public purpose' irrespective of whether it is executed by private companies or Government or a combination of both and would not require any consent. Gateway has been opened to loosen the restrictions on acquisition of irrigated and agriculture land by giving States the discretionary power to decide its limits. The fact that his dilution was inserted under pressure from State Governments (also the Standing Committee) clearly indicates that 'development' would outweigh the need for protecting agricultural land. The much publicized inclusion of provision of employment to one member of the affected family in the rehabilitation package been negated by incorporating the provision of financial compensation in the event of inability of land requiring agency to do so. This provides the latter with easiest escape route from its responsibility to provide employment. Even the provision relating to higher compensation in the schedule I would fail to materialize as it has been diluted by subjecting it to a sliding scale depending upon the distance of acquired land from the urban centre which would be fixed by the State Government. The acquisition of land in case of urgency still retains the wide ambit of its applicability which extends to national security, defence and natural calamities. Every need of defence cannot justify application of urgency clause as, for example, acquisition for peace time operations and requirements which are of no urgent nature such as housing units, golf courses, play grounds, firing ranges etc. There is no justification to waive provision of Social Impact Assessment, consultation with Gram Sabha, Public hearing on objections raised in respect of them. By keeping 13 Central Land Acquisition Acts out of the purview of 2013 Act would leave three-fourth of the acquisition untouched and the affected persons would fail to get relief. The Act merely promises application of provision of compensation and rehabilitation contained in the 2013 Act to these laws within a year through a notification but the process of acquisition contained in the 2013 Act would not apply of them. The provision of SIA has even been exempted in relation to irrigation projects for which there is little justification. The restrictions on acquisition of land in Scheduled Area have been so diluted that it would provide no deterrence. By prefixing 'as far as possible' to the restriction it provides the acquiring agency a huge escape route to ignore it. Tribals with a population of 8 per cent have been the greatest victims of acquisition with a share of nearly 45 per cent of total acquisition so far (MORD, 2004). The 2013 Act only provides cosmetic relief to them.

Notwithstanding this critique, the 2013 law is an improvement over the 1894 Act and 2007 and 2009 Bills introduced in the Parliament in terms of entitlements it provides to the affected persons. However, its implementation needed to be watched over a sufficient period of time to assess whether the positive benefits, if any, accrue to the affected persons. The Act could not be enforced immediately as rules had to be framed by the Central and State Governments. While this process was under way, a major reversal of its architecture was resorted to by the newly elected NDA Government. It enacted an ordinance amending the Act of 2013 nullifying virtually all the major provisions which were the outcome of long political struggle and a decade long extensive and unprecedented nationwide consultations, debates in Parliament, and reports of the two parliamentary Standing Committees. The ordinance virtually brought back the situation to a state that prevailed at the time of operation of the 1894 law. This change was justified on the ground (without any substantial evidence) that many difficulties were being experienced in its implementation. Ironically, the Government claimed that amendments were made to protect the interests of the affected families. The Land Acquisition Amendment Ordinance, 2014 made nine changes. These were (1) No consent of affected persons would be required in five categories of projects (i) defense (ii) rural infrastructure (iii) affordable housing (iv) industrial corridors and (v) infrastructure projects including Public Private Partnership projects where the Central Government owns the land (2) No Social Impact Assessment would be required for above mentioned five categories of projects, (3) There would be no restriction on acquisition of multi-cropped land in respect of above five category of projects, (4) The restriction on acquisition of land for private hospitals and educational institutions was removed and such land acquisition would also be treated as public purpose, (5) Land Acquisition for private entities confined to only companies registered under section 3 of the Companies Act 1956 in the 2013 Act, was now expanded to include private entity proprietorships, partnerships, corporations and non-profit organizations and any entity under any law for the time being in force, (6) retrospective application of the 2013 Act was permitted to land acquired under 1894 Act five years or more prior to it but not taken possession of or for which compensation was not paid. The ordinance excluded from the period of 5 years any period or periods during which land acquisition proceedings were held up due to a stay order or injunction or the period specified in the award of a Tribunal for taking possession or where possession has been taken but compensation is lying deposited in the court or any other account maintained for this purpose, (7) The provision for prosecution of officials found guilty of violation of the Act has been subjected to prior sanction of the Government, (8) The five year period for return of unutilized land to the land owners has been extended until the period specified for setting up of the project, (8) The period within which Central Government can issue directions has been extended from 2 years to five years, (9) The compensation, rehabilitation and resettlement provisions in 13 Central Laws were brought in consonance with The Right to Fair Compensation and Transparency in Land Acquisition, Rehabilitation and Resettlement Act, 2013.

The 2014 ordinance was replaced by a Bill (2015) with minor changes and introduced in the Lok Sabha and passed in March 2015. It was then introduced in the Rajya Sabha where it was referred to the Standing Committee for scrutiny. The report of the Committee has not yet been submitted.

From the nature of amendments proposed it would be evident that the structural changes in 1894 Act attempted by the Government after a long period of people's struggle and unprecedented consultation with the stake holders were reversed taking the situation back to the period of unfettered acquisition without pre-acquisition scrutiny, and with collector, once again, exercising unchecked authority to determine what constitutes 'public purpose', the quantum of legitimate requirement for a project and the speed with which it can be acquired (Ramesh and Khan, 2015). The five fold separate categorization of purposes for which consent clause and social impact assessment has been exempted is bereft of any logic and rationale as some of these purposes overlap with purposes already included in the list of exempted purposes in the 2013 Act. The purposes included in this categorization make the exemption of the applicability these provisions so expandable as to virtually include any project which the Government wants to take up or promote. Its objective is to knock off the 'consent' clause (which limited the exercise of 'Eminent Domain') altogether from acquisition of any project for private companies and ppps so as to enable declaration of such acquisition also as public purpose. The exemption from application of 'Social Impact Assessment' requirement not only removes any pre-acquisition scrutiny of its cost and benefit, its rationale as pubic purpose and quantum to minimize the extent of displacement but also the participation of likely affected persons in its process so as to democratize decision making. Even worse, it prevents an objective assessment to be made of the number of affected persons, particularly the livelihood losers and those dependent upon land but whose names are not found in the record of rights. The change would make it difficult to rehabilitate and resettle livelihood losers, the most vulnerable category in displacement. The amendments undo even the much diluted restrictions on acquisition of irrigated multi-cropped land to safeguard food security. This makes it clear that growth fundamentalism triumphs over concerns of food production. The amendments relating to retrospective application of 2013 Act clearly tilt in favour of the acquiring project agencies and are intended to protect their interests at the cost of the affected persons by depriving them of the limited protection from financial loss provided by the provision in the 2013 Act. The same intent is reflected in the amendment relating to return of unutilized land so as let it remain with the project agency much longer. The acquiring authority can specify a longer period for completion of a project so as to retain the acquired land. The amendment requiring prior sanction of Government for prosecuting a Government servant guilty of offence under the Act is retrograde and wipes out the modicum of accountability introduced in the 2013 Act and would fail to check delay, inaction, wrong action and removes the element the fear in bureaucracy involved in the implementation of the Act of possible legal culpability in their actions. The extension of period for Central Government to issue directions or remove difficulties in the law underlines the danger that, in the garb of removing difficulties, directions may be issued further diluting whatever remains of the beneficial provisions in the 2013 Act so as to smoothen the process of acquisition for the benefit of the requiring agencies. Altogether, the changes made are clearly intended to remove any possible delay in the acquisition or increase in transaction or opportunity cost for the requiring agencies. The amendments aggressively respond to pressure from corporations, bureaucracy, politicians and neo-liberal economists who consider, without any evidence, 2013 Act as serious bottleneck to growth and show little empathy with the displaced persons. This shows the powerlessness of the affected people in their fight for justice against the State (Saxena, 2015).

Conclusion

Given the strong opposition to the 2014 ordinance, NDA Government allowed it to lapse and did not repromulgate it since it could not muster necessary support in Rajya Sabha. It, however, let it be known that State could enact their own law on acquisition on the lines of 2014 ordinance since they had the concurrent power to legislate on the subject. Taking a cue from this, Rajasthan Government enacted a law on acquisition broadly on the lines of 2014 ordinance. Other States are taking similar measures to bypass relax/dilute the provisions of the 2013 Act so as to simplify and speed up the process of acquisition and reduce its costs to the industry States have also adopted measures to find other ways to take land from the peasants and do away with the process of acquisition altogether such as voluntary land pooling arrangement in Andhra Pradesh and Gujarat and direct purchase from the land owners to escape the responsibility of resettlement and rehabilitation of affected persons. In addition, discretionary powers given by the 2013 Act to States under many Provisions is being used to relax their rigour or exempt certain projects from their application. Altogether, it is the State whether in the centre or in the provinces, which is depriving the land dependent people from the extremely modest gains they had won after long years of struggle and sacrifice. Some of the changes now being introdocued by the States may turn out to be worse for the land and livelihood losers than what the 1894 Act delivered to them over a period of time. What is abundantly clear is that the process of depeasantisation is being aggressively pushed by the State in alliance with the Capital. The survival of peasantry is bleak and has no one to look up to for Justice. The persons affected by this drive are doomed to join the reserve army of destitute labour for survival

REFERENCES

Campaign for People's Control over Natural Resources. 2001. *The Land Acquisition, Rehabilitation and Resettlement Bill, 2000*. Dharwad: Samaj Parivartan Samudaya.

Cernea, M. 1998. 'Impoverishment or Social Justice? A Model for Planning Resettlement.' In *Development Projects and Impoverishment Risks: Resettling Project-Affected People in India*, edited by H M Mathur and D Marsden. New Delhi: Oxford University Press.

Fernandes, W. 2006[a]. 'Development Induced Displacement and Tribal Women.' In *Tribal Development in India: The Contemporary Debate*, edited by G C Rath. New Delhi: Sage Publications.

Fernandes, W. 2006. 'Liberalization and Development Induced Displacement.' *Social Change* 36, No. 1:109-123.

Fernandes, W and V Paranjape, eds. 1997. *Rehabilitation Policy and Law in India*. New Delhi: Indian Social Institute.

Lok Sabha. 2008[a]. *The Land Acquisition (Amendment) Bill 2007*. Secretariat Thirty Ninth Report of Standing Committee on Rural Development (2007-08), October, 2008.

Lok Sabha. 2008[b] Secretariat. *The Rehabilitation and Resettlement Bill, 2007*. Fortieth Report of the Standing Committee on Rural Development (2007-08), October, 2008.

Lok Sabha Secretariat. 2012. *The Land Acquisition, Rehabilitation and Resettlement Bill 2011*. Thirty First Report of Standing Committee on Rural Development, May 2012.

Mahapatra, L K. 1999. *Resettlement, Impoverishment and Reconstruction in India*. New Delhi: Vikas Publishing House.

Mathur, H M. 1997. *Managing Projects that Involve Resettlement: Case Studies from Rajasthan, India*. Washington: IBRD/World Bank, Economic Development Institute.

Ministry of Law and Justice. 2013. *The Right to Fair Compensation and Transparency in Land Acquisition, Rehabilitation and Resettlement Act, 2013*. No. 30 of 2013.

Ministry of Law and Justice. 2014. *The Right to Fair Compensation and Transparency in Land Acquisition Rehabilitation and Resettlement (Amendment) Ordinance*. 2014.

Ministry of Rural Development (MORD). 2004. *Report of the Expert Groups on Prevention of Alienation of Tribal Land and its Restoration*. Government of India.

Ministry of Rural Development. 2007[a]. *The Land Acquisition (Amendment) Bill, 2007*. Bill No. 97.

Ministry of Rural Development. 2007[b]. *The National Rehabilitation and*

Resettlement Policy, 2007. Government of India.

Ministry of Rural Development. 2007[c]. *The Rehabilitation and Resettlement Bill, 2007.* Bill No. 98 of 2007.

Ministry of Rural Development. 2009[a]. *The Land Acquisition (Amendment) Bill, 2009.* Bill No. 97-C of 2007 as passed by Lok Sabha on February 25, 2009.

Ministry of Rural Development. 2009[b]. *The Rehabilitation and Resettlement Bill 2009.* Bill No. 98-C of 2007 as passed by Lok Sabha on February 25, 2009.

Ministry of Rural Development. 2011[a]. *The Draft Land Acquisition Rehabilitation and Resettlement Bill, 2011.* August, 2011

Ministry of Rural Development. 2011[b]. *The Land Acquisition, Rehabilitation and Resettlement Bill, 2011.* Bill No. 77 of 2011 as introduced in the Lok Sabha, on September, 7.

Parsuraman, S. 1999. *Development Dilemma.* UK: Macmillan.

Planning Commission. 2003. *The Tenth Five Year Plan.* Government of India.

Ramesh, Jairam and Muhammad Ali Khan. 2015. *Legislating for Justices: The Making of the 2013 Land Acquisition Law.* New Delhi: Oxford.

Shanmukham, K. 2011. *Law of Land Acquisition and Compensation.* New Delhi: Butterworth.

Upadhyay, Sanjay and Raman, Bhavani. 1998. *Land Acquisition and Public Purpose.* New Delhi: The Other Media.

5

Social Impact Assessment (and Social Inclusion): A Critique of National Rehabilitation and Resettlement Policy (NRRP) - 2007

Rudra Prasad Sahoo

Introduction

Social Impact Assessment (SIA) is considered as a tool to assist communities to determine their development priorities. In common parlance, development, is generally understood as a right to which all people should have access. But at the same time people's right to development also means they have a right to be protected from development's negative effects, like arbitrary eviction, forced displacement and the loss of economic, political, civil, and human rights. This idea is echoed in Article 1 of the 1986 Declaration on 'The Right to Development', which states that, '*The right to development is an inalienable human right by virtue of which every human person and all people are entitled to participate in, contribute to and enjoy economic, social, cultural and political development, in which all human rights and fundamental freedoms can be fully realized. The human rights to development also imply the full realization of the right of the peoples to self-determination, which includes subject to the relevant provisions of both International Covenants on Human Rights, the exercise of their inalienable rights to full sovereignty over all their natural wealth and resources*'[1]. This approach to, development is seen as a paradigm shift in the development discourse which clearly lays stress on both generating benefits and imposing costs. Among its greatest costs has been the displacement of millions of vulnerable people due to implementation of developmental projects. It has been marked that, the victims of development-induced displacement never got due justice. This is because the negative effects of development-induced displacement may be every bit as grave as those faced by people displaced by other forces. They may be receive some compensation from the government or authorities who are involved in the development projects but their community resources, and social bonding are hardly ever restored in the resettlement and rehabilitation process. To address these issues and the negative impact of such development on innocent people, some international covenants came into force in the recent decades. Out of the many covenants, Rio Declaration on Environment and Development, 1992 is an important one among them which emphasized the need for environmental assessment before undertaking new projects. Principle 1, of this declaration proclaims *that, 'Human beings are at the center of concerns for sustainable development. They are entitled to a healthy and productive life in harmony with nature'.* Likewise principle 17 of the same declaration states that, *'Environmental Impact Assessment (EIA), as a national instrument shall be undertaken for proposed activities that are likely to have a significant adverse impact on the environment and are subject to a decision of a competent national authority'*[2].

The above-mentioned declarations are nothing but expressions of the concern to minimize the negative effect of development projects both on environment and society as a whole. So, in the planning and implementation process of any development projects, the *Guiding Principles* would be, authorities must first explore all feasible alternatives to avoid displacement altogether. Further if the displacement is unavoidable, then attempts should be made to, minimize displacement along with its adverse consequences. In all instances, displacement should not threaten life, dignity, liberty, or security; rather they should be equally protected by providing conditions of adequate shelter, safety, nutrition, and health to who suffer a lot due to displacement. But it is unfortunate that most of the projects undertaken in the name of development today have negative effects not only on the ecology but also on human settlements and the social fabric of human relations and on their cultural composition.

Now in the ongoing debate on development discourse, the issue of forceful displacement issue is a major concern. Because the human suffering created by development projects through displacement of the large disadvantaged section of society needs to be supported through a favourable policy. It will better, if a SIA could be done prior to carrying out the developmental projects as then , perhaps a proper balance between the ecology and human settlement can be maintained and there will be no major disturbance in that particular geographical location.

This paper is an attempt to focus how to minimize the negative impact of developmental projects through SIA and it will provide the critics of the present National Rehabilitation and Resettlement Policy (NRRP), 2007 formulated by Department of Land Resources, Ministry of Rural Development, Government of India for its methods to arrive at better results. So the paper is divided into four major parts. The first part deals with what is SIA and its evolution as a concept. The second part deals with the SIA response to social development concerns and the stages of SIA. And it also deals with the methodology and scope and how it will serve as a tool for social development by measuring and analyzing the social costs of ongoing project in a particular human settlement and how it will affect their access to living and livelihood. The third part deals with SIA and NRRP-2007. The fourth part presents a critical analysis of NRRP-2007 in the light of new innovations in social and cultural thinking. The fifth part deals with some suggestions and recommendations. The last part deals with the conclusion.

1. SIA: Evolution as a Concept

In the past too, developmental projects carried out by the State or different agencies did use to result in some human misery. But their (social) impact has not been adequately recorded. The projects like dams and reservoirs, mining, power and industrial plants and hazardous waste disposal sites result in some kind of social impact (in the form of risks to the health of individual, groups and communities and to their livelihood patterns). So it is better to understand what exactly is meant by social impact. Armour (1992) defines social impact as changes that occur in: people's way of life (how they live, work, play and interact with one another on a day to day basis) and their culture (shared beliefs, customs and values) and their community (its cohesion, stability, character, services and facilities)[3]. The Inter-organizational Committee on Principles and Guidelines for SIA (IOCGPSIA, 2003) define social impacts as 'the consequences to human population of any public or private actions that alter the ways in which people live, work, play, relate to one another, organize to meet their needs, and generally cope as members of society. The term also includes cultural impacts involving changes to the norms, values and beliefs that guide and rationalize their cognition of themselves and their society'[4]. As a result of development projects, people experience these changes which involve a significant impact on their lives.

To minimize the negative effects of a developmental project, the assessment of social impact is unavoidable. But assessing the response of human communities to a policy drive intervention (as we call a developmental project) is not new. Assessment of this type of impact goes back to 1969, when the United States adopted the National Environmental Policy Act (NEPA)[5]. The passage of NEPA of 1969 made it a requirement to produce environmental impact statements for special types of projects. But the term 'SIA' was first used when the Department of the Interior prepared the Environment Impact Statement (EIS) for the Trans-Alaska pipeline in 1973 in the United States The EIS was done in response to the requirement made in NEPA to understand the impact of this project on human environment[6]. This SIA was made under the broader umbrella of environmental assessment to identify the social consequences of a developmental project.

During this period, the Inter-organizational Committee on Guidelines and Principles for Social Impact Assessment defined SIA 'in terms of efforts to assess or estimate, in advance, the social consequences that are likely to follow specific policy actions (including programmes and the adoption of new policies), and specific government actions (including buildings, large projects and leasing large tracts of land for resources extraction)'[7]. This definition is more popular and is favoured because it possesses the core concept of SIA, which has been found in other definitions as well.

An important change came in the understanding of SIA, when the CEQ suggested regulations for implementing the procedural provisions of NEPA (US Council on Environment Quality, 1986). The CEQ noted that the 'human environment' mentioned in NEPA is to be interpreted to include 'the natural and physical environment and the relationship of people with that environment'. It means the agencies which are involved in undertaking developmental projects need to assess the historic, cultural, economic, aesthetic, and social or health effects...whether direct, indirect or cumulative[8]. With this interpretation and changed meaning, SIA arrived at a new phase. During 1980s countries like Australia, New Zealand developed marked interest to adopt the SIA tool for their developmental project initiatives particularly on indigenous land. Its importance was deeply realized and as a result of that an International Association for Impact Assessment was formed in the year 1981.

At this stage everybody irrespective of their nationality, acknowledged the growing need of the SIA to understand the complexity of the needs of the human community and the negative impacts of planned intervention. So checking the consequences of the negative effect and the search for positive result is the determining goal of SIA[9].

Despite its overwhelming recognition, Van clay Franck feels that this type of assessment has limited scope because this is purely a bureaucratic exercise and there is no chance for public participation. Even Burdge and Robertson (1998) say public involvement is a key component of SIA because this is the medium by which the affected community can provide systematic inputs to the decision making[10]. In acknowledgement of these deficiencies, the SIA community revised the International Principles for SIA by coming up with a new definition in 2003 which was more democratic, participatory and constructivist in its understanding and elaboration.

The International Principles for SIA (2003) define, 'SIA is the process of analyzing, monitoring and managing the intended or unintended social consequences, both positive or negative of planned interventions (Policies, Programs, Plans, Projects) and any social change processes invoked by those interventions. Its primary purpose is to bring about a more sustainable and equitable biophysical and human environment'[11]. SIA ensures that development interventions can be tackled in two ways. The first is to be informed of and take into account the key relevant social issues and second, to incorporate a participation strategy for involving a wide range of stakeholders.

In general, SIA can be understood as a framework for evaluation of all impacts on humans and on all the ways in which people and communities interact with their socio-cultural, economic and environmental surroundings. The starting point for the SIA elements of the study is an investigation of the social characteristics of the project area: the size and location of populations, ethnicity, livelihoods and income, infrastructure, education and public health, and cultural sites. However, the focus of the SIA is on the consequences of resettlement, since the most significant social impacts arise from this. SIA is typically applied to the consequences of planned interventions. The techniques might also be used to consider the social impacts of other types of events such as disasters, climate change, demographic change and epidemics.

In any development project, the consequences may be direct or indirect; there may be short- term impact or long-term changes; so SIA helps us to explain how a proposed action will change the lives of people in the communities. Consideration should be given to the indirect, long-term or cumulative impacts involving interactions between communities and the environment. For example, the growth of local populations may lead to shortages of livelihood opportunities and as a result of this, over a longer period of time, excessive pressure may build on natural resources which leads to unsustainable environmental management practices, which in their turn may result in environmental degradation and associated hazards/risks. (Increases in population size and density are by themselves likely to increase the risk from the existing hazards unless the existing protective measures and emergency services are reinforced). A secondary impact of mitigation measures may be changes in the relationships between social groups. For example, the construction of a dam or reservoir to control downstream flooding might lead to tensions between different water users such as farmers, recreational users such as fishermen or those who make their living transporting goods and people by water. In addition, SIA must be integrated with health impact assessment in the early phase of planning process. Health impact here can be dealt with two risk factors. These are: one related to occupational health hazard and second related to community health impact in the project area. Health is understood in broad terms, encompassing social, economic, cultural and psychological well-being and the ability to adapt to the stresses of daily life. Health Impact Assessment (HIA) therefore considers the underlying determinants of health (e.g. employment and working conditions, physical environments, health services, education and coping skills), using checklists of indicators of changes in health risks. The Guidelines recommend investigating a wide range of health factors related to project interventions: exposure and effects on factors related to project interventions; hazardous agents, environmental factors, exposure and effects on physical health, healthcare services and the quality of the ageing of the members of the society. Health inequality is a central issue and identification of the most vulnerable groups is very important.

However, widening the scope of the assessment in such ways does have practical implications in terms of capacity, resources and data access. The more immediate and direct impacts are likely to be easier to identify and assess. Moreover, the SIA should focus on the most important social impacts. SIA teams should also be clear from the very beginning about the areas and communities under investigation. In a nutshell, SIA, is a concept based on the notion that decision makers should understand the consequences of their decision before they act and the people affected shall not only be appraised of the effects, but also should have the opportunity to participate in designing their future (IOCPGSIA 2003)[12]. Some writers Beard, 1973; Biswas,1973, say, 'the inclusion of social factor in resources planning consideration introduces great complexity into the planning process but its omission may have also serious consequences on the effectiveness of the entire planning effort'[13]. Further, to elaborate it means a growth-centric development initiative undertaken by different agencies must develop an action plan in such a way that the social and cultural ethos of people will not be violated and at the same time their traditional social and cultural milieu should be in harmony with their environment.

2. Social Impact Assessment Response to Social Development Concerns

Social impacts are impacts of developmental interventions on human settlements. Such impacts not only need to be identified and measured but also need to be managed in such a way that the positive externalities are magnified and the negative ones minimized.

SIA is predicated on the notion that development interventions have social ramifications and it is imperative that decision makers understand the consequences of their decisions before they act and affected people must get the opportunity to participate in designing their future. Developmental initiatives informed by social assessment alleviate poverty, enhance inclusion and build ownership while minimizing and compensating adverse social impacts on the vulnerable and the poor.

There are certain methods to be followed while undertaking SIA. These are the experiences of expert groups of different fields of knowledge consisting of anthropologist, sociologists, economists, psychologists and public planners. They provide a blueprint to assess some minimum conditions to achieve better results.

1.1 Stages of SIA

Step 1: Baseline Conditions

In most of the developmental projects, the project area is demarcated in the map but the impact area is not often coterminous with the project area. So once the project area is identified, representatives from each group should be systematically interviewed to determine potential areas of concern/impact, and the ways each representative might be involved in the planning decision process. Public meetings by themselves are inadequate for collecting information about public perceptions. Survey data can be used to define the potentially affected population. In this first step, a public involvement programme will facilitate the environmental and SIA process. The baseline conditions will help to understand the existing conditions and past trends associated with the human environment in which the proposed activity is to take place. The social impacts and their significance are situation-specific. The relevant human environment may be a more dispersed collection of interested and affected public, interest groups, organizations and institutions[14]. The category of social impact which need investigation are as follows:

- Population change/characteristics
- Community and institutional structures
- Political and social resources
- Community, individual and family changes
- Community resources.
- Issue of Social Justice

Step 2: Public Involvement

The public include those who are going to displaced by the proposed project and the persons whose land will be used in the project area, the people whose land is not taken but who are living near the project area and the persons who are debarred from community services as a result of the proposed project. The stakeholders must be identified and representation will have to be given to all these victim groups who are affected by the proposed project directly or indirectly. The people who are affected by the project and are excluded due to their persistent linguistic, cultural and economic barriers must be involved in decision making process not in the form of a passive agent but in the form of active interaction where communication will flow from both ways between the implementing agencies and the affected groups[15].

Step 3: Project Description and Identification of Alternatives

In this stage, the proposed action is described in detail to enable identification of the data requirements to frame the SIA. This should include:

- Location
- Land requirements
- Needs for ancillary facilities (roads, transmission lines, sewer and water lines)
- Construction schedule
- Size of the workforce (construction and operation, by year or month)
- Facility size and shape
- Need for a local workforce
- Institutional resources

These steps are listed looking into the CEQ regulation guideline[16]. Data relating to social history of the area and present demographic, social, cultural, political and economic conditions will be gathered in this stage so that it will provide clues to understand differentiated impacts on different categories of people.

Step 4: Screening

Screening is done to determine the boundaries of SIA. It is concerned with selecting 'developments' that require assessment and avoiding 'developments' that do not require any assessment. It involves making a proposal on the 'developments' in terms of its impact on people and of its relative significance[17]. A certain level of basic information about the proposal and its location is required for this purpose. Screening procedures employed can be based on the already existing legal frameworks and can be executed in consultation with the stakeholder.

Step 5: Scoping

After the initial screening, the SIA variables need to be selected for further assessment. Consideration needs to be given both to the impacts perceived by the acting agency and to those perceived by the affected groups and communities. The principal methods to be used by experts are reviews of the existing social science literature, public scoping, public surveys and public participation techniques. It is important for the views of affected people to be taken into consideration. Ideally, all affected people or groups contribute to the selection of the variables assessed through either a participatory process or by reviews made by responsible officials.

Relevant criteria for selecting significant impacts include the,

- Probability of the event occurring
- Number of people including indigenous populations that will be affected
- Duration of impacts (long term vs short term)
- Value of benefits and costs to impacted groups (intensity of impacts)
- Extent to which the impact is reversible or can be mitigated
- Likelihood of causing subsequent impacts
- Relevance to present and future policy decision
- Uncertainty over possible effects
- Presence or absence of controversy over the issue

The above criteria are mentioned in detail in CEQ regulations[18]. After the direct impacts have been estimated, how the affected people will respond in terms of attitudes and actions must be taken into account. Their attitude before implementation predicts their attitude afterwards, though there are increasing data which show that fears are often exaggerated and that expected benefits fail to meet expectations. The actions of affected groups can be estimated using comparable cases and consultations and interviews. A lot depends on the nature of local leadership (and the objectives and strategies of these leaders) which makes such assessment highly uncertain. However, such an exercise enables policy makers to be aware of potential problems and unexpected results. This step is also important because adoption and response of affected parties can have consequences of their own- whether for the agency that is responsible for taking action (as when political protests stall a proposal) or for the affected communities, whether in the short-term or in the long-term.

Patterns in the previous assessment guide this analysis and expert judgment along with field investigations are used to see whether the case study follows the typical patterns or is it developing uniquely. Affected people are incorporated in the decision making process and their assessment is critical to the success of this step.

Step 6: Predicting Responses to Impacts

'Social impacts' refer to the consequences to human populations of any public or private actions that alter the ways in which people live, work, play, relate to one another, organize to meet their needs and generally cope as members of society. The term also includes cultural impacts involving changes to the norms, values, and beliefs that guide and rationalize their cognition of themselves and their society.

Adverse social impacts could be in the form of:

- Loss of land
- Loss of structures
- Loss of livelihood
- Loss of crops/trees
- Loss of access to community infrastructure/public utility lines.[19]

All these are very much considered as economic issues. But it has also social implications which determine life in the society for people's existence, their survival and for building self-esteem among their fellow beings.

Step 7: Mitigation, Management & Monitoring

SIA is not only a mechanism to forecast impact but also it identifies the means to mitigate the adverse impacts. If the impact is to be too severe then it is better not to consider the project. And if the predicted impact is minimal and can be managed, then mitigation measures must be taking into consideration. This could be in the form of:

- Modifying an action related to the project
- Changing the operational and designing part of the project
- Compensation for the impact by providing suitable alternative facilities, opportunities and resources.

Even though they are not immediately adopted but identification of mitigation measures is essential. These measures are comprehensive in form because it also includes risk mitigation strategies[20].

Social Management Plan (SMP) is a must and a part of Social Impact Assessment (SIA) methodology which includes the following:

- Enumeration of the project affected person's families
- Measures to minimize resettlement
- Consultation and involvement of project affected peoples (PAP)
- Entitlement framework
- Institutional arrangement

Institutions are a vital part of delivery mechanism of a state. Institutions have to address the social inclusion aspect. Social Inclusion means removal of institutional barrier and providing incentives to increase the access of different developmental opportunities to individual and vulnerable groups.

Monitoring programme is generally required because it will perform the task of identifying deviation from the proposed action and any important unanticipated impacts. This should track project and programme development and compare real impacts with the projected ones. It should spell out (to the degree possible) the nature and extent of additional steps that should take place when unanticipated impacts. The purpose of this monitoring progamme is also to compare the real impact of development programme with the projected one. Only then it can spell out the nature and extent of the additional steps it will take when an unanticipated impact or those large than the projections occur.[21]

3. SIA and NRRP-2007

The Government of India, Ministry of Rural Development, and Department of Land Resources has formulated a National Rehabilitation and Resettlement Policy, 2007 which is published in the Gazette of India in October 31, 2007. In this policy framework, an entire chapter is devoted to SIA. In Chapter 4 details the policy document clearly lays out the details about the SIA of projects.

The very first clause deals with the number of people involuntarily displaced from the project affected area. The clause 4.1 states that when a new project or expansion of an existing project which involves involuntary displacement of four hundred or more family in plain areas, or two hundred or more families en masse in tribal or hilly areas, DDP blocks (It means a block identified under the Desert Development Programme)[22] or areas mentioned in the Schedule V or Schedule VI to the Constitution, the appropriate Government shall ensure that a SIA study is carried out in the proposed affected areas in such manner as may be prescribed.

4.2.1. It is stated that above SIA report shall be prepared, considering various alternatives.

4.2.2. While undertaking a SIA study, due consideration will be given to the impact that the project will have on public and community properties, assets and infrastructure, particularly, roads, public transport, drainage, sanitation, sources of safe drinking water, sources of drinking water for cattle, community ponds, grazing land, plantations, public utilities, such as post offices, fair price shops, etc as also food storage godowns, electricity supply, healthcare facilities, schools and educational/training facilities, places of worship, land for traditional tribal institutions, and burial and cremation grounds, etc.

4.2.3. The appropriate government may specify that the ameliorative measures, which will need to be undertaken for addressing the said impact for a component, may not be less than what is provided in a scheme or programme, if the Central Government or a State Government is in operation in that area.

4.3.1. Where it is required as per the provisions of any law, rules, regulations or guidelines it will be necessary to undertake environmental impact assessment also.

4.3.2. In cases where both EIA and SIA are required, the public hearing done in the project affected area for EIA shall also cover issues related to SIA. Such public hearings shall be organized by the appropriate government.

4.3.3. Where there is no requirement for EIA, the SIA report shall be made available to the public through a public hearing.

4.4.1. The SIA report shall be examined by an independent multi-disciplinary expert group constituted for the purpose by the appropriate government. Two non-official social science and rehabilitation experts, the secretary/secretaries of the department(s) concerned with the welfare of Scheduled Castes and Scheduled Tribes of the appropriate government or his (their) representative (s), and a representative of the requiring body shall be nominated by the appropriate government to serve on this expert group.

4.4.2. Where both EIA and SIA are required, a copy of the SIA report shall be made available to the agency prescribed in respect of environmental impact assessment by the Ministry of Environment and Forests, and a copy of the SIA report shall be shared with the expert group mentioned in paragraph 4.4.1.

4.5. The SIA clearance shall be accorded as per the procedure and within the time limits.

4.6. The SIA clearance shall be mandatory for all projects involving involuntary displacement.

4.7. The Ministry of projects involving emergency acquisition of minimum area of land in connection with national security, may be exempted from the provisions of the Chapter, with due institutional safeguards, as may be prescribed, for protecting the interests of the affected families and achieving the broad objectives of this policy. The details of these lists are elaborated in the Gazette of India and along with this a Chapter 5 deals with appointment, power and function of Administrator and Commissioner for Rehabilitation and Resettlement.

4. Issue and Critical Analysis

Major strengths of NRRP-2007 are as follows.

1. For the first time, SIA introduced for displaced persons.
2. Consultation with Gram Sabha or public hearing is mandatory.
3. Principle of rehabilitation before displacement.
4. Option for shares in companies implementing projects to affected families.
5. Housing benefits to all affected families include landless labourers.
6. Monthly pensions to all types of venerable sections and groups who are going to be displaced due to any development project.
7. Monetary benefit linked to consumer price index to be revised at periodic level. Spoke about Peripheral development should also be considered.
8. Ombudsman for grievances reduction.
9. Lastly, a National Rehabilitation Commission shall be set up by the Central Government to look after the rehabilitation and resettlement issues of project-affected families.

But there are policy pitfalls found in some areas which need some clarifications to strengthen the existing policy. These are as follows:

- In this policy, it is mentioned that only where 400 and more people in the plains and 200 or more people in tribal area are residing and involuntary displacement is to take place an SIA study will be carried out. So SIA will not be done if displacements below these figures occur in a particular locality.
- It is important that plans are prepared, reviewed and approved before the land acquisition is initiated and that it is done before any of the Affected Person's gets adversely

affected. The policy implicitly addresses rural and not urban settlements.

- The policy does not address some basic issues pertinent to urban settlements for example relocation of affected commercial properties to proper locations.
- Compensation will be made available depending on the losses of income during transition.
- The policy document does not clearly state that the physical infrastructure will be improved or at least maintained after resettlement. Also the houses or the plots provided to the projected affected people are very small. It is also not clear how and where the institutional details will work out. This is also materially not consistent.
- The policy only deals with economic rehabilitation and does not focus much on the Land Acquisition Act.

5. Suggestions and Recommendations

There are some recent major changes taking place in social science discourses which need to be given due importance for the betterment of vulnerable and disadvantaged sections of the society. One such thing is what Peter Berger and Thomas Luckmann wrote about in the social construction of reality. From this reading, one can probably conceive that their work is probably another attempt to integrate the two social theories of Durkheim and Weber. Focusing on Durkheim's analysis on the integrative aspects of social structure, and methodological individualism focused on by Weber, which deal with individual actions as being the basis of social action and structure[23]. Berger and Luckmann's idea of society can be represented by one word they use many times throughout the book, 'dialectic'. Humans are viewed to be engaged in the perpetual cycle of the 'dialectic' of creating the objective reality socially, while internalizing these very created realities as their own subjectively. As they call their approaches the 'sociology of knowledge', they pay a great deal of attention to the role of knowledge in constructing these objective and subjective realities. It is extremely critical to understand that when Berger and Luckmann talk about knowledge, they are not just discussing knowledge based upon ideology, theoretical knowledge, or a type of scientific knowledge, but rather about everything that humans take part in and within their everyday lives.[24]

The model represented by Berger and Luckmann depicts reality as a social phenomenon. The external actions of individuals become transformed into society as an objective reality that then may be internalized as moral norms and prescriptions, or otherwise known as individuals as a social product. Therefore, this means that reality is not fixed, but rather it is open to constant reinterpretation. The outcome of this social construction of reality is dependent on structures of inequality and relations of power. Though the social construction of reality is dependent upon both inequality and relations of power, it is impossible for power to have the capability to determine reality, because of the unknown consequences of any exercise of power and the interpretive nature of reality.

Socially constructed reality is the biggest influence on what we perceive as reality and how we perceive it, especially in the world as we know it today. An individual lacks knowledge, when he takes birth in the society. We gradually get to know very basic things, such as how to eat, drink, and sleep. Other than that, humans have to be reared, or raised, and we do this from our vision and hearing. We see the environment and learn the difference between what is right and wrong. We can perceive images that go on around us like no other specie can. As a result of this ability to see, we become constantly self-improving creatures to learn and develop ourselves around our environment.

Any social issue requires some amount of sensitivity because the social reality as we perceive must be looked through the broader lens of humanism. Achieving objective reality in social sphere is extremely difficult. Therefore, it is said, objectivity in social sphere is context specific and it is based on inter-subjective and intra-subjective (experience) relationships. Therefore human sensitivity for fellow beings is to be treated with empathy. The people for whom this SIA is going to be done are subjects and not material object. This subjective treatment if mooted out to those projects affected person than it will assume that SIA will achieve its goal and contribute to human progress.

Another issue which needs to be incorporated in NRRP policy is that the concept of impact equity must be analyzed. This will clearly identify who will win and who will lose and emphasize vulnerabilities of underrepresented groups. In addition to this, SIA must include not only EIA but also the HIA.

6. Conclusion

As of now, many existing theories are being criticized because the walls of metanarrative or grand theories and monolithic development discourses have failed to satisfy the need of human beings. So to lead a life full with dignity and freedom, a change is required. This alone can bring an alternative to fit into this realm of thought, which can provide some hope. Thus, crucial to this are the diffusion of democratic norms and belief in change. Therefore challenging traditional hegemonies and using the public sphere and the public as the central figure in the arena of change is unavoidable. Recently, the major failures of the current development system in delivering the goods in socio-economic terms and the consequent rise in discontent and unrest have led to exclusion and polarization in the society. The problem of integration is not just that the country has followed a path and model of development but it has created two Indias. One is concerned with resources and institutions and the other is left to fend for itself. In order to make SIA a reality we must fight a multifaceted struggle for justice, autonomy and dignity. So social ordering will not derive its end from the market and the narrow monetary end of profit; it must place emphasis on humane governance involving institutions to recognize the basic human values for which the civilization exists.

NOTES

1. United Nations General Assembly , Declaration on the Right to Development,1986, Declaration on the Right to Development adopted by UN General Assembly Resolution 41/128 on December 4, 1986 http://www.un.org/documents/ga/res/41/a41r128.htm]

2. 1992, Rio Declaration on Environment and Development, http://www.unep.org/Documents.Multilingual/Default.asp?documentid=78&articleid=1163

3. Armour, A. 1992. 'The Challenge of Assessing Social Impacts', Social Impacts.' *The Social Impact Management Bulletin*1, No.4: 4. http://www.newcastle.nsw.gov.au/__data/assets/pdf_file/0005/5576/social_impact_assessment_policy.pdf.

4. *Social Impact Assessment (A module).* Anthropological Survey of India, Calcutta, pp. 12-13, http://www.ansi.gov.in/download/SIA-%20Draft_Manaul.pdf.

5. Guideline and Principles for Social Impact Assessment by the Interorganizational Committee on Guideline and Principles for Social Impact Assessment, 1993, p. 1.

6. Social, Cultural, Economic Impact Assessments: A Literature Review (2002), prepared for The Office of Emergency and Remedial Review (2002), US Environmental Protection Agency, p.1 http://www.epa.gov/superfund/policy/pdfs/SILitRev Final.pdf.

7. Vanclay Frank, Engaging Community with Social Impact Assessment: SIA as a Social assurance process Interorganizational Committee, 1994, p. 108.

8. Opp. No. 6, p.1.

9. Western, J. and M Lynch. 2000. 'Overview of the SIA process' in Social Impact Analysis: An Applied Anthropology Manual', edited by L R Goldman. New York: Berg, 35-62.

10. Burdge, Rabel J. and A Robertson Robert. 1998. 'Social Impact Assessment and the Public Involvement Process.' In *A Conceptual Approach to Social Impact Assessment (revised edition): Collection of writings by Rabel J Burdge and Colleagues,* edited by Rabel J Burdge. Middleton, WI: Social Ecology Press ,183-192.

11. Vanclay, F. 2005, 'Principle for Social Impact Assessment : A Critical Comparison between International and US documents, *Environment Impact Assessment Review*, Vol. 25.

12. IOCGPSIA. 2003. 'Principle and Guidelines for Social Impact Assessment in USA.' *Impact Assessment and Project Appraisal* 21, No. 3: 231-250.

13. Dunning, C Mark. 'A Systematic Approach to Social Impact Assessment. http://www.edra.org/sites/default/files/publications/EDRA05-v2-Dunning-59-64.pdf

14. Opp. No. 4, p. 18.

15. Ibid.

16. Guidelines and Principles for Social Impact Assessment, 1994,

May. prepared by the Interorganizational Committee on Guidelines and Principle for Social Impact Assessment, U.S Department of Commerce National Oceanic and Atmospheric Administration National Marine Fisheries Service, available at: http://www.nmfs.noaa.gov/sfa/social_impact_guide.htm.

17. Social Impact Assessment (A Module) Anthropological Survey of India. 2010. Calcutta, p. 23. Available at: http://www.socialassessment.com/documents/KudatWorks/2010/2010-SIA-Draft_Manual-Ayse-Kudat-citations.pdf.

18. Opp. No. 16

19. Mishra, Vivek .Social Impact Assessment Methodology, available at: http://rlarrdc.org.in/images/Social%20Impact%20Assessment%20Methodology.pdf.

20. Benson Charlotte and John Twigg with Tiziana Rossetto, 2007. 'Tools for Mainstreaming Disaster Risk Reduction: Guidance Notes for Development Organizations,' The International Federation of Red Cross and Red Crescent Societies/Provention Consortium, Switzerland, p. 135. Available at: http://www.preventionweb.net/files/1066_toolsformainstreaming DRR.pdf.

21. A Comprehensive Guide for Social Impact Assessment. 2006. Center for Good Governance, pp.18-19. Available at: http://unpan1.un.org/intradoc/groups/public/documents/cgg/unpan026197.pdf.

22. National Rehabilitation and Resettlement Policy, 2007, p. 37 Published in Gazette of India, Extraordinary, Part 1, Section 1, October 31.

23. Berger, Peter L. and Thomas Luckmann. 1991. *The Social Construction of Reality: A Treatise in the Sociology of knowledge.'* Penguin Books, US, p. 30.

24. Ibid., p. 49.

REFERENCE

Beard, L R. 1973. 'Status of Water Resources Systems Analysis.' *Journal of the Hydraulics Division* 99, No. 04: 559-565.

Becker, H A. 1997. *Social Impact Assessment: Method and Experience in Europe, North America and the Developing World.* London: UCL Press.

Benson, Charlotte, John Twigg and Tiziana Rossetto. 2007. *Tools for Mainstreaming Disaster Risk Reduction: Guidance Note for Development Organization.* The International Federation of Red Cross and Red Crescent Societies/Provention Consortium,

Geneva, Switzerland. http://www.proventionconsortium.org/ mainstreaming_tools.

Biswas, A K. 1973. 'Socio-Economic Considerations in Water Resources Planning.' *Journal of the American Water Resources Association 09*, No. 04: 746-754.

Breeze C H and K Lock. 2001. *Health Impact Assessment as a Part of Strategic Environmental Assessment*. Copenhagen, WHO Regional Office for Europe. http://www.hiagateway.org.uk/http://www.who.int/heli/impacts/impactdirectory/en/index1.html.

Burdge, R J. 2004. *A Community Guide to Social Impact Assessment*. Middleton, USA: Social Ecology Press.

Government of India. 2007. *The National Rehabilitation and Resettlement Policy, 2007*. Land Reforms Division, Department of Land Resources, New Delhi.

National Rehabilitation and Resettlement Policy, 2007, Published in the Gazette of India, dated October 31, 2007. http://www.dolr.nic.in/NRRP2007.pdf,

Robinson, W C. 2004. 'Minimizing Development-Induced Displacement.' http://www.migrationinformation.org/feature/display.cfm?ID=194.

Sadler, Barry. and Mc Cabe, Mery, eds. 2002. *Environmental Impact Assessment – Training Resources Manual*. United Nation Environment Programme, Geneva, Switzerland. http://www.unep.ch/etu/publication/EIAMan_2edition_toc.htm

Vanclay, F. 2003. 'Social Impact Assessment: International Principles.' *Impact Assessment and project Appraisal 21*, No. 1:5-11. http://www.iaia.org.

World Bank. 2003. *Social Analysis Source Book: Incorporating Social Dimensions into Bank-Supported Projects*. Washington, DC: Social Development Department.

6

Uprooting the Earthworms - Resisting the Land-grabs

Felix Padel

A Total Disconnect

'We have sought an explanation from the Government about people who have been displaced in the name of development: how many have been properly rehabilitated? You have not provided them with jobs; you have not rehabilitated them at all. How can you again displace more people? Where will you relocate them and what jobs will you give them?' (Bhagaban Majhi, for the Kashipur movement, Das 2005)

My previous essays with Samarendra Das (2008, 2011) have drawn attention to a total disconnect between policy and practice regarding R and R (Resettlement and Rehabilitation). Millions of small-scale farmers have been uprooted from their land and communities without the compensation and improvements in living conditions that they were promised. After fifty years, families displaced by the Rourkela Steel Plant/ Mandira dam, and hundreds of similar projects, are still waiting for proper compensation in terms of land they were promised.

> 'On being displaced, people meet the same fate everywhere – buli-buli-buli-buli-bulichhanti (they are on the streets/wander/get lost)..... If they are displaced they will be packed tightly in houses built by Posco, far from the river, getting at most coolie jobs for a few years of construction'. (Villagers in Nolia Sahi, Samadrusti, 2009)

The problem is therefore at two levels. On the one hand, new 'generous' R and R policies turn out to be anything but, since they do not offer land for land, and cash compensation soon morphs into debt in the hands of village people not used to handling bank accounts and loan offers. Social Impact Assessments are barely carried out at all, forming at best a very subsidiary component in some Environment Impact Assessments, but without any weight or substance (Mathur, 2011).

And even if the policies were as good as claimed, in practice they have rarely if ever been enforced, due to the yawning gap between policy and practice. For example, companies' job offers, after an initial labour-intensive phase, become opaque: invariably, local people are left unemployed while outside migrant workers get most jobs, especially those with higher salaries. Moreover, the shift from agriculture to industry redefines skilled cultivators as 'unskilled', so that even 'training courses' bring people who have been skilled cultivators only one or two rungs at most up the ladder of employability, in a labour system that is degrading, exhausting and dangerous, where market economics is rigged against the labourer, and the price of a human life is often very cheap.

Overall, a rapid drop in people's quality of life characterizes the situation for the vast majority of displaced people. Numerous key problems find almost no place in mainstream R and R discourse, such as corruption, the role of goondas, illegal liquor shops and prostitution, or even proper analysis or monitoring of people's lives in resettlement colonies. Often, it's up to journalists to record the outrages, since official discourse avoids all mention—e.g. of an estimated 500 prostitutes and numerous illegal liquor shops at Damanjodi, Nalco's prime resettlement colony, often described as exemplary (Perry, 2010). These problems, and other reasons for the disconnect between policy and practice, are systemic, as we shall see.

Yet instead of first trying to resettle and rehabilitate the millions already displaced without proper compensation, millions more displacement is planned - not only by numerous new mega-displacement projects, but also via 'restriction of access' (Cernea, 2011), by rivers drying up or becoming polluted, by war and communal conflict, and by the entry of agri-business that favours big farmers and intensive cash crops at the expense of small farmers, whose way of life is defined as 'unsustainable' by current economic criteria, even though it is the epitome of long-term sustainability as defined by ecological criteria, and the maintenance of an economy still rooted in local ecology.

> We are tribal farmers. We are earthworms. Like fish that die when taken out of water, a cultivator dies when his land is taken away from him. So we won't leave our land. We want permanent [i.e. long-term] development (Bhagaban Manjhi, one of the leaders of the Kashipur movement against the Utkal Alumina Project, in an interview to Das and Das, 2005).

One focus of this paper is to draw attention to the element of community-death or soul-death, rarely understood by 'educated' people for whom roots in a community tied to a piece of land is barely even a memory, but articulated with devastating clarity by displaced people themselves. Bringing voices of displaced people has value in its own right, since they are so numerous yet so little heard. For example, Subrat Sahu's film *DAM-aged* features interviews with people in the atrociously neglected communities around the Upper Indravati reservoir. This also draws critical attention to the messy resource frontier of today's development wars.

What would be real development for people in India's poorest areas? How are people standing up to the corporate invasions and land-grabs?

Between what a company or development project promises and what actually happens, we have seen that a reality gap exists (Padel and Das, 2011). Briefly, promises of jobs and an all-round rise in quality of life have been systematically betrayed. In practice, displaced people have faced wholesale neglect.

The disconnect of mainstream society from displaced people operates at several levels. The neglect represents a fundamental injustice, congruent with the historic injustice towards tribal people which a recent Supreme Court judgement has drawn attention to as needing to be undone (http://www.the hindu.com/opinion/op-ed/article1081343.ece). But even the subject of displacement is subject to neglect and distortion, with

'R and R' a frequent euphemism for displacement, even though genuine rehabilitation has rarely been achieved.

The disconnect also mirrors the lack of dialogue between what Jairam Ramesh has called 'two cultures' – essentially economics and ecology (C P Snow's original 1959 'The Two Cultures' essay drew attention to the split between arts and science). The two cultures consist of very different groups, with very different value systems. One is propagated by an elite of economists, bankers, businessmen and financiers-including the IMF/WB economists who orchestrate World Bank loans, and everyone who believes in their system (which includes a large proportion of the middle classes)-and ecology as expressed by a broad alliance of people's movements, based in local communities fighting displacement, as well as professionals in many walks of life.

One of the great ironies of development-induced displacement is that projects termed 'development' have caused and are causing millions of people a marked decline in their quality of life.

Another is that many of the communities facing displacement have an economy still interwoven with ecology, representing ancient traditions at the core of India's culture of food cultivation-systems that have sustained over centuries, now threatened with enforced extinction as 'uneconomic!'

Exterminating Earthworms

This is especially so since a high proportion of displaced families are (or were) small-scale cultivators, using largely organic methods of subsistence-based farming practices. Green revolution agriculture, that uses large doses of fertilizers and pesticides, has damaged and polluted the groundwater in Punjab so intensely that 97 per cent of villages are now classed as water-scarce (Dutt, 2010). Many species of birds, as well as insects and earthworms, have witnessed a massive decline.

Since a 'new green revolution' based on GM and biotechnology threatens to compound the displacement of small farmers along with their indigenous cultivation techniques throughout India, the assault on the country's earthworms and on Adivasis, who often identify with earthworms in their bond with the soil, are closely interlinked.

Earthworms are the key to 'living soil'-the subject of Darwin's last research and book (1881). Thousands of farmers tempted into Green Revolution fertilizer-based methods have found themselves complicit in a holocaust of worms.

> This is what had happened to Upendra; he was told by the Government, the companies and many others that if he spent his money on agricultural chemicals he would make more money. He tried it and it worked. For five years his yield increased, the more he spent, the more he used and the more he seemed to make. Little did Upendra know that the reason for this was the combined efforts of the natural richness of the soil and the chemical fertilizers' boosting effects. While this was happening nothing was being put back into the soil. The chemicals were killing his soil, the worms and other organisms... all the life of the soil. Soon there was nothing left and his yield went down. Now he had nothing but the hybrid seed and chemicals to produce his crop and year after year he began to pay more and more to the companies while, now knowingly destroying his soil. (Taylor, 2011).

The condition of the land remained unchanged until he started working actively with worms, breeding them in compost to bring back the nutrients to his starved soil. Fertilizers kill earthworms within a few hours of application to fields. And what life-forms do pesticides kill? Punjab witnesses a silent spring already, yet Rachel Carson, the visionary scientist who issued the first major warning against fertilizer-pesticide-intensive agriculture in *Silent Spring* (1962) was the subject of vicious attacks and attempts to discredit her meticulous research by the chemical industries (Laura Orlando, 2002).

So plans for a new Green Revolution in Eastern India, and MoUs recently signed between Monsanto, Du Pont and other multinational biotech/seed companies, by State Governments including Odisha and Rajasthan spell grave danger of accelerating the already rapid displacement of small-scale cultivators from the land, by promoting hybrid rice and other new cash crops—in a context where the role of unrepayable debts to seed companies is already a major cause of farmers' suicides, and where farmers in Punjab are committing suicide due to the legacy of the Green Revolution, in the land's infertility and a vast depletion of ground-water. (Living Farms, 2010).

Displacement of human communities is closely interwoven with a variety of assaults on the fabric of natural life known as the ecosystem. The two are part of the same process. Displacement is not only caused by 'development projects'. If about 60 million people have officially been involuntarily displaced and resettled to make way for dams, mines and factories, uncounted numbers have been displaced by other causes too: internecine conflicts and communal conflicts, displacing thousands in South Chhattisgarh, Kandhamal, etc.; depletion of water resources—always-depended-on rivers drying up from dams, etc., or dangerously polluted, and groundwater levels sinking and polluted; 'restriction of access' in national parks, etc.; the gradual takeover of Adivasi lands by money-lenders and liquor-sellers, which has been recorded for over 150 years, and still takes place on a large scale, though illegal, morphing into the takeover of lands by seed companies, etc.; and housing developments displacing thousands of slum-dwellers in cities.

The disconnect is blatant in a lot of World Bank and corporate literature, promising a reduction in poverty, even as eyewitnesses from the ground report violent tactics used against people resisting displacement, and a huge increase in the poverty of people displaced.

Adivasi Economics

'You take us to be poor. But we're not. We live in harmony and cooperation with each other... We get good crops from Mother Earth. Clouds give us water... We produce many kinds of grains with our own efforts, and we don't need money. We use seeds produced by us... The lands in Gujarat (offered in compensation to people being displaced in MP) *are addicted to artificial susbtances. You cannot have a crop there without hybrid seeds.* (i.e., chemical fertilizers and pesticides have spoilt the land's natural fertility, and larger amounts need to be used each year).

You people live in separate houses. You don't bother about the joy or suffering of each other. But we live on the support of our kith and kin. We all work together….in the spirit of Laha *(communal labour) we construct a house in just one day… How does such fellow-feeling prevail in our villages? For we help each other. We enjoy equal standing. We've been born in our village. Our* Nara *(umbilical cord) is buried here)'* (Baba Mahariya, 2001).

Mainstream economists have long described small-scale farmers, whose main focus is subsistence farming, as 'uneconomic'. This was as much the case in Scotland, where "uneconomic" was an excuse for the Highland Clearances that removed tens of thousands of crofters off their land, as it is in India today.

So are Adivasis 'uneconomic'? What do they mean when they call themselves earthworms?

Marshall Sahlins' *Stoneage Economics* (1973) shows that, far from stereotypes dwelling in hunter-gatherer societies as enmeshed in scarcity, these actually made up 'the original affluent society'. Communities dismissed as 'primitive' tend to have a lot more leisure time, and use it a lot more productively.

This holds true for adivasis. Working hard in the fields during certain seasons, in mid-winter and the hot season they have major festivals, and traditional culture puts great emphasis on social life of villages visiting each other, dances and songs, intertwined with communal labour exchange, and working on each other's fields. The distinction between work and leisure is quite differently formulated in an Adivasi economy.

The Adivasi mode of production links them with the forest, mountains and rivers, so movements to maintain their culture and communities and conservation movements often work alongside each other, though occasional clashes take place on issues such as sanctuaries, which have caused some very painful cases of displacement.

Adivasi society is founded on systems of exchange, including reciprocity in the kinship system, brideprice, 'marriage by capture', but also in terms of a give-and-take relationship with the spirit-world realm of nature, ancestors and 'devatas'. Blood sacrifice is regularly offered to the spirits, and plays an important part in adivasi economics as well as communal relations and diet, since the sacrificed animal is always eaten. Cultivation is usually carried out using a system of labour exchange.

But a declining number of communities still have control over their environment and economy. Since British times, *Adivasi* communities have been preyed upon by a system of endemic exploitation that constantly eats away at *Adivasi* land-rights.

The term 'Adivasis', defining the 'Scheduled Tribes' as 'original dwellers' or 'Aborigines', was apparently first used in the Jharkhand movement during the 1930s by Jaipal Singh, when he formed the Adivasi Mahasabha. A Supreme Court judgement of 5 January 2011, in the case of a Bhil woman beaten and paraded naked in Maharashtra, records the need to correct historic injustice towards *Adivasis* and affirms the status of *Adivasis* in terms of their indigeneity. India has not officially recognized *Adivasis* as 'indigenous people', partly because it may seem invidious to term 92 per cent of India's population as 'old immigrants'. This non-recognition also has the effect of making it difficult to apply UN legislation protecting indigenous people in India. Nevertheless, this issue of indigeneity has been taken up vociferously by organizations such as BAMCEF, who promote the term 'Mulnivasis' to cover STs, SCs and OBCs (Backward and Minority Communities Employees Federation, http://www.mulnivasibamcef.org/pages/about.asp).

The Fifth Schedule of India's Constitution is meant to uphold tribal rights and cultures, especially through the non-alienability of their land. The PESA Act and Samatha Judgement extended this principle, which has nevertheless been repeatedly bypassed, among other means by the claim that displacement-projects are in the national interest.

Seventy-Five groups are still classified as PTGs (Primitive Tribal Groups). A 2002 report from the Ministry of Tribal Affairs on *Development of Primitive Tribal Groups*, still defines them using the concepts 'primitive' and 'backward' (http://164.100.24.208/ls/CommitteeR/Labour&Wel/33.pdf). This classification was made supposedly in order to protect them from exploitation. Yet the social evolutionism inherent in 'primitive' and 'backward' implies an intention to try and reduce these groups and 'bring them into the mainstream' – in distinction to the recognition of difference. This has been evident in the case of the Dongria Kondhs, a PTG who came into international news for their resistance to Vedanta's planned bauxite mine in Niyamgiri, where they live. Their administration is managed through the Dongria Kondh Development Agency, who have overseen an extensive road building programme into the heart of the Niyamgiri range, in line with Vedanta mining plans.

Many Adivasis still live in areas of great biodiversity. This is because Adivasi economics is still firmly rooted in long-term symbiosis with the local ecology. This has enabled them to live amidst biodiversity, and profit from it in their mix of cultivation, gathering and hunting, without destroying it or even (until some years ago) depleting it.

Uprooting Adivasis involves different elements. If the commodification of land and resources is one major element, the grounds for this were laid when British officials made a conscious effort to tie tribal people into the markets and a dependence on outside tastes. Markets were promoted from early British times. For example, G E Russell, a senior administrator from Madras who oversaw the first invasion/conquest of the Kondhs in what is now Kandhamahal, wrote of promoting markets so as to give the Kondhs *'new tastes and new wants'* since this *'will, in time, afford us the best hold we can have on their fidelity as subjects, by rendering them dependent upon us for what will, in time, become necessities of life'* (Padel, 2010).

Displacement Projects

The reality gap between what R and R is supposed to do-raise people's living-and what displacement actually does—devastate their standard of living—reflects a similar reality gap as that between the 'two cultures' of banks, economists and corporations on the one hand, and movements resisting the land-grabs on the other. The tendency is for consequences on the greater population, and even consequences on the natural environment, to be simply discounted, or treated as unimportant.

How does one weigh the value of huge sums invested by

companies taking over land and resources, and the value of communities who have always lived on this land, and managed it for agriculture and forest produce? There is incommensurability here (Martinez-Alier, 2012). On one side, a view where only what can be measured is real, and only what is profitable counts; on the other, a long-term vision and practice of cultivating food through respect for the land – the essence, perhaps, of Indian culture, expressed through old and tested methods of cultivation.

On the corporate side, at least it has become increasingly obvious to many people that real profits come only to the controlling elite and those who accommodate them. Yet this does not stop the clearances, and the scale is awesome. In 2005, when the MoU signing spree for mineral projects gathered momentum, Jharkhand's Government under Arjun Munda signed fifty, and a similar number were signed in Chhattisgarh and Odisha. Tata's MoU for a five million tonne steel plant in Bastar district was signed in June 2005 – the same month that Salwa Judum started its anti-Maoist campaign of burning villages and, in effect, civil war, which has displaced at least 200,000 people (Perspectives, 2008; CSE, 2008).

The scale and number of displacement projects is awesome. The land-grab/real estate/land speculation aspect has if anything become even more blatant than it was. It was already apparent in, for example, Tata's land acquisition near Gopalpur during the 1990s, that displaced 19 villages, who had tried hard to resist; the plant has not even started to be built yet. It is also apparent in the case of the land Tata wants at Kalinganagar, where it is well known that Tata bought land from IDCO at about ten times the price that IDCO paid to the tribal villagers. The escalating violence against protesters of the Bisthapit Birodhi Jan Manch, and against those whose houses were demolished in Baligutha and other villages, and the smear campaign against the BBJM (including allegations of Maoist instigation) are deeply worrying.

Mining and other companies frequently try to acquire far more land than they need for a project. Vedanta University is a classic example of this. It is a blatant feature of many SEZ projects, such as Reliance's 25,000 acre SEZ in Jhajjar and Gurgaon districts of Haryana, and its 35,000 acre SEZ in Pen-Uran-Penvel taluks of Raigad District, near Mumbai. Over 100 SEZs have been approved and several hundred more are planned—a massive series of takeovers of precious water and electricity, as well as land; receiving massive tax-breaks, special deregulation of labour laws, and draconian power structures to bypass normal democratic forms.

When one starts to enter the world of countless personal stories of upheaval that displacement involves, it is not surprising to find that people's non-violent resistance movements are strong in many places.

Many major displacement-projects are extremely controversial. Polavaram Dam in Andhra threatens to displace over 250 villages—over 200,000 people, and has been fought through the courts as well as in resistance campaigns on the ground.

The Jaitapur nuclear power plant in South Maharashtra, near the sea, threatens many villages of farmers as well as fishermen, and the security situation has become very tense, since a large cross-section of the population refuses to go along with the plan. In many projects like this, it is not only the direct displacement that people object to, it is also being forced to live dangerously close to a dangerously polluting plant. Nuclear plants emit radiation regularly as well as in periodic accidents, while workers there have repeatedly been shown to be at high risk of exposure (Ghanekar September 2010 and January 2011). In this case, a joint venture with France's star company Areva is at stake.

Jairam Ramesh's clearances as well as refusals represent a historic landmark in India's environmental history—especially coming after several years of A Raja as environment minister (Krishna, November 2010). His clearance of Posco is particularly controversial, since MoEF reports have exposed—in this and other cases—multiple illegalities in procedure (Bidwai, 2011; Mittal, 2011; Bera, 2011). These include shoddy EIAs and absent or highly manipulated Public Hearings. It's good that this prevalence of irregularities is coming more clearly to light, since many projects have been cleared on the basis of appallingly sub-standard EIAs, and Public Hearings that were held under extreme pressure or badly misreported. In the Posco case, an independent group has written a report questioning the conventional figures done of economic benefits, jobs, etc., (Mining Zone, 2010). This goes into welcome detail on the jobs that the Posco Steel-plant-cum-port would destroy—in this case a very large number, since betel-vine cultivation gives a good income and an estimated 22,000 people stand to lose their livelihoods if the project goes ahead.

Coal mines have been another particularly controversial issue, with Jairam attempting to classify nine major coal blocks as 'no-go areas' due to the extensive forest above them. A major reason for the extremely large number of new coal mines and thermal power plants, as well as new nuclear power plants and new big dams (e.g. the Par-Tapi-Narmada river interlinking dam project on the Gujarat-Maharashtra border, Lower Suktel in Odisha, many huge ones in Arunachal, as well as some new big ones in the western Himalayas also) being planned is that India faces a serious power shortage.

The impact of coal mining is generally less known about than the higher-grade minerals, though its impact on communities and ecosystems is probably just as dire. Uncounted thousands of families are uprooted each year to make way for new coal mines or expanding old ones. Several open-cast coal mines in Jharkhand now occupy as much as 35 sq km.

In the case of the Highland Clearances during the nineteenth century, thousands of displaced highlanders emigrated to America, Australia and other colonies, while thousands served in the colonial army, and thousands in Britain's mines and factories. Thousands died in poverty. For the twenty-first century Adivasis, there are even fewer options. Many migrate to do coolie labour in far-off places, often in cities, where they join massive slum populations. Over half of Mumbai's population live in slums according to the 2001 Census (6.25 million people out of a total of 11.9 million, Perspectives, 2008).

These slum populations also face periodic demolition drives against their homes that have become increasingly severe recently, as the cost of 'real estate' escalates. In Delhi, Commonwealth Games constructions forced evictions and demolitions that displaced an estimated 200,000 people (Housing and Land Right Network, February 2011; http:// www.business-standard.com/india/news/2-lakh-people-in-delhi-displaced-due-to-cwg-report/125010/on).

A similar pattern has been reported from Kolkata and Bhubaneswar, among other cities (Satyabrata, 2011).

In Mumbai, Mandala, East Golibar and other slums face demolition drives from companies trying to build new foreign-funded skyscrapers, even though here too communities have built homes and make ends meet in dire circumstances, such as a serious shortage of water (Iqbal January 2, 2011, Kumaran January 16, 2011). These drives continue even after residents won a court case against Shivalik Ventures for forging inhabitants' signatures (Iqbal, November 27, 2010, Khar East Andolan February 2 and 4, 2011), with great brutality, and apparent collusion by police. The 'reality gap' between what is promised and what happens is as gross in cities as in remote rural areas, and shows in promotional literature. In Golibar, sixty-nine colonies are faced with demolition to make way for a plan outlined by Unitech, a group tainted in the 2G spectrum scam, for a *'project that has the vision to develop mixed use integrated development of Residential Skyscrapers, State of Art Commercial buildings, High-end Retail and Hospitality ventures'. – Or 'Santa City', according to Unitech's website, 'the flagship project of Unitech in Mumbai in partnership with Shivalik Ventures. Spread over 140 acres, this is one of the single largest slum rehabilitation projects in Mumbai'.*

As many as 800,000 slum-dwellers face eviction from expansion plans for Mumbai's controversial new airport (Iqbal, 2010). Problems affecting rural displacement are often even worse for the urban poor, with less than a third resettled, and usually no question of cash compensation—resettlement is for those with the right documents, and only after payment of at least Rs. 7,000. Colonies are often as much as forty five kms outside the city, making travel to city work places extremely hard; water access and amenities are often appalling

(Perspectives, 2009). In other words, brutal demolition drives displace tens of thousands of families each year, with no compensation, and with no R and R at all for well over half of them.

Dismantling Social Structure

Communities and cultures are destroyed when villagers are removed from the land. Increasingly, people recognize this is what is at stake, which is why they fight with everything they have- non-violently at first, recognizing the powers against them are strong and violent.

Statistics on the Human Development Index (HDI) do not necessarily capture either the drastic drop in people's quality of life, or the extinction of cultures and communities. HDI has been used since the 1990s by UNDP to evaluate development not only by economic advances but also improvements in human well-being. Initially opposed by Amartya Sen as too complex to measure, it focuses on three areas: life expectancy/ health, education and income. Assumptions of uniformity are a major problem here, especially in dealing with tribal communities, who may have a relatively short life expectancy combined with a rich quality of life, and who may be illiterate while possessing a large amount of traditional knowledge, with a low income just because until recently, their economy was based more on exchange than money.

Raising the HDI can be made to seem consistent however with the image of Corporate Social Responsibility (CSR) as increasing local people's well-being, promoted by Vedanta, Tata, Posco and other mining companies, even while this presents an extraordinary contrast to the reality on the ground. Displaced people face a loss of community, and of the freedom to control their labour and environment, which especially affects women, who have a large amount of freedom over their labour and income in a traditional village, that they lose in a resettlement colony.

The essence of much displacement needs understanding in terms of cultural genocide – the killing of cultures (Padel and Das, 2008), since every aspect of Adivasis' social structure is effectively destroyed:

- kinship and community culture
- system of cultivation, self-employment
- cult of local natural features, system of values overturned
- power structure – losing control of their environment
- material culture: locally made items give way to mass-produced bought items

Feedback from the 'Oustees' and 'PAPs' (Project Affected Persons), though placed at the top of new R and R policies, is nowhere promoted. R and R is a totally top-down system. The corruption, intimidation and exploitation which occur at every stage of a 'development project' and R and R process, and the environmental degradation involved, are not properly recognized. Nor is the dividing of communities, even though this is clearly observable wherever there is displacement (Bera, 2011).

Relinking Economy with Ecology

One of the most painful aspects of displacement is the delinking of people's economy from an all-round embedding in ecology. In many ways, the Adivasi society—and this applies to many non-tribal communities also-is based on an ecological awareness in tune with long-term sustainability, worked out in extensive systems of ecological knowledge. This is true of tribal and indigenous societies worldwide-ecology-economy fine-tuned to each other. Yet the dispossession and invasion by mainstream society has often been so extreme, that systems still in place 50-200 years ago exist often under severe stress.

The Dongria Kondhs are one community whose preservation of their environment and attuning of economy to ecology is not in question. When their leader Lado Sikoka called the invading companies *asurmane* (demons) at the Belamba Public Hearing in Lanjigarh, April 25, 2009, this is a voice we rarely hear coming to the surface:

> We won't give up Niyamgiri for any price... Niyamgiri is not a pile of money... We won't tolerate Niyamgiri being dug up. They have bought Niyamgiri from the Government, but it doesn't belong to the Government, it belongs to Adivasis... How many

lies they tell! We won't fear them, even though it seems that the demons of mythology (asurmane) have returned' (Samadrusti, http://www.youtube.com/watch?v=ipHmVee_uXw&feature= related).

Displacement needs bringing into much more central focus, as a basic problem of received models of development. The combination of impoverishment (in the name of reducing poverty!), cultural genocide and injustice is a potent mix. Displacement needs to be seen as a major cause of the Maoist conflict. Of course, when movements for justice and against displacement get public support from Maoists, this acts as a kiss of death. This has happened in the case of movements against steel plants in Bastar, in the case of the Chasi Mulya Adivasi Sangho in Narayanpatna area of Koraput, that focused on reclaiming Adivasi lands lost through liquor selling and moneylending, and also in the case of Santal Adivasi People's Committee Against Police Atrocities, that started out over resistance to a Jindal Steel Plant SEZ in West Midnapur district of West Bengal.

Perhaps real development should be conceived in terms of restoring people to their villages, and an economy linked firmly to ecology. Unless such links are restored, there seems little hope of correcting the historic injustice done to displaced people, and to Adivasis in general. The 'freedom' of companies to take over land, extract resources too quickly, and destroy ecosystems, is more of a 'free for all', that tramples ordinary villagers underfoot. How far have we come from Gandhi's vision of village India, where self-reliance on small-scale industries gives full employment, and food security is based on a system where food is mostly consumed near the place it is grown? And from the aim of land redistribution and land ceilings central to the vision of newly Independent India? The land-grabs of big corporations and SEZs contradict this blueprint.

A lot of evidence indicates that the economics of these projects is not being worked out through a holistic appraisal of costs and benefits, but in terms of short-term gain, and driven by foreign debts and 'moneylender colonialism' from the World Bank and similar institutions (Padel and Das, 2010). We have seen that new GoI and State level R and R policies, though promoted as 'very generous packages' are actually highly inadequate, and do not begin to tackle the reality gap between policy and practice (Padel and Das, 2011). It is significant that the UNDP and DFID played a key role in drafting these policies, which have to be in place to give an air of legitimacy to the land-grabs represented by large amounts of FDI. In effect, foreign investors, in the form of companies and banks, as well as hedge funds, private equity funds, and other non-transparent institutions, are buying up rights to India's resources. All the evidence suggests that water, minerals, forests and biodiversity are getting depleted at a dangerous and accelerating rate. Assaults on the ecosystem form part of the same process as mass displacement of long-established communities.

In this context, one can argue that people's movements against further displacement offer hope of a model of real development that can only come by resisting the takeovers. Clearances for projects such as Posco steel-plant and port, Jaitapur nuclear power station and many others – after hopes were raised and multiple illegalities in clearances exposed - show immense pressure from business and financial interests. Anti-displacement movements are making a stand not just for themselves, but for future generations.

At least the manipulation in Public Hearings, EIAs and other features of the clearance process are increasingly recognized in Government reports (e.g. MoEF reports on Vedanta and Posco projects), and there is a recognition of the need to implement the Panchayat Raj scheme outlined in the PESA Act. But there are millions of displaced people awaiting compensation and justice. As Bhagaban says, how can we think of displacing more people until this happens?

The World Bank's latest major loans to India, agreed in Jan 2011, are for $1.5 billion, to fund a massive programme of road expansion on 24,000 kms of roads. A total of $40 billion of new loans are being taken by the Indian Government, for 747,000 kms (Jagota and Gangopadhyaya, 2011).

Throughout Odisha, Jharkhand and other States, avenues of old trees are being cut to build wide new roads - this is another land-grab in itself, and facilitates an 'opening up' of remote areas to many shades of land-grab. Signposting to the ports is a prominent feature of the expanded roads, and understanding the linkage with numerous mining and other projects, it is hard not to see this road-building programme, and the new debts taken on to expand the roads, as a rape of the country's resources, that converts fertile fields and long-established villages into wastelands.

Is India's present high growth rate based on a rapid extraction of the country's resources? Isn't foreign investment aimed at making a profit out of India? Isn't it therefore the high growth rate and foreign investment and debt that drives the displacement?

In effect, what is doing the displacing, ultimately, is money; and the opening of village India to 'the market'. As Adivasis express this (Padel and Das, 2010) 'We are being flooded out with money'.

REFERENCES

Bera, Sayantan. 2011. 'POSCO Unplugged'. *Down To Earth*. Retrieved February 11, 2011 from http://www.downtoearth.org.in/content/posco-unplugged.

Bidwai, Praful. 2011. 'Scorching the Earth'. *Frontline* 28, No. 4. Retrieved February 12-25, 2011 from http://www.frontline.in/stories/20110225280409600.htm.

Centre for Science and Environment. 2008. *Rich Lands, Poor People: Is Sustainable Mining possible?* Delhi: CSE.

Cernea, M M. 2011. 'Broadening the Definition of "Population Displacement": Geography and Economics in Conservation Policy.' In *Resettling Displaced People*, edited by H M Mathur. New Delhi: Routledge and Council for Social Development. 85-119.

Darwin, Charles. 1881. *The Formation of Vegetable Mould through the Actions of Worms with Observations on their Habits*. McLean, Virginia: IndyPublish.com.

Das, Samarendra. and Amarendra Das. 2005. *Matiro Poko, Company Loko* (Earthworm, Company Man), Documentary Film, from sdasorisa@hotmail.co.uk.

Dutt, Umendra. 2010. 'A Dying Civilization called Punjab.' Ama Chasa Katha (Odia) 20-21: 27-34.

Ghanekar, N M. 2010. 'The Nuclear Park at Jaitapur will be Huge. So will the Human Cost.' *Tehelka*. Retrieved 18 September 2010 fromhttp://www.tehelka.com/story_main46.asp? filename= Ne180910The_nuclear.asp.

_____. 2011. 'Villagers up the Ante against Jaitapur's N-plant.' *Tehelka*. Retrieved January 18 2011 from http://www.tehelka.com/ story_main47.asp? filename=Ws241110ENVIRONMENT.asp.

Iqbal, Javed. 2010. 'Invisible Cities Part 1: A Short History of a Slum.' *The New Indian Express*. Retrieved October 29 2010 from http:// www.rethinkingindia.com/new/aggregator/sources/4.

_____. 2010. 'Invisible Cities Part 3: The ABC of Slum Demolition.' *The New Indian Express*. Retrieved November 27 2010 from http:/ /www.rethinkingindia.com/new/aggregator/sources/4.

_____. 2011. 'Invisible Cities Part 5: A Place called Mandala.' Retrieved January 2, 2011 from http://moonchasing.wordpress.com/2011/ 01/02/invisible-cities-part-five-a-place-called-mandala/.

Housing and Land Rights Network. 2010. *Planned Dispossession: Forced Evictions and the 2010 Commonwealth Games*. Delhi: HLRN.

Jagota, Mukesh and Gangopadhyaya, A. 2011. 'World Bank Pledges nearly $2 billion to India.' *Wall Street Journal*, New York. Retrieved September 7, 2015 from http://online.wsj.com/article/ SB10001424052748703959104576081543105440036.html.

Khar East Andolan. 2011. 'The Robot Returns: Demolition Day Again' (February 2, 2011); 'Home for 40 years, Rubble Now' (February 4, 2011), Mumbai. Retrieved October 7, 2015 from http:// khareastandolan.wordpress.com/.

Krishna, Gopal. 2010. 'At Play in the Fields of the Lord.' *Tehelka*. Retrieved November 24, 2010 from http://www.tehelka.com/ story_main47.asp?filename= Ws241110ENVIRONMENT.asp.

Kumaran, Uttarika. 2011. 'A Day in the Life of the Waterless of Mumbai." *DNA*. Retrieved January 16, 2011 from http:// www.dnaindia.com/mumbai/report_a-day-in-the-life-of-the- waterless-in-mumbai_1495030.

Living Farms. 2010. *Green Revolution in Eastern India: Which Way Forward!* Bhubaneswar: Living Farms.

Mahariya, Baba. 2001. 'Development: at Whose Cost? An Adivasi on Dislocation and Development.' In *Beyond Mud Walls: Indian Social Realities*, edited by K C Yadav. Delhi: Hope India.

Martinez-Alier, Joan. 2012. 'Environmental Justice and Economic De- growth: An Alliance between two Movements.' *Capitalism Nature Socialism* 23, No.1: 51-73.

Mathur, H M. 2011. *Resettling Displaced People: Policy and Practice in India*. Delhi: Routledge and Council for Social Development.

Mining Zone People's Solidarity Group. 2010. 'Iron and Steel: the POSCO-India Story.' Retrieved October 7, 2015 from http://miningzone.org/wp-content/uploads/2010/10/Iron-and-Steal.pdf.

Mittal, Tusha. 2011. 'Loopholes in Ministry's Posco Verdict?' *Tehelka.* Retrieved February 1, 2011 from http://www.tehelka.com/story_main48.asp? filename= Ws010211ENVIRONMENT.asp.

Orlando, Laura. 2002. 'Industry Attacks on Dissent: From Carson to Oprah.' *Dollars and Sense: Real World Economics.* Retrieved October 7, 2015 from http://www.dollarsandsense.org/archives/2002/0302orlando.html.

Padel, Felix. 2010. *Sacrificing People: Invasions of a Tribal Landscape.* Delhi: Orient BlackSwan.

Padel, Felix. and Das, Samarendra. 2008. 'Cultural Genocide: The Real Impact of Development-Induced Displacement.' In *India: Social Development Report: Development and Displacement*, edited by H M Mathur. New Delhi: Oxford University Press and Council for Social Development.

_____. 2010. *Out of this Earth: East India Adivasis and the Aluminum Cartel.* Orient Delhi: BlackSwan.

_____. 2011. 'Resettlement Realities: The Gulf between Policy and Practice.' In *Resettling Displaced People Policy and Practice in India*, edited by H M Mathur. Delhi: Routledge and Council for Social Development.

Perry, K E G. 2010. 'Secrets and Lies: Tackling HIV among Sex-Workers in India.' *The Guardian*, UK. Retrieved December 7, 2010 from http://www.guardian.co.uk/global-development/2010/dec/07/india-prostitution-hiv.

Perspectives. 2008. *Abandoned: Development and Displacement.* Delhi: Perspectives.

Perspective Team. 2009. Abandoned: Development and Displacement. Delhi: Perspective (2nd Edition) (Review at https://www.scribed.com/document/22564083/Abandoned-Development-and-Displacement-Review-in-EPW).

Ramesh, Jairam. 2010. 'The Two Cultures Revisited: the Environment-Development Debate in India.' *Economic and Political Weekly* 45, No. 42:13-16.

Sahlins, Marshall. 1972. *Stoneage Economics.* London: Tavistock.

Sahu, S Kumar. 2009. *DAM-Aged.* Documentary Film. Available from subrat69@gmail.com.

Samadrusti 2009. 'Nolia Sahi – a Fishing Village.' Retrieved October 7, 2015 from http://www.youtube.com/watch?v=Pe-

DWR3rTdg&feature=player_embedded.
Satyabrata. 2011. 'Slum Dwellers in Bhubaneswar Fight the Police.'
Radical Notes. Retrieved January 31, 2011 from http://
radicalnotes.com/journal/2011/01/31/slum-dwellers-in-
bhubaneswar-fight-the-police-a-report/.
Taylor, Jason. 2011. 'Upendra has Worms.' Retrieved October 7, 2015
from http://www.thesourceproject.blogspot.com/

7

Assessing Institutionalized Capacities for Reducing the Impact of Development-Induced Displacement in India

Charu Singh
Sujit Kumar Mishra

1.0 Background

The established law on land acquisition is loaded against landowners irrespective of their economic status or the fact that they may be exclusively dependent on land for survival. This thoughtlessness has resulted in violent displacements of large populations, mostly tribal and farmers, since Independence. Increased attention, in the recent past, by the activists, the academia and the media to successful (adequate and sustainable) rehabilitation of such people affected by the development projects is compelling the Government to draw up legislations in favour of the local people who get adversely affected by the grand projects for 'national' development). In spite of the initiatives taken by the authorities that the poignant fact remains that more than ever before, development-induced displacements face massive resistances from the local people, often resulting in violent clashes with the State and project officials, inevitably resulting in stalling the projects or even abandoning them altogether. The latest example is that of the South Korean steel giant, Posco which had to abandon two of its gigantic projects in Karnataka after protests from the local people. Land acquisition hit a roadblock in 2011 when about 2,500 farmers launched an agitation under the guidance of the popular Lingayat Seer, Tontadarya Swami. The move to acquire 3,382 acre land owned by the farmers was abandoned under pressure of continued agitation and the State Government finally relented to halt the acquisition in 2011. Posco's 70,000 crore project (later scaled down to 47,000 crore) in Jagatsinhpur, Odisha is almost a case study of how not to go about acquiring land. The State Government signed a MoU with Posco in 2005 to set up a steel plant, which was scheduled to start production by 2011. After signing the MoU, the Government decided to displace the locals occupying over 4,000 acres in a rich agrarian area, leading to anti-industry agitation and inordinate delays. The struggle by the local people against the project is still on, aptly supported by human rights activists, scholars, students and a section of the media. These tumultuous altercations result in anguish for not just the potential oustees but also the project proponents. 'There is no point in signing MoUs with fifty steel companies when you cannot provide land', said an official of Posco (*Hindustan Times*, July 23, 2013).

It is now common knowledge that a host of factors lead to the successful rehabilitation and resettlement of the Project-Affected People - PAPs, whether displaced or adversely affected but not displaced. These factors classically include proper implementation of a policy, proper monitoring of the process, equitable distribution of rehabilitation benefits, sharing of information at the grassroot level and decision making power at the bottom level. Experiences from the world over have shown that the last two factors, namely, information sharing with the local people and collective decision making – both of which are to be realised at the grassroot level, are the two most crucial factors. Unfortunately in India, innumerable case-studies have revealed that the written word in the resettlement/rehabilitation policy does not translate into practice. For instance, the resettlement blueprint for Rengali Dam project in Odisha was acclaimed to be one of the best resettlement frameworks designed for the local people likely to be displaced by the dam construction. Yet the policy turned out to be a failure at the implementation level simply because the two aforementioned factors were given little importance. This could have been prevented if a solution had been evolved collectively by the State, the project proponents and the local people through open and transparent ways, in other words, through effective sharing of information. Effective sharing of facts leads to effective decision-making, which normally brings forth an adaptive solution in a sustainable manner. This paper attempts to bring to the reader a detailed discussion regarding the same.

2.0 What has Failed in the Indian Context?

This is a big question to address. From the literature of development-induced displacement, the authors have understood the following three critical issues[1], which have failed the resettlement and rehabilitation efforts in the Indian context. The three issues are: (i) faulty valuation of land, (ii) blinkered implementation, and (iii) skewed government intervention.

2.1 Faulty Land Valuation

The basis on which the valuation of land has been done in India is demonstrably arbitrary and skewed against those most requiring of the State's protection (Mishra, 2005; ASCI, 2009). It is also established through several studies that there is desperate want of baseline data on pre-displacement villages (Mishra, 2002). The obvious result is unscientific land valuation, which fails to conform to the norms of the Land Acquisition Act. Examples are plenty, such as the Rengali Multi-Purpose Dam Project, Hirakud Dam Project, etc. In most cases, the valuation strategy that evolved did not focus on providing a means of livelihood to the affected people.

2.2 Blinkered Implementation

There was a gap noticed between the date of 4(1) acquisition and the date of final payment (in some cases more than ten years). Study of Kannabiran and Mishra (2016) has depicted lucidly this gap from three study villages—Charla, Ghanamal and Kairakuni in Mahanadi Coal Field Limited, Jharsuguda, Odisha. The details of land acquisition procedure in the above three villages are presented in Table 1.

Table 1: Land Acquisition Process in the Study Villages

S. No.	Name of the Villages	Date of 4 (1) Notification	Date of Payment
1	Charla	1983	1991, 1992, 1995
2	Ghanamal	1983	1991, 1994
3	Kairakuni	1985	1986, 1995, 2005

Source: Kannabiran and Mishra (2016)

Only marginal number households complained against injustice met by them to the land acquisition officer (LAO) or collector. The chief reason for this was their poor knowledge about the land acquisition procedure. A gap of at least 8 years had been observed in all the above cases (except few cases of the village Kairakuni). It was the toughest times for the victims to survive since they were not supposed do any productive activities once they had received the 4(1) notice.

2.3 Skewed Government Intervention

Taking the example of the famous Rengali Dam built across the Brahmani River (Mishra, 2011), one notices that the entire process of land valuation polarised the local community into effectively two categories of people - the powerful land owning rich group and the assorted weaker sections of the displaced community. During the land valuation process the valuation of lands belonging to the more powerful and frequently wealthier group saw higher compenzation figures as opposed to the marginalized groups who remained silent observers to the process. In the disbursement of land, maximum benefit went to the powerful section of the people. Benefits disbursed could thus be termed 'skewed', 'biased', even 'feudal'. The more powerful members of the displaced community were able to challenge compensation awards, and make complex arguments that clearly influenced the process of land valuation. For example, it was sometimes argued that the water from the village river or pond was used to irrigate their lands and produce two crops. The court was persuaded by this argument thereby awarding an enhanced compensation in several cases. These cases of people receiving enhanced compensation were limited to the already affluent groups. Some of them were even able to successfully point that they needed to be compensated for the changed business environment at the resettlement site. The landless and asset less were not able to articulate their predicaments in such sophisticated arguments and, as a result, failed to avail the benefits of enhanced valuation of their land.

3.0 Consequences: Battles Lines Drawn

The obvious consequence stemming from the institutional mechanism flaws discussed above is intense social agitation, which often takes an ugly violent shape, as verified by innumerable cases of the recent past. Battle lines get drawn between the project proponents (often backed by the State) on one side and the displaced/yet to be displaced local community opposing them. Examples from the recent past lie in abundance: the most infamous being the TATA Motors project at Singur in Hoogly district, West Bengal and the Vedanta bauxite mining project in Niyamgiri hills of Odisha (Chandra, 2008). The Polavaram dam in Andhra Pradesh, the Koel Karo hydro-electricity project in Jharkhand, the Inchampalli multi-purpose project initiated jointly by the three State Governments of Maharashtra, Andhra Pradesh and Chhattisgarh, the Tehri dam project, Hirakud dam and Rengali dam etc. are the other cases in point (Bondla and Rao, 2010; *Down to Earth*, 2003; *Economic and Political Weekly*, 1985; Nayak, 2010; Baboo, 1991; Nath and Agrawal, 1987; Nath, 1998).

The root cause does not just lie in the aforementioned reasons but also in the history of displacement vis-à-vis rehabilitation and resettlement since Independence. The high-handedness of the Indian state in ousting tribal groups, which are otherwise considered by the State as forming the 'vulnerable group' requiring special status and special benefits, is glaring. Tribal populations have been displaced multiple times over the years since Independence in the name of 'development', prompting social action groups (formal/informal) to actively participate in the social agitations against projects involving displacements from their land. These groups have strengthened the morale of the oustees by not only lending support to their cause but also by intelligently articulating the concerns of the PAPs before the media, the Government and the civil society as a whole.

Table 2 shows the spurt in the number of advocacy organizations in so far as development vis-à-vis environment and displacement related issues are concerned. One can spot the tremendous growth rate: for instance, the numbers of organizations concerned with issues of human rights violations have grown rapidly from 33 to 190 between the four-decade periods from 1953-1993.

Table 2: Status of Non-Governmental Advocacy Organizations

| S. No. | Year | | Areas | |
		Human Rights	Environment	Development
1	1953	33	02	03
2	1963	38	05	02
3	1973	41	10	07
4	1983	79	26	13
5	1993	190	123	47

Source: Nayak (2010); Akundy and Mishra (2012)

The past couple of years have witnessed innumerable discourses in the academia as well as the policy-making sector, both national and international, highlighting the plight of the ousted and what solutions could be envisaged to alleviate them of their deplorable condition after displacement. The wide coverage the social issue has begun receiving all over the world has been made possible by the association of NGOs/CSOs. In fact, the active involvement and exchanges among these social action groups have contributed to the global spread of best practises, assessing institutionalised capacities and suggesting ways of improving them.

4.0 Existing Institutional Mechanisms for Resettlement

It is interesting to note that in a country like India where millions of people have been displaced (sometimes being subjected to multiple displacements) by several development projects, there has been a near vacuum of standards to ensure the *appropriateness* and *practicality* of rehabilitation and/or resettlement programmes (henceforth, R&R). 'Appropriateness' to suggest its suitability for the people displaced, that is, is it even relevant to the livelihoods and the life-styles of the oustees? The 'practicality' of any R&R plan is measured against its possibility to deliver – is it even possible in the given context and if 'yes' then how soon?

Current literature on development-induced displacement falls under two broad categories: the first-group primarily calls attention to the consequences of displacement, whereas the second-group stresses upon the causes of displacement. For the former group, resettlement becomes the central issue around which explanations/resolutions are sought. For the latter group of scholars, minimizations of causes of displacement occupy the core theme. On a proper analysis of the existing literature, one tends to observe that the first group of researchers envision primarily *ex-post* development in their works, while the second group concentrate largely on *ex-ante* strategies. The authors are of the view that more often than not, ex-ante strategies are preferred to ex-post strategies since the ex-ante approaches are preventive in nature and in contrast to the curative ex-post line of attack. Nevertheless, one point clear from the literature of development-induced displacement is that whenever there is change, it is succeeded by tumultuous life-changing drastic impacts. This has especially been very true for the Indian tribal and rural populations in cases of mineral excavation and dam building projects. However, since we are not in a position to avoid the implementation of large development projects, displacement is inevitable. The only thing we can do is to avoid its tumultuous impact so that the vulnerability of the affected people gets reduced to as much extent as possible. Hence, it is very critical to establish an efficient, relevant and speedy institutional mechanism, which aids in bringing back the life of the displaced groups to normalcy. The mechanism constitutive of Acts, guidelines, policies, procedures and strategies has come to be formalised very recently, since the turn of this century. Besides the aforementioned activism of CSOs, one of the contributing factors has also been the material and intellectual investment. Yet field studies indicate that the outcomes in terms of successful and sustainable resettlement are not satisfactory.

One of the reasons the authors have identified is the gaps in linking each component of the institutional mechanism. There are the over-arching legislations, which provide the ambit within which plans have to be designed, procedures and strategies have to be worked out keeping in mind the specific socio-cultural context of the group(s) to be rehabilitated and/or resettled. A proposition inter-linking the various facets is submitted in Figure 1

Figure 1: Interlinked Institutional Mechanisms

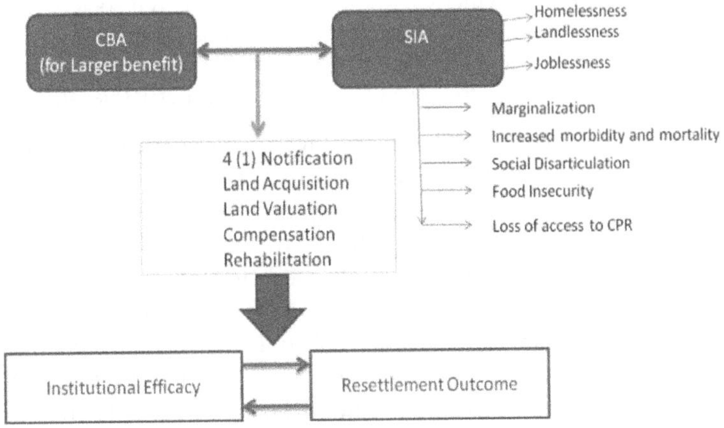

4.1 First Stage of the Institutional Mechanism

The conception of any project starts with the Cost – Benefit Analysis (CBA). This instrument is generally helpful to calculate the benefit to be generated from a project with respect to a cost for a certain period of time. It gives an indicative valuation of benefit to the respective cost. Policy makers then compare the benefit to be generated with the cost in order to check the feasibility. They accept the project if the benefit incurred from the projects outweighs the cost. However CBA as an institutional mechanism is skewed on its application part. It largely concentrates on the total impact, completely ignoring the distribution pattern of the costs vis-à-vis the benefits.

Next, the tool, designed for the easy implementation of land acquisition is the concept of 'Eminent Domain'. Large sections of the people rely on agricultural land—the pivot of the rural economy—either directly or indirectly to earn living. The Land Acquisition Act (LAA) 1894 was the commonly available act in India to deal with the acquisition of the affected/displaced people. The guiding principle of the act is the concept of 'Eminent Domain', which has its roots in the work of 17th century Dutch jurist Hugo Grotius who suggested:

> The property of subject is under the eminent domain of the state or he who acts for it may use and even alienate and destroy such property not only in cases of extreme necessity, …….. for end of public utility, to which ends those who found civil society must be supposed to have intended that private ends should give way. But it is to be added that when this is done the state is bound to make good the loss to those who lose their property (Desai, 2011).

Notwithstanding the dependence fact, the doctrine of 'Eminent Domain' enables the state acquires any kind private land for public purpose (for a cogent critique of the jurisprudence of eminent domain, see Ramanathan, 2011). The different important notions that have been used by this framework are 'State', 'acquisition of any land' and 'larger public interest', where provision of compensation is found as the only connecting indicator among these issues (See Desai, 2011). We have a clear distinction here categorising the people into the following types: (i) households with a legal possession of land; (ii) people enjoying land without any legal right over it; (iii) tenant households; and (iv) landless households with livelihoods[2]. So far as the issue of compensation is concerned, the Land Acquisition Act of 1894 admits only the first category. The LAA is completely silent about the rest.

Till 2013, the acquisition of land in India was administered by Land Acquisition Act 1894. The historic Right to Fair Compensation and Transparency in Land Acquisition, Rehabilitation and Resettlement Bill (2012), commonly known as the Land Acquisition Bill, has received the assent of the President on September 27, 2013. The Bill seeks to replace a 119-year-old legislation - the archaic Land Acquisition Act, which suffered from countless shortcomings, including silence on the issue of resettlement and rehabilitation of those displaced by acquisition of land. However, much remains to be seen in terms of its actualization once the Act comes into force on the date stated date of January 01, 2014. Although the act was regarded as pro-poor, certain issues remained unsorted. For instance, there was no address to the fear of arbitrary valuation of market price of the land acquired (Verma, 2015). However, the National Democratic Alliance (NDA) Government virtually nullified this act. In place of the former act, it passed a LARR Ordinance on December 29, 2014.Several amendments for land acquisitions were included in the ordinance, on the grounds that the LARR Act, 2013 was complicated and anti-development (Jaitley, 2015; Verma, 2015).

4.2 Second Stage of the Institutional Mechanism: Status of Rehabilitation Policies in India

Until recently, India had no policy on resettlement and rehabilitation needed after involuntary displacement. The Indian Government started the policy drafting process only in the 1980s, almost forty years after its formal pledge to respect and protect the 'dignity of life' of every citizen—rich or poor, urban, tribal or rural. Policy formulation took a new turn in 1993 when, in the wake of the World Bank's withdrawal from the Sardar Sarovar project on the Narmada, the Ministry of Rural Development prepared a draft pertaining to R&R, revised it in 1994 and yet again in 1998. The draft was finalized in 2003 and published in 2004. Titled the 'National Policy on Resettlement and Rehabilitation' (please note that it was not an Act but a Policy, not forceable in any court of law), it was criticized on numerous aspects, like failure to emphasize a non- displacing or least displacing option for project execution and no provision for assessing the social, economic, cultural or demographic impacts of projects that involved involuntary displacement. The policy was critiqued for its limited applicability given that it outlined to set forward a high threshold of 500 families or more *en masse* in plain areas and 250 families *en masse* in hilly areas, DDP blocks (Desert Development Programme Blocks) and areas mentioned in Schedule V and Schedule VI of the Constitution of India. The policy did not prescribe any time limits for completion of R&R activities and also failed to specifically highlight provisions that addressed concerns of the Scheduled Castes and Scheduled Tribes. In addition, it lacked gender sensitivity. Failure to address concerns of vulnerable sections on the one hand and inadequate provision to redress grievances on the other brought the Policy under a downpour of criticism from the civil society, the academia as well as several sections of the bureaucracy. The sharpest criticism was for want of improving the standards of living of the affected families upon resettlement—an important concern the policy did not emphasize at all.

This prompted the Government to introduce a new policy framework in 2007 for providing better resettlement and rehabilitation opportunities to those affected by development-induced displacement. Currently, the existence of the National Resettlement and Rehabilitation Policy of 2007 has been a leap much ahead of its predecessor, the National Policy on Resettlement and Rehabilitation (2003). A landmark and highly progressive change from 2003 to 2007 is visible in the intent of the 2007 Policy—that its Preamble recognises the mental trauma and socio-cultural consequences for persons of both project-induced displacements as well as displacements caused by natural disasters. In theory, the National Rehabilitation and Resettlement Policy (NRRP) 2007 is applicable to all sites where involuntary displacement takes place. It has scored over its predecessor on several counts: amending the threshold level for inclusion of displaced persons under the Policy from 500 to 400 families en masse in plain areas, and 200 families en masse in hilly or tribal areas, DDP blocks and areas specified under the Fifth and Sixth Schedules of the Constitution. For the time in our country, an R&R policy of the magnitude and stature of a national policy has recognised not only directly affected families/individuals but also indirectly affected persons, that is, those who may not directly lose land yet are adversely affected by acquisition of it. For example, landless labourers, rural artisans, manual workers are now defined under the title 'non-agricultural labourer' by NRRP 2007.

A few states had evolved rehabilitation policies before the NRRP 2007 for projects launched within their jurisdiction. Maharashtra in western India, Madhya Pradesh in central India and Karnataka in south India had enacted laws on the rehabilitation of irrigation-displaced persons during the 1980s. In the 1990 decade, Odisha in eastern India and Rajasthan in western India too formulated policies for persons displaced by irrigation projects. Even private sector companies dealing in acquisition of vast tracts of land, required for their operations, framed policies for the individuals/families they were responsible for displacing. Coal India Limited (CIL) and the National Thermal Power Corporation (NTPC) promulgated their sectoral resettlement policies within the 1990 period. NTPC has revised its policy in 2005 (in view of the enactment of NRRP 2003) and the National Hydro-Power Corporation (NHPC) has finalized its policy in 2006. There are reasons to believe that, except the Maharashtra Act, all the other states' and sectoral policies were prepared at the suggestion of the World Bank, which was a co-financer in the development projects launched in the said states and sectors. These state and sectoral policies were borrowed heavily from, while drafting the NRRP 2007. They in fact form its backbone. The contributions have resulted in positive outcomes for R&R, such as expanded objectives, redefined scope, concern for the vulnerable, transparency for participation, grievance redress and monitoring and incorporation of the clause of social impact assessment.

4.2.1 Definition of 'Development Project'

According to the section 3(t) of the NRRP 2007, 'project' refers to an act involving involuntary displacement of people, irrespective of the number of persons affected. A question arises here about the development communities who inhabit in the vicinity of the mining areas, bearing all the negative consequences of development.

Definition of 'Project' and the 'Mining Communities'

The case of Padmana Naik of the Mahanadi Coalfield Limited (MCL) in Angul, Odisha is illustrative. Naik who was a daily wage worker had to stop working when he began getting severe stomach pain which kept increasing daily. He also started running a fever as he had been working in a smoky and dusty environment. Treatment at a local hospital failed to provide relief and he was shifted to the Cuttack Medical College of Odisha where he was diagnosed with cancer. He started treatment there spending around Rs 20,000 for it. Though he has returned to his village, the weakness caused due to the prolonged illness has made him incapable of working anymore. His son who is also a daily wage earner and unable to afford the expensive treatment required for cancer is taking care of his father. The MCL certainly has moral responsibility in this case because the environment which caused Naik's ailment is the result of the MCL's mining activities.

4.2.2 Still Follows 'Eminent Domain'

The concept of 'Land Acquisition' is mentioned in the section 3 (m) in the NRRP 2007 policy.

> 'land acquisition' or 'acquisition of land' means acquisition of land under the Land Acquisition Act, 1894 (1 of 1894), as amended from time to time, or any other law of the Union or a State for the time being in force.

'Old wine in a new bottle' is a befitting metaphor for the new definition of land acquisition. The policy of 2007 upholds the sovereign power of the State to apply the principle of 'eminent domain' to forcibly acquire any property in any part of the country on the pretext of 'Public purpose'. The clause 7.18 of NRRP 2007 deals with the urgency as per the section 17 of the Land Acquisition Act, 1894 or similar provision of any other Act of the Union or a State for the time being in force. It also provides for putting displaced people in 'transit and temporary accommodation, pending rehabilitation and resettlement scheme or plan'.

4.2.3 Social Impact Assessment and the Impoverishment Risk Model

The Social Impacts Assessment (henceforth, SIA) as a mechanism identifies the perils—socio-economic, socio-political, socio-cultural, socio-environmental—that a person, family, community may face in the event of its displacement. The core objective of conducting SIA is to identify risks, develop counter strategies against the identified risks and necessarily include the strategies in the rehabilitation action plan meant for the PAPs. In India, SIA has been conducted as part of the Environment Impact Assessment (EIA) clearance required from the Ministry of Environment and Forests. This was until the inception of NRRP 2007, which mandates the inclusion of SIA in the following words:

> 'Wherever it is desired to undertake a new project or expansion of an existing project, which involves involuntary displacement of 400 hundred or more families, en masse in plain areas, or two hundred or more families en masse in tribal or hilly areas, DDP blocks or areas mentioned in the Schedule V or Schedule VI to the Constitution, the appropriate Government shall ensure that a Social Impact Assessment (SIA) study is carried out in the proposed affected areas in such manner as may be prescribed'. (Section 4.1 in Chapter IV *Social Impact Assessment*)

SIA has therefore become institutionalized as a mechanism, indispensable to the projects requiring displacements and consequent rehabilitations of people. Data generated through SIA is especially useful for the preparation of resettlement action plans (RAPs).

SIA as a mechanism has close association with the Impoverishment Risk and Reconstruction (IRR) Model propounded by Michael Cernea, the American-Romanian social scientist who introduced sociological and anthropological approaches into the World Bank. Cernea marked out the eight most common impoverishment risks an individual is confronted with upon being displaced. In his extremely popular IRR Model (1996), the identified threats are listed as the following: (i) landlessness (ii) joblessness (iii) homelessness (iv) marginalization (v) food insecurity (vi) increased morbidity and mortality (vii) loss of access to common property (viii) social disarticulation. Relying on much of worldwide displacement research works and his own field experience, Cernea has proposed this conceptual model to mitigate the occurrences of abject impoverishment that local people suffer. How can the livelihoods as well as socio-cultural lives of displaced people be reconstructed is the basic concern this model seeks to address. Enormously useful for policy makers and project planners, the model anticipates the major displacement hazards, explains the behavioural responses of displaced people and can efficiently guide the reconstruction plans and processes.

4.2.4 The Question of 'Consultation'

It is a commendable step of the state that it has included the concept 'consultation' with the affected people/victims in various places of the NRRP 2007. Let us scrutinize the term 'consultation' used in various places of the policy document in favour of the victims.

Clause 5.5: Subject to any general or special order of the appropriate Government, the Administrator for Rehabilitation and Resettlement shall perform the following functions and duties: (ii): hold *consultation* with the affected families while preparing a rehabilitation and resettlement scheme or plan; (v) prepare a budget including estimated expenditure of various components of acquisition of land, rehabilitation and resettlement activities or programmes in *consultation* with representatives of the affected families and the requiring body;

Clause 6.14.1: After completion of baseline survey and census of the affected families and assessment of the requirement of land for resettlement, as mentioned in paragraphs 6.3 and 6.12, the Administrator for Rehabilitation and Resettlement shall prepare a draft scheme or plan for the rehabilitation and resettlement of the affected families after *consultation* with the representatives of the affected families including women and the representative of the requiring body

Clause 6.15.2: The *consultation* with the Gram Sabha or the Panchayats at the appropriate level in. the Scheduled Areas under Schedule V of the Constitution shall be in accordance with the provisions of the Provisions of the Panchayats

(Extension to the Scheduled Areas) Act, 1996 (40 of 1996).

Clause 7.21.2: The concerned Gram Sabha or the Panchayats at the appropriate level in the Scheduled Areas under Schedule V of the Constitution or as the case may be, Councils in the Schedule VI Areas shall be consulted in all Cases of land acquisition in such areas including land acquisition in cases of urgency, before issue of a notification under the Land Acquisition Act, 1894 or any other Act of the Union or a State for the time being in force under which land acquisition is undertaken, and the *consultation* shall be in accordance with the provisions of the Provisions of the Panchayats (Extension to the Scheduled Areas) Act, 1996 and other relevant laws. Further, in cases of involuntary displacement of two hundred or more Scheduled Tribes families from the Scheduled Areas, the concerned Tribes Advisory Councils (TACs) may also be consulted.

If we analyze, this concept has been used in all the four places as a 'demand side' parameter. 'Consultation' and 'Consent' are completely two different concepts. The victims own no right to say 'no' when the project site is identified. From our elaborate discussions with the local inhabitants and activists, it became clear that consultation was just the spreading of information about the project in a monopolized manner to the affected people. In this crucial process, where obtaining consent plays a vital role in the resettlement process, our study finds the absence of negotiation element from the entire regulatory mechanism. So, it is essential to create a system which will negotiate with the state by exploring how community perception and concerns reflect in the development policy in India and what mechanisms should be evolved to make the current policies sustainable with a special emphasis on social justice and equity.

4.2.5 Provisions for the Scheduled Tribes

At first, the section b (iii) component of the clause 3.1 cites the criteria to get included into the affected family category and that is as follows:

Any agricultural or non-agricultural labourer, landless

person (not having homestead land, agricultural land, or either homestead or agricultural land), rural artisan, small trader or self-employed person; who has been residing or engaged in any trade, business, occupation or vocation continuously for a period of not less than three years preceding the date of declaration of the affected area, and who has been deprived of earning his livelihood or alienated wholly or substantially from the main source of his trade, business, occupation or vocation because of the acquisition of land in the affected area or being involuntarily displaced for any other reason.

Secondly, as far as resettlement is concerned, the clause 1.5 of the NRRP 2007 says about the 'sizable number' of the displaced people. In the present context, the sizable number is involuntary displacement of 200 or more ST families from the Scheduled Area. Most of the times, it seems quite difficult to find 200 ST families together in a single tract since they migrate from time to time for shifting cultivation.

In the third place, 2 (c) of the clause explains the 'protection of rights' of the weaker sections of the society, and 5.5 (iii) narrates about the 'interests of the adversely affected persons of ST and weaker section'. However, the indicators to be included to the protection of rights and interests of the tribal are missing from the policy document.

Fourthly, the qualification of the expert group is a major component under SIA. The group is entitled to examine the SIA report and there are two non-official social science and rehabilitation experts: the Secretary/Secretaries of the department(s) concerning the welfare of Scheduled Castes and Scheduled Tribes of the appropriate Government or his (their) representative(s), and a representative of the requiring body. We can see here the seriousness of the issue by the 'either or' criterion decided by the state i.e. 'the Secretary/Secretaries of the department(s) concerned with the welfare of Scheduled Castes and Scheduled Tribes of the appropriate Government or his (their) representative(s)'.

5.0 Efficacy of Institutional Mechanisms

Studies of Mathur (2011), Mishra (2005), Garkipati (2000),

Scudder (2005), etc. have discussed features of a successful and sustainable R&R programme. After a review of works pertaining to the subject, the authors consider three categories of variables, which together determine the outcome of a resettlement-rehabilitation. The three categories are - (i) external factors (ii) equity factor, and (iii) endogenous institutional mechanism. Together, they provide the 'incentive structure' for appropriate outcomes to emerge. A detailed framework listing the components of each category have been given in Figure 2.

Figure 2: Efficacy Criteria of Institutional Mechanisms

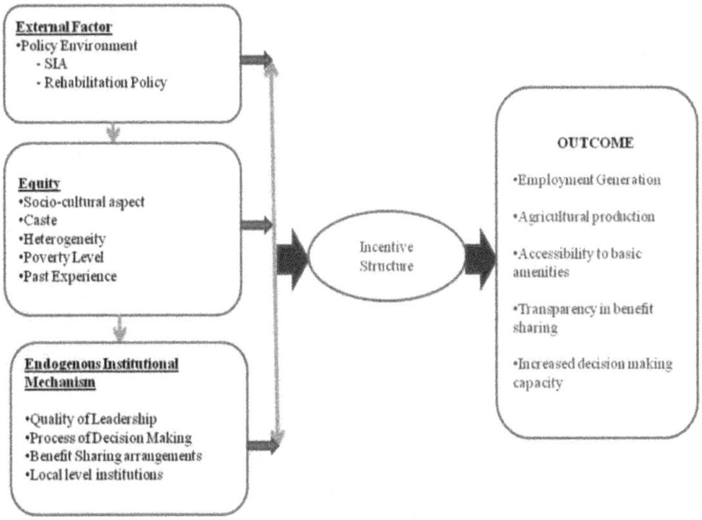

5.1 External Factors

Policy environment is crucial for apt rehabilitation outcomes. Policies can lead to institutional innovations or the disintegration of existing ones. For example, in independent India, centralised policies of not involving local people have not only led to breakdown of local institutions but also resulted in the degradation of resources (Reddy, 1996). In the present context, the two interlinked factors constituting the policy environment are SIA and NRRP 2007.

5.2 Equity Factor

Equity is always measured between two individuals or groups of people in terms of the difference between them or the gaps in their incomes, resource levels and quality of life. A very urgent issue to be addressed in the present context of volatile land acquisition environment is the equity factor through appropriate inclusions in the national legislation. What good is an R&R mechanism if it fails to address the equity concerns in social terms too? Therefore, inclusions should not be limited to a one-time fair monetary compensation; rather, the concerns of bringing sustainable equity in economic as well as the social lives of the displaced people ought to be the overriding factor.

Irrespective of the concept of equity adopted by the project authorities, compensation must also aim to reflect the true losses incurred by the displaced people. Compensation is still the main financial instrument used for 'restoring' those dispossessed and displaced (Cernea, 2007). For years, these have been the basic problems arising in all types of development interventions, especially the land-based projects. The two major questions that arise over here are: (i) who will decide about the compensation? and (ii) what are the components of adequate compensation? These are the major undecided factors in all kinds of resettlement studies.

5.3 Endogenous Institutional Mechanism

Quality of leadership, the course of decision-making, benefit sharing arrangements and involvement of local level institutions are the various indicators proposed. The role of leadership is becoming increasingly crucial as the politico-economic transformation in most of the societies is giving rise to individualistic and self-centered behaviour. Similarly, it is observed, in the context of disaster management, that in some instances the performance is good in the presence of good leaders at village level (Mishra 2009). Added to this observation is the fact that people should be made aware of the benefits and the sharing arrangements. It is no mystery that efficient decision making leads to a high-quality outcome. Historically, local level institutions are embedded in the community system since they have evolved in response to the specific needs of the community with negligible support from outside. Embedded institutions are found to be more robust and efficient when compared to the formal and imposed institutional arrangements (Reddy and Reddy, 2002).

6.0 The Road Ahead

The reality of development projects is that these projects have destabilized the material and socio-cultural bases of the affected people by destroying their livelihoods and life-styles concurrently. This paper has made a humble attempt at explaining the inter associations between the legislations, the IRR model, tools of SIA and CBA—as the chief institutional mechanisms for accurate assessment and mitigation of the displacement impacts arising out of development projects. The study finds the policy framework for institutional capacity as evolved by the Government of India as having both merits and demerits. In the first place, there are several indications of institutional improvement, the most important being the system of SIA—an ex-ante risk diagnosis mechanism. Also the grass-roots participation of communities has been recognised through the involvement of village councils. Communication between planners and resettlers is instrumental for effective early warning and for making possible joint preventive activities. Cernea (1996) uses the term 'communication' in its broad sense, which means transparent information (regarding the causes of displacement and its likely impact); consultation between planners and affected groups of resettlers, hosts and their organizations; and genuine participation in finding acceptable solutions.

As a result of economic growth, current attempts at decentralization and the adoption of modern information technologies, the administrative set-up has undergone a character change. The new class of bureaucrats and technocrats dealing with R&R are younger, computer literate, systematic and more inclined to deliver results. Field studies have shown that enhanced transparency and accountability is visible on the ground. The fusion of the LAA with the prescriptive national policy to guide rehabilitation and resettlement into a singular piece of legislation (GoI 2013), while also attempting to fine-tune the clauses is a welcome step on the road ahead.

However, certain aspects still need a revision: An effective communication requires high quality, two-way communication network between those at risk and those with expertise and resources to help. From primary field visits, the study identified a mismatch between policy intention and its practice (Mishra, 2005). This results in sub-optimal outcomes. Here, the community initiatives, reflected through a sound collective action process, were found to be better than that of the Government initiatives. Dependable baseline vulnerability and capacity data, prior to a project, is a necessity in successfully planning relief and rehabilitation responses. The Central/State authorities should maintain a database of baseline information with special reference to land type, pattern of yield and yield rate of different types of land of all the potential villages to be affected. What's more, it would avoid arbitrariness and vagueness. A uniform model for the purpose of valuation of land compensation would go a long way in ensuring at least economic satisfaction for the oustees.

The authors recommend that as part of its R&R mechanism, each State should ensure taking care of the livelihood needs of the displaced people during the period of transition from the original habitation to the relocated place. In this sense, rehabilitation should precede resettlement. Koenig (2002) and Erickson (1999) rightly stress that in depth knowledge of the rehabilitated area, its climate and biological factors are needed before shifting to the new place.

NOTES

1. See Mishra, S.K (2011).
2. See Reddy (1992).

BIBLIOGRAPHY

Akundy, A. and S K Mishra. 2012. 'People's Responses to the State Policies of Resettlement - The Case of Ultra Mega Power Plant in Orissa.' *Journal of Socio-Economic Development* 14, No. 02: 202-214.

ASCI (Administrative Staff College of India). 2009. *Impact Assessment Study- R & R in Orissa.* New Delhi: United Nation Development Programme (UNDP).

Baboo, B. 1991. 'State Policies and People's Response: Lessons from Hirakud Dam.' *Economic and Political Weekly* 26, No. 41: 2373-79.

Barnabas, A P. 1985. 'Development Policies and Human Deprivation.' *Indian Journal of Public Administration* 31, No. 04: 1269-77.

Behura, N K. 1989. 'Socio-Economic Problems and Social Change among the Relocatees of Rengali Dam- A Case Study.' *Man and Life* 15, No. 1-2: 1-22.

Bondla, D J N. and N S Rao. 2010. 'Resistance against Polavaram.' *Economic and Political Weekly* 45, No. 32: 93-95.

Centre for Science and Environment. 1999. *The Citizens' Fifth Report: National Overview.* New Delhi: CSE.

Cernea, M M. 2007. 'Financing for Development- Benefit - Sharing Mechanisms in Population Resettlement.' *Economic and Political Weekly* 42, No. 12:1033-46.

Cernea, M M. 1990. 'From Unused Social Knowledge to Policy Creation: The Case of Population Resettlement.' *Development Discussion Paper No. 342.* Cambridge: Harvard Institute for International Development.

Cernea, M M. 1995. 'Understanding and Preventing Impoverishment from Displacement: Reflections on the State of Knowledge.' Keynote address presented at the International Conference on Development-induced Displacement and Impoverishment, held at the University of Oxford, 3–7 January 1995.

Cernea, M M. 1996. 'Public Policy Responses to Development Induced Population Displacements.' *Economic and Political Weekly* 31, No. 24: 1515-1523.

Cernea, M M. 1997. 'The Risks and Reconstruction Model for Resettling Displaced Populations.' *World Development* 25, No. 10: 1569-87.

Cernea, M M. 1999. 'Why Economic Analysis is Essential to Resettlement: A Sociologist's View.' In *The Economics of Involuntary Displacement,* edited by M M Cernea. Washington, DC: The World Bank.

Chandra, N K. 2008. 'Tata Motors in Singur: A Step towards Industrialization or Pauperization?' *Economic and Political Weekly* 43, No. 50: 36-51.

CSD (Council for Social Development). 2010. *Social Impact Assessment Report of a Research Project on Social Impact Assessment of R and R Policies and Packages in India.* New Delhi: Council for Social Development.

De Wet, Chris. 2000. 'Can Everybody Win? Economic Development and Population Displacement.' Paper presented at Workshop on Involuntary Resettlement: Risks, Rio de Janeiro, 1-3 August 2000.

Desai, M. 2011. 'Land Acquisition Law and the Proposed Changes.' *Economic and Political Weekly* 46, Nos. 26 & 27: 95-100.

Down to Earth. 2003. 'Koel-Karo: Jharkhand Leaders Renege, But Tribal Collectivism Holds forth.' *Down to Earth (Coverage)*, July 31, 2003. Retrieved December 22, 2016 from http://www.downtoearth. org.in/coverage/koelkaro-jharkhand-13200.

Dwivedi, R. 1999. 'Displacement, Risks and Resistance: Local Perception and Actions in the Sardar Sarovar.' *Development and Change* 30: 43-78.

Economic and Political Weekly. 1985. 'Anti- People Development- Case of Inchampalli Project.' *Economic and Political Weekly* 20, No. 22: 952- 954.

Erickson, J H. 1999. 'Comparing the Economic Planning for Voluntary and Involuntary Resettlement.' In *The Economics of Involuntary Resettlement: Questions and Challenges*, edited by M M Cernea. Washington, DC: The World Bank.

Fernandes, W. 2008. 'Indian's Forced Displacement Policy and Practice, Is Compensation up to its Functions?' In *Can Compensation Prevent Impoverishment? Reforming Resettlement through Investment and Benefit Sharing*, edited by M M Cernea and H M Mathur. USA: Oxford University Press.

Fernandes, W. and V Paranjpye. 1997. 'Hundred Years of Involuntary Displacement in India: Is the Rehabilitation Policy an Adequate Response?' In *Rehabilitation Policy and Law in India: A Right to Livelihood*, edited by W Fernandes and V Paranjpye. New Delhi: Indian Social Institute.

Garg, S. 1998. 'Resettlement in the Upper Indravati Project: A Case Study.' In *Development Projects and Impoverishment Risk*, edited by H M Mathur and D Marsden. Delhi: Oxford University Press.

Garikipati, S. 2000. *An Economic Perspective on Resettlement of Population Displaced by Large Dams: The Case of the Sardar Sarovar Project Displaced, India.* PhD Thesis, University of Cambridge.

Government of India. 2013. *The Right to Fair Compensation and Transparency in Land Acquisition, Rehabilitation and Resettlement Act, 2013.* No. 30 of 2013, Ministry of Law & Justice, India.

Government of Orissa. 2000. *Land Acquisition Status in Rengali Dam, Rengali Dam Site.* Government of Orissa.

Hemadri, R. 1999. 'Dam, Displacement, Policy and Law in India.' Contributing Paper, prepared for Thematic Review, Social Issue

1.3, Displacement, Resettlement, Rehabilitation, Reparation and Development, World Commission on Dams.

Hindustan Times, July 23, 2013

Jaitley, A. 2015. 'Amendments to the Land Acquisition Law- The Real Picture,' Retrieved December 29, 2015 from http://www.bjp.org/en/media-resources/press-releases/.

Kannabiran, K. and S K Mishra. 2016. *Measuring Institutionalised Capacities for Development Projects in India*. New Delhi: Indian Council of Social Science Research.

Khagram, S. 2004. *Dams and Development: Transnational Struggle for Water and Power*. New Delhi: Oxford University Press.

Koenig, D. 1997. *Competition among Maliar Elites in the Manantali Resettlement Project: The Impacts on Local Development*. Urban Anthropology and Studies of Cultural Systems and World Economic Development, 26, 3-4.

Kothari, S. and A Bharati. 1984. 'Displaced.' *The Illustrated Weekly of India*, February 24: 40-45.

Mahapatra, L K 1991. 'Development for Whom? Depriving the Dispossessed Tribals.' *Social Action* 41, No. 03: 271-288.

Mahapatra, L K. 1990. 'Rehabilitation of Tribals Affected by Major Dams and Other Projects in Orissa.' In *A Report on the Workshop on Rehabilitation of Person Displaced by Development Projects*, edited by A P Fernandez. Bangalore and Myrada: Institute of Social and Economic Change.

Mathur, H M. 2011. 'Social Impact Assessment: A Tool for Planning Better Resettlement.' *Social Change* 41, No. 01: 97–120.

Mishra, A. 2013. 'Rule of Thumb.' *Business Today*, September 15, 2013. Retrieved December 22, 2016 from http://www.businesstoday.in/magazine/features/orissa-niyamgiri-rejects-vedanta-entry-impact-reasons/story/197972.html.

Mishra, S K. 2009. *Estimation of Externality Costs of Electricity Generation from Coal: An OH- Markal Extension Dissertation*. PhD Thesis, The Ohio State University, United State of America.

Mishra, S K. 2002. *Development and Displacement: A Case Study in Rengali Dam in Orissa, India*. PhD Thesis, University of Hyderabad, India.

Mishra, S K. 2005. 'Impact of Rehabilitation Policy and Low Crop Yield: A Case Study of Rengali Dam in Orissa, India.' *Economic and Political Weekly* 40, No. 60: 2688-2691.

Mishra, S K. 2011. 'Compulsory Land Acquisition in Orissa: Policy and Praxis.' In *Development-induced Displacement, Rehabilitation and Resettlement in India: Current Issues and Challenges*, edited by S Somayaji and S Talwar. New Delhi: Routledge.

Nath , G B. and Agrawal, K S. 1987. *Politics of Agitation against Rengali Dam Project: A Case Study.* ISSC Seminar, Sambalpur University, Orissa.

Nath, G B. 1998. *Socio-Economic Re-Survey of a Village Submerged Under Rengali Dam Project.* New Delhi: Indian Council of Social Science Research.

Nayak, A K. 2010. 'Big Dams and Protests in India: A Study of Hirakud Dam.' *Economic and Political Weekly* 45, No. 02: 69- 73.

Ota, A B. 1996. 'Countering the Impoverishment Risk: The Case of Rengali Dam Project.' In *Involuntary Displacement in Dam Projects,* edited by A B Ota and A Agnihotri. New Delhi: Prachi Prakashan.

Ota, A B. 1998. 'Countering the Impoverishment Risk: The Case of Rengali Dam Project.' In *Development Projects and Impoverishment Risks Resettling Project–Affected People in India,* edited by H M Mathur and D Marsden. Delhi: Oxford University Press.

Oza, N. 1997. 'Marginalization, Protests and Political Action–Tribal and Sardar Sarovar Project.' *Economic and Political Weekly* 32, No. 29: 1790-1793.

Palit, C. 2004. 'Short-changing the Displaced- National Rehabilitation Policy.' *Economic and Political Weekly* 39, No. 27: 2961- 63.

Pandey, B. 1998. *Depriving the Unprivileged for Development.* Bhubaneswar: Institute for Socio-Economic Development.

Paranjpye, V. 1987. 'Dams and Their Dangers.' *Seminar* 333: 40-43.

Patnaik, S M. 1996. *Displacement Rehabilitation and Social Change.* Tribal Studies of India Series, New Delhi: Inter India Publications.

Ramanathan, U. 2011. 'Land Acquisition, Eminent Domain and the 2011 Bill.' *Economic and Political Weekly* 46, Nos. 44 & 45: 10-14.

Rangachari, et.al. 2000. *Large Dams: The Indian Country Study,* Chennai: Madras Institute of Development Studies.

Rao, K N. 2006. 'Integral to State's Good.' In *Perspectives on Polavaram A Major Irrigation Project on Godavari,* edited by B Gujja, S Ramakrishna, V Goud and Sivaramakrishna. New Delhi: Academic Foundation.

Rao, R S. 1995. *Towards Understanding Semi-Feudal, Semi-Colonial Society.* Hyderabad: Perspective.

Reddy, V R. 1996. *A Study of Willingness and Ability to Pay for Water.* Institute of Development Studies, Jaipur.

Reddy, D N. and K M Reddy. 1998. 'River Valley Projects and Rehabilitation Policy: The Andhra Pradesh Experience.' *The Administrator* 43: 177- 192.

Reddy, K M. 1992. *Some Aspect of Rehabilitation Policy of the State Government with Reference to Major Irrigation Projects: A Case Study* of *Sriramsagar and Srisailam*. PhD Thesis, Kakatiya University, India.

Reddy, V R. and P P Reddy. 2002. 'Water Institutions: Is Formalization the Answer? A Study of Water User Associations in Andhra Pradesh.' *Indian Journal of Agricultural Economics* 57, No. 03: 519-34

Reddy, V R. 1996. *A Study of Willingness and Ability to Pay for Water*. Project Report, Institute of Development Studies, Jaipur.

Rew, A., E Fisher. and B Pandey. 2000. *Addressing Policy Constraints and Improving Outcomes in Development-induced Displacement and Resettlement Projects*. DFID, Oxford: Refugee Studies Centre, University of Oxford.

Sahoo, R. 2003. 'National Rehabilitation Policy: Many Loopholes.' *Economic and Political Weekly* 38, No. 06: 510 - 512.

Satyanarayana, G. 1999. *Development, Displacement and Rehabilitation*. New Delhi and Jaipur: Rawat Publications.

Scudder, T. 2005. *The Future of Large Dams: Dealing with Social, Environmental, Institutional and Political Costs*, London: Earthscan.

Sharma, M. 2009. 'Passages from Nature to Nationalism: Sunderlal Bahuguna and Tehri Dam Opposition in Garhwal.' *Economic and Political Weekly* 44, No. 08: 35-42.

Supakar, K. 2004. *Itihaasra Parihaas* (Oriya) First Part, Sambalpur: Orissa.

Vaswani, K. 1992. 'Rehabilitation Laws and Policies: A Critical Look.' In *Big Dams, Displaced People*, edited by E G Thukral. New Delhi: Sage Publications.

Verma, S. 2015. 'Subverting the Land Acquisition Act, 2013,' *Economic and Political Weekly* 50, No. 37: 18-21.

8

Neo-Liberal Development, Displacement, and Exclusion: Tribal Resistance to Vedanta

Satyapriya Rout
Pratyusna Patnaik

I. Introduction

Development, in its various *avatars*, has surely been the most powerful influence structuring the social and economic transformations in the non-western world in this century, especially after decolonization and post-World War II period. One of the reasons for the seemingly increasing influence of development has been its 'power to transform old worlds and the power to imagine new ones' (Crush, 1995). Starting from post-Second World War period, when the newly decolonized nations began aspiring for rapid economic growth with active support from the First World, till today, the concept of development has occupied the centre of public policy discourse for most developing nations. Sivaramakrishnan and Agrawal (2003) in their attempt to underscore the relation between nation-state and development discourse within the framework of modernity, identify two broad phases of public policy concerning development practice and discourse in the post-colonial era. The first phase witnessed the growing influence of international Keynesianism, based on state mediated capitalism, and the emergence of international financial institutions like the World Bank and International Monetary Fund. In this phase, central state was viewed as playing a pivotal role in planning and implementing development policies and programmes, and, therefore, international institutions of development and reconstruction focused on the central state as an important factor in transforming social relations and modes of production in societies. The second phase of policy discourse in the context of development started in the late 1970s, as failures of the central state in delivering development become more prominent. This was the phase of deregulated neo-liberal capitalism, which also coincided with dismantling of the Second World and the regimes of socialism as a political and economic system. The Third World, in such a situation, responded with a set of prescriptions for development that simultaneously followed two courses, often contradictory to each other. While on the one hand, it emphasized the neo-liberal ideology of privatization, Liberalization, export promotion and openness to international market, on the other hand, recognizing the limits of these policy innovations to address issues of equity, it advocated idioms of decentralization and community participation to argue for a dismantling of the State (Agrawal and Ostrom, 2001; Sivaramakrishnan and Agrawal, 2003).

The new development paradigm that has emerged since mid-1980s, as a modification to the second phase of post-colonial development debate, therefore, places a high value on local governance and community participation in delivering development. This new paradigm, while on the one hand emphasizes issues of inclusion, participation, and devolution of decision making, on the other, has created scope for structural reforms that provide an appropriate institutional framework to reduce the imposition of state institutions (Veltmeyer, 1997). What has emerged in the process is that of decentralization, which tries to fulfil the institutional void at the local level to ensure inclusion, participation, local service delivery and better developmental outcomes.

Recognizing the need for greater democratization and progressive inclusion, many governments carried out political reforms ensuring decentralization to promote empowerment and inclusion. In its attempts for democratization, the Indian State enacted the 73rd Constitutional Amendment Act in 1993, making provisions for devolution of power to the local levels, and gave a Constitutional status to the Panchayats. Further, in its commitment to introduce the process of decentralization reforms in the tribal regions of the country, Government of India in December 1997 enacted the 'The Provisions of the Panchayats (Extension to Scheduled Areas) Act' (PESA Act), which paved the way for inclusion and self-governance in the nine states that come under the Fifth Schedule of the Indian Constitution. The PESA Act has attempted to vest legislative consultative power in the Gram Sabha, especially in matters relating to development and planning, acquisition of land for development projects, management of local natural resources, grant of mining licenses, and adjudication of disputes in accordance with prevalent traditions and customs.

In this context of neo-liberal capitalist development and the resulting displacement, marginalization and exclusion the paper aims to narrate the lived experiences of tribal people, which describe their agony, sufferings and marginalization, in the context of Odisha's Vedanta project. In the process, the paper also attempts to examine how marginalization and exclusion are manifested in the process of development and development-induced displacement. Land acquisition for neo-liberal capitalist development, involuntary displacement of Scheduled Tribes and the resulting resistance to development in the Vedanta Alumina Project of Lanjigarh in the Kalahandi district of Odisha form the wider context within which the present study is situated. The empirical work for the research is carried out in two Gram Panchayats, i.e. Lanjigarh Panchayat and Batelima Panchayat of the Lanjigarh Block in Kalahandi district, which were subjected to displacement, and were the hotbed of the resistance against the Vedanta Project. Besides displacement and resistance to development due to Vedanta, the Lanjigarh Block has also a political significance, which made it more appropriate for the present study, i.e., its position within the Fifth Schedule area of the Indian Constitution, with several protective laws including that of PESA for safeguarding the tribal interests.

A combination of case study method, group discussion and in-depth interviews was carried out to gather the empirical data for the paper. We viewed the two Panchayats taken for study as socio-political organizations, within which tribal social organization is embedded rather than just as political units. To collect the field data, interviews were conducted with the present and past representatives of the two Panchayats and other key informants, such as local tribal leaders, tribal youth, and a few tribal women, who had participated actively in the anti-Vednata struggle. Further, in-depth discussions were also carried out with the members of Civil Society Groups like *Niyamgiri Surakshya Samiti* and *Green Kalahandi* at Lanjigarh and Bhawanlpatha to gain a wider perspective of the tribal resistance to Vedanta. Besides, the primary source, information from various reports, local newspapers and brochures used during the tribal mobilization was also gathered, which served the material for the present paper.

The paper is divided into six sections, which includes the discussions in the introduction. The second section discusses the current practice of development neo-liberal capitalist development and the consequent marginalization, exclusion and tribal conflict over development, which forms the point of departure for the present research. The third section unveils Vedanta's intrusion into Odisha and the tribal hinterland of Lanjigarh in Kalahandi, and the fourth unfolds the case of two Panchayats, where the empirical work was carried out. The fifth section explains the manifestation of exclusion and marginalization of tribal people of Lanjigarh in the context displacement due to the Vedanta Project, and the sixth section concludes the paper with a critical question as to what is meant by development and how far would people's voice matter in development.

II. THE POINT OF DEPARTURE

Development Practice, Marginalization, Exclusion and Conflict

The post-1980 efforts towards decentralization and subsequent devolution of power for inclusion of marginalized groups that intend to empower the local communities as opposed to a centralized state, have also paradoxically coexisted with neo-liberal policies of capitalist development, which has increased the power of the state over local communities. The rapid economic growth agenda of neo-liberalism and globalization has resulted in monopolization and exploitation of natural resources to feed the process of development. The tendency of the State to monopolize and consolidate its power over the natural resource base is quite visible with its support for the process of development, which is now characterized by huge expansion of energy and resource intensive industrial activities, and major developmental projects like construction of big dams, forest exploitation, mining, energy intensive commercial agriculture, etc. The greater demand for natural resources by the process of development has led to monopolization of the resources by the State, and narrowing down of the natural resource base for survival of economically poor and powerless, either by direct transfer of resources away from their basic needs or by destruction of the essential ecological processes that ensure renewability of the life supporting natural resources (Bandyopadhyay and Shiva, 1988). In such a context of resource capture by the State to continue its project of rapid economic growth and deprivation of local communities from these resources, the State has often been successful in using the ideology of development as an effective instrument to legitimize exploitation.

The pattern of development that the State has followed ever since independence, and more intensively with its neo-liberal agendas of 1980s and 1990s has resulted in fundamentally altering two crucial bases of production: land and water, upon which survival of majority of economically poor, powerless and marginalized groups depend (Baviskar, 1995). The most significant life support system beyond clean air, are the common pool resources, such as water, forest and land on which the majority of the tribal and economically poor people of India depend for their survival. The response of local and tribal communities to this new threat to survival, which is being created by the very process of development, has often manifested through virulent economic conflicts between the tribal communities, whose resources and livelihoods are now threatened by the rapid economic growth agenda, and the State and its allies who are actively pursuing these. Such economic conflicts over development, mostly involving tribal and marginalized communities, have been on the rise in India recently, and have emerged as a serious challenge to the current practice and discourse of development as well as efforts towards institutionalization of local Government initiatives.

An understanding of the conflicts arising out of the development process and its impact on local communities and marginalized groups and the efforts for their inclusion in local governance is incomplete without exploring the very nature of development, which is creating alienation and exclusion of the tribal and other marginalized communities. The current practice of development not only excludes and alienates the tribal and other marginalized communities by way of threatening them of losing the resources on which their survival depends, but also through an unequal sharing of the fruits of development. The Indian national development ever since independence has been a process where the tribal and other marginalized communities have borne the cost of development and sacrificed their lives and livelihood, whereas the benefits of development have been cornered by the elites. The bulk of development policies, justified in the national interest, actually diminished the ability of the poor to control and gainfully use the natural resource base, and safeguarded the interests of capitalists, merchants, industrialists and rich farmers (Baviskar, 1995). Madhav Gadgil and Ramchandra Guha from their excellent analysis of use and abuse of nature for the purpose of development mention that 'the strategy of development, willingly or unwillingly sacrificed the interests of the bulk of the rural population—landless labour, small and marginal farmers, artisans, nomads and various aboriginal communities—whose dependence on nature was a far more direct one' (Gadgil and Guha, 1992).

The current practice of development, manifested through rapid economic growth, increasing industrialization and uncontrolled resource capture to support it, demands capture of resources to be used as raw materials in the process of development. However, these resources are used as life support systems for the marginalized groups, whose survival depends upon these resources. Therefore, much of the development conflicts that have emerged recently are in fact struggles of tribal and marginalized groups in defence of their traditional rights over land, water, forest and other common resources. However, these conflicts should not be understood just as who captures the resources, rather they are conflicts involving issues of how and for what purpose they are captured. Developmental conflicts may therefore be understood as continuing struggles over the process of production and extraction of resources, and issues concerning resource capture, mode of resource use and technology adopted for its extraction (Gadgil and Guha, 1992). To agree with Baviskar (1995), these conflicts have been contestations between two versions of economy – 'political economy of profit' pursed by the State and its allies and 'moral economy of need' practised by the tribal and marginalized communities for their survival. To put it precisely, these conflicts over the process of development had their origin in 'lopsided, iniquitous and environmentally destructive process of development' (Guha and Martinez-Alier, 1997). Development conflicts may therefore be approached as a response of the tribal and marginalized groups against the process of marginalization, exclusion and alienation of these communities from the very process of development.

III. Vedanta's Journey into Odisha[1]

Vedanta Resources is a British based multinational mining company with operations in India, Zambia, Australia and Armenia. Vedanta's core business is linked to the production of copper, zinc and aluminium in India, which are used by a large gamut of industries. Vedanta Alumina Limited (VAL), which has its operations in Lanjigarh in the Kalahandi District of Odisha, is an associate company of globally diversified and London Stock Exchange-listed metal and mining group Vedanta Resources PCL. Vedanta Alumina's journey into Odisha dates back to April 1997, when the State-Owned Odisha Mining Corporation signed a Memorandum of Understanding (MoU) with Sterlite India, an associate of Vedanta, to extend the right to mine bauxite in the Niyamgiri Hills of Lanjigarh in Kalahandi district of Odisha. However, during July, 1997, the Supreme Court of India challenged mining on protected forest land in the Scheduled Areas of Andhra Pradesh in its famous Samatha judgment. The Supreme Court of India held that the provisions of the Fifth Schedule also applied to the transfer of private or Government land in the Scheduled Areas to the non-tribals. The Court ordered for establishment of a committee, made up of senior Government officials at the state level to consider the feasibility of permitting the industry to carry on mining operations and if necessary to place it before a cabinet sub-committee to take appropriate action. The Court also held that similar committees should be set up in other states where similar acts do not totally prohibit granting of mining leases of the land in scheduled areas and also suggested that it would be useful for the Central Government to take a policy decision and enact a suitable law in light of the Court's guideline to ensure a consistent scheme throughout the country in respect of tribal land and mining. Such an act of judicial activism protecting the interests of tribals resulted in halting of the mining initiative by Sterlite India in Kalahandi's Lanjigarh.

After almost five years, in July 2002, Government of Odisha announced that the decision of the Supreme Court in the Samatha Case in Andhra Pradesh was not relevant to Odisha, and the state's existing laws were sufficient enough to protect the tribal communities; and proceeded with the Vedanta refinery-mining project. Subsequently, Sterlite India commissioned the rapid Environmental Impact Assessment (EIA) study in August 2002, and the first phase of compulsory land acquisition began for Vedanta's Lanjigarh refinery. By the first quarter of the year 2003, the executive summary of the EIA report was ready, and the Odisha State Pollution Control Board (OSPCB) conducted two public hearings on the refinery-mining project, following which Sterlite India sought environmental clearance from the Ministry of Environment and Forest (MoEF) for the refinery-mining project. From its planning phase, the bauxite mining and alumina refinery were conceptualized as one project, where the bauxite was supposed to be mined from

Niyamgiri Hills, and transported to the foothills to be refined at the Lanjigarh Refinery. However, by 2004, the mining and refinery project was effectively separated into two projects to avoid legal hassles.

On October 5, 2004 the Odisha Mining Corporation signed a new agreement with Vedanta Alumina for an 'integrated project' including the Lanjigarh Refinery, the Niyamgiri bauxite mining, and another bauxite mining at Karlapet or elsewhere in the State, and an aluminium smelter in northern Odisha. The Vedanta Aluminium, subsequently, started construction of Lanjigarh refinery and certain elements of mining project, although it had not obtained the required regulatory clearances. Besides, there were several other violations by Vedanta Aluminium such as clearing forest land and encroaching village common land without required clearances. In 2006, the Vedanta Aluminium completed construction of the refinery and commenced the trial operation using bauxite brought from Korba in the neighbouring state of Chhattisgarh, and from other states. The refinery moved on to full operation in 2007.

The Vedanta refinery at Lanjigarh is located in a 750 hectare complex. Land acquisition for this refinery was initiated in June 2002 when the Kalahandi District Collector's office sent a letter to affected landowners of 12 villagers of the Lanjigarh area, namely: Bundel, Borbhata, Kothadwar, Bandhaguda, Sindbahali, Basantpada, Jagannathpur, Kinari, Kappaguda, Belamba, Boringpadar and Turiguda. The letter declared that the District Administration intended to compulsorily acquire 391 hectares of private land and 628 hectares of common village land for Vedanta's refinery factory at Lanjigarh. The letter also explained that the families to be fully displaced would be compensated and resettled, while the families, whose lands would be taken over, would be compensated. It was informed to the people that complaints against this land acquisition notice could be filed at the office of the Revenue Inspector at Lanjigarh by June 22, 2002. Two public meetings were convened by the Kalahandi District Administration at Lanjigarh and Batelima on 26 June 2002, and within two weeks of this meeting land acquisition started in Lanjigarh.

IV. Unfolding the Research Locales

The empirical work for the present research was carried out in two Panchayats, i.e., Lanjigarh and Batelima of Lanjigarh Block of the Kalahandi District of the State of Odisha. It would, therefore, be appropriate to introduce the study of the Panchayats with a brief description about the Kalahandi District, as well as about the Lanjigarh Block.

4.1. Kalahandi District: A Profile

Kalahandi District is in south-western part of Odisha, and is situated between 19^0 3 to 21^0 5 North latitude and 80^0 30' to 84^0 47' East longitude. Kalahandi is bordered to the north by the State of Chhattisgarh and the districts of Bolangir and Nuapada, to the South by the districts of Rayagada, to the West by the districts of Nabarangapur and Raipur (Chhattisgarh), and to the East by the districts of Rayagada, Kandhamal and Boudh. The District headquarters is Bhawanipatna Town, which is on the eastern border. Kalahandi has a substantial chunk of population who belong to the SC and ST category. As per the 2001 census, the total population of the ST in the District is 29 per cent of the total population of the district, out of which 1,88,646 are male and 1,93,927 are female. A striking feature of ST population in the district is that they comprise a very small percentage of the urban population. Bhawanipatna Municipality has 6 per cent of the population that falls under the category of STs. Similarly, the Junagarh NAC has only 4 per cent of the total population and Kesinga NAC has 12 per cent of the total population that fall under ST category.

4.2 Profile of the Lanjigarh Block

The Lanjigarh Block occupies the western part of the Kalahandi District, and is situated at 19^0 43' North latitude and 83^0 22' East longitude. The Lanjigarh Block is bordered by Rayagada district in the West, Narla and M Rampur Block in the North, Bhawanipatna in the East and T Rampur and part of Rayagada district in the South. There are 21 Gram Panchayats in the Lanjigarh Block, which are constituted out of 848 villages. The basic population data of the panchayats of Lanjigarh Block is given below in the table (Table 1).

Table 1: Basic Population Data of the Panchayats of Lanjigarh Block

Name of the Panchayat	No. of Villages	No. of Households	Total Population	ST Population	SC Population
Bandhapari	43	1204	5272	2472	1793
Batelima	10	372	1759	1063	153
Bengaon	27	810	3680	2261	1124
Bhatangpadar	30	456	2041	1516	505
Bhurtigarh	22	647	2451	1809	327
Bijepur	35	822	3760	2359	973
Biswanathpur	16	1263	5305	1503	1178
Champadeipur	18	1090	4804	1480	1050
Chatrapur	15	969	4210	1651	1066
Gobardhanpur	9	1014	4062	1390	693
Gunduri	34	633	2624	1732	707
Kamarda	19	1018	3779	2205	558
Kankatru	24	718	3226	1532	1107
Lakhbahali	22	817	3792	2282	1119
Lanji	33	944	4301	2674	1052
Lanjigarh	28	1444	6101	2450	1420
Lanjigarh Road	19	1252	4668	1166	1237
Malijubang	18	531	2270	1421	371
Pahadapadar	13	710	3195	2088	749
Pokharibandh	23	547	2264	653	677
Trilochanpur	24	323	1474	930	279

Source: Census of India, 2001

Lanjigarh Block has the second highest tribal concentration in the District, with 49 per cent tribal population. The Block is only next to T Rampur with its tribal population of 57 per cent. The two most important tribal groups concentrated in the region are those of Dangaria Kandh and Kutia Kandh. While the Dangaria Kandh stay inside the Niyamgiri Hills, and mostly carry out horticulture and shifting cultivation, the Kutia Kandhs are dependent upon mostly settled agriculture and stay in the foothill villages.

4.3. The Panchayats Studied

The Lanjigarh Panchayat. The Lanjigarh Panchayat, which is now home to the Vedanta Alumina Project, consists of twenty-eight villages, out of which twenty-one are inhabited villages. Out of these twenty-one villages, there are three large villages, i.e., Balabhadrapur, Jagannathpur and Lanjigarh, which are demographically as well as politically important in the Panchayat. The Panchayat has a total population of 6,100 as per the 2001 Census. The Lanjigarh has a predominance of Scheduled Tribe population, which constitutes 49 per cent of the total population. The Scheduled Castes also constitute a sizable number with 24 per cent of the total population (Table 2). Except for the Lanjigarh Village, which also happens to be the Block Headquarters, the other villages are not so well connected with the main road. A narrow *pukka* road connects Lanjigarh Village with the nearby Muniguda town of Rayagada District and Bhawanipatna of the Kalahandi District. The rest of the villages are connected with each other through kuccha roads. Further, there are some grocery, cloth and other shops at the Lanjigarh Village, making it the market place for the locality.

The Lanjigarh Panchayat is divided into fifteen wards, out of which eight are reserved for Scheduled Tribe category (including women); and the post of the President of the Panchayat is reserved for Scheduled Tribe Women's category as per norms of the PESA Act, 1996. The current President's post is occupied by Ms. Saraswati Munda, belonging to the *Munda* tribe. She is educated up to class eight, and has been holding the position since 2007. A personal interview with the President revealed that she had neither any interest in politics before contesting the election, nor any exposure to village politics. Her Father-law, who was the ex-Sarpanch of the Gram Panchayat, persuaded her to contest the election, so as to keep someone from their family in the Panchayat.

Before Saraswati Munda was elected as the President of the Panchayat in 2007, the post was held by one Mr Banamali Majhi from 2003 to 2007. The land acquisition process started during his tenure as the President. Initially, Mr Banamali Majhi was opposed to the land acquisition for the Vedanta Project and had organized the tribal community to resist against it. But later, Mr Majhi changed his position and supported the land acquisition process. Towards the later part of his tenure, Mr Majhi lost his popularity and support in the Panchayat due to such a change of stance and subsequent betrayal of the community members. In the 2007 Panchayat election, there were three candidates for the post of the President, out of which one was Mr Banamali Majhi's daughter-in-law. However, the lost popularity and lack of public support due to his support to the Vedanta Aluminium Company came in the way of the victory of his daughter-in-law; and Ms Saraswati Munda was declared elected to the post of President in 2007 election.

Table 2: Basic Population Data for Lanjigarh Gram Panchayat

Name of the Village	No. of Households	Total Population	ST Population	SC Population
Balabhadra Pur	102	458	136	87
Balipadar	40	160	80	47
Banigaon	26	129	129	0
Barabhata	17	72	1	0
Bhatajhari	26	104	101	0
Dangargarh	1	4	4	0
Denga Saragi	23	91	91	0
Gaipata	34	126	120	0
Jagannathpur	164	725	354	308
Jamchuan	13	58	58	0
Kadambaguda	29	120	0	0
Kadhibadi	48	203	112	16
Kokasur	19	78	65	0
Kothadwara	11	33	33	0
Kothasama	50	198	177	19
Lanjigarh	685	2913	471	839
Rengopali	53	210	176	33
Semilivata	41	168	160	5
Sindhbahali	23	97	92	0
Tangarkana	38	153	90	57
Total	1,443	6,100	2,450	1,411

The Batelima Panchayat. The Batelima Panchayat is adjacent to the Lanjigarh Panchayat and also constitutes the site of land acquisition for the Vedanta Project. The Panchayat has ten villages, out of which one is an uninhabited village. The Batelima Panchayat is numerically preponderant with Scheduled Tribe population, which constitutes more than 60 per cent of the total population. Out of the nine inhabited villages, Banipanga and Kinari are completely Scheduled Tribe villages. Similarly, Rusbundel and Ketundeli villages are also predominated by the Scheduled Tribe population (Table 3).

The Batelima Panchayat consists of eleven wards, out of which ten are reserved for Scheduled Tribe category (including women), and the post of the President is reserved for Scheduled Tribe Women's category as per norms of the PESA Act, 1996. The current President post is held by Ms Jagadi Majhi, belonging to the *Kandh* tribe. The present sarpanch Ms Jagadi Majhi is the daughter-in-law of Mr Daisingh Majhi, who happens to the ex-Sarpanch of the Panchayat, and one of the leaders of the tribal community. Like the President of the Lanjigarh Panchayat, Ms Jagadi Majhi of the Batelima Panchayat was also observed to be little interested in politics and had no experience and exposure to the village politics before contesting the election. It was clearly observed that reservation of the president's post for ST women's category brought her in to the position, which she is holding right now.

Ms Jagadi Majhi serving as the Sarpanch of the Batelima Panchayat since 2007. Before her, one Mr Andrue Majhi of Rasbundel village served as the President of the Batelima panchayat for the period of 2003–2007. It was in his tenure as the President, the land acquisition process for the Vedanta Company and the subsequent conflict over it started in the locality. In the beginning, Mr Andrue Majhi opposed the process of land acquisition and led the tribal struggle against it. However, later Mr Andrue Majhi changed his position and supported the land acquisition by the company. The local people as well as the other members of the Panchayat were of the opinion that Mr Andrue was lured by the company to support its activities and thus, betrayed his own community. By the 2007

Panchayat election, Mr Andrue Majhi had already lost his public support and faith of people, and therefore, was not successful in getting one of his family Members elected to the post. In the 2007 election, out of three candidates, including the family member of Mr Andrue Majhi, Ms Jagadi Majhi won the election.

Table 3: Basic Population Data for Batelima Gram Panchayat

Name of the Village	No. of Households	Total Population	ST Population	SC Population
Banipanga	26	122	122	0
Basantapada	131	649	258	68
Batelima	60	276	56	57
Belamba	34	176	152	24
Kapaguda	46	199	171	0
Kinari	32	134	134	0
Kutendeli	16	90	86	4
Parbatipur	8	29	2	0
Rasbundel	19	84	82	0
Total	372	1,759	1,063	153

V. Development, Displacement and Exclusion in Lanjigarh

Development, understood as modernization through rapid industrialization and increased utilization of natural resources as input so as to derive maximum output and accelerated economic growth, have been the predominant phenomena since 1950s, with decolonization and emergence of new nation states in the developing societies. Burdened with the problems of underdevelopment, backwardness and poverty on the one hand, which were directly related to the preceding centuries of colonial rule, and fascinated on the other hand with the achievements of growth oriented modernity of the First World countries, the Third World societies uncritically accepted the western model of development. Rather than utilization of natural resources as input in the process of development, what was more striking was the speed with which such resources were harnessed, unmindful of the dependence of the local and tribal communities on these resources for their life and livelihood. Such a process of development has, from its very inception, undermined and marginalized these local and tribal communities, and has ignored and systematically denied them access to these resources. Subsequently, with the adoption of liberalization policies in the early 1990s, the new multi-national capitalist interests have joined hands with the nation state in further marginalizing the interests of these communities. In such a context of marginalization, exclusion and resource extraction, resistance to development has emerged as a natural response to ensure life and livelihood and to combat threats of survival.

Resource extraction for industrialization and the consequent tribal resistance to such a process owe their origin to the colonial period. The colonial intervention in natural resources of India led to a conflict over vital natural resources like water and forests and induced new forms of poverty and deprivation among the tribal communities.[2] Control and consolidation of monopolistic rights over natural resources, and subsequent changes in endowments and entitlements over these resources by the British came in conflict over the locals' and tribals' age-old rights and practices related to natural resources. Such a process of resource alienation generated a local response through which people tried to regain control over local natural resources. The indigo movement in eastern India, the Deccan movement for land rights or the forest movement in Western Ghats, the central Indian hills or the lower Himalayas, were the obvious expressions of protest generated by these newly created conflicts (Bandyopadhyay and Shiva, 1988).

These local protests in defence of traditional rights could not grow independent of the national struggle against colonialism and, therefore, got merged with it in the distance hope that decolonization would bring relative autonomy and greater local control of means of livelihood, i.e., the local natural resources. With decolonization and formation of new nation states, resolution of these developments-induced natural resource conflicts and the related livelihood insecurity and exclusion appeared possible. However in practice, political independence did not provide legitimate access to and control over these natural resources to the local tribal communities. With the end of colonialism and colonial control of natural resources, the *slogan* for rapid industrialization became the new development bandwagon for modern India, and State monopoly over natural resources and consequent marginalization and exclusion of scheduled tribes continued as usual, with the only exception that this time the enemy was the own nation state instead of a colonial ruler. This inexorable logic of resource exploitation, exhaustion and alienation integral to the classical model of economic development based on resource intensive technologies led Gandhi to seek an alternative path of development for India when he wrote: '*God forbid that India should ever take to industrialism after the manner of the West. The economic imperialism of a single tiny island kingdom (England) is today keeping the world in chains. If an entire nation of 300 million took to similar economic exploitation, it would strip the world bare like locusts*' (Gandhi, 1928).

Writing on India's national development, Gadgil and Guha (1992) mention about the alternative theoretical choices available during the time of independence for choosing a model of development. However Indian nationalists guided by modernists like Pandit Nehru chose the industrialized path of resource-intensive development, and as a consequence, resource extraction and marginalization of scheduled tribals continued at an ever increasing speed. As the scale of economic development activities escalated from one five-year plan to another, the disruption of the ecological processes that maintained the productivity of the natural resource base and livelihood of local tribal communities started becoming more and more apparent. In the absence of ecologically enlightened resource management methods, the pressure of poverty and underdevelopment enhanced the pace of economic development, industrialization and exhaustion of natural resource base, with the hope that economic development would trickle down to all sections of society and would result in a quick improvement in the standard of living for all, as in the case of Western Europe. However, such a model of achieving infinite growth with a finite environment, apart from exhausting the natural resource base and degrading the environment, also resulted in livelihood insecurity, marginalization and exclusion of the Scheduled Tribes from the very process of development. For example, commercial forestry made more revenues by making more timber and pulpwood available in the market but in the process reduced the multipurpose biomass productivity or damaged the hydrology of the forests. People dependent on non-timber biomass outputs of the forests like leaves, twigs, fruits, nuts, medicines, oils, etc., were unable to sustain themselves, in the face of commercial exploitation of forests. Further, the changed hydrological character of the forests affected both the micro-climate and the stream flows disturbing the hydrological stability and affecting agricultural production (Bandyopadhyay and Shiva, 1988).

Examples like this are not uncommon in the India's development terrain. The resource capture by the State and its allies, justified in the name of national development, has always resulted in livelihood insecurity, marginalization and exclusion of Scheduled Tribes, and has challenged their cultural integrity. The situation has become more severe for the tribal communities in the wake of globalization and liberalization, when the private capitalist interests have joined hands with the nation-state to carry forward its mandate of rapid industrialization. From the national development paradigm of 1950s by the welfare state to the neo-liberal development paradigm of 1990s by the globalized State, development has meant nothing more than alienation and exclusion for the tribals. And it is essential, therefore, to understand that such incidents of marginalization, exclusion and cultural dilution, created by ecological degradation and economic deprivation, have in turn resulted in virulent conflicts over development and environment in many parts of our country. Vedanta's proposed mining at Niyamgiri and the refinery plant at Lanjigarh are just few other examples of tribal marginalization, exclusion and resistance in defence of traditional livelihood patterns. We elaborate in the following paragraphs the manifestations of such a process of marginalization and exclusion as a result of capitalist intrusion into the tribal hinterland in Lanjigarh.

5.1 Proposed Mining at Niyamgiri as 'Cultural Genocide'

The English word 'genocide' comes from the original Greek word *'genos'* meaning people, race, stock, and the Latin word *'cidium'* meaning cutting or killing. Lexicographically, it is defined as 'the deliberate or systematic destruction in whole or in part of an ethnic, racial, religious or national group' (Funk, 2010). The term was coined by Raphael Lemkin, a Polish-Jewish legal scholar, in 1944, to describe the Nazi treatment of Jews. Padel and Das (2010) highlight that the process of genocide involves two levels of what is killed: 'the physical extermination and the killing of a culture'. Agreeing with Padel and Das (2010), we argue here that what is happening at Lanjigarh under the veil of development is a systematic and strategic attempt to exterminate and extinguish the traditional culture of the *Dongria Kondh* community, which is deep-rooted in the two important resources – 'Land' and 'Forest' – with which their life, livelihood and cultural existence depend upon, and which they are in the process of losing due to the Vedanta's operations in the area.

The Lanjigarh area is primarily inhabited by *Kondh* tribe and Scheduled Castes. The 2001 Census data reveals that the STs and SCs comprise almost three-fourths of the total population with 49 and 24 per cent of the total population respectively. *Kondhs* of Lanjigarh are mainly divided into two categories: *Kutia Kondh* and *Dongria Kondh*. The *Kutia Kondh* live in the foothills of Niyamgiri and the plains, and mostly carry out settled agriculture, and in some cases shifting cultivation. The *Dongria Kondh*s are settled around the Niyamgiri Hills, the proposed site for Vedanta's mining operations, and are engaged mostly in horticultural activities and practise shifting cultivation. The *Dongria Kondh*, is a unique Primitive Tribal Group (PTG)[3], and can be compared with the endangered *Jarawas* of the Andamans. The total population of the *Dongria Kondh* as reported in 2001 Census amounted to be only 7,500 (Samantara, 2006).

The Niyamgiri Hills, whose top is proposed to be mined for extracting bauxite by Vedanta, is the most sacred entity for the *Kondhs* of Lanjigarh. The tribes worship the *Niyam Raja*, a deity, believed by them to be living in the top of the Niyamgiri Hills. The entire area inhabited by the *Kondhs* is thought to be the kingdom belonging to the *Niyam Raja*. It is believed this deity provides water, which sustain all plants, animals and human life in the vicinity. Below is the picture of the Niyamgiri Hill – the sacred hill, with which the tribals associate their culture, existence and value of life; and paradoxically also the site for Vedanta's mining operations.

(Picture taken by the researcher in December 2010, showing the Niyamgiri Hills, the adobe of tribal deity, and the erected pillars and the conveyer belt to transport bauxite from the hill top to the refinery at Lanjigarh)

Besides worshipping the Niyamgiri Hills (the Forest), the tribes of the locality also worship *Dharni Penu* or the mother earth (the Land). In almost every village, one can see a place of worship with a wooden structure (see the picture below). The tribals worship the hills (the Forest) and the earth (the Land) at this place of worship and often offer animal sacrifices. For the *Dongria*, worship in any occasion begins with first an offering to their prime deity – the *Niyam Raja*.

(Photo taken by the researcher in Sindh Bahali Village in Lanjigarh Gram Panchayat during field study in December 2010)

The Niyamgiri Hills form a biologically rich and diverse habitat, which the tribes in the region rely on for food, fuel wood, forest produces, timber, and medicinal plants. Almost all tribals in the region associate Niyamgiri Hills with their life and livelihood. The streams flowing from the hills form the source of water for them. The tribals grow crops in the hills. They also earn a livelihood by selling forest produces procured from the Niyamgiri Hills at nearby Lanjigarh market. The top of the Niyamgiri Hills is referred to as the *'Kaman Jungle'* by the *Dongria*, is the most sacred place for them. As per the beliefs of the local tribals, cutting forests from this hilltop, which is the abode of the tribal deity, is a loss of their cultural identity, integrity and above all tribal sovereignty enjoyed in the reign of *Niyam Raja*. Therefore, the hilltop is protected by the tribals with their religious and cultural beliefs. They believe that it is the *Niyam Raja* himself who loves the trees and animals, and therefore, the tribals do not hunt or cut trees from this hilltop. It is the same forest area, which is very much sacred for the local tribes, and is associated with their life, existence and livelihood, that is proposed to be mined by the Vedanta now. For the local tribes, digging the hilltop is an assault on their basic values of existence on this earth, murder of their cultural integrity with the hills and attack on their tribal identity and sovereignty, which they believe to have gained under the reign of *Niyam Raja* in the area. The case materials that we gathered from the Lanjigarh area the above claims.

During the fieldwork, we interacted with Mr Kumiti Majhi of the Jagannathpur village of Lanjigarh Panchayat and the Convener of the *Niyamgiri Surakshya Samiti* – an organization for saving the Niyamgiri Hills. Kumuti Majhi, aged about 55 years, is from Jagannathpur village of Lanjigarh Panchayat, and belongs to *Kutia Kondh* tribe. Kumuti possess the traditional knowledge of several medicinal plants, and can also predict the weather as well as the future for the local tribals based upon his knowledge and understanding of the position of planets and stars. He has assumed a new role in the last one decade of playing a pivotal role in protecting, what he calls his *'ma'* and *'mati'*, .i.e., mother and soil/earth. Since the Vedanta's intrusion into the area, he has spearheaded an organization called *'Niyamgiri Surakshya Samiti'* to save the Niyamgiri Hills from the clutches of Vedanta. Highlighting the importance of Niyamgiri Hills in the tribal life, culture, and value, Kumiti reiterates:

> '... we are the subjects of the King Niyam Raja. Niyam Raja reigns this kingdom, and resides in the Niyamgiri Hills. He is our prime deity, supreme creator, and responsible for our very existence in this tribal land. Niyam Raja brings us happiness, and provides us everything that is required for human life with his blessings, and has made us who we are today. Niyam Raja treats the tribal people like his children and provides food, water and shelter. Our life, culture, songs, dance and very existence as human beings are related to the Niyamgiri Hills. The springs, from which we fetch water, come from the top of the Niyamgiri Hills, and is a blessing of the Niyam Raja. Tribal people are self-sufficient here because of the Niyamgiri Hills, which provides food and water to survive, land for cultivation, herbs and medicinal plants for saving life in cases of illness. Even though the tribal people clear some forest for cultivation, large trees are never cut from the hill, and especially

people here do not touch the top of the hills, since we believe that the hilltop is the adobe for the Niyam Raja. Now the Vedanta Company wants to mine bauxite from Niyamgiri. This will lead to cutting down of lot of trees from the hill top. Any destruction of trees and the hill is an attack on tribal culture, beliefs and religion. If we don't have Niyamgiri Hill, whom shall we worship? Vedanta and the State are now trying to destruct our identity, cultural practices, and the very essence of life here in this tribal land as a human being ...'

Kumuti's worries just voice the tribal concerns over development. What we could gather from the discussions with Kumuti Majhi is that tribals give a symbolic meaning to the Niyamgiri Hills and cannot imagine being a tribal without the Niyamgiri Hills. Life without Niyamgiri will be completely different for the tribals, since they associate their culture with the Niyamgiri Hills, and again being tribal as a distinct identity is essentially related to their culture and cultural practices.

The tribal people's socio-economic and political systems are fundamental to their culture, which is deep-rooted in their 'Land' and 'Forest'. And when displaced from the land and denied access to the forest, the socio-economic and political systems of the tribal people are subsequently destroyed. Losing land and forest brings the end to the culture of the *Dongria*, which they have cherished inside the Niyamgiri Hills for generations. The proposed mining and the industrialization may bring development for the rest of the society, but for tribals— as we learnt from them—have nothing to offer other than bringing about a cultural genocide. And to agree with Padel and Das (2010), 'underlying this cultural genocide is the invaders' total lack of respect for tribal people's traditions and connections with the land and the forest'.

5.2 Proposed Mining, Tribal Exclusion and Concerns for Life and Livelihood

One of the strands of exclusion, as it can be gleamed from the theoretical and conceptual discussion on the subject, is its linkages with loss of employment.[4] Even in the European countries, where the term exclusion first originated, exclusion is associated with unemployment and joblessness. The term 'exclusion', in fact, originated in the context of prolonged and large scale employment difficulties in European countries, which gave rise to criticisms of the welfare systems for failing to prevent poverty (Loury, 1999). Exclusion, in this framework, is located in people's access to labour market, where access to labour market is considered something as not just providing income, but rather integration with the State and society. It is in this context that Duffy (1998) makes a conceptual distinction between poverty and exclusion: the former being understood as lack of income because of limited access to labour market, whereas the latter gives a broader meaning to limited access to labour market in terms of lack of inclusion and integration with the economic order. Viewed from this perspective, we may say with certainty that capitalist intervention in the tribal hinterland of Lanjigarh is associated with loss of livelihood and life-supporting systems, and thus generates exclusion.

The proposed mining of bauxite at Niyamgiri Hills threatens to undermine the traditional land rights and religious-cultural beliefs of the *Kondh* tribe in general and the *Dongria Kondh* in particular. It also poses serious threats to their right to sustainable and adequate standard of living, by alienating their sources of water, food and livelihood. Regardless of their knowledge about the geology and hydrology, many of our respondents showed concern about availability of water if the mining activities take place. Some of the Panchayat representatives whom we interviewed as well as the tribal people from several villages had the same concern about the future availability of water. We cite here the excerpts of the interview with Mr Sri Majhi, the representative from Jagannathpur village to the Lanjigarh Panchayat:

'We never associate water with rainfall or monsoon. The streams and springs from the mountain are our major water source. Even though, now some people have wells in their houses, and the Government has constructed a few tubewells in some villages, we uneducated tribals at least know this much that the source of all water is the Niyamgiri Hills. The bauxite mining in the Niyamgiri Hills will disturb our water availability. If the company (Vedanta) takes away the Niyamgiri Hill from us, we will lose our life-supporting system, as we will not have adequate access to food and water.'

Such concerns about disturbances in the availability of water and food are not out of the context. The Niyamgiri Hill is the source of two perennial rivers in the region: Vamsadhara and Nagavali. Therefore, any disturbance of the water structure of the Hills and its capacity to recharge ground water will have a serious impact in the entire region. Besides, concerns over availability of water and food, the tribals also have a serious concern over traditional land rights. Many tribal households in this region practise shifting cultivation with customary rights over land. In the absence of any legal ownership of the land, the hill tracts are used by tribal families based upon their traditional rights and customary law, which are mutually agreed upon by all the members of the community. It is a matter of great concern that the tribals will lose their traditional and customary right to land in the hills, and further to worsen the condition, will not get any settlement benefits in the absence of any legal claim of ownership over the land. This forms an important manifestation of exclusion of the Scheduled Tribes in the region, whose sources of livelihood associated with the proposed mining site, are now under threat.

Besides cultivation, the tribals of Lanjigarh area also look upon the hills and mountains as a source from which they collect non-timber forest produces and earn a livelihood by selling them in the market. Now with the proposals for mining, they fear about the closure of such a source of livelihood. Tribals, an otherwise self-sufficient community, now apprehend an increased dependence on the market in the absence of access to forests and hills, their source of self-sufficiency. Such an increased dependence on the market would also lead to increased poverty for the tribal communities in the absence of any source of cash income.

5.3 Construction of Refinery Factory and Livelihood Insecurity

Exclusion and marginalization of Scheduled Tribes become more apparent when we look at the situation in the Lanjigarh Panchayat, where Vedanta's refinery unit is in operation. The issue which again and again comes to the forefront while discussing the exclusion of tribals in Lanjigarh is that of acquisition of land for construction of the refinery unit. It is however, true that some land-losers got cash compensation from Vedanta in exchange of their acquired land as per the existing resettlement and rehabilitation framework. But such a process of cash compensation for loss of land does not reveal the true picture of increasing livelihood insecurity and the emerging exclusion of the tribal people. We shall discuss here two aspects to make our point clear.

Who are the Land-losers?

The tribal people of Lanjigarh differ from those of the State and/or the company as to who are the land-losers in Lanjigarh or for that matter any development project which involves appropriation of land. The tribal people have a different connotation for land. For many tribal people, land that they use and cultivate is not private property with some sort of legal claims over it. The tribals in Lanjigarh, who utilize the forest land for shifting cultivation, never bothered about having a legal claim over it, since their access to land was governed by their traditional and customary rights. Besides, as we have pointed out earlier, many tribal people used the forest land for horticultural activities and for collecting non-timber forest produces. Therefore, private ownership over land did not matter much for them, and what governed their access to the land were their traditional use and access rights. However, for the Government records, all these lands, which the tribals used for sustaining their livelihood, are non-private or Government lands, and on which private individuals have limited or no say. The existing legal framework, while acquiring these lands, never take into account the likely livelihood uncertainties of those people and communities who depended upon these land. The cash compensation provision for legal land-losers by Vedanta offered nothing to those many tribals, who obviously lost land, but which they could not claim as their own private land. The very concept of land-losers had different meanings for the tribals and the Vedanta and/or the State. For Vedanta as well as the

State, a family can claim itself a land-loser if they could establish some legal claims of ownership over the land, which has been taken over by Vedanta. Even the Odisha Resettlement and Rehabilitation (R and R) Policy, 2006, which depends upon the colonial Land Acquisition Act, 1894 and the colonial concept of 'eminent domain' for appropriating land, considers the people, who do not have land deeds (*patta*) to the land they cultivate and occupy as 'encroachers on government land'. And these encroachers are not considered as land-losers and are not entitled for compensation for the land they lose in the process of land acquisition. However, for the tribal people, all are land-losers, since the land taken up for or would likely to be taken up for the company belonged to the tribals of the region.

Changing Patron-Client Institutions and Resultant Livelihood Insecurity

The second point that we would like to highlight about the resultant livelihood insecurity and exclusion of tribals relates to those tribals who worked as tenants and agricultural labourers in the lands of non-tribal landlords of the Lanjigarh. Over the years, feudalistic agrarian relations had developed in the Lanjigarh region, with strong presence of the institution of patron-client relationship.[5] The non-tribal landlords of Lanjigarh had land in several villages, which was actually cultivated by the tribal tenants. Some of the tribals with whom we interacted during the fieldwork had some sweet memories to cherish about the long-standing patron-client relationship with the landlord family. The landlord family extended help and fulfilled several obligations to the tenants in case of need. However, Lanjigarh areas being hilly and with limited facility for irrigation, the productivity of these lands was very low, and the returns to the landlord were minimal. When the proposal for establishment of Vedanta's factory mooted, these non-tribal landlord families were the first ones to support it as they could envision a foreseeable cash benefit, out of the land acquisition process. Subsequently, during the time of land acquisition, these families received modest cash compensation from Vedanta in return of surrender of their land to the company. This served as mutual gain for the company and the landlords, as the former got local supporters who would make the process of land acquisition comfortable, and the latter got heavy economic rewards for their otherwise less-productive land. But in the process, it was the tribal tenants, who got excluded and marginalized, as neither the company nor the landlords had anything to offer to these tenants. With the loss of the tenancy/land which they were cultivating, also ended to the long standing patron-client relations which they had established with the landlord's family. We cite here the excerpts of a respondent in the Belamba village in Batelima Panchayat, who stated the following:

The Mahakud family of Lanjigarh had their land in many nearby villages. Since they had large quantities of land, they gave land to the tribal people to cultivate on tenancy basis. As per the tenancy agreement between the Mahakuds and the tribals, each shared the produce from the land. Both the tribals and the Mahakud's depended upon each other. This has led to healthy relations between the tenant families with the zamindar family. In case of need we used to look upto the zamindar family for help, and they used to oblige us. Even though on certain occasions, we had to work for their family without any payment, but at times of festivals and marriages, the zamindar's family used to help us. We shared a good mutual relationship. But now things have changed. The Mahakuds have given their land to the Vedanta, and have received a huge amount of money in return. We as tenants had a stake in their land and used to get benefit out of it. But now, we can't claim any stake in their money, and nor it is going to benefit us in any way. Earlier we the tribals used to get benefit from them, since we cultivated their land. It was the land, which governed our relationship with the Mahakuds. Now we do not cultivate their land as they have given it to Vedanta. So now, we cannot go to them for any help, nor will they oblige us for anything.

Such an observation highlights an important aspect of tribal exclusion in Lanjigarh. It's not only that tribals didn't get any benefit out of Vedanta's operation; rather they lost the benefits which earlier they used to get from the traditional patron-client bonds. Their zamindar no longer remained their patron, to whom they could look up to for help during need. Now these families lost their livelihood of cultivating the landlord's land, and had to search for an alternative livelihood in the changing circumstances. This loss of livelihood also meant increased conditions of poverty, and it led to their exclusion.

VI. Conclusion

The above explanation of the industrialized mode of development in the tribal hinterland and the resulting exclusion and marginalization of the tribal communities raises two pertinent questions: 'What is development?' and 'Does people's voice matter in development?' While in theory, development is defined as a process which will give people the ability to control their own lives and lead to empowerment, in practice, what we observed is that it led to a situation where the tribals lost control over their life and livelihood. The tribals' actual experience of development quite contradicts what we may have gained from the text-bookish knowledge on the concept. With respect to people's voice in development, as we came to learn from Lanjigarh, the tribals' voice was never taken into account and their interests and concerns were sacrificed in the name of industrialization, economic growth and national development. Even though both national and international laws talk about consultation with local people before implementation of any development project, proper public consultation was not done in the case of Vedanta's operations. Further, the prolonged tribal resistance in the region also echoes the voice of the local tribals against the Vedanta's mining operations in the region. We therefore, can comprehend the unwillingness of the neo-liberal development process to listen to and take into consideration the voices of people, which further limits their choices and leads to their disempowerment.

Acknowledgement

This article is part of a project funded by Local Governance Initiative in South Asia (*LoGin*) – a programme of Swiss Agency for Development Cooperation (SDC), Embassy of Switzerland, New Delhi, whose support the authors gratefully acknowledge.

NOTES

1. This section is based upon materials gathered from Amnesty International's (2010) study on Vedanta titled *'Don't mine us Out of Existence'*.
2. Guha (1989) in his work *The Unquiet Woods: Ecological Change and Peasant Resistance in the Himalayas'* analyses the colonial exploitation of India's forests. Guha highlights that large scale extraction of India's forest wealth continued during the colonial period to meet three strategic requirements of the colonial state: expanding railway network, increased agricultural revenue, and increased requirement of good quality timber to build war ships. For details of colonial treatment of India's forest resources, see Guha, 1983, 1985, and 1990.
3. Today they are known as Particularly Vulnerable Tribal Group (PVTG) instead of PTG.
4. For a conceptual discussion on 'exclusion' and 'inclusion', see: Bhalla and Lapeyre, 1997; De Hann, 1998, Sen, 1997, Silver, 1994; IILS, 1997; Kabeer, 2000, IDS, 1998).
5. For details on the concept of patron-client relations see, Kaufman, 1974; Eisenstadd and Roniger, 1980; Stein, 1984; Michie, 1981; Scott, 1972.

REFERENCES

Agrawal, A. and E Ostrom. 2001. 'Collective Action, Property Rights, and Decentralization in Resource Use in India and Nepal.' *Politics and Society* 29, No. 4: 485-514.

Amnesty International. 2010. *Don't Mine us out of Existence: Bauxite Mine and Refinery Devastate Lives in India.* London: Amnesty International Publication.

Bandyopadhyay, Jayanta. and Vandana, Shiva. 1988. 'Political Economy of Ecology Movements.' *Economic and Political Weekly* 23, No. 24: 1223-32.

Baviskar, Amita. 1995. *In the Belly of the River: Tribal Conflicts over Development in the Narmada Valley.* New Delhi: Oxford University Press.

Bhalla, A. and Lapeyre, F. 1997. 'Social Exclusion: Towards an Analytical and Operational Framework.' *Development and Change* 28, No. 3: 413-33.

Census of India, 2001. Government of India, New Delhi.

Crush, Johathan, ed. 1995. *Power of Development.* London: Routledge.

De Haan, A. 1998. 'Social Exclusion: An Alternative Concept for the

Study of Deprivation?' *IDS-Bulletin* 29, No. 1: 10-19.

Duffy, K. 1998. 'Free Markets, Poverty and Social Exclusion.' In *Coping with Homelessness*, edited by Dragana, Avramov. Aldershot: Ashgate Publishing.

Eisenstadt, S.N. and Roniger, L. 1980. 'Patron Client Relations as a Model of Structuring Social Exchange.' *Comparative Studies in Society and History* 22, No. 1: 42-77.

Funk, M T. 2010. *Victims' Rights and Advocacy in the International Criminal Court*. Oxford, England: Oxford University Press.

Gadgil, Madhav. and R Guha. 1992. *This Fissured Land: An Ecological History of India*. Delhi: Oxford University Press.

Gandhi, M K. 1928. *Young India*. Ahmedabad: Navajivan Publishing House.

Guha, R. 1983. 'Forestry in British and Post British India: A Historical Analysis.' *Economic and Political Weekly* 18, No. 44: 1882–96 and 18, Nos. 45-46: 1940–47.

Guha, R. 1985. 'Scientific Forestry and Social Change in Uttarakhand.' *Economic and Political Weekly* 20, Nos. 45-47: 1939–52.

Guha, R. 1989. *The Unquiet Woods: Ecological Change and Peasant Resistance in Himalayas*. Delhi: Oxford University Press.

Guha, Ramachandra. 1990. 'An Early Environmental Debate: The Making of the 1878 Forest Act.' *Indian Economic and Social History Review* 27, No. 1: 65–84.

Guha, Ramchandra., and Martinez Allier, J. 1997. *Varieties of Environmentalism: Essays North and South*. Delhi: Oxford University Press.

Institute of Development Studies (IDS). 1998. 'Poverty and Social Exclusion in North and South.' *IDS Bulletin* 29, No. 1: 1-93.

International Institute for Labour Studies (IILS). 1997. *Social Exclusion and Anti-poverty Policy: A Debate*. Research Series No. 10. Geneva: International Institute for Labour Studies.

Kabeer, N. 2000. 'Social Exclusion, Poverty and Discrimination: Towards an Analytical Framework.' *IDS Bulletin* 31, No. 4: 83-97.

Kaufman, R R. 1974. 'The Patron-Client Concept and Macro-Politics: Prospects and Problems'. *Comparative Studies in Society and History* 16, No. 3: 284–308.

Loury, G C. 1999. *Social Exclusion and the Ethnic Groups: Challenges to Economics*. Paper Presented at the Annual World Bank Conference on Development Economics, Washington, D.C, April 28-30, 1999.

Michie, B H. 1981. 'The Transformation of Agrarian Patron-Client Relations: Illustrations from India.' *American Ethnologist* 8, No. 1: 21–40.

Padel, F. and S Das. 2010. *Out of This Earth: East India Adivasis and the Aluminium Cartel*. New Delhi: Orient Blackswan.

Samantara, P. 2006. *Niyamgiri Waiting for Justice*. Berhampur, Odisha: Lokshakti Abhiya, Odisha Unit.

Scott, J C. 1972. 'Patron Client Politics and Political Change in Southeast Asia.' *The American Political Science Review* 66, No. 1: 91-113.

Sen, A. 1997. 'Inequality, Unemployment and Contemporary Europe.' *International Labour Review* 136, No. 2: 155-172.

Silver, H. 1994. 'Social Exclusion and Social Solidarity: Three Paradigms'. *International Labour Review* 133, Nos. 5-6: 531-78.

Sivaramakrishnan, K. and A Agrawal. 2003. 'Regional Modernities in Stories and Practices of Development'. In *Regional Modernities: The Cultural Politics of Development in India*, edited by K Sivaramakrishnan and Arun Agrawal. New Delhi: Oxford University Press.

Stein, H F. 1984. 'A Note on Patron-Client Theory.' *Ethos* 12, No. 1: 30–36.

Veltmeyer, Henry. 1997. 'Latin America in the New World Order.' *Canadian Journal of Sociology* 22, No. 2: 207–29.

9

Dispossession for Development: Some Recent Experiences in Uttar Pradesh

Bhaskar Majumder

All the post-Second World War decolonized economies are chasing the industrialized world for 'development'. For these economies, development follows from conversion of natural resources to extend the frontier of production-cum-consumption. Specifically, it aims at lessening dependence on nature and sets the agenda of industrialization. The core of industrialization is the conscious application of advanced technologies to increasing human productivity, diminishing the limitations imposed by nature, and raising the standards of living (Magill, 1997). The origin of industrialization is located in prehistory but the fundamental changes associated with industrialization are usually derived from the Industrial Revolution in the United Kingdom (UK) that began in the late eighteenth century and subsequently spread to other countries and continents (Deane, 1984). Setting up of industries needed land. This required State intervention - land had to be acquired by the State, because such land-to-be-acquired would be large by area and its impact multiple and long-term relative to land-in-use for agricultural and residential purposes. Between 1870 and 1914, more than 50 million people had to leave Europe for US, Canada, Australia, New Zealand, South Africa, Argentina, and Brazil for resettlement after being displaced from the agricultural sector. The displacement was driven by both the push factor of 'land scarce' Europe and the pull factor of 'land abundant' Americas in particular (Nayyar, 2002). In Russia, planned industrialization after the 1917 Revolution led to millions of peasants being evicted from land and shunted into urban industries, mining, hydroelectric projects, thousands of collective farms (kolkhozy), and State farms (sovkhozy). In Japan the path of industrialization based on the post-Meiji Restoration in 1868 ended Japanese feudalism (Magill, 1997). The percentage of population working on land gradually declined not only in the UK and the US but also in Japan and China, particularly since the days of the first Industrial Revolution in the UK. Around 1,600 AD 2.76 per cent of the total land was enclosed and 50,000 persons out of a total population of around four million were evicted in the UK. In China since the 1950s around ten million people have been displaced due to hydraulic and hydroelectric projects alone (Sarkar, 2007).

Most of the post-Second World War decolonized countries accepted industrialization as an inescapable route for development shown by the British Industrial Revolution. The economic policy of the State in favour of industrialization shows not only technological advancement but also an emerging production relationship weighted in favour of the controllers of capital and technology and against manual workers based on land and hence was different from the agrarian economy that preceded it. Industrialization provides the space for the workers to get united as a working class to come out from the local economy based inertia and start realizing their own strength (Plum, 1977). In a frame of Darwinism, it breaks isolation and localization in favour of tying multiple locations by the investment-production-employment chain. In the economic advancement of India, modern industry was supposed to dissolve the hereditary divisions of labour based on the rigid caste system and thus remove the 'decisive impediments to Indian progress and Indian power'. Industrialization was seen as not only inescapable but also a step forward in breaking the 'self-sufficient inertia of the villages' (Marx, 2006).

This paper deals with the dilemma in development associated with industrialization. Any path of development will carry with it unequal consequences for people located at different layers of the society. The paper focuses on the displacement of people following acquisition of land by the State for industrialization. Land acquisition has an immediate effect of displacing people from the land that earlier provided them sustainable livelihood. We have cited a few examples of land acquisition of the recent past for industrialization in India in this paper. The role of the State as the catalyst in land acquisition is juxtaposed in the light of that ground reality ultimately to look into the safeguards by rehabilitation and resettlement of the displaced people.

The rest of the paper is structured into the following sections. In Section I, the economy of India is seen as a case of delayed industrialization. In Section II, we analyze dispossession by acquisition of agricultural land for industrialization and livelihood of people dependent on land in India. In Section III, we present the changes in the law on land acquisition in India and the role of the State. Finally, in Section IV, we propose safeguards in case land is acquired for industrialization.

I. India as a Case of Delayed Industrialization

In India, while the absolute number of population working on land increased, the percentage of population remained more or less unchanged during the post-independence sixty years. Its agriculture is characterized by a monotonically declining land-man ratio, low labour productivity measured by money value of product and declining share of agriculture in national income over time. During the early decades of planning, the Indian economy went in for setting up of capital-intensive industries remote from the final consumption point of the people living at the bottom of the economic ladder and imported technology for production of goods for the economic elite that left little scope for employment of the people who could have been released from agriculture. Thus, the capital accumulation-led industrialization via release of surplus labourers from agriculture for absorption in industry did not work. In addition to being attached to land, the inherited skills of the workers which are not much relevant to industries, prolonged the limited role of industries for employment of labourers released from land. This led to delayed industrialization in India since other countries were in no mood to wait for India to catch up.

Development became production-centred by transformation of natural resources following collective collection-cum-consumption by human beings who have been living as natural members of the world since pre-historic times. In the early stages of human civilization nature provided enough resources to fulfil the basic needs of life. Later applied Darwinism led to discontinuation of collection as the dominant mode of fulfilling needs. The forest-based living did not resist the emerging agricultural mode of living, and subsequent development of agro-industries. Since the scope for agriculture is limited by the size of land and its uses by type and frequency, the question arose about setting up of industries by location and time. As opposed to limited flexibility in locating agricultural practices, an industrial set up has higher flexibility by its location and change. Generally industrialization is backed by the availability of raw materials, market size-cum-access, transport and communication, availability of physical infrastructure, own industry concentration or clusters of firms for externality advantages and inter-industry linkages. Annihilation of agricultural land and agriculturists' displacement are natural corollaries.

With the urban boundaries expanding to grab rural areas that circumscribe cities, agricultural land shrinks by area. This may lead to reduction in total agricultural output because of shrinkage in total cultivable land unless compensated by intensive farming. For countries like India that are delayed in industrialization, there is now limited non-cultivated cultivable land. This may invite imbalances between agriculture and industry, because unless agriculture is developed enough to ensure food self-sufficiency, industry may fail to develop on a sustained basis. This is in addition to the home market constraint —because of inadequate expansion of rural market for industrial goods—that industries in India are subjected to (Majumder,

1989). The dual constraints that India faces in the context of land acquisition for industrialization are the impossibility to rely on import of food grains as a dependable avenue to feed more than 1000 million people at the beginning of the twenty-first century and the limited possibility to rely on export of industrial goods.

II. Dispossession by Acquisition of Agricultural Land for Industrialization in India

Late starting countries like India on the trajectory of industrialization relative to the path traversed by the countries called industrialized today face several economic problems due to the falling carrying capacity of land. The demographic condition in India in 1951 showed a size of population more than that of any country in the world, excepting China, in time fifty years ahead of 1951. The land-man ratio in India is declining fast because of, apart from the natural increase in population, service sector-led urbanization for both private and public purposes and conversion of agricultural land for non-agricultural purposes. People settled in the rural regions have a history of moving out because of various push and pull factors. Apart from the natural shift of agricultural land to non-agricultural purposes, there is the State-sponsored shift empowered by the 1894 Land Acquisition Act formulated and implemented during the colonial rule. This Act empowers the State Government to acquire any land from private hands for public purposes decided by the State (GOI, The Land Acquisition Act, 1894). Development, thus, has a tendency to displace the people at the bottom from the trajectory of development.

Acquisition of agricultural land for industrial purposes in India is not new. Since independence, the State has been executing a 'top down' approach in development by setting up large industries and projects like mines, dams, ports, plants and expansion of road and rail network, each of which displaced people. Heavy industrialization was at the core of India's planned development and hence large areas had to be acquired. Looking at the scenario by States in India, the State of Odisha used 40,000 hectares of land for industry between 1951 and 1995. The State of West Bengal used two million hectares of land between 1947 and 2000 for industry. The private corporate sector, often the Transnational Corporations, have been targeting mining land and hills in the States of Odisha, Jharkhand, and Chhattisgarh in India. For example, Posco, the world's fourth largest South Korean steel company, signed an MOU with the Government of Odisha in 2005 to set up a plant near Paradip Port in Odisha's Jagatsinghpur district that would produce 12 million tonnes of steel per annum. The project cost is estimated at $12 billion (Rs. 55,200 crore). The Government of Odisha on July 09, 2010 announced a Rs. 70 crore rehabilitation package for the 3,000 people who will be displaced by land acquisition (*Hindustan Times*, Lucknow, July 10, 2010). Mostly the mineral-rich and Government land-abundant less industrialized States are being targeted for acquisition of land. Vedanta Aluminium's $1.7 billion proposal to mine bauxite in the Niyamgiri Hills in Odisha that is destined to oust the local tribal community violated forest and environment laws, as reported by the National Advisory Council (*The Hindu*, August 24, 2010, p. 1). Construction of dams to feed drought-prone areas, of which the Narmada Dam Project is notoriously known for the disputes around the Narmada River that flows into the Arabian Sea after passing through the States of MP, Gujarat, and Maharashtra, led to displacement of people. The acquisition is not only for public sector units but also for private players like Reliance, ESSAR, and Jaypee for both power generation and mining that inescapably displace people (Sharma and Singh, 2009).

Since independence, around sixty million persons have been victims of displacement in India (Fernandes, 2007). Of this, development projects like dams and canals displaced 70.9 per cent up to 1989. For industrial set-ups it was 6.4 per cent. Overall 25.5 per cent of the displaced people could be rehabilitated that is well distributed by projects (Fernandes, Das and Rao, 1989). Displacement by declaration and payment of money as compensation does not make it voluntary. This is for many reasons. One is that the displaceable people rooted at the bottommost layer of the economic ladder by monetary parameters do not understand the intricacies of industrialization. The other is that many of them do not have land rights on paper. They are neither made part of the decision-making processes ex-ante nor do they have the capacity to negotiate vis-a-vis the section having the power to manoeuvre. These displaceable people are the consequence of development —earlier thought of as the cause of underdevelopment.

Land was never thought to be a factor of production in industry, either because land was abundant in supply relative to what was required or because the required land area was insignificant relative to the available land area of any particular economy. The relatively less area required for setting up of industries was also because of its high-tech nature that moves away from dependence on land by area. But after a point, land claims more scarcity-value because of, among others, the requirement for setting up or extension of industries. This takes two faces—first, near the market-cum-urban areas, and second, by selection of mining areas, forests and hills. The immediate consequence is similar—the displacement of the people living in the villages near the urban areas, and the displacement of the people living in the forests and hills remote from the urban areas. The remote consequence remains dependent on the location of rehabilitation and resettlement.

Land acquisition actually implies acquisition of a physical area that covers cultivable soil area, plus plantations, water bodies, residential buildings, animal sheds and many other assets that 'land by area and volume' carry. More than being a means of production, land is a base of livelihood that provides the space for self-employment and allied activities. Moreover, for the people rooted in the villages in India, land has cultural value immeasurable by economic parameters.

The nature of displacement may be exogenous due to wars, partitions, droughts, floods, landslides, cyclones, and earthquakes. What we are concerned with is displacement for endogenous reasons like land acquisition by the State for industrialization. The proximity to market-cum-physical infrastructure for location of industries means people settled by housing and land-based occupations are displaced. While landowners give up land in the process of acquisition by the State, landless people are deprived twice, once by not getting the opportunity to work on land as agricultural labourers and the other by not being eligible for compensation. Obviously, the landless people dependent mainly on Common Property Resources (CPRs) are outside the purview of compensation of any type. One of the major reasons why people remain rooted in rural region in India is CPRs for livelihood. Access to and uses of CPRs in India are delinked from 'property rights' under capitalism. While use-value of CPRs remains unpaid by any individual because of its non-marketability and non-excludability, the individual fails to be compensated for loss of access to CPRs following land acquisition.

The immediate victims in global technological advancement are the local people living at the bottom of the socio-economic ladder. These people continue to practise spatial socially inherited caste-cum-gender division of labour that fails to break the low productivity-cum-small scale trap. These people remain displaceable and are displaced by execution of development projects which are usually State-sponsored and characterized by high capital-intensity and high capital-output ratio. Development thus occurs by capital accumulation for A and dispossession of physical means of production for B. In the context of land acquisition, following Section 38A, Land Acquisition Act 1894, land can be acquired for a private limited company for the purposes of developing dwelling houses for its workers and for the provision of related facilities (Lobo and Kumar, 2009). The workers in the payroll of the industry are not generally the local workers earlier engaged in agriculture and related activities displaced by land acquisition but the workers drawn from a distance. As a consequence of long-term stagnation understood as stability at the bottommost level of the economy, B fails to develop the capacity to be a partner in the decision-making processes of development projects planned by A. This failure gets prolonged for the multiple boundaries erected against B by obstructive education, power language (English by colonial inheritance), caste, community, height-weight-colour of the person, gender, access to institutions, and the domain of privileges. The additional factors that prolong the vulnerability of B are ignorance, immobility and tradition-custom-belief. B remains confined to a traditional society as fait accompli. As a corollary, B fails to foresee changes. In the same process often B stands for anti-development or symbolizes anti-change. What B fails to communicate is an unequal impact of development planning executed by the State that goes decidedly against it; it benefits the already privileged A by the power of the purse, education and free walk on the corridors of power; it goes against the B group people who are rooted, tradition-bound, and localized. Development (accumulation) of A and displacement (dispossession) of B go together.

We cite here three examples of actual and attempted land acquisition in India, two for National Thermal Power Corporation (NTPC) representing the public sector and one for Reliance Energy Limited in the private sector, all for generation of electricity.

Example I: Meja, District Allahabad, UP: A Case of Completed Acquisition

In the power sector, the NTPC Ltd. and Uttar Pradesh Rajya Vidyut Nigam Ltd. (UPRVUNL) on November 22, 2007 signed a Memorandum of Understanding (MoU) to set up a thermal power plant of 1,320 MW at Kohrarghat of Meja Tehsil in Allahabad District of East UP. The Government of UP acquired a total land area of 2,500 acres for setting up the plant covering seven villages, namely, Kohrar, Bhagdeva, Esauta, Mai Khurd, Salaiya Kala, Salaiya Khurd, and Patai Dandi that reportedly affected the livelihood of 469 settled households. The displacement had an immediate adverse impact on community support-cum-social integration by loss of cultivable land, houses, wells, common grazing land, fruit trees and timber trees. This adversely affected agricultural output and food security (self-production lost) and security of domestic animals. Loss of CPR led to loss of fodder, and fuel. The worst hit were the landless stone quarry workers living at the bottom of the social hierarchy like the Nishads, Mushahars, Kols, Chamars, Pasis, Dhaikars, Domars, Pals, and Muslims, who had no entitlement for compensation post-loss of only source of livelihood.

Most of the displaced persons in this case received compensation. The major reasons for pending or delayed payment of compensations were court cases, 'speed money' asked for by the Land Reforms Officer (Lekhpal), disputes related to canals, outstanding bank loans of the displaced persons, errors in names written on the bank cheque book, objections raised by the displaced against the compensation money offered, disputes between Treasury and Senior Land Reforms Officer (SLRO), official apathy, family disputes, and instances of expiry of validity by date shown on the bank cheque book. The loss of Common Property Resources (CPRs) remains unaddressed perhaps because it is owned by no single individual.

Most of the project-affected households were rehabilitated by caste-cluster type housing. For example, the Mallahs (thirty-five fishermen households) along with a few Mushahars have been rehabilitated at Nai Basti in Jhariyahi at an altitude of around 50 ft. above normal road-level, from their earlier settlement at Amhwa at Mai Khurd. The Jadavs (cattle rearing community) have been rehabilitated at Nai Basti, Jadav Nagar, Koyaltara having a dry canal. Both the caste-communities demanded rehabilitation at a safe distance from Brahmins and Thakurs, the two most dominant castes by local power structure in Uttar Pradesh. However, the approach road to new location has remained non-motorable. No provision has been made for rehabilitation of domestic animals in the new settlement for Mallahas for absence of animal sheds and the absence of grazing land. The Mallahas have got two functioning hand pumps for potable water. The original inhabitants (Thakurs) at the location of rehabilitation of Mallahs initially expressed hostility to the resettlement of displaced persons, but following the intervention of police, harmony has been restored. Access to elementary education has remained undisturbed in the new location because of the proximity to the same school where the children had been enrolled earlier before displacement. The resettled women face problems in absence of proper public space for sanitation. The households displaced by land acquisition expect to be employed by the MUNPL.

Example II: Dadri, Ghaziabad District, UP: A Case of Aborted Acquisition

To set up a 3500 MW gas-based power plant with an estimated project cost of Rs. 25,000 cr. in Dadri region in Ghaziabad district, Hapur tehsil, in western UP, the Government of Uttar Pradesh (UP) acquired about 1,011 hectares of land in 2004 in seven villages for Reliance Energy Generation Ltd. (REGL). The villages were Dehra, Jadopur, Bajhera Khurd, Kakrana, and Dhaulana. The other two affected villages, namely, Nandlalpur and Baharmandpur, were found to be uninhabited. Most of the land acquired was fertile under multi-cropping used for agricultural purposes. Pasture or common grazing land was not acquired. The major assets covered in land acquisition were canals, ponds and wells. On July13, 2007 the GOI gave environmental clearance to the project.

Land acquisition in Dadri was estimated to have led to displacement of over 6,000 families. The rate of compensation was fixed at Rs. 150 per sq. yard that was more than the market rate prevailing there before land acquisition. The market rate immediately after land acquisition was Rs. 300 at the minimum and Rs. 400 at the maximum. The loss to the cultivators for surrendering product value per year was enormous while revenue loss on account of land rent was marginal (Majumder, 2007). The rate of compensation offered was twelve times the output value calculated at current price.

The farmers formed an association called Maharana Pratap Sangram Sangharsh Samiti to protest against the acquisition and claimed a compensation of Rs. 500 per sq metre. They also staged a demonstration in front of the Collector's Office in August 2004. On January 3, 2006 the farmers expressed their dissent against the rate of compensation. On December 30, 2006 Reliance Energy Ltd. decided to start the construction work by using a JCB machine to dig the fields of Sripal Singh in Jadopur village. The farmers protested against it but the administration ignored the protest and applied the 'Urgency Clause' of 1894 LA Act. Following the protests against low rate of compensation, and based on the magnitude of loss of fertile agricultural land, the Allahabad High Court Division Bench on December 4, 2009, cancelled the acquisition of land of 2,500 acres, quashing urgency powers to acquire land exercised by the-then Government. It passed an order acting on writ petitions filed by the farmers and the former Prime Minister, V P Singh, claiming that the petitioners were forced to sign on documents and accept the meagre compensation offered by the Collector. The Court said that the farmers had the option to refund the compensation received.

Example III: Tanda, District Ambedkar Nagar, UP: A Case of People's Struggle

Set up in 1980-81 by the UP State Electricity Board (UPSEB) under the Government of UP, the power plant was transferred on January 15, 2000 to NTPC Ltd. under the Government of India with a capacity of 440 MW. The geographic area of the plant on the banks of Sarayu River has remained the same since it was set up. In 2009, after 9 years of its transfer of ownership, the NTPC, Tanda thought of its expansion by acquisition of land from adjoining nine villages, namely, Samariya, Husainpur Sudhana, Salarpur Rajpur, Keshopur Pachpokhra, Hasimpur, Sarifpur, Kakrahi, Ashopur, and Ladanpur. The argument for acquisition of adjoining land was based on capacity expansion-cum-cost-minimization for the NTPC, Tanda. The locally settled people could hardly cope up with the fact that after seventeen long years, NTPC would wake up for capacity expansion of the plant by land annexation. The time-span was long enough to make settled people understand that no more land was going to be acquired and hence made them go ahead with constructing pucca residential houses. The people identified two decades ago, settled in the selected villages for acquisition and after they had been displaced elsewhere earlier also. That means they are facing the threat of repetitive displacement in different locations. Initially, the small and marginal farmers having no productive assets and those whose cultivable land was being adversely affected by dumping of fly ash by the power plant expressed their willingness to give up land in exchange of compensation. Some of the households with double settlements, housing at a long distance from the identified land to be acquired and socially oppressed households expressed willingness to give up land. Representatives of Gram Panchayats kept silent on the issue. Subsequently, following the agitation against land acquisition in Agra-Mathura region in West UP for construction of Expressway and its media coverage led to mass mobilization of affected people against land acquisition. The potential victims by mid-2010 became adamant not to give up land. An organization, namely, 'Kisan Mazdoor Sava Samity' came into action against land acquisition in the targeted villages. There is virtual curfew declared by the displaceable people ('Janta Curfew' displayed on banners at the entry point on the villages from the main road) in some of the targeted villages where the NTPC officials and the State Authorities feel compelled to abstain from visiting the villages physically. The State is, however, in the process of negotiating the rate of compensation and has already applied its 'Urgency Clause' through a notification to acquire land. The rate of compensation-to-be-fixed is being influenced by the demonstration effect from recent land acquisition-cum-compensation from affluent regions like NOIDA region in UP (Source: Informal conversation with district officials and local people).

Such displacements, as and when they occur, will have unwelcome impacts on social relations, will impose social Darwinism by the State, empower industrial capitalists by enhancing their unhindered access to natural resources, convert marginal and small landowners into manual labour-based wage workers (supposedly unfit for industrial jobs), expand labour size in informal sector, impose forced migration to urban areas, and cause slumization. Fixing and paying cash as compensation to the displaced is a poor substitute for life-saving land for the land-dependent people. Urban-type resettlement does not help the villagers because the domestic animals need common space (CPRs) for grazing. Since village space is horizontal while urban space is vertical, the difference explained by population density, urbanization does not help the people accustomed to the village mode of living of the recent past. In absence of re-creation of similar village life elsewhere by rehabilitation of the displaced, the villagers feel robbed off their earlier livelihood. Nearby rehabilitation could be the solution but not bankable because of unanticipated further expansion of the industrial plant. The once displaced people remain vulnerable by 'future' unanticipated displacement.

In case of land acquisition in Meja, the social shock was minimal because of the barren nature of land given up, the low population density and the revealed aspiration of the PAPs to get physical infrastructure like concrete roads and electricity, and gain from the possibility of being employed in industry. In case of Dadri, the PAPs initially failed to understand the gravity of the situation, and once understood took support from polity and subsequently the judiciary to avoid giving up land. In case of Tanda, the protest against displacement is on. In Meja there was no protest organization unlike in Dadri and Tanda. In Meja and Dadri it was a new initiative for setting up of the plant, while in Tanda it was for extension of an already set up plant. Each situation has a common cause but the manifestations are different by the types of protests, and it is difficult to predict the spatial consequences of State action for land acquisition.

In the power structure, industry is well ahead of agriculture. The State considers agriculture as a source of surplus to feed industry by both food and intermediate inputs. Hence, the State does not hesitate to acquire land for industrial purposes that show 'forward' movement in history. Nowhere in history has land used for industrial purposes been acquired for agricultural purposes because the accepted trajectory is conversion of rural region into urban region, conversion of agriculture into industry, hiking the economy above subsistence level, and shifting from nature-dependence to man-dependence.

III. Changes in Law on Land Acquisition in India: Role of the State

Article 31 Section A of the Constitution of India (Compulsory Acquisition of Property) empowers the State to acquire land based on payment of compensation at a rate which shall not be less than the market value prevailing (The Constitution of India, p. 14). Nearly after a century, the first Land Acquisition Act 1894 was comprehensively amended in 1984. The conference of the revenue secretaries of States followed in July 1989 that endorsed the major provisions of the 1984 Amendment. The Draft National Policy for Rehabilitation of Persons (1996) of the Ministry of Rural Development, GOI, acknowledged that cash compensation was not an acceptable proposition for most of the tribal people. The 1996 Policy observed that 'majority of our mineral resources, including coal, iron ore, and manganese reserves are located in the remote and backward regions mostly inhabited by tribals (GOI, 1996). While tribals constitute 8.08 per cent of India's population, they constitute more than 40.0 per cent of the project affected population; another 22 per cent of the PAPs are dalits, and the rest, including the above, are rural poor (Lobo and Kumar, 2009). After a decade, the GOI approved the National Policy on Rehabilitation and Resettlement, 2007, replacing the earlier National Policy on Resettlement and Rehabilitation for Project Affected Families, 2003 (Chakrabarty and Dhar, 2010).

The Government of India introduced The Land Acquisition (Amendment) Bill, 2007 in the Lok Sabha (Lower House of Indian Parliament) on November 30, 2007 duly signed by the Minister of Rural Development, Sri Raghuvansh Prasad Singh, that was a Bill 'further to amend the Land Acquisition Act, 1894' (Source: Bill No. 97 of 2007, Lok Sabha, website). The Bill 2007 pledged to make the process of land acquisition transparent through Notification in the Official Gazette and in two daily newspapers circulating in that locality. The 2007 Bill stated that the appropriate Government shall, for the purpose of providing speedy disposal of disputes relating to land acquisition, set up, by notification in the Official Gazette, the Land Acquisition Compensation Disputes Settlement Authority. The Bill 2007 mentioned that the Collector of the concerned District, before acquisition ascertain the intended land use and take into account the value of the land of the intended category in the adjoining areas, for the purpose of determination of the market value of the land being acquired. The determination of market value of land being acquired is pledged to include 'the market value of the buildings and other immovable property or assets attached to the land or building which are to be acquired', 'the value of trees and plants', 'the value of the standing crops damaged during the process of land acquisition proceedings'. The Collector has to ensure that physical possession of the land is taken over and the amount of compensation is paid within a period of sixty days commencing from the date of the award.

The Bill 2007 was passed and published on September 27, 2013, called 'The Right to Fair Compensation and Transparency in Land Acquisition, Rehabilitation and Resettlement Act, 2013' that came into force from January 1, 2014.

The Act 2013 acknowledged that the acquisition of land would lead to displacement of people, deprive them of their livelihood and shelter, restrict their access to their traditional resource base, and uproot them from their socio-cultural environment. Land acquisition would have traumatic psychological and socio-cultural consequences for the affected people, which call for protecting their rights, including those of the weaker sections of society, particularly tribals, and tenants. Rehabilitation and resettlement of the persons and families affected by involuntary acquisition of private land and immovable property was considered in the Act to be of paramount importance. Following the Act 2013, 'public purpose' restricts 'the scope of land acquisition under the Act to provision of land for strategic purposes relating to naval, military and air force works or any other work vital to the State, and for infrastructure projects like generation, transmission or supply of electricity, construction of roads, highways, bridges, airports, ports, rail systems or mining activities, water supply project, irrigation project, sanitation and sewerage system, any other public facility as may be notified in this regard by the Central Government in the Official Gazette' where the benefits accrue to the general public. The expression 'person interested' in the principal Act (1894) is proposed to be expanded in the new Act (2013) 'to include tribals and other traditional forest dwellers, who have lost any traditional rights recognized under the Scheduled Tribes and Other Traditional Forest Dwellers (Recognition of Forest Rights) Act, 2006 and expanded to include 'persons having tenancy rights' under the relevant State laws.

The Act 2013 pledged to make the process of land acquisition transparent through a Notification in the Official Gazette and two daily newspapers circulating in that locality. The 2013 Act stated that the appropriate Government shall, for the purpose of providing speedy disposal of disputes relating to land acquisition, set up, by notification in the Official Gazette, the Land Acquisition, Compensation Rehabilitation and Resettlement Settlement Authority. The Act 2013 mentioned that the Collector of the concerned District, before acquisition ascertain the intended land use and take into account the value of the land of the intended category in the adjoining areas, for the purpose of determination of the market value of the land being acquired.

State of UP: Changes in Land Acquisition Policy

On April 1, 1976 the UP Industrial Area Development Act came into force. Under this Act, the State Government is empowered to 'declare' the industrial development area; Section 3 empowers the Government to constitute an authority by a notification; the Act empowers the authority to acquire the land by direct purchase or through State under the provisions of the 1894 Land Acquisition Act. Under Section 7 of the said Act, the authority is empowered to allot its properties, by way of lease or otherwise, on such terms and conditions as it may deem fit (Nand Kishore Gupta and Others vs. State of UP and Others, Civil Appeal No. 7468 of 2010). Because of litigations in the courts of law and public outcry, on September 3, 2010 the Government of UP declared its Land Acquisition Policy that announced provisions for various facilities for farmers at the time of acquisition of their land:

- Payment of a lump sum, which is at present Rs. 1,85,000 equivalent to the daily agricultural wages over a period of five years, to each of the families of farmers being rendered landless because of land acquisition by the UP Government.
- Under the new policy, each farmer whose land is to be acquired shall receive an annuity of Rs. 20,000 per acre per year for 33 years in addition to the compensation amount.

- Assured increase at the rate of Rs. 600 per acre per annum on the Annuity of Rs. 20,000 per acre per annum, payable every year in the month of July.
- In the case of a farmer unwilling of availing the Annuity, he/she shall be given a lump sum Rehabilitation Grant at the rate of Rs. 2,40,000 per acre.
- In the event of land acquisition for a company, the farmer shall have the option of a share of the company equivalent to 25 per cent of the lump sum rehabilitation grant payable to him.
- If land is being acquired under any 'Land Development Scheme', the affected farmers shall be allotted 7 per cent of the acquired land for residential purposes. The issued plot shall have a minimum land area of 120 sq. meters and maximum area limit shall be set by the related Authority.
- One member from each of the families to be rendered landless completely, due to land acquisition under the 'and for development' project, will be provided with employment, consistent with his/her qualification, in the concessionaire company.
- Provision of 17.5 per cent reservation in the allotment of plots, on the acquired land to the affected farmers, in the event of any land acquisition by the development authority for its housing schemes.
- Land acquisition shall be done under the 'Karar Niyamavali' (Press Information Bureau, Information & Public Relations Department, Government of UP; *Hindustan Times*, Lucknow, 11 September 2010).

A Critique (Of State Determinism)

The catalyst in land acquisition is the State in India. The 'person interested' in the context of land acquisition by the State includes all those going to be affected by land acquisition of a particular zone. De facto, the 'person interested' category would cover the tribals, the original settlers on land who generally do not possess any land records (even many of them being not at all aware of any such needed records), the small and marginal farmers, the tenants and sharecroppers, and the agricultural wage-workers (settled in the locality and migrants). These 'interested' persons generally do not express their interests. While the migrant agricultural workers living on the bottommost plank are disempowered by the new Bill by not being allowed to ask the District Collector for payment of any compensation when his employer's plot of land is lost by acquisition for purposes other than agriculture, the employer by being a small farmer is disempowered by being on the queue to receive compensation, the time distance between acquisition and compensation being sixty days. It is beyond the capacity of tribals and dalits (socio-economically downtrodden in Indian society), unless politically mobilized, to raise voice for a compensation equal to 30 per cent mark up of prevailing market rate. The small and marginal farmers may feel shaky to move the courts and remain content with whatever cash compensation they are offered. Judiciary by its cobweb nature may itself be a trap for them. Fear factor works for the holders of petty property lest it is also lost in the process of bargaining and negotiating with the administrative authority. 'Public purpose' incorporated and interpreted by the State either gets camouflaged by 'silence of the displaced' or manifests itself in public response to land acquisition by protest. While 'silence' ensures easy implementation of the project by fixing the rate of money compensation from the player it is offered to, protest is not prolonged in the absence of political mobilization. The trade-off between the interests of the lightweight large public and the heavyweight few elite is weighted in favour of the latter.

For launching projects in cities, the State aims for vertical measures like constructing flyovers for surface transport, tunnels underground for metro rail and tube rail so that buildings and other assets possessed by the urban civil society, both public and private, are not affected; however, when it comes to rural areas, the State targets horizontal expansion by acquisition of private and collective cultivable land and hence eviction of vulnerable people. It is arguable that the State historically followed similar measures for conversion of rural areas into urban areas in India and abroad. All the areas identified as urban today are conversions of rural areas. But in the twenty-first century the role of civil society, by public response, is sharply different from earlier centuries by size and density of population, economic engagement under compulsions, democracy and the voice of people. The extent of displacement is more acute today because of land-scarcity relative to land area required for rehabilitation. The question of 'prior informed consent' thus becomes relevant now which might have been not relevant earlier. The State takes pre-emptive measures by 'inclusion' in the safety net of social welfare of those who the State took initiatives to throw out of the development trajectory. Since high growth via industrialization is urgent for operationalization of the trickle down mechanism, the State first evicts people from land by its acquisition, makes them expendable and then catches them in the safety net. The objects caught in the net are never asked if they had the right to self-determination in the development map. The map is drawn and guarded by the State.

While the inherited skills of the people settled in land-based occupations become irrelevant for industrial employment, the very acquisition of land for industrialization kills the inherited skills or indigenous knowledge of the displaceable people. These people accept their vulnerability in a new situation imposed on them by losing their self-esteem. The local village economy does not take a national shape by market-technology linkages. In parallel, technological revolution requires a large space to operate which industries provide by 'flow input flow output' technology. The harbingers of the new situation are the controllers of capital, the safety of that capital ensured by the State.

It takes more than a generation for households to find the space to get settled by developing social relations. These inter-generational social relations are destroyed by land acquisition. Such plots of land are often under multi-cropping. By acquiring such fertile land, the development strategy of the State imposes 'rural displacement-led urban slumization'. Extension of the urban boundary by such acquisition subsidizes the better off by assured supply of cheap labour from the 'newly displaced' villagers converted to urban slum dwellers. Both land and necessary labour thus are carved out by one single step of land acquisition for the industry-cum-urban economy.

In case of Nand Kishore Gupta & Others vs State of UP and Others (Writ Petition No. 31314 of 2009), the High Court, in the judgment dated November 30, 2009 took the view that 'the scales of justice must tilt towards the right to development of the millions who will be benefited from the road and the development of the area, as against the human rights of thirty-five petitioners therein, whose main complaint was that they were not heard before the declaration under Section 6 of the Act (Nand Kishore Gupta and Others vs State of UP and Others, Civil Appeal No. 7468 of 2010). In the interest of development, thus, land acquisition from villages is an accepted proposition; living in villages and livelihood by cultivation is a losing proposition. The calculated trade off between development of the majority and human rights of the minority is really baffling. The confusion perhaps is solved by the observation that the concern of the State as the governing entity and the concern of the governed society are not necessarily synonymous. The State represents the ideology of the dominant political society and camouflages it by the declaration of a 'democratic republic'. The State remains strong internally by imposition of laws it formulates for non-or-restricted access of the original settlers in forests and on land who are the initial insiders to the resources. The State is strengthened as a protector of forests and land. On the other hand, the State has a tendency to allow private capital to extract and convert natural resources, including land, into consumable goods for the mainstream. The sections that are considered not-in-the-mainstream at present constituted the original stream in the past. These constituents of the original stream were the tribals and the dalits who distanced themselves from the institution of private property understood by 'excludability'. The sections are now evicted who protected these resources as the life-support system since the pre-historic times not backed by any State laws. By acquisition of land, collective social ownership-cum-use is surrendered – what gets supreme is the State authority.

Land carries a dual meaning by uses by the people. Land essentially has a precautionary value as opposed to immediate exchange value to its holders. For the State, land is a resource for conversion into gross domestic product. In the view of the affected people, it is displacement and loss of livelihood. The ultimate decision-maker is the State that calculates the costs and benefits of land acquisition. The State is the ultimate protector of the citizens. Hence, forced injustice is ruled out from the action-plan of the State.

Even if the outcome of the industrialization initiatives by the State is positive by accelerating growth in GDP, the time span between displacement and the final GDP outcome is long and displacement is often repetitive to lead to the misery of many. Stagnation or decline of the village economy in India is also put forward as an argument for the dispossession of the village income-poor (Bannerjee-Guha, 2010). It is, however, difficult to understand how dispossession of the income-poor in the village economy of India can be seen as a panacea for lifting the poor above poverty or changing the economy of village India. Misery of one section of the society cannot be compensated by the affluence of the other section. To the contrary – the affluence of one section is because it is extracted from the misery of the other section in society.

The fact is that State is not the owner of natural resources. State can at best be the custodian of natural resources that belong to people. State as an institution is itself accountable to the nation, the latter accepting the State as a political institution. The State can show the guiding principles of how the resources are to be conserved by optimal use and if needed for future by non-use at present. The State has no reason to be in a hurry to allow extraction of all natural resources now to convert into GDP-based growth. In fact, non-exhausting physical resources indicate the base of sustaining growth.

IV. Safeguards in Land Acquisition for Industrialization

We offer the following safeguards in land acquisition for industrialization in India:

- The farmers whose self-consumption is more than 50.0

per cent of self-production of foodgrains should be exempted from giving up land under distress; otherwise such farmers may face the compulsion to become net buyers of foodgrains at a subsequent price higher than the initial sale price.

- The target for land acquisition by the State has to be the absentee landlords, the landowners with 'distress-free' double settlements and the big landowners. The land that remains idle as estate and *'benami'* should be acquired.

- The State has to select barren land far from human settlements for acquisition for industrialization.

- There has to be pre-project participation of people of the going-to-be affected zone as equal partners in the decision-making processes in 'public interest'.

- Even if land-dependent people give consent to give up land, it is to be examined by an autonomous body if the future of the nation will be endangered by deforestation, diminishing water table, emission of gas and other health hazards. It is also to be examined if the rooted people gave consent out of fear and political pressure or for immediate urgency to get lumpsum amounts of money as compensation.

- The real resources of a country are land, rivers, mines, forests, the coastal belt, and above all the people. A national 'Resource Protection Policy' has to be formulated by the State to preserve these resources.

- Paying one-time money compensation is no solution for the people who live with land, domestic animals, water, hills, and forests. The people unsettled in the rural region by land acquisition have to be materially rehabilitated within a reasonable radius through employment programmes.

- CPRs lost have to be re-created at the site of rehabilitation.

- There has to be national Land Census on a regular basis. All land records have to be computerized and put on websites for the public.

- There has to be a Land Rights Commission (LRC) to work as a vigilante over the activities of the Government so far as land market is concerned.
- The corporate sector as the beneficiary of land acquisition has to shoulder Corporate Social Responsibility (CSR) by adoption of one or a cluster of rehabilitation zones.
- The compensation has to cover land price post-acquisition plus the cost of surrendering domestic animals and other productive assets plus the cost for surrendered opportunities to have access to common spaces (CPR) plus the cost for security loss.
- At least 50 per cent of India's total non-water non-forest surface area has to remain reserved for agriculture for production of food and cash crops. A national policy for Protected Agricultural Zone (PAZ) needs to be formulated in this regard.

For the persons who are displaced by land acquisition, the Government should in a time-bound manner,

- ensure food security by provision of BPL cards to the displaced families,
- ensure re-schooling of children, in case the rehabilitation site is more than two km. away from the location of displacement,
- open up formal and informal vocational institutions at the resettlement site for the displaced, or alternatively, arrange entry of eligible youth from the displaced families in nearby vocational institutions at zero cost,
- develop physical infrastructure like motorable link roads in a reasonable time-span at the rehabilitation zone,
- develop co-operatives for the displaced potential entrepreneurs for credit with no property mortgage,
- provide low-cost rural housing along with animal sheds to the displaced at the resettlement site,
- promote resources for repetitive, durable and multiple uses for development of agro-industries in the resettlement zone, and

- ensure social security, particularly of displaced women, in the new location.

Overall, in addition to a National Policy on Land Acquisition by prior provision of R&R, there has to be regional planning in advance for industrialization.

Acknowledgement

I thank M G Gupta, Tinku Paul, G N Jha, S Jaiswal, and A Singh for the field work. The author is indebted to the anonymous referee on the article for his valuable comments. The usual disclaimer applies.

REFERENCES

Bannerjee-Guha, Swapna. 2010. 'Revisiting Accumulation by Dispossession: Neoliberalizing Mumbai.' In *Accumulation by Dispossession*, edited by S Bannerjee-Guha. New Delhi: Sage Publications.

Chakrabarti, Anjan. and Dhar, Anup. 2010. *Dislocation and Resettlement in Development, From Third World to the World of the Third.* London and New York: Routledge.

Constitution of India. 1982. As Amended up to the Constitution (45th Amendment) Act. Central Law Agency, Allahabad.

Deane, Phyllis. 1984. *The First Industrial Revolution.* UK: Cambridge University Press.

Fernandes, W. 2007. 'Singur and the Displacement Scenario.' *Economic and Political Weekly* 42, No. 3: 203-06.

Fernandes, W., J C Das. and S Rao. 1989. *Displacement and Rehabilitation – An Estimate of Extent and Prospects.* New Delhi: Indian Social Institute.

GOI, *Forest (Conservation) Act, 1980 (with amendments made in 1988).* Ministry of Environment and Forest. Government of India, New Delhi.

GOI, *The Land Acquisition Act, 1894 (As amended up to 1985).* Ministry of Law and Justice. Government of India, New Delhi.

GOI, Ministry of Rural Development, 1996, Draft National Policy for Rehabilitation of Persons, New Delhi. (Cited in *Economic & Political Weekly* 31, No. 24: 1541-1545).

Hindustan Times. 2010. July 10, 12 and September 11. Lucknow, India.

Lobo, Lancy. and S Kumar. 2009. *Land Acquisition, Displacement and Resettlement in Gujarat, 1947-2004.* New Delhi: Sage Publications.

Lok Sabha, *The Land Acquisition (Amendment) Bill, 2007 (Bill No. 97 of 2007)*. Government of India, New Delhi.

Magill, F N, ed. 1997. *International Encyclopaedia of Economics*. Vol. I and II. London.

Majumder, Bhaskar. 1989. *Economic Planning and Industrial Growth in India, 1951-1981: Selected Internal and External Issues and Options*. DPhil Thesis, University of Calcutta, Calcutta.

Majumder, Bhaskar. 2007. *Development Hydra, Two Cases of Forced Industrialization in India*. Mimeo. Allahabad, India: G B Pant Social Science Institute.

Marx, Karl. 2006. 'The Future Results of the British Rule in India.' In *Globalization and Violence*, edited by P James and D Phillip. London: Sage Publications.

Nayyar, Deepak. 2002. 'Cross-border Movements of People.' In *Governing Globalization, Issues and Institutions*, edited by D Nayyar. New Delhi: Oxford University Press.

Plum, Warner. 1977. *Industrialization and Mass Poverty: Points from two Centuries of Debate* (Translated from the German by Lux Furtmuller). Friedrich-Ebert-Stiftung, Bonn, Federal Republic of Germany.

Press Information Bureau, Information and Public Relations Department, Government of Uttar Pradesh.

Reports of National Commission on Labour (2002-1991-1967). 2003. New Delhi: Academic Foundation.

Sarkar, Abhirup. 2007. 'Development and Displacement, Land Acquisition in West Bengal.' *Economic and Political Weekly* 42, No. 16: 1435-42.

Sharma, R N. and S R Singh. 2009. 'Displacement in Singrauli Region: Entitlements and Rehabilitation.' *Economic and Political Weekly* 44, No. 51: 62-69.

Supreme Court of India Judgment. 2010. Civil Appeal No. 7468 of 2010 (Nand Kishore Gupta and Others vs. State of UP and Others). Supreme Court of India.

World Commission on Dams. 2000. *Dams and Development, A New Framework for Decision-Making*. London: Earthscan Publications Limited.

10

Displacement of Tribal People in the Name of Development: A Case Study of Indira Sagar Project in Andhra Pradesh

K Anil Kumar

Introduction

In many developing countries, population displacement because of development projects has been a prominent feature in tribal, rural and urban areas. Population displacement because of development projects poses one of the major challenges facing Governments in developing countries because displaced people are not resettled and rehabilitated. The main method used by many Governments in dealing with population displacement is through payment of cash compensation. Cash compensation has been criticized by scholars and donor organizations as having limited capacity to improve and/or restore the livelihood of the displaced households.

Economic development tends to depend on the creation of new infrastructure in order to cater to the increasing needs of growing population. It often involves acquisition of land and other assets, which can adversely affect the socio-economic well-being of the people as well as of the communities they live in. The impacts of development projects include physical relocation, disruption of livelihood and potential breakdown of communities (WB, 2004). The number of people displaced by programmes and projects intended to promote national, regional, and local development are substantial, accounting for nearly 10 million people per year throughout the world; over the last 20 years this would mean 200 million people were displaced (Cernea, 2000).

In India, the construction of large dams has been causing human displacement and resettlement. In many cases, indigenous groups of people are forced to move due to these development projects and are at a risk of losing their homes, lands, livelihoods, social networks and rights to customary land. This can cause impoverishment and marginalization of the tribal people. Constructing dams is usually initiated by the State and multinational organizations and the State follows a top-down approach.

The indigenous groups of people are not well considered during the planning process and their wishes about the development and resettlement are not properly acknowledged. A majority of the displaced people have not been properly resettled or given adequate compensation. This may eventually result in lack of integration and rootlessness in their new settlements.

In Andhra Pradesh during the year 2004, the Government has about thirty irrigation projects in progress on a massive scale under the programme 'JALAYAGNAM' (irrigation initiative). 'JALAYAGNAM', as the word speaks is a ritual for water utilization. It has been implemented by Hon. Chief Minister of Andhra Pradesh as a election promise to the cultivating people of state to bring 73 lakh acres under irrigation in five years. This project accords the highest priority for the development of irrigation infrastructure, particularly in backward and drought prone areas by taking up this program in a big way. Jalayagnam includes a number of irrigation projects by construction of reservoirs and lift irrigation systems for lifting water from major rivers, particularly from Godavari to provide immediate irrigation benefits. Twenty-six major and medium irrigation projects costing Rs. 46,000 crore (Revised to Rs. 67, 823 crore) are taken up for execution. Out of this, eight projects are programmed to be completed within two years and the balance eighteen projects within five years. In addition to these twenty-six projects, it is proposed to construct several other major irrigation projects like *Polavaram, Pranahitha* and *Chevella* and it is estimated that about Rs.1.00 lakh crore would be needed to complete all these projects. Eight of these projects were to be completed before the kharif season of 2006. The irrigation projects in progress now without any integrated planning, comprehension of the complex issues involved, or any systematic river basin planning.

The irrigation projects in Andhra Pradesh are emerging as new sources of displacement of the people from their lands. The Scheduled Tribes, Scheduled Castes, and Backward Castes of Andhra Pradesh have been the disproportionate victims of developments projects. Displaced people are never properly compensated. There is the loss of familiar surrounds. There is loss of preferred livelihoods. There is the trauma, uncertainty and insecurity of the unknown. The record of AP Government on resettlement and rehabilitation is appalling. In this context, this paper attempts to find out the problems of displacement and issues of rehabilitation and resettlement. Secondly, the paper also highlight the policy issues that focus on cash compensation sufficiently prevent displacement and impoverishment. It is an empirical study of Indira Sagar Project (Polavaram) in Andhra Pradesh. The study was conducted during the year 2009-2010. In-depth interviews and focus group discussions were conducted among the displaced communities and with Government officials. Research findings revealed that there were various impacts experienced by displaced households economically and socially.

Displacement for Development

Displacement or the involuntary relocation of people has come to be acknowledged as one among the most significant negative impacts of large water resources development projects such as dams. While many countries have benefited from the large dams, their construction and operation have led to significant, and negative social and human impacts. The unfavourably affected populations include directly relocated families, host communities where families get resettled, and those communities downstream of dams. It is estimated that nearly 40.80 million people have been displaced worldwide due to the reservoirs created by large dams. A World Bank review of 192 projects worldwide for the period 1986 to 1993, estimated that 4 million people were displaced annually by 300 dams on an average by large dams. In India alone, it is estimated that some 21 million to 42 million people have been displaced by dams and reservoirs. In China, by the late 1980s, some 10.2 million people were officially recognized as 'reservoir resettlers' while the unofficial estimates put the number much higher. China and India, the world's two most populous countries, have built about 57 per cent of the world's large dams and also account for the largest number of people resettled (World Commission on Dams, 2000). India, with about 4,200 operational dams since independence, has the dubious distinction of having 30-50 million dam induced displaced people; further the displacement due to large river valley projects in forested and tribal areas is an exceptionally devastating one leading to the loss of access to natural resources and cultural heritage.

Large dams over 10-15 metres in height became possible with advanced engineering practices in the 1850s. Prime Minister Jawaharlal Nehru early on called dams temples of modern India, but by 1958 he had become disillusioned with the excesses of dam building and began to call them a disease of giganticism. Between independence and the mid-1990s, India had 4,129 large dams and associated large-scale irrigation projects completed or under construction. In India, tribal people, Scheduled Castes, the poor and vulnerable are the losers when a dam is built. Their homes and ancestral places are submerged, their livelihoods are destroyed and their free access to common resources, such as rivers, grasslands, forests and wetlands is taken away from them. Displacees are never adequately compensated. They do not have resources to fall back on. They suffer major traumas. Malnutrition, disease and death stalk them. Impoverishment is the normal outcome for them. A reasonable estimate for those displaced by dams and associated development projects in India since Independence is 50 million. Including canal, backwater, livelihood and other non-submergence and indirect displaces, the figure is nearly 100 million.

It has been pointed out that a large majority of those displaced belong to the poor and deprived classes. At present, the figures appearing in official as well as unofficial records are based on hypotheses. A recent estimate suggests that at least 55 per cent of those displaced across India are tribal people (Government of India, 2004). It is largely this group that is paying for the development of India. Due to the large-scale of development projects, millions of indigenous people have been uprooted from their lands and homes, and have lost livelihoods and community structures to make way for projects. A majority of the displaced people have not been properly resettled or given adequate compensation.

Most of the displacement has been involuntary. Communities affected are usually the last to hear about the development projects and their displacement, and thus they rarely participate in the planning and implementation process. Many of the communities may have a historically deep relationship with the land but legally their rights to the land are informal and thus disregarded (Nixon, 2010). In the national rhetoric, the displacement is seen as a sacrifice for the greater good and development. However, it fails to acknowledge the basic human rights to land and resources of those affected and falsely portrays the resettlement as a reward for their suffering (WCD, 2000). Needless to say, most communities strongly oppose the resettlement. Many disputes also occur about who is responsible for the social component of the displacement. The State should be the one to safeguard the rights of all its citizens, but when the State is also the perpetrator, the question becomes tricky. The private sector also regards displacement and resettlement as the responsibility of the State (Morvaridi, 2008). It may also not be the best actor in ensuring poverty reduction and the sustainable management of resources. Many problems emerge with displacement such as drastic changes in livelihoods, loss of autonomy, indigenousness, traditions and established community networks. It is generally known that displacement causes disruption and loss of assets both within the community and for the individuals and a greater likelihood for impoverishment and reduced access to rights and entitlements (Morvaridi, 2008). In many cases, the displaced people have little or no say in deciding over the displacement and although the projects usually have a plan for resettling the displaced people, it is mostly created without consulting the affected people. The displacement is a heavy burden on its own and many of the other negative consequences only emerge after the resettlement process. It is also important to shift from focusing on the needs of the displaced to a more rights based approach of displacement and resettlement. This includes active participation in the whole process of resettlement, rights to secure livelihoods, autonomy, land tenure rights and rights to self-sufficiency and citizenship (Grabska and Mehta, 2008). In essence, this comes down to acknowledging the rights of the displaced in deciding over their own lives and futures. As has been proven in many global instances, some displacement, even for the sake of development, may be inevitable. However the negative consequences of displacement could be mitigated or even avoided. This needs a thorough social impact assessment, the consultation of the people affected as well as a comprehensive resettlement plan. The rights of the people should be respected and not violated. In most cases, this has not happened and the situation after the displacement and resettlement has been neglected or forgotten. Especially with developing countries such as Sudan which are already entangled in webs of continuing conflicts the resources, capacity and financial means cannot always support a comprehensive social resettlement plan. When the people affected by displacement are already marginalized and peripheral, it is highly unlikely that they will be better off after the displacement.

History of Dams and Displacement in Andhra Pradesh

The magnitude of displacement is very high in Andhra Pradesh. Several development projects, unlike in most other states in India, were initiated in the erstwhile Nizam-ruled State. Nawab Ali Jung Bahadur formed an irrigation development department in 1886 to combat the problems of floods and famines. By 1925, the department provided irrigation to about 7,000 acres through minor irrigation works besides launching an intensive drive to construct large and medium dams. Two major irrigation projects, viz., Nizam Sagar and Tungabhadra were initiated during the pre-state formation era under the regimes of Nizams and the British respectively. Nizam Sagar project (on river Manjira lower, a tributary of river Godavari) was constructed during the period 1923-31 by the erstwhile princely state of Hyderabad, in Banswada Taluk of Nizamabad District. At the time of conception and execution, it was not only the largest in the State but also one of the biggest projects in India. It was intended to irrigate 2,75,000 acres serving 326 villages spread over four taluks in Nizamabad District. The construction of the dam and the creation of the reservoir affected forty villages in two taluks, viz., Yellareddy and Andole. A total of 5,037 houses in these villages got submerged. In addition, lands to the extent of 20,140 acres were acquired. In all 35,274 acres of land, including 15,135 acres of crown wasteland were inundated.

Tungabhadra project was an inter-state project actually proposed by the then Madras Government to the Indian Irrigation Commission 1901-03. The project was delayed by fifty years of prolonged negotiations for sharing the waters between the two states, and due to the long delay in project design, the notification for land acquisition was issued by the then Government of Madras only in 1941; and Hyderabad Government did so in 1945. Three districts, Bellary, Raichur, and Dharwar, were affected by this project. 37 villages were submerged in water in Hyderabad State. The number of families and persons affected in these 37 villages stood at 5,225 and 30,000 respectively.

Nagarjuna Sagar project was launched in 1955 as a joint project between Andhra and Hyderabad States, and was completed in the mid 1960s. The dam affected 57 villages in two districts, viz., Nalgonda and Guntur. In all 25,000 people, comprising 5,098 families, were displaced. Most of them belonged to the tribal communities, viz., Lambada and Chenchu. About 2,05,948 acres of land were acquired for the project. Yeleru Reservoir project resulted in submergence of 10 villages, some of them partly and some fully in Mandals. A total number of 2,326 families from 8 villages were affected due to the submergence. Some of the project affected families refused to move to the sites allotted to them because their new sites were located adjacent to a burial ground. Some of the families could not get relocated until the project took off as they did not want to leave their lands. As a result, they dispersed to the nearest places when submergence occurred rather than to the places they were allotted.

Sri Ram Sagar is a major irrigation project meant to serve 6 districts of the then Telangana region of the State. The project was intended to irrigate a total area of 16.109 lakh acres in Stage-I and 8.930 lakh acres in Stage-II. However, more than three decades after the completion of the reservoir, it is only providing irrigation for about 5 lakh acres. As many as 91 villages of 2 districts, Nizamabad and Adilabad, were affected due to the main project dam. In addition, 26 villages were affected under the balancing lower Maner Dam reservoir. In all, 117 villages with 47,599 families were affected. An area of 1,52,493 acres had been acquired for the reservoir construction. Yeleswaram Dam was built in the 1980s for serving the Vizag Steel Plant with water through a dedicated canal. This water supply, due partly to losses from the canal, has proven to be not adequate, and the plant is now drawing water from the Godavari via the Kaniti balancing reservoir. Surampalem and Kovvada are the two medium irrigation projects that have displaced villages during the year 2004-06.

There are 185 numbers of large dams under major, medium and minor irrigation sectors in the State of Andhra Pradesh that are constructed in the river sub-basins of Krishna, Godavari, Penna and other minor basins spread over in 23 districts of Andhra Pradesh. As soon as the Congress Party came back to power in Andhra Pradesh in May 2004, it embarked on a Jala Yagnam, Water Workshop, campaign to provide as many irrigation facilities as possible for the struggling farmers during its five year term in power. Construction of irrigation projects has been taken up on a massive scale in Andhra Pradesh. Twenty-six major and medium irrigation projects were taken up for execution. Out of this, 8 projects are programmed to be completed within 2 years and the balance 18 projects within 5 years. In addition to these 26 projects, it is proposed to construct several other major irrigation projects like Polavaram, Pranahitha and Chevella. The major issue facing tribal communities today is the continuing process of displacement. The tribals of Andhra Pradesh have been the disproportionate victims of displacement due to the so-called development projects such as setting up of industrial projects, construction of dams, and mining, etc. Development projects in Andhra Pradesh are emerging as new sources of displacement in the Scheduled Areas. Because of development projects as well as the process of displacement, many tribal communities in Andhra Pradesh have been uprooted from their land resources. The previous record of Andhra Pradesh Government on resettlement and rehabilitation is appalling. Various case studies show a progression from quite decent treatment of the displacees, by the Nizam State, with policies ensuring they shared in the benefits of dam projects, to a significant dilution of benefits. From the 1980s, resettlement and rehabilitation in Andhra Pradesh were typified by inaction and confusion or, perhaps charitably, by relative neglect-with a minority of people receiving some compensation but never enough.

Indira Sagar Project (Polavaram Project)

The Indira Sagar Project is a major multipurpose irrigation project which is under construction across the Godavari River at Ramaiahpet village in Polavaram Mandal, West Godavari District. The dam is to be constructed straight across the Godavari River some 15 km north of Rajmundhry in East Godavari District. The dam will be constructed at a level of 150 feet (47 m). The submergence will stretch along the Sabari River, a tributary to Godavari, up to the borders of Orissa and Chhattisgarh. Polavaram is a major project on the Godavari River named after the closest town in West Godavari District of Andhra Pradesh. Despite the lack of clearance from Central Government agencies and ministries, the Chief Minister went ahead with the foundation stone ceremony for the construction of the Right Main Canal on November 8, 2004 and the endeavour was renamed the Indira Sagar Project.

The cost of the project according to the official AP figures is Rs. 8,194.4 crore for capital works and Rs. 2,655.9 crore for economic rehabilitation, giving a total of Rs. 10,850.3 crore. No base year is given for these estimates. Another unsubstantiated figure of Rs. 13,000 crore has some currency; it may or may not be the 2005 estimate. It is relevant to note that the ILR calculated a cost for the Right Canal of Rs. 1,484 crore based at 1994-95 prices, whereas the Andhra Pradesh Government estimate above includes Rs. 1,613 crore for the same capital works, an increase of 8.7 per cent. This indicates the year of the estimate was likely to be in the second half of the 1990s. Consequently, a 2005 estimate of Rs. 13,000 crore for the project is probably an underestimate. Both figures—Rs. 10,850 crore and Rs. 13,000 crore—will be used in attempting to extrapolate the project's actual cost. Recently the Chief Minister put this as high as 20,000 crore ($ 4,590 million). This Multi-Purpose Dam on Godavari River would irrigate 7.2 lakh acres and provide more than 80 TMC water for drinking and industry. In 2009 National Water Commission approved the project at an estimated cost of Rs. 16,010.45 crore which has skyrocketed to Rs. 20,000 crore by 2015. Since 2004 the State Government has spent Rs. 5,700 crore on the project. Andhra Pradesh Reorganization Act declared Polavaram as a national project. Fifty per cent of the canal work has been completed till date and the reservoir work has to start. An ordinance was passed to merge villages from 7 mandals of Telangana into Andhra Pradesh. Polavaram ordinance merging the project-affected villages in the residuary Andhra Pradesh State was accepted by the Parliament in July 2014. Seven mandals from Khammam District of Telangana have been transferred to Andhra Pradesh. Four mandals from Bhadrachalam Revenue Division namely, Chinturu, Kunavaram, Vararamachandrapuram, Bhadrachalam (excluding the Bhadrachalam Revenue Village) were transferred to East Godavari District. Three mandals from Palvancha Revenue Division namely, Kukunoor, Velerupadu, Burgampadu (except 12 villages namely, Pinapaka, Morampalli, Banjara, Burgampadu, Naginiprolu, Krishnasagar, Tekula, Sarapaka, Iravendi, Motepattinagar, Uppusaka, Nakiripeta and

Sompalli), have been added to West Godavari District. This came into force as the 16th Lok Sabha has passed the Polavaram Ordinance Bill with the voice vote on July 11, 2014. The State Government is taking all necessary steps to complete the Polavaram Project by 2018. Honourable Chief Minister N Chandrababu Naidu is also trying to raise the funds from the Central Government for completion of the projects at the earliest. Participating in the 'Janmabhoomi Maa Vooru' programme at Chenchupet on January 5, 2016, Honourable Chief Minister said works were going on at a brisk pace on the Polavaram Right Main Canal and the main project (Polavaram Dam) would be completed as per the schedule in spite of some hurdles. The Irrigation Minister of Andhra Pradesh D Umamaheswara Rao has said works on the right bank canal of Polavaram project will be completed by June 2017 which will provide drinking as well as irrigation water to East Godavari and Visakhapatnam Districts of the State. The State Government has been negotiating with the Austrian Government for financial support to the project.

The project will involve a large displacement of 30,607 families (1,28,913 people as per the 1991 Census) in 292 villages according to the designs made during the 1980s. These were later modified and the 2003 designs are expected to reduce the submergence to 276 villages (1,17,034 people as per the 2001 Census) in seven Mandals[1] of Khammam and one Mandal each of East and West Godavari Districts in Andhra Pradesh. It is by far the largest project in India in terms of geographical displacement of disadvantaged groups, i.e. indigenous people

Table 1: Villages, Families and Population Affected under Submergence

Name of the State	Number of resettlements	Number of project affected families	Number of population affected
Andhra Pradesh	276	44,574	1,77,275
Chattisgarh	16	2,335	11,766
Odisha	11	1,002	6,316

Source: SPWD, 2012.

or tribals in the Scheduled Districts of three states viz. Andhra Pradesh, Odisha and Chhattisgarh. In the beginning of the project, the State of Andhra Pradesh conceded before the Appellate Authority that the impacts of the dam were estimated as per 2001 Census. The details are given below in the Table 1

Out of the above, 14.9 per cent are Scheduled Castes, 48.7 per cent Scheduled Tribes, 17.4 per cent Backward Classes and the balance 18.9 per cent fall in other categories.

The inhabitants of 276 habitations (147 revenue villages and 129 hamlets) spread over 9 Mandals in 3 districts face displacement because of the project. The brunt of the problem is faced by Khammam District wherein 205 habitations (122 revenue villages and 83 hamlets) spread over 7 Mandals face displacement. Among all the 9 Mandals, the greatest extent of displacement occurs in Kukkunur and Kunavaram Mandals. The least affected is Boorgampadu Mandal. 75.7 per cent of the affected population (8,818 out of 11,654) in Chintoor Mandal belongs to Scheduled Tribes. Among the affected population of Polavaram Mandal, 61.1 per cent belongs to Scheduled Tribes.

Centre for Economic and Social Studies (CESS) has conducted a systematic and reliable study to assess the number of households and the number of project-affected people and nature and extent of damage caused to immovable property in the project-affected areas. The Government of Andhra Pradesh developed rehabilitation and resettlement package has been prepared on the basis of data provided by the survey. According to the survey, the number of families likely to be affected are 27,798 with a population of 1,17,034 in Andhra Pradesh. About 75,000 acres of cultivated land will be submerged besides an area to the extent of about 20,000 acres of fallow land and some thousand acres of forest land. Among the households 13,401 (18 per cent) represented tribals, followed by 6,077 (21 per cent) BC, 4,246 (15 per cent) SC and 4,074 (15 per cent) OCs. Further, analysis of the data made available under this showed that out of the 276 settlements, 23 per cent of them were fully inhabited by tribals. In another 24 per cent of the settlements tribal population constituted 90 per cent to 99 per cent; in another 20 per cent settlements, the tribal concentration was between 50 to 89 per cent and in the rest 33 per cent settlements the concentration of tribal population was less than 50 per cent. The survey also provided information about the extent of land held by the households. In West Godavari, 56 per cent (1,176 households) owned land with an average holding of 3.81 acres and the rest are landless. While in East Godavari, those who held land constituted 53 per cent of the households (1,526) with an average holding of 4.39 acres. While in Khammam, 57 per cent of the households (12,922) own land leaving the rest 43 per cent landless. In Khammam, the average land holding is 4.95 acres per household. In East Godavari 47 per cent of the households were landless and among them 43 per cent of them worked as labourers and 2 per cent were engaged in service, 1 per cent were in artisanal activities and the rest 1 per cent were in trade and business. While in West Godavari out of the 44 per cent of the landless, 38 per cent engaged in wage labour, 3 per cent each were in service and artisanal activities, and the rest were in trade and business. While in Khammam out of the 43 per cent of the households, 33 per cent were engaged in wage labour, 3 per cent were in service, 2 per cent in artisanal activities and the rest in trade and business (CESS, 1996).

Godavari Basin Details

Godavari Basin extends over an area of 312,812 km^2, which is nearly 9.5 per cent of the total geographical area of the country. The details of the lie of the basin are given in Table 2.

Table 2: Godavari Basin Lies in the following States

S. No	Name of the State	Area (Square Km)	Share in the Geographical Area (Per cent)
1	Maharashtra	1,52,199	48.65
2	Andhra Pradesh	73,201	23.40
3	Chattisgarh	39,087	12.49
4	Madhya Pradesh	26,168	8.63
5	Odisha	17,752	5.67
6	Karnataka	4,405	1.41

Source: http://www.sakti.in/godavaribasin/basindetails.htm
https://saktiblog.wordpress.com/2011/09/page/2/

The Godavari, the Perennial River of India is the fourth largest river in India. It flows in the southern India and is considered to be one of the seven sacred rivers. The Godavari, throughout its entire length, is sacred to the Hindus. Godavari River rises near Trayambak near Nasik, Northeast of Mumbai in the State of Maharashtra at an elevation of 1,067 m and flows for a length of about 1,465 km (910 miles) before falling into the Bay of Bengal. It flows for 692 kms before entering Andhra Pradesh at Basara in Adilabad District. It flows through the Eastern Ghats and emerges at Polavaram to flow into the plains. At Dhawaleswaram, the river divides into two branches, the Gautami and Vasishta. Between the two lies the Godavari Central Delta. The two arms split into branches as they approach the sea dividing the Central Delta into a number of islands. These branches are said to have been made by seven great 'Rishis' after whom they are named. Godavari is known as the Ganga of the South. Asia's largest Lift irrigation project named Vishnupuri Prakalp is constructed on the river just 5 km away from Nanded city.

Figure 1: Map of Godavari River Basin

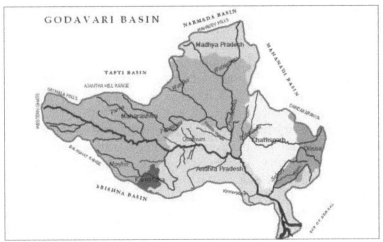

Source: http://www.sakti.in/godavaribasin/basindetails.htm
https://saktiblog.wordpress.com/2011/09/page/2/

The Godavari Basin is bounded on the North by the *Satmala* Hills, the Ajanta Range and the Mahadeo Hills, on the South and East by the Eastern Ghats and on the West by the Western Ghats. It is roughly triangular in shape and the main river itself runs practically along the base of the triangle.

Godavari Basin: Characteristics

The Godavari Basin receives the major part of its rainfall during the South-West monsoon period. The other rainy seasons are not so well defined and well spread as the South-West monsoon season. They contribute about 16 per cent of the total annual rainfall in the Godavari Basin. The annual rainfall of Godavari Basin varies from 3,000 mm to 600 mm. The Godavari Basin has a tropical climate. The mean annual surface temperature in the Western Ghats area is about 24°C, and it increases gradually towards the East and attains a maximum of 29.4°C on the East Coast. During January, the mean daily minimum temperature increases from West to East from 15°C on the Western Ghats to about 18°C on the East Coast. The mean maximum daily temperature generally exceeds 30°C in the western part of the Godavari Basin and it is only slightly less than 30°C in the Eastern part. The population of the Basin, based on 2001 census was 60.6 million out of which about 75 per cent live in rural and remaining 25 per cent in urban areas. The density of population is around 194 persons per sq. km. Nearly 40 per cent of workforce is engaged in cultivation, 30 per cent as agricultural labour and balance 30 per cent in mining, manufacturing etc.

Except for the hills forming the watershed around the basin, the entire drainage basin of the river Godavari comprises undulating country, a series of ridges and valleys interspersed with low hill ranges. Large flat areas which are characteristic of the Indo-Gangetic plains are scarce except in the delta. The Sahyadri ranges of Western Ghats form the Western edge of the basin. The interior of the basin is a plateau divided into a series of valleys sloping generally towards East. The Eastern Ghats, which form the Eastern boundary, are not so well defined as the Sahyadri range on the West. The northern boundary of the basin comprises tablelands with varying elevations. Large stretches of plains interspersed by hill ranges lie to the South.

Figure 2: Map of River Godavari from Brahmagiri to Bay of Bengal

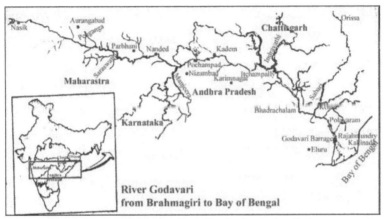

Source: http://www.sakti.in/godavaribasin/basindetails.htm
https://saktiblog.wordpress.com/2011/09/page/2/

The Krishna and the Godavari Rivers traverse 1,280 kilometres (592 km in Andhra Pradesh) and 1,460 kilometres (772 km in Andhra Pradesh) respectively from the Western Ghats to the Bay of Bengal. In engineer-speak, Krishna water is overutilized (i.e. no more is available) and Godavari water is underutilized. Table below shows that the Godavari and Krishna Rivers account for 84 per cent of the river water available in Andhra Pradesh. In this text, TMC means thousand million cubic feet – the most commonly used unit in India; one unit is a very large quantity of water. On the Krishna River, Andhra Pradesh receives much less than half the available water. On the Godavari River, Andhra Pradesh receives virtually all the water (more than three-quarters of which comes from tributaries within Andhra Pradesh).

Methodology of the Study

The study was undertaken in 3 districts of Andhra Pradesh viz East Godavari, West Godavari and Khamam. The research is exploratory. It seeks to find out the impact of displacement on livelihood of the displaced households (community). A case study strategy was used for the study as it allows a researcher to provide detailed description of an existing problem. Qualitative methods were used to collect information to answer the raised questions. Purposive sampling technique was used to select the targeted population for the study.

To ascertain the impact of displacement on the livelihood of the displaced households a field study was conducted in tribal dominated villages in the State of Andhra Pradesh. The Polavaram Dam Project victims are covered under this study. In order to get a representative sample, purposive and simple random sampling techniques were used. The respondents included; households who relocated from Polavaram, those who are still living at Polavaram and key Government officials who were involved in the planning and implementation of the Polavaram Dam. For the purpose of the study to select the samples, the following steps and stages were administered. To begin with, from each district one or more Mandals were selected, wherever the displacement is on the higher side. Thus Devipatnam from East Godavari, and Polavaram from West Godavari were selected. Information about socio-economic profiles of the affected villages from all the three districts were collected.

In-depth interviews were conducted as the main tool for data collection for household respondents. Focus group discussions and observations were also used as methods for data collection at community level while only key informants' interviews were used for Government officials. The in-depth interviews were used in order to generate an in-depth understanding of displacement impacts on the livelihoods of households. The study also made use of secondary data including journals, articles, books, policies as well as use of internet sources for data collection. The unit of analysis was the households which have been displaced. The study mainly focused on households in the study location as elaborated in the study sample.

All the 3 villages were relocated in one new colony which

Table 3: Socio-economic Details of the Study Villages

S. No	Name of the Reservoir/ Dam	Name of the Villages	Name of the Mandal & District	Total HHs and Population		Social Category	
				HH	Pop	Category	Sub-Caste
1	Indira Sagar	Paragasanipadu D Ravilanka Bodugudem (Peda Bheempalli)	Devipatnam, East Godavari	200	600	ST, SC & OC	Koya, Mala, Madiga and Kapu
2	Indira Sagar Dam	Ramayyapeta	Polavaram, West Godavari	490	1200	BC, ST, SC & OC	Kapu Velama, Koya, Mala, Madiga & Kapu
		Devaragondi	Polavaram, West Godavari	160	400	ST	Koya
		Mamidigondi	Polavaram, West Godavari	100	300	ST	Koya
		Pydipaka	Polavaram, West Godavari	450	1000	BC, SC & OC	Mixed population
		Singanapalli	Polavaram, West Godavari	180	400	ST, BC, SC & OC	Mixed all Castes
		Chegontipalli	Polavaram, West Godavari	300	815	ST	Koya
3	Indira Sagar Khammam	Kondaigudem	Kunavaram	62	230	ST, SC BC	Koya, Mala, Kapu
		Sabari Raigudem	VR Puram	74	248	ST, SC BC	Koya, Mala, Kapu

Source: From Field Study

is known Peda Bheempalli colony. Compensation to agricultural land was not equally distributed to those who should have got it. From the three villages some of the families are staying in old villages because at the new colony, some of the basic amenities were not provided. Most of the villages are yet to be relocated and the process of compensation going on since five years has not yet been completed.

The villages/settlements studied from East Godavari are (1) Bodigudem (2) D. Ravilanka (3) Pargasanipadu (Villages which are selected from Devipatnam Mandal displaced by Polavaram Dam). The villages studied in West Godavari were (4) Pydipaka (5) Ramayyapeta (6) Devargondi (7) Totagondi (8) Chegondapalli (9) Mamidigondi (10) Singannapalli (11) Pydipaka and the villages studied from Khamam District are (12) Kondaigudem and (13) Sabari Raigudem.

In the District of East Godavari all the 3 villages which are selected for study were relocated in one new colony which is known as Peda Bheempalli colony. Compensation for agricultural land was not equally distributed to those who should have got it. From the 3 villages some of the families are staying in old villages because at the new colony, some of the basic amenities were not provided. Most of the villages are yet to be relocated and the process of compensation going on since five year has not yet been completed.

The study was conducted in the above villages/settlements. The number of households was listed down and all the villages were categorized into two types of settlements such as partially relocated villages and yet to be relocated villages. For the purpose of study the partially and yet to be relocated villages were selected as sample villages from the Mandals where the displacement of tribal people was on the higher side. Thus altogether selected villages were studied in detail. The study included collection of both primary and secondary data.

Data was collected from the village communities and as well from the Government officials by using various anthropological tools and techniques such as observation, key informants, interviews and focus group discussions. The secondary source of data was collected from journals, articles, books, policy

Table 4: Compensation details of the Study Villages

Name of the District	Name of the Mandal	Name of the Panchayat	Name of the Affected village	Total House holds	Status of relocation, Partially-2) Yet to be-3)	Name of the Project				Details of the Compensation									
						Name of the Reservoir	Starting date	Ending date	GO	Amount (Rs)					Land to Land (in Acres)		18 years package only for boys		Home-stead
										ST Land less	ST Land holders	Others landless	Others land holders	Empl- oys	ST Landless	ST Land Holders	Land less	Land Holders	
	Devipatnam	China Ramanayy-apeta	D Ravilanka	81	2	Indira Sagar	2005	Not completed	58 & 68	157200	107200	125200	7520	5000	0	6.10	157200	125200	0.05
		Padipalli	Paragasanipadu	61	2														
		Chinaraman ayyapeta	Bodigudem	20	2														
West Godavari	Polavaram	Polavaram	Ramayyapeta	360	3	Indira Sagar	2006	Not completed	68	130200	140200	130200	1402	5000	0	6.10	130200	140200	0.05
		Mamidigondi	Devaragondi	85	3					170200	120200	130200	1402	5000	0	6.10	For ST 170200 For others-130200	For ST 120200 For others-140200	0.05
Khammam	Kunavaram	Suchiregula-gudem	Kondagudem	62	3	Indira Sagar	2006	Not completed	68	0	0	0	0	0	0	6.10	0	0	0
	V.R.Puram	Ramavaram	SRaigudem	74	3				68	0	0	0	0	0	0	0	0	0	0
		Total		1070															

Source: From Field Study

Table 5: Package details of G.O.Ms. No. 58 and 68

Offered Benefits	GO 58					GO 68							18 years package offered					
	ST Land less households	ST land holders	SC,BC and OC landless households	SC,BC and OC land holders	Employs (Govt)	ST Land less households	ST land holders	ST Land less households	ST land holders	SC, BC & OC landless households	SC,BC and OC land holders	Employys (Govt)	ST Land less households	ST land holders	ST Land less households	ST land holders	SC,BC and OC land less households	SC,BC and OC land holders / Remarks
Home stead	0.05 cents	0.05 cents	0.05 cents	0.05 cents	0.05 cents	0.05 cents	0.05 cents	0.05 cents	0.05 cents	0.05 cents	0.05 cents	0.05 cents	0.05 cents	0.05 cents	0.05 cents	0.05 cents	0.05 cents	0.05 cents
New house construction	40000	40000	40000	40000		50000	50000	50000	50000	50000	50000	-	50000	50000	50000	50000	50000	50000
Individual Toilet	-	-	-	-	-	3000	3000	3000	3000	3000	3000	-	3000	3000	3000	3000	3000	3000
Cattle shed	3000	3000	3000	3000		3000	3000	3000	3000	3000	3000		3000	3000	3000	3000	3000	3000
Transport cost	5000	5000	5000	5000	5000	5000	5000	5000	5000	5000	5000	5000	5000	5000	5000	5000	5000	5000
Loss of labor day (625 days x Rs. 80 per day)	40000	-	4000	-		50000	-	50000	60000	50000	60000		50000	-	50000	60000	50000	60000
Additional labor days (240 days x Rs. 80)	15360	15360	15360	15360		19200	19200	19200	19200	19200	19200		19200	19200	19200	19200	19200	19200
Loss of NTFP 500 days x Rs. 80)	32000	32000	-	-		40000	40000	-	-	-	-		40000	40000	-	-	-	-
Total	135360	95360	103360	63360	5000	170200	120200	130200	140200	130200	140200	5000	170200	120200	130200	140200	130200	140200

Source: http://www.sakti.in/godavaribasin/basindetails.htm
https://saktiblog.wordpress.com/2011/09/page/2/

documents and from the source internet.

In each selected village the respective heads of the households were contacted and collected required primary data were with the help of an interview schedule. In the above villages focus group discussions were conducted in each village involving 8-10 members each. The focus group discussions involved women's group and local NGOs. Similar methods used to get respondents for interviews were applied for the focus group discussions. Observations were also used in order to document the general living conditions of the displaced households.

More Recent Official Views

(1) The Social Welfare Department of the Government of Andhra Pradesh enunciated the following guidelines for resettlement and rehabilitation as per G O No 64 dated April 18,1990.

   I. Whenever or not it is unavoidable to take up schemes involving submergence of total lands, rehabilitation should be taken up on a land-to-land basis, and if the extent of land lost by a tribal family cannot be entirely made good by alternative land, it must be ensured that some land is provided so that the family is not completely uprooted from its traditional occupation.

   II. If adequate land cannot be provided, employment should be provided to at least one member of each family displaced. The list of displaced tribals and their dependents should be put on the rolls of the project and, if necessary, they should be sent for requisite training.

The only comment that can be made on this G O is that while the intentions implicit in the first clause are unexceptionable, the second clause, if taken as an alternative to the first, has the effect of completely diluting the former. It would be desirable if the second clause is read only as complementary to the first and not as a substitute.

(2) The Ministry of Rural Development, Government of India circulated an approach paper on R R Policies and elicited the views of the State Government during 1995. Among the

many good guidelines presented therein, the following are particularly noteworthy:

    I. For purpose of compensation, the Government should go by the price of land in the nearest command area and not by the registration price of land in the area of submergence.

    II. Land to land on a one-to-one basis should be considered the ideal basis of rehabilitation. But where it is not possible, every effort should be made to provide land on a proportional basis to members of the Scheduled Tribes, Scheduled Castes and other weaker sections who have been mainly dependent on land for their livelihood. Even those who had customary or usufuctory rights in land should be recognized for this purpose.

    III. When the displaced person has to buy land at a higher cost per unit area than the compensation he has received for the land lost by him, the difference between the two has to be treated as ex-gratia payment.

    IV. Where neither land nor secure employment has been provided, the oustee should be paid resettlement grant or subsistence allowance on a monthly basis, until he is helped to find an alternative source of livelihood.

    V. Unskilled and semi-skilled jobs and Class III and Class IV Services in the project should be reserved for the displaced persons with special provisions for the STs and SCs.

    VI. Tribal communities should be strictly settled in the area of their choice, after providing them full information about the resettlement sites and giving them the opportunity for physical inspection of the same.

    VII. When the displaced persons have to purchase lands on their own, they should be exempted from payment of stamp duty and registration fee.

The Response of Andhra Pradesh Government

The above suggestions from the Ministry of Rural Development have evoked from the Andhra Pradesh State Government a response which can be only described as cold or cut-and-dried. Stated briefly, it is as follows:

I. The suggestions ton provide land for land to the displaced persons is not acceptable. The State Government is also not agreeable to its involvement in the purchase of private lands by the displaced persons either on their own or through the land purchase committee. However, in regard to displaced persons belonging to Scheduled Tribes, Government land can be assigned subject to availability.

II. The question of providing exemption from stamp duty and registration fee on the lands purchased by the displaced persons does not arise.

III. Subsistence allowance will be paid only for six months.

IV. The State Government is not in favour of reservation of jobs for the displaced persons.

V. The State Government is not in favour of giving any preference to the displaced persons in allotment of shops or contracts.

3) Recent Clarification by the Department of Irrigation, Government of Andhra Pradesh

In response to some of our queries about the available vacant lands, the Secretary (Projects), Department of Irrigation communicated to us the decision taken at a meeting held in his chambers on April 4, 1996. It reads as follows: 'What is required (at this stage) is a statement of RR Policy and the commitment of the Government to allot land wherever available. If no land is available, a committee with the District Collector as Chairman can assist displaced families in purchasing private lands from rehabilitation funds'.

What needs to be pointed out at this stage is the enormous divergence of views between the last two communications. Both these communications, we are informed, do not have the status of Government Orders. It is hoped that there would not be such wide fluctuations of views in the future and the State Government would stand steadfast and stick to forward-looking humanitarian views on resettlement and rehabilitation.

G O Ms No 64 of 1990 Issued by Government of Andhra Pradesh

Consolidating the instructions of various earlier G Os related to displacement of tribals, Social Welfare (T) Department, Government of Andhra Pradesh released G O Ms No 64 of 1990. The G O says that 'The dispossession and displacement of tribals on numerous counts is mounting in these sensitive areas, which is creating conditions of discontent and unrest in some of the scheduled areas'. Saying that, 'The Government has carefully considered the entire question of acquisition of land for public purposes and rehabilitation of tribal people in the Scheduled Areas to ensure that the tribal people in scheduled areas enjoy the safeguards envisaged for them under the Constitution of India and their interests are not compromised on any count whatsoever', the G O contains the following major provisions:

- There should be no displacement of tribals or any disturbance of tribal way of life in the execution of any developmental project.
- Construction of new major and medium irrigation projects shall be avoided to the extent possible so as to avoid submergence of tribal lands.
- Plans for rehabilitation shall be prepared in association with the people adversely affected and it must be ensured that the people are fully compensated and rehabilitated completely.
- Entire cost of rehabilitation shall be in the first charge on the project. In other words, rehabilitation shall be completed first before project execution.
- Wherever it is unavoidable to take up a scheme involving submergence of tribal lands, rehabilitation shall be taken up on land-to-land basis, at least for a part of the land lost in submergence.
- If adequate land cannot be provided, employment (in the project or in other projects or in Government) should be provided at least to one of the members of each family displaced.

- A substantial training programme of entrepreneurial skills for displaced tribals, with follow-up in helping and getting financial support, marketing outlets, supply of raw materials etc., shall be built up at the time of execution of the project.

Though the GO clearly states that the instructions apply to all those projects already executed or being executed in tribal areas, no effort was made to implement this GO in any project during later years. Some of the submerged villages in Yeleru Project, viz., D Kristavaram in Addatheegala Mandal, Ramuladeva-puram and Lingavaram in Gangavaram Mandal, were under Notified Scheduled Areas. Neither a comprehensive rehabilitation plan nor any one of the above provisions was implemented in these villages. Still, authorities did not bother to apply the provisions of this GO to compensate the sacrifice of people of those villages.

Andhra Pradesh Resettlement and Rehabilitation Policy 2005

Government of Andhra Pradesh came out with a Policy on Resettlement and Rehabilitation (R & R) for the Project Affected Families on April 8, 2005. The Policy was released in the form of GO No 68 of Irrigation and CAD (Projects Wing) Department. While releasing the Policy, Government boasted of it as the one offering best resettlement and rehabilitation package in the country. The proposed R & R Policy has, in fact, a few good elements but falls short in many areas.

The Policy assumes great significance in the light of Andhra Pradesh Government vigorously pursuing to complete as many as 34 irrigation projects by year 2009. An irrigation project, such as Polavaram in West Godavari District, is going to cause huge human displacement depriving the local tribes of their shelter and means of livelihood. Submergence in tribal and forest areas will result in irrecoverable ecological destruction and affect the cultural identity of ethnic tribes. In Polavaram alone, an estimated 2,00,000 people—of which at least 50 per cent are tribes—will be displaced from 276 villages. About 1,61,775 acres of land will be lost in dam submergence, including about 8,000 acres of forest resources.

As usual, this policy also recommends land-to-land compensation in case of Project Affected Families (PAFs) belonging to ST community. This policy stands separately from earlier GOs only in providing wage compensation to landless people. A random study of various projects implemented during 1990 to 2005 revealed that the provisions of GO No 64 of 1990 were never implemented in any irrigation project executed during this period. Therefore, this policy is no different from earlier ones unless it is implemented in its true spirit.

While the GO 68 of Andhra Pradesh in many respects is a copy of the National Policy on Rehabilitation and Resettlement 2003, in reality, the package is very similar to the relatively 'standard model' floating around the Government bureaucracy in India. It is a quasi-legal document outlining amounts of compensation, definitions and administrative structures. The second half of the Volume 2 document provides the 'rehabilitation and resettlement plan', that is, fleshes out the policy in GO No 68, provides a budget and predictably focuses on organization and management, training of Government officers (a tidbit for displacees), monitoring and administrative procedures. There are at least nine Government agencies involved. The structure, management, coordination and monitoring procedures appear weak. Therefore, there is plenty of room for confusion, 'buck passing', siphoning off of money and general inaction. The whole package and the details for implementation are sketchy. What is aggravating about GO No 68 in general terms is not that it has been patched together from a 'standard package', but that it is missing about three-quarters of the content necessary for implementation. In other words, there are fine vague phrases about what is intended, there are some legalistic definitions, there are some specific compensation items and some basic administrative structures, but there is nothing whatever on how the programme can be delivered.

The National Thermal Power Corporation (NTPC), New Delhi by contrast formulated a rehabilitation and resettlement policy in 2005 based on the same 'standard model' which is recognizably similar. While this document is longer and denser, it is also clear and succinct. It hangs together logically, in a way that GO No 68 does not. Where the NTPC policy stands out is in its guidelines and mechanisms for implementation. They are specific, but flexible, and are designed to deal with complex issues. The policy also prescribes mechanisms for participation, and in particular appears to treat villagers with dignity and as partners in the process, rather than as 'objects'. This is not to say that the NTPC policy is ideal, nor that the words on paper will actually be implemented in the field, but it is many years ahead of GO No 68. Implementation is where the Government of Andhra Pradesh misses the point completely. No matter how good the content of any rehabilitation and resettlement policy is, if the process is not implemented properly then the quality of the promised package is irrelevant.

Andhra Pradesh Government has achieved quality rehabilitation and resettlement. Since 1980, rehabilitation and resettlement implementation has been characterized by bumbling confusion, ineptitude and inadequacy. The current AP Government's rehabilitation and resettlement package G O No 68 and plan for implementation are destined to produce the same outcomes. As argued by the World Commission on Dams in 2000, The World Bank and many other authorities and agencies, it is no longer acceptable to treat 'oustees' as a nuisance. As N Subba Reddy said in 1996 of the Chief Engineer, the Government of Andhra Pradesh's approach to rehabilitation and resettlement is backward and not consonant with contemporary thinking at international and national levels.

One of the Objectives of the Policy is stated to be 'to minimize displacement by exploring non-displacing or least-displacing alternatives' to the project designs. The policy sounds quite optimistic but the Government violated its own Policy in case of Polavaram project. The technical committee formulated to examine alternatives to Polavaram Dam, brushed aside all the alternative designs proposed by eminent engineers like Sri Hanumantha Rao and Sri Dharma Rao without following a systematic and transparent evaluation methodology.

The Policy recommends including a time schedule for resettlement of PAFs in the rehabilitation and resettlement plans prepared by the District Collector concerned. But, there is no mention of any time schedule for rehabilitation aspects of rehabilitation and resettlement package such as allotment of alternative agricultural land and training and skill development activities for landless and artisans among PAFs. In projects, like Yeleru and Sri Ram Sagar (SRSP), proper resettlement and rehabilitation are still not complete after decades of project execution. This is an important aspect that all the rehabilitation and resettlement activities shall be time-bound with a reasonable time period in order to do justice to the Project Affected Families. Therefore, rehabilitation and resettlement plans should be developed with a detailed time schedule for each and every aspect of the package, not just for resettlement.

As a whole, the Policy is comparable to 'old wine in new bottle'. The sincerity of Government to translate it into action is the matter of real concern. Government should prove its commitment to the best R & R efforts by demonstrating it in on-going projects such as Polavaram.

Apart from financial and economic considerations, human dignity and human rights must find a place in the thinking of Government. Until 'oustees' are treated as valuable human beings, whose homes, land, livelihood and way of life are valuable, then no dam should be built. Until they are given as much caring attention and compensation, in terms of physical property, livelihoods, location and spiritual well-being, to make up for their loss, then no dam should be built. That is the bottom line.

Findings of the study

The Indira Sagar Project (earlier Polavaram Project) is a major multipurpose irrigation project which is under construction across the Godavari River at Ramaiahpet village in Polavaram Mandal, West Godavari District. 276 habitations (147 revenue villages and 129 hamlets) spread over nine mandals in three districts seven mandals of Khammam and one mandal each of East and West Godavari Districts will face displacement of people and habitats because of the project. About 2,00,000, people going to be displace out of which 14.9 per cent are Scheduled Castes, 48.7 per cent Scheduled Tribes, 17.4 per cent

Table 6: Compensation for the Acquisition of the Assets (House, Agricultural Land and Trees)

Name of the Reservoir/ Major irrigation Project	House (The household valuation is based on measurements)			Land (Per Acre)				Trees (Toddy, Cashew, Coconut, Mango and others)
				Own		Assign		
	Kutcha	Pucca	Semi-Pucca	Wet	Dry	Wet	Dry	
Surampalem Reservoir	1000 to 10000	5000 to 1000000 and above	5000 to 50000	35000	35000	25000	25000	150 to 1000
Bhupathipalem Reservoir	1000 to 10000	5000 to 1000000 and above	5000 to 50000	35000	35000	25000	25000	150 to 1000
Musurumilli Reservoir	1000 to 10000	5000 to 1000000 and above	5000 to 50000	35000	35000	25000	25000	150 to 1000
Major irrigation Project – East Godavari	Valuation not done	Valuation not done	Valuation not done	Valuation not done	Valuation not done	Valuation not done	Valuation not done	150 to 1000
Major irrigation Project – West Godavari	1000 to 10000	5000- 1000000 and above	5000 to 50000	185000	185000	185000	185000	150 to 1000
Major irrigation Project - Khammam	Valuation not done	Valuation not done	Valuation not done	1015000	1015000	Valuation not done	Valuation not done	150 to 1500

Source: From Field Study

Backward Classes and the balance 18.9 per cent fall in other categories.

Despite the lack of clearance from the Central Government agencies and ministries, the present Government went ahead with the foundation-stone ceremony for the construction of the Right Main Canal on November 8, 2004 and the endeavour was renamed the Indira Sagar Project.

The brunt of the problem is faced by Khammam District wherein 205 habitations (122 revenue villages and 83 hamlets) spread over seven Mandals will face displacement. Among all the 9 Mandals, the greatest extent of displacement occurs in Kukkunur and Kunavaram Mandals.

The least affected is Boorgampadu Mandal. 75.7 per cent of the affected population (8,818 out of 11,654) in Chintoor Mandal belongs to Scheduled Tribes. Among the affected population of Polavaram Mandal, 61.1 per cent belong to Scheduled Tribes.

From the focus group discussion with the selected villagers on Polavaram project the following issues came up. Government officials did not make any serious efforts to explain about the details of R&R package and they did not even translate them in to the local language. Government has not served any kind of notice to the households to vacate their places. They were not sensitized about Polavaram project. The three villages Paragasanipadu, D Ravilanka, Bodugudem were relocated in one colony (Peda Bheempally colony).

The new colony Peda Bheempally was a model housing colony for the displaced people. In this colony, most of the affected villagers partially shifted because the work of project had slowed. And the other reason is allotment of agricultural land for families is given very far from the colony. Compensation of Rs. 3,000 per cattle shed was not sufficient for the families. There was also problem of grazing land for cattle. Compensation of Rs. 5,000 for transportation to relocate was not sufficient due to the long distance for shifting to the new location. The quality of house construction was not satisfactory. In the new colony, there was little opportunity for daily wage labour. After shifting to the new colony, families were suffering because it was daily wages work. Apart from this, the new colony was constructed neither near to forest nor to the town. People's dependency on forest was become very low. Government has not allotted a piece of land for the purpose of a grave yard.

At the time of acquisition land from the villagers, the officials with the help of local NGOs convened the Gram Sabha meetings in the villages Ramayyapeta, Devaragondi, Mamidigondi, Pydipaka, Singanapalli, and Chegontipalli. The officials at the time of acquisition of land committed themselves to implement the rehabilitation and resettlement package as early as possible but until now they have not completed the implementation of rehabilitation and resettlement package. The people have been waiting for the compensation without cultivation of their lands for the last eight years. From the above villages, some of the families have shifted to the new location. Compensation has not been paid to many of the families. For the village Ramayyapeta so far Government has not shown any land for the construction of houses. In the rehabilitation and resettlement package for the non-tribals (Ramayyapeta village) Government only allotted a land for the construction of their houses. In the village Ramayyapeta families received the documents of land for house construction but officials until now have not shown the land to them. The above villagers thought of cultivating their land till the relocation but they did not get permission to cultivate their fields. For 5 to 6 years families have been working on whatever little agricultural work that comes their way. And they are just waiting when the Government will relocate them. In Khammam District Government promised to the villagers that they would give land as land compensation but until now Government has not shown any land to them. In some cases, the land selected for compensation is located very far from the original habitat and too far away from the forests for example the villages D Ravilanka, Bodigudem, Pargasanipadu, Devaragondi and Mamidigondi .

In the study area, issues relating to forest and land are acting as major obstacles to the speedy implementation of the project. In the study villages, most of the project affected families are tribals. For them land and forests are very essential for their bare minimum sustenance. Apart from wage labour, most of the villagers earned their living by undertaking collection of Minor Forest Produce (MFP) and agriculture. Though there are certain restrictions, their dependency on forest is still intact.

From the study it is found that the newly constructed colonies for relocation lack most basic amenities for example Donepalli, and D Ravilanka villages. Although they lack most of these facilities, they lead a contended life with whatever resources they have. On the other hand, people said that for centuries they have been living there and they have emotional attachment to the forests and the land. It is that is forcing the tribals to stay in their old locations where several generations thrived and survived. Similarly in the study area it was reported those who don't have land are relocating, while others who possessed agricultural land are not ready to relocate because they are emotionally attached to the original place.

According to the study, most of the potential project oustees live below poverty line and they depend on wage labour followed by collection of MFP and agriculture for their sustenance. The project affected people were of the opinion that they should be properly relocated where there is forests. Otherwise they will suffer from further marginalization. Though certain legislations permit the free access of the tribals to the forest resources certain limits have been laid down. The study showed that their dependency on forest for their very survival largely remains intact. Therefore measures need to be taken to see that even after relocation they continue to get the same benefits from the forests.

Tribal villages in the submerged area fall under Scheduled Areas notified in the Fifth Schedule of the constitution. Under the 73rd Constitution Amendment Act (CAA), land can be acquired for the projects in such areas with the consent of local bodies which pass resolutions to that effect. Forceful takeover of the land from the Fifth Schedule area amounts to violation of the of the Constitution as it deprives them of control and ownership of natural resources and land essential for their way of life. But in the case of Indira Sagar Project Government is acquiring land from Fifth Schedule Areas unauthorizedly.

Development opportunities in terms of basic services and model facilities need not necessarily attract the tribals to voluntarily leave their original habitat and resettle in an alien area. The relocated area should have more or less similar environment for the tribal people to enable them to continue to enjoy the traditional customs, beliefs, practices and way of life.

In all the three districts model colonies have come up. The older generation is particularly not happy with the houses that they have constructed for them. According to them the rooms are too small, and there is no backyard space for vegetable cultivation; the plinth provided of the toilet-cum-bathrooms is too small and no provision has been made to construct sheds for the cattle owned by them. In situations like this, there is the need to look into individual, collective and community interests to overcome such problems.

In the study area, most of the homestead land is in the name of the community. Respondents have occupied Government land and private land without any Patta and some of them are cultivating in such lands. If they get displaced they will get deprived of the ownership rights that they enjoy now. In some cases, the land selected for compensation is located very far from the original habitat and too far away from the forest for instance D Ravilanka, Bodigudem, and Pargasanipadu villages. It may be true that land selected for compensation is within the Scheduled Areas, but it is very far from the forest. Therefore it is necessary that compensatory land should be identified and given very near to their nearby place or near a forest area.

According to the R & R package, an amount of Rs. 3,000 was earmarked for the construction of a cattle shed. However no provision has been made for land to construct the shed. An amount of Rs. 5,000 was earmarked for the transportation of personal belonging of the Project Affected People (PAF) to the place of relocation. Distance, location of the house and mode of transport available in the locality for transport of the household items need to be also taken into consideration while fixing the transportation cost.

In the Rehabilitation and Resettlement package, those who have completed 18 years are eligible for an independent house.

Therefore there is the need to put a cut off age while deciding on the allotment of houses to the oustees. This is because a man who is 17 years old and on being shifted gets married at the age of 18 years is not eligible for an independent house. In the tribal area they can occupy any community land and construct their own house. But in the new settlement area this is not possible. Therefore the cut off age for allotting independent houses should be brought down from the existing 18 years.

As per the earlier Rehabilitation and Resettlement policy order, the tribals are not entitled for complete land-to-land compensation. It is restricted to 6.2 acres or 2.5 hectares and the rest of the compensation for land is paid in terms of cash. But it is felt that full land-to-land compensation need to be given to the tribals. The relocation area should have more or less similar environment for the tribal people to enable them to continue to enjoy the traditional customs, beliefs, practices and way of life.

Conclusion

After independence, when India initiated development projects in different parts of the country, no specific policy was formulated either by the Central or the State Government to address the issue of displacement of people that took place. In the past, Rehabilitation and Resettlement policy of the displaced people was based on ad hoc plans, resolutions and orders, passed for specific States or even projects when the need arose. Different State Governments and Ministries of Central Government followed different policies on rehabilitation and resettlement in the absence of a national rehabilitation and resettlement policy. So far, States such as Maharastra, MP and Karnataka have resettlement legislation. Most State Governments rely not only on law or universal policies, but on ad hoc administrative instructions, in conformity with bureaucratic preference for what is described as 'case-by-case approach'.

As a result of this ad hoc approach, many of the displaced were left out in receiving the legitimate compensation for their losses. Until 2004, there was no broad policy that could guide the rehabilitation efforts of State sponsored projects in irrigation, power, mining etc. The rehabilitation and resettlement policies for the Project Affected Families at the national level was formulated according to the notification No. A C Q 13011/4/2004 of the Ministry of Rural Development for the first time to address the problems of the displaced due to the increasing number of development projects in the country. A few months after this notification, a Draft National Rehabilitation Policy (NRP) 2006 was under circulation. The Draft (NRP) 2006 is an attempt to improve upon some of the provisions of the National Rehabilitation and Resettlement Policy of 2003 for the benefit of the Project Affected People (PAP), particularly the marginalized sections of the community, which are soft targets in any development project that displaces people.

Past rehabilitation experiences in various projects reveal that they are far from satisfactory. In several cases, project displaced people have been languishing in abject poverty and living without basic amenities even after 25 years of relocating to settlement areas. Issues surrounding dam and reservoir building, as well as other large infrastructure development projects, and involuntary human displacement, remain fervently contested in both Andhra Pradesh and India. They are particularly significant where development projects have routinely involved significant dislocations of populations.

The State of Andhra Pradesh has its rehabilitation and resettlement policy through its GO MS No 68 of the irrigation and Canal Ayacut Development (CAD) department, issued on April 8, 2005. If we compare Draft NRP 2006, with the GO 68 of AP we see that the GO 68 of AP in many respects is a copy of the National Policy on Rehabilitation and Resettlement 2003. It was common for States to have policies on 'The Eminent Domain', many of which dealt solely with the legal process of expropriation, a number of which outlined compensation mechanisms, but none of which dealt in detail with resettlement in ways that would prevent impoverishment. Millions of people were affected by displacement caused due to the submergence of their native habitations. Most of these people were deprived of satisfactory resettlement and rehabilitation due to the absence of comprehensive policies and the lack of commitment in practice. Policies of Governments on resettlement and rehabilitation released over the past few years stand as examples to say that Governments are becoming sensitive to the displacement issue. But, what is essential and yet to be proved is the commitment of Governments in establishing 'best practices' in resettlement and rehabilitation. These issues involve complex interrelationships between economic, environmental, social, technical, political and cultural factors. Gender issues in involuntary resettlement have not received enough attention in development planning in India and in many other developing nations.

On the basis of interviews with the affected people of the Polavaram Project. The R&R package is not properly implemented. The R&R package doesn't provide an adequate land compensation, neglects payment of cash compensation, unequal redistribution of costs and benefits. Agriculture and forest is the main source of livelihood of the people in the displacement area. Agricultural land is the most important productive asset for the tribals and non-tribals. There is symbiotic relationship between forest and tribe. Forest plays an important role in enhancing livelihood requirements and in maintaining ecological balance. It provides products for both marketing and self-consumption during the lean season. Ultimately the people who will be displaced by the Polavaram Project will be deprived of the main sources of their livelihood that is land and forest. Lack of proper implementation of R&R policy people loses a source of income and employment opportunities.

NOTES

1. Tehsil is an administrative division in India and denotes a sub-district. In some States, they are also known as talukas or mandals. Tehsil is generally a land area that serves as the administrative centre to a city or a town and includes towns and sometimes villages. Within a tehsil's jurisdiction, the tehsil offices exercise some fiscal and administrative power over the municipalities and the villages. A tehsil officer is known as Tahsildar or at times Talukdar. At times, tehsils are also known as 'blocks'.

REFERENCES

Biksham, Gujja., S Ramakrishna., V Goud. and Sivarama Krishna. 2006. *Perspectives on Polavaram: A Major Irrigation Project on Godavari.* New Delhi: Academic Foundation and WWF-India.

Cernea, M M. 2000. 'Risks, Safeguards and Reconstruction: A Model for Population Displacement and Resettlement.' In *Risks and Reconstruction: Experiences of Resettlers and Refugees,* edited by M M Cernea and C McDowell (pp. 11-55). Washington, DC: The World Bank.

Government of India. 2004. *National Policy on Resettlement and Rehabilitation for Project Affected Families-*2003. Gazette of India, Extraordinary Part I, Section I, No-46, 17 February 2004.

Government of Andhra Pradesh. 2005. *Indirasagar (Polavaram): A Multipurpose Major Irrigation* Project. Volume I (Environmental Impact Assessment (EIA) and Environmental Management Plan (EMP). Irrigation and CAD Department, Government of Andhra Pradesh; Volume II (Resettlement and Rehabilitation Project Affected Persons Economic Rehabilitation Plan (PAPERP)). Agricultural Finance Corporation, Government of Andhra Pradesh.

Grabska, K. and L Mehta. 2008. *Forced Displacement. Why Rights Matter.* Great Britain: Palgrave Macmillan.

Mathur, H M. 1999. *The Impoverishment Potential of Development Projects-Resettlement Requires Risk Analysis.* Frankfurt: Development and Cooperation (6) Deutsche Stiftung fur Internationale Entwicklung.

Mathur, H M. and Marsden, eds. 1998. *Development Projects and Impoverishment Risks: Resettling Project-Affected People in India.* Delhi: Oxford University Press.

Morvaridi, B. 2008. 'Rights and Development-Induced Displacement: Risk Management or Social Protection?' In *Forced Displacement: Why Rights Matter,* edited by K Grabska and L Mehta. New York: Palgrave Macmillan.

Nixon, R. 2010. 'Unimagined Communities: Developmental Refugees, Megadams and Monumental Modernity.' *New Formations* 69: 62-80.

Reddy, N S. 1996. *Polavaram Project: Report on Resettlement and Rehabilitation of the Displaced.* Hyderabad: Centre for Economic and Social Studies.

SPWD, 2012. *Forest and Common Land Acquisition: Estimated Forecast and Lessons of Case Studies from 6 States.* New Delhi: SPWD. Washington, DC: Rights and Resources Initiative.

World Bank. 2004. *Involuntary Resettlement Sourcebook – Planning and Implementation in Development Projects*. Washington: The World Bank, available at http://www.wds.worldbank.org/servlet/WDSContentServer/WDSP/IB/1996/03/01/000009265_3980728143956/Rendered/PDF/multi_page.pdf.

World Commission on Dams. 2000. *Dams and Displacement: A New Framework for Decision-Making*. London and Sterling, Virginia: Earthscan Publications, Limited.

http://www.sakti.in/godavaribasin/basindetails.htm.

https://saktiblog.wordpress.com/2011/09/page/2/.

11

R and R and Environmental Compliance in Sardar Sarovar Project

D C Sah
Shubhru Singh Tomar

The Sardar Sarovar Project is part of a gigantic scheme seeking to build more than 3,000 dams, including 30 big dams, on Narmada. A mega project costing Rs. 84,080 million in 1986-87 prices (revised Rs. 145,985 million in 1992 prices), Sardar Sarovar Project is supposed to irrigate 1.8 million hectares of agricultural land and provide drinking water to 4,720 villages and 131 urban centres. It would generate additional agricultural output worth Rs. 14,000 million, apart from generating 1,450 MW power. The project has been controversial since its inception[1]. The controversy started in late 1960s on sharing the benefits and cost of the project between Gujarat, Madhya Pradesh and Maharashtra. This was followed by an agitation for the Relocation and Rehabilitation policy for the project between 1982 and 1987. During late 1980s and early 1990s, the project again remained controversial owing to the estimations of social and environmental costs and economic benefits. The opponents of Sardar Sarovar Project argue that this project hides its social and environmental costs and overestimates its benefits and believe that even under heroic assumptions this project is nothing but an environmental disaster. These activists have been critical of the tech-economic feasibility of the project. Their criticism has also been directed at (i) the large area of submergence, (ii) the destruction of forest and wildlife, (iii) the interruptive approach to the natural flow of river and resultant sedimentation, (iv) the problems of water-logging and salinity, (v) the seismic problems due to the large reservoir, and (vi) the risk of water borne diseases to downstream population. Anyone who is following the SSP debate would substantiate the fact that the second generation R and R problems created because of SSP are equally important. The fates of over 40,000 project affected persons (PAPs)[2], who have been displaced, do need concentrated efforts. The violation of rights to livelihood of some of these PAPs, who have poor quality land, has been in debate.

The debate on relocation and rehabilitation of tribals in Narmada valley is informed by numerous sources including print and electronic media, the State, the Greens, Morse and Berger Independent Committee, the pro and anti-dam activists, tribals in submerging zones and the rich landowner beneficiaries of the project, interests of Gujarat State and concerns of Madhya Pradesh Government. Each of these agencies has its own perspective and source of information.

More often, the aim of these agencies is either to discredit R and R, making it an impossibility, or proclaim that everything with respect to R and R is as planned. The facts are in between the two extremes. The Sardar Sarovar Project, because of these, has been controversial since its inception. Of late, the right to livelihood of PAPs has become a moot question wherein the insensitivity of the major agents towards grassroots needs has allowed the judiciary to play an active role.

Human rights of the poor, for one or the other reason, have always been disregarded by the Indian State under the guise that these rights have different meanings for different societies and the western concepts cannot be imposed on us. This argument is unique to states that have little sensitivity for human misery. Unfortunate as it may seem, the State and the civil society have failed in protecting the livelihood rights of a section of PAPs. Consequently, the Supreme Court interpreted some of the rights buried under Directive Principles and made them enforceable.

Sardar Sarovar Project is also one of the development projects in India that has received attention and scrutiny to an extent that it has changed the rules of how projects would be formulated, examined for its socio-economic and environmental viability and executed so that human displacement is minimized. This paper has the aim to document some of the controversies associated with SSP and important lessons from the project, so that the mistakes committed in SSP can be avoided in the future development projects.

Institutional Innovations in SSP

It may be argued that the emergence of NGOs sensitive to actual needs of the PAPs has changed the political process of empowering the poor[3]. In fact, shedding of the built-in inertia to act with humane values in the case of SSP is an outcome of a combination of forces: a strong grassroots movement and the initiative of the civil society[4]; an in-depth understanding by academicians of socio-cultural needs of the affected people to generate alternatives in policy formulation; and pressure by the foreign funding agency—the World Bank—to allow for various options have played an important role in developing an acceptable R and R policy. It is least likely that such interplay of forces can be accommodated in many development projects so that a just R and R becomes part of the project. For, not only the existence but also a change in the nature of initiative from various participants could result in a different R and R policy frame.

In a normative sense, after accepting the R and R package, the first institutional intervention was to introduce accountability in land acquisition and relocation. Barring a few exceptions on the front of providing land, the State and the NGOs did a creditable job; PAPs did get what was due to them in terms of land and infrastructure. But a policy frame cannot solve all the problems of the society; it, nonetheless, reflects the concerns we have and the type of society we believe in.

Viewing the R and R with the backdrop of SSP experiences, there are many positive features also. The land for land policy of compensation is one of the most important of all. By accepting land for land, subjectivity in price fixing can safely be avoided. Tribal groups residing often in remote undulating areas, sustain themselves under low yield equilibrium. Cultivating larger area compensates for the low yields. Through the R and R policy, the procedure of compensating on quality based pricing of land —which results not only in subjectivity in price fixation but also in meager compensation to PAPs — has been avoided.

Planning development projects with sensitivity needs establishment of strong linkages with those processes and institutions that identify and address the disequilibria created by the projects. First, the lack of provisions in the project design to monitor second generation environmental problems and their remedial measures may render the project non-functional, for such problems become threats to environment and the people. This happens over time especially when no specific organization is formally responsible for providing remedial measures. It is desirable to make provisions to avoid such occurrences as an essential part of the project document itself. Such a measure will not only compel the planners to identify second generation environmental problems to the maximum extent at the planning stage, but would also call for fund allocation in order to respond to such problems as and when they arise. Secondly, in the prevalent paradigm of development, market plays an important role. PAPs who are mainly tribal people are unfamiliar with market forces and remain alienated from these processes. Consequently they are required to bear a variety of associated costs without being benefited. This increases economic inequality not only between hosts and new settlers but also among resettlers. Provisions necessary for economic integration are also missing from the present R and R policy of Sardar Sarovar Project. Development has been so isolated from displacement in the present R and R policy that these issues are not even recognized. What is, therefore, needed is a Development Policy wherein Displacement and Rehabilitation become part of a policy frame.

The R and R policy of the SSP has subdivided the implementation plan into a relocation plan and a resettlement plan. In doing so, it has disassociated the relocation process from the project construction. The R and R policy states that this plan would be ready at least a year before the start of land acquisition. In the process, as experiences show, relocation takes place simultaneously with submergence. This is referred to as *pari passu*. The problem with *pari passu* is that project authorities turn indifferent to the needs of PAPs as time passes. But the *pari passu* mode clause cannot be avoided. Thus, a project should commence only after ensuring equal treatment and package to early as well as late resettlers.

The early years of relocation were of extreme hardship to the oustees owing to the breaking up of usual informal exchange structures of submerging villages. To mitigate this hardship, the relocated households have cultivation rights till submergence commences without resorting to an official sanction. This economic support may ease hardship associated with early shocks of relocation. Also, the process of acquiring land in the command area for relocated PAPs should be complete before the commencement of the project. Though, to some extent, this will restrict the choice of site for resettlement by the oustees, it will smoothen the planning of the relocation process.

Relocation and Rehabilitation
Relocation: The First Generation Problems

The relocation policy of SSP is one of the best in the country. But this policy, as has been reported earlier, was accepted by the GOG (Government of Gujarat) after a prolonged struggle. The relocation from the submerging villages, however, started before the acceptance of the R and R policy. Early resettlers did not immediately shift to new sites; over 70 per cent of them took over 5 years to make the new site their home. During this period they commuted to and fro or members of households split between locations. By and large, the social interaction between the host and new settlers have remained cordial. Visiting each other during sickness, death, marriages, and religious occasions was common. But whatever common property resources got depleted due to the arrival of new settlers or when social groups were dissimilar and unknown to each other, the relationship between the two become occasionally tense.

The commitments made by the State at the time of relocation have been fulfilled to a large extent: only 4 per cent of oustees have not received agricultural land. Since these oustees have been recognized as PAPs, they are in the process of acquiring all the benefits available to PAPs, including allocation of agricultural land. Barring a few exceptions like PAPs in Malu, Piparvati, Ambavadi, Chikda and Kali-Talavadi, the PAPs are satisfied with the quality of their land. Education, road and transport, healthcare services and institutions like input and output markets are highly appreciated by the PAPs. There is on the whole no deterioration in the living standards of PAPs after relocation. Going by the condition of early resettlers, it can be argued that the tribals who were relatively better exposed to the market are slowly getting adjusted to the new socio-cultural changes. The supportive structure to facilitate their participation in the modern economy is weak, which continues to keep them in a disadvantageous position compared to those who have been part of the system for a longer period. They do feel a loss of identity and security. But that feeling is not strong and pronounced. On the whole, despite irritants and complaints, at the subjective level they seem to be happy. They are, however, unhappy about fuel and fodder availability, tin-shed transit houses and frequent disruptions in drinking water facilities. Submerging villages had traditional healthcare services which were provided mainly by Bhuva; alternative services were totally lacking in these submerging villages. After relocation, traditional healthcare services are being largely replaced by non-traditional services like sub-primary health centres, visit of health workers and private practitioners. Despite these, PAPs relocated in 45 out of 120 new sites have to travel about 6 to 10 kms before reaching a health provider. Moreover, though the health seeking practices have been considerably influenced by allopathic services, PAPs' perceptions about diseases are still guided by their experiences of submerging villages. Another noticeably improved service is the educational facility in the new sites compared to the submerging villages. Not only schools were inaccessible in the submerging villages, but also a sizeable population of schoolgoing children were engaged in cattle grazing and agriculture. Consequently, literacy rates were low. About 25 per cent of males and 6 per cent of females were literate in submerging villages. In new sites about 41 per cent males and about 18 per cent females are literate. Nonetheless, fragmentation of families, agricultural land to major sons, lack of access to fuel and fodder, high prices of land, relocation sites outside the command area, short-changing in land, fragmented and encumbered plots, non-functional hand-pumps and lack of access to drinking water, hardships of tin-shed dwelling, and institutional isolation were some of the major first generation problems faced by early resettlers. The State was quick to solve these first generation problems. Serious though these problems are, the existing R and R policy has provisions to tackle them. More serious are the second generation rehabilitation problems for which no such provisions exist. As will be seen in the next section, the Bhil, Nayka and Vasava tribes of interior submerging villages are finding it difficult to adapt to new agriculture. Even during normal years about two out of every ten PAPs allocated face access failure to minimum nutrients. Although the relocation of over 80 per cent of PAPs was achieved quite successfully, their rehabilitation has just started and its success calls for a fresh investigation for policy review and revision.

Rehabilitation: Second Generation Problems

About 20 per cent of all the relocated households (2981) feel that their land quality is not adequate and needs mechanical or chemical treatment (Ambavadi, Piparvati, Chikda 1 and 2, Dabhavan and other new sites located outside the command area of Narmada have these problems). About 13 per cent of the households believe that they received less land than what was due to them. About 9 per cent of the households had their land under canals or roads (households located in Karshnapura, Malu 1, Pania 1 and 2 have this problem). About 4 per cent households reported that their agricultural land remains waterlogged during the rainy season (this is a serious problem for households located in Kanteshwar, Kali-Talavadi, Pansoli, Malu 1 and 2, and Sanoli). The surplus generated in agriculture during normal years is insufficient to sustain them during abnormal years. During years of severe yield fluctuations, PAPs' adjustment mechanism revolves around the judicious use of foodstocks, past savings, borrowings, casual and agricultural labouring and migration. In this adjustment mechanism, the State support has been marginal. There are other impoverishment risks identified and these are: the plight of the less exposed tribes principally those from interior submerging villages; the access failure to minimum nutrition even during normal years; the commercialization and consumerism; the pressures on land and short-term land transactions.

Economic Activities

While agriculture has become the major economic activity after relocation, the proportion of population engaged as casual or agricultural labour has come down. The reduced importance assigned to labouring activities is not because of the lack of opportunities but because cultivation on their own land is making it possible to adequately provide for family needs. It is only in distress conditions that some of the family members of relocated households have to take up casual or agricultural labour. Two other processes are worth noting: first, due to the improved extension support relating to stall-feeding of milch animals and judicious relocation of land for food and fodder, animal husbandry has regained its lost importance. Secondly, owing to paucity of fuel and fodder in new sites, their collection have become time-consuming activities.

Agricultural Production

The trends of crop diversification as observed after relocation reveal a shift from subsistence farming towards high value crop production for markets. This crop diversification is, however, not uniform across locations. Increased access to irrigation apart from locational advantage has been the driving force behind this change. Although there is about a twofold improvement in crop yields in comparison to yields in their submerging villages, the yields in some years and on some farms are lower than either the best of the yields or the district average. To make the matter worse, during two consecutive abnormal agricultural years, the farmers have been unable to sustain the impact. Borrowing, depletion of animal stock, migration and going for non-farm labouring during these years is a natural outcome. This indicates the vulnerability of dry land agriculture where low yields could result owing to marginal weather changes. Despite the fact that the extension wing of SSPA is providing support to bring appropriate cropping pattern changes and selection of seed varieties to suit the local soil-moisture, the support is not viable enough to minimize the crop losses. The need is to insulate the local agrarian economy from the vagaries of monsoon.

Market Links

The use of market purchase inputs has increased over the years, but the input use is much below their recommended rates. Another emerging feature of input linkage is the slowly increasing integration of production with the credit markets. In the case of output marketing, not only the proportion of PAPs selling the crops has increased but the proportion of total produce sold has also increased significantly. Unfortunately, the surplus marketed by this group (low intake) of PAPs is relatively high. Cash needs and the demonstration effect of host villagers may be responsible for forcing this vulnerable group of PAPs to market their food crops relatively more rather than keeping them for self-consumption.

Pressures on Land

Pressure on land has forced the PAPs to augment their land resources by multiple cropping. About 16 per cent of the cultivable area is double-cropped. Though irrigation is important, in the diversified farms, multiple cropping on dry land is three times more than the multiple cropping in irrigated areas. While irrigation is instrumental for diversification, it is the quality of irrigation which governs diversification. Two other obstacles in crop diversification are the lack of exposure to modem technology and the labour availability.

The crop diversification instead of adversely affecting food security, has brought positive changes in terms of increased farm yield, additional surplus for non-food expenditure, less market dependence and increased calorie intake for all farms other than cotton dominated farms. But in the absence of a viable technology, the crop diversification could not decisively reduce yield risks. Although the economy as a whole could absorb the seasonally unemployed in the farm sector, the pace and intensity of employment in the vicinity is not robust enough to bear the employment imperatives of poor agriculture. Consequently, some of the family members have to seasonally migrate to distant places. Seasonal migration supports the consumption levels of the households' non-migrating members at a reasonable level. In order to get the best out of their unproductive land, some affected PAPs have developed new institutions unknown to them in their submerging villages. Short term land transactions — like sharecropping, fixed rent or land mortgage — are some of such institutions developed in new sites to address the market failures.

Food and Calorie Intake

Measured through simple indicators like average consumption intake and access to amenities, it seems that over the years, the PAPs have not experienced a deterioration in their level of living compared to their submerging villages. Nevertheless, at the margin about 20 per cent PAPs even during normal years do not consume minimum nutrients. During abnormal years this figure shoots up to over 50 per cent. The findings on food consumption reveal that during bad years, yield variations have adversely affected the food availability, and consumption of cereals and protein has been affected adversely. Findings also show that the PAPs have learned to sustain one bad year using their own coping mechanism. This is a paradox of early development when growth is accompanied with recurring yield variations, increased vulnerability and access failure to food to some. The overall impact of low yield of two consecutive years forces a sizeable reduction in consumption and calorie intake. During the summer months the effect is severe. This is the most vulnerable period because the food stocks would have depleted and the new crop is still to arrive. The R and R policy will have to devise strategies to provide short-term relief and employment support to check this access failure to food so that yield fluctuations in the future are sustained with minimum adverse consumption disruptions. In the long run, however, the local economy has to be insulated from the vagaries of monsoon.

Expenditure

At current prices, the total annual expenditure of the households has increased about two and a half times when compared to the expenditure level of the submerging villages. The improved purchasing power of households after relocation is undisputed even at constant prices. The increased productivity of land is a major reason. But such improvement drains when productivity falls. This may be happening even during a normal year in the case of PAPs with poor agricultural yields. Relocation has also resulted in bringing changes in relative importance of various heads in the expenditure pattern. Improvement in agricultural production has resulted in the fall of the share of day-today expenditure on food purchase and due to the overall increase in income, share of asset formation has improved substantially. Nonetheless, the tendency of low income trap, where a large proportion of expenditure is on food items, sets in again when there is a crop failure.

Perceptions about Economic Condition

During a normal year, about 90 per cent of the PAPs report that their economic condition has either improved or has remained the same compared to what it was in their submerging villages. Not surprisingly, during the abnormal years, a large proportion of PAPs reported significant deterioration in their economic condition. These findings should be interpreted with caution. For, these do not necessarily reflect the pre and post-relocation comparison of the economic condition of PAPs. The findings, in fact, indicate their importance of contemporary experiences in shaping these perceptions: Farm production of households which are dissatisfied is significantly lower, and PAPs who were unable to feed their members from self-production have also reported deterioration in their economic condition. Those PAPs who have to resort relatively more to casual and agricultural labour are also the PAPs who have negative perceptions about their economic condition. On the other hand, the PAPs who perceive an improvement in their economic condition have significantly higher income and calorie intake, depend much less on market purchases for food, and do not have to fall back on casual and agricultural labour compared to those PAPs who believe that their economic condition has deteriorated. These tendencies shall further strengthen if farm income can be insulated from the vagaries of monsoon through appropriate policy interventions.

Performance of Different Tribes

Evidence reveals that after relocation, the Nayaka, Bhil and Vasava tribes have less diversified cropping pattern and lower yields compared to Tadvi and Rathwa. The former tribes have less than 24 per cent of gross cropped areas allocated to non-traditional commercial crops and superior cereals, whereas the latter group has between 33 and 44 per cent area allocated to these. Production is also higher on farms operated by Tadvi and Rathwa. Among the relocated households there is a small group of PAPs who were landless in their submerging villages. These people were mainly in interior villages of Zone II and III. These households in their submerging villages depended on agriculture as their subsidiary occupation; their main occupation was animal husbandry and labouring. After relocation, about a third of these PAPs could not adjust to agricultural practices of new sites. Inputs used by the tribal groups like Nayaka, Bhil and Vasava reveal that these PAPs have yet to establish strong links with the input market. The bulk of their farming is with family labour and homegrown seeds. Purchased input, seed, fertilisers and chemicals, used on their farms are about a third to half of purchase inputs used by Tadvi and Rathwa: Fertiliser use is about a third on the farms of Nayka, Bhil and Vasava compared to Rathwa managed farms. The same is the situation with other market purchased inputs, plant protection chemicals and hired labour A low input use is reflected in the agricultural production of the PAPs coming from submerging zones II and

III. The farm production of Nayaka, Bhil and Vasava is about half of the production obtained by Rathwa, who not only produce relatively efficiently but also do not have to rely on large market purchases for their food consumption. The calorie intake amongst the tribes coming from interior zones also reveal constraints. This variation in calorie intake is mainly governed by the variation in pulse and cereals consumption. The low farm production also reflected in the capability of different groups to invest on various items like consumer items, health and education and assets.

The apprehension expressed in the last section that the condition of the oustees of Zone II and III after the relocation is unlikely to be as satisfactory as observed on the farms of Tadvi and Bhil than the condition of the PAPs of Zone I has come true. The tribes Bhil and Nayaka are the worst hit due to their inability to assimilate with the mainstream groups.

Missing Rights in SSP

When the R and R policy of Sardar Sarovar Project proclaims that the tribal community would, strictly, be settled in the area of their choice, it empowered the State to break the social fabric associated with the village, peer group and family[6]. The relocation process could be seen from two different angles; first, the traditional social linkages and economic institutions in the submerging villages had an important place in the life of oustees. These arrangements had helped in the sustenance of the society in submerging villages. The randomness of relocation and absence of the traditional arrangements at the new sites could make the oustees vulnerable to exploitation. Second, the existing policy is inappropriate. The people associated with resettling the oustees may defend the policy and the process by reiterating that the decision of shifting is an individual decision. The strength of the argument is drawn from the fact that the tribal village is not a homogeneous unit; Even in a *falia* (hamlet of a village), people do not always want to shift together. And since the oustees may be shown land in different locations, their moving to the new sites is voluntary, for oustees have preferred the land they want to cultivate in the new sites. The argument could have been accepted if there were methods in avoiding the randomness of the relocation.

It may be argued that the R and R policy of SSP provides avenues and instruments of choosing the new site. The fact is that oustees certainly may have a choice; to choose the best amongst the worst. Thus, the migration in the absence of proper social and economic arrangements may not only be involuntary but also an outcome of the policy frame incapable of safeguarding the risks of social disruption. This is what can be termed as lack of interaction within a rigid policy frame.

The lack of interaction among agents was not only present in site selection but also in the gender issues. While interpreting 'member dependent on land', unmarried women, widows and divorcees need to be identified as adult members. This is just not a question of justice and equality, but also reflects the attitude of policy makers towards the needs and participation of women. This attitude further manifests in the form of ignoring the gender perspective in choosing relocation sites, selection of sites for house plots, locating drinking water sources (pumps and wells) at the new sites etc. In tribal communities, female participation in day to day decision making as also in economic activity is equal to that of the male. Patriarchal norms of non-tribal societies restrict mutual decision making. Revisions recognizing women's needs and concerns, and ensuring their participation in decision making have to be incorporated in the R and R policy. In fact, the relocation and rehabilitation must be recognized as a participatory processes and this must be realized by policy makers through appropriate and effective interventions. The term participation has been used here as the right of the displaced to participate in a process which is affecting their livelihood. This also presupposes that there exists mutual trust between institutions involved in R and R and the affected community. This may result in better living conditions with respect to choices of migration, identification of new sites, agricultural land, house plots and location of social amenities. The proposition was well founded, but the reality shows that though the interaction between the State and the civil society existed, it was missing at the community level. Exclusion and marginalization was the obvious outcome.

The experience of SSP has shown that well-intended policy statements remain unimplemented owing to the failure of identifying instruments for their execution. The R and R policy of SSP also lacks necessary linkages that make such a policy implementable. For example, with respect to land rights of the PAPs, and their cultural losses, the policy does not ensure how the right for entitlement of land free from encumbrance would be enforced. Neither is the policy spelling out as to how cultural losses owing to relocation and social and economic integration with the mainstream would be taken care of. Almost always these statements show well-intended concerns but these have emerged as rhetoric that clearly lacks the necessary institutional arrangements for their implementation. And thus, when land rights are being discussed in the R and R policy, issues like the following need checking:

- the size of allotted agricultural land
- if canal, road, or any other project is not on the land allotted to a PAP
- whether the same land which was shown to PAP has been allotted to him
- for encumbrance on it
- if an issue like the right of a minor in the father's property clashing with the right of a major son, has remained outside the purview of the present policy. This creates ambiguity in the minds of PAPs about their status as landholders. Therefore, identification of institutions which have to carry out such verifications cannot be overemphasized.

The PAPs despite being tribal, are not a monolithic entity[7]; they vary significantly in terms of their languages, customs, beliefs, perceptions, needs and capabilities. The SSP has failed to address the needs of groups which remained unexposed to the market economy and modern agriculture - the Bhil, Nayaka and Vasava tribes of Zones II and III. The extension wing neither differentiates between the hosts and PAPs, nor among different groups in tribal population.

Relocation allows only movable heritage to shift along with the displaced. Relocation of PAPs as a community demands reconstructing immobile cultural icons in the new site. This is possible when (a) it is recognised that the community has to be relocated rather than the PAPs, and (b) freedom of cultural necessities becomes part of the development process. Both the above prerequisites are difficult to achieve, for one, we keep on forgetting the concept of heterogeneity amongst the PAPs, and for the other, there may not be many social scientists who may like to be associated with the process of identification of relevant necessities—social, cultural and economic—to be included in the development process. Empowering the PAPs is a process which may not fascinate many social scientists, for the research agenda in this case is guided by tangential pressures from funding agencies and the *publish or perish* syndrome from peer groups. Having cautioned about the dangers, the help of trained social scientists—anthropologists, sociologists and economists —in the process of planning itself is not considered an undesirable option. In fact, such inclusion may improve the chances of identifying meaningful alternatives.

For providing amenities in the relocation sites, the R and R policy of SSP states that water supply for drinking and cattle, fodder and grazing land, schools, approach roads, electricity connection, health centres, religious places, cemeteries and graveyards, *Panchayat* house, etc. should be made available. More often these facilities are linked to a minimum number of relocated families. The relocation process, as experiences have proven, does not always contain the minimum number of specified families required for the provision of a particular facility at a new site. This easily leads to non-compliances in providing these amenities. Another major problem in the new sites has been the lack of maintenance of created services. This not only marginalized the inhabitants but also results in the exit of NGOs from the R and R scene.[8]

India is a signatory to ILO Convention 107 adopted in 1957 as a convention concerning the protection and integration of tribal population. The ILO convention affirms the right of tribal people to their land and proclaims that if they are displaced due to national interests, the displaced will be provided with land suitable for their present needs and future development. We in India also believe that people are free and equal in dignity and that all people contribute to the diversity and the richness of Indian culture. Any doctrine of cultural superiority, therefore, is legally invalid and socially unjust. Despite the fact that the relocation package of SSP reflects the idea that relocation will not adversely affect the standard of living, and also reflects the development of human rights, the displacement due to SSP has had reporting of human rights violations. The first serious protest against the violation of human rights originated from Manibeli (PUCL 1993). The PUCL (People's Union for Civil Liberties) report viewed the process of relocation infringement on the right to life, rights to information, right to struggle, as well as the violation of NWDT (Narmada Water Dispute Tribunal) recommendations. This was followed by a Gujarat PUCL (1993) report which found the findings of PUCL report factually incorrect and concluded that allegations of coercion were baseless. The Gujarat PUCL cited the findings of Fact Finding Team's report on Manibeli incident (Acharya et. al, 1992). The Fact Finding Team observed that there was a rupture of dialogue between the two groups who are socially and culturally the same. Their differences have been aggravated by the intervention of outside agencies. Police intervention became inevitable to help the group who wanted to shift to new site. Bulldozers were used more for operational purposes than intimidation. The committee found no visible signs of violence nor was any violence reported by any party during the operations. Police was not used for any dismantling or shifting operations. There are also other citings of human rights violations which range from rights of non-PAPs (Soni and Appa 1993), right to struggle, violation of Court Orders (HRCN, 1993), right not to be forcibly evicted, right not to be forcibly staying, right to information and right not to be physically harassed (Bhatia 1997). These reports from pro and anti dam groups are equally persuasive. But when Bhatia reported of forced eviction from an Antras submerging village of Gujarat where thirty families were refusing to shift and violence against Budiben—

a PAP of Antras and Narmada Bacho Andolan activist—and her subsequent rape to psychologically threaten her to shift, and forced stay of Malu PAPs who wanted to shift to their submerging villages Gadher and Vadgam, the drama was being staged for collection of pieces of evidence to stop the dam project. Neither the text was mediocre in nature nor were the sentiments behind it trivial. But the way the whole set of evidence served the ideology, a sense of patronage towards PAPs was more dominating than the possibility of rehabilitation.

But more disturbingly evidence confirms that abnormal weather in the region results in severe yield fluctuations which in turn affect the rights to livelihood. The food security implications are serious if the PAPs have also experienced yield stagnation for two consecutive years. Even during normal years, risks involved in technology adoption are so high that PAPs, by and large, have preferred to avoid adopting the new agricultural technology in dry areas. As a result, the cushion available from good years is not enough to neutralize the risk of food insecurity during abnormal years. Erratic weather induces wide yield fluctuations. During abnormal years, nearly half of the PAPs face total crop failure. The yield of major crops registers a sizeable fall and, households' access to foodgrains reduces by about 20 per cent, and the level of consumption and calorie intake fall by about 17 per cent (Sah, 1997). In scarcity years, PAPs' coping mechanism revolves around (a) reducing farm expenditure, (b) decision of household members to work as casual and agricultural labour, (c) seasonal migration of some family members, and (d) borrowings and distress sale of cattle. But these adjustments are not enough to maintain the households' calorie intakes. The role of the State in the PAPs' coping mechanism has been marginal. Moreover, agricultural growth in this dry zone is riddled with moderate increase in production and recurring crop failure. The pressure on land is immense and agriculture alone is unable to sustain the households' consumption in a weather cycle[9].

Pressure on land forced the PAPs to augment their land resources by multiple cropping. A fifth of the cultivable area is double-cropped (Sah, 1998). Though irrigation is important, in the diversified farms, the extent of multiple cropping on dry land is three times more than that in the irrigated area. While irrigation is consequential for diversification, it is the quality of irrigation which governs diversification. Two other obstacles to crop diversification are lack of exposure to modern technology, enabling access to extension support, and constraints in labour availability. The process of crop diversification has been left to PAPs, wherein the role of State as an agent of change with NGOs as its catalyst is negligible.

Crop diversification, instead of adversely affecting food security, has brought about positive changes in terms of increased farm yield, additional surplus for non-food expenditure, less market dependence and increased calorie intake for all farms, other than cotton dominated farms. But in the absence of a viable technology, crop diversification could not reduce yield risks. Since the understanding on the new technology varied amongst different tribes, Tadvi and Rathwa did well to adapt it to their needs but Vasava, Bhil and Nayaka were unable to adopt the technology. This increased inequality between tribes. Moreover, the economy as a whole, though, could absorb the seasonally unemployed in the farm sector, the pace and intensity of growth of the non-agricultural sector in the vicinity is not robust enough to bear the employment imperatives of crop failure. Consequently, some of family members have to migrate to distant places for some time[10]. Seasonal migration supports the consumption levels of households' non-migrating members at a respectable level. In order to get the best out of their unproductive land[11], some PAPs have developed institutions unknown to them in their respective submerging villages. Short term land transactions like sharecropping, fixed rent or land mortgage[12] are such institutions developed in the new sites owing to market failure.

The PAPs' consumption response to income changes is similar to the one observed in case of the mainstream society: a decline in the share of food in total family budget. Although cereals and pulses still account for over three-fourths of the total calorie intake, superior cereals are replacing coarse cereals among all the income groups, more so during abnormal years.

This substitution is more an upshot of the availability of superior cereals through PDS rather than a matter of choice. What is most disturbing is the fact that even during normal years about a fifth of PAPs have reported per capita intake of less than 2,000 calories per day. During abnormal years, the calorie intake of half of the PAPs remains below this norm. Not only the incidence of poverty is high during these abnormal years, but also the intake gap within the vulnerable group of the poor further deteriorates and inequality indices show a sharp increase. In order to bridge the poverty gap, a mixed policy focusing on rapid agricultural growth and expansion of non-farm employment is desirable.

These second generation problems of involuntary migration were known to the policy makers, and yet inaction on their part for strengthening the coping mechanism of PAPs only indicates their insensitivity. State, it seems, instead of participating at the time of the short-term shocks, believed that their interaction with community at the time of these crises was outside the R and R purview.

Decision Making

In order to utilize the findings of information support for policy reorientation, it would be mandatory on the part of the project authority to participate in the discussion and dissemination of field realities. This dissemination would lead to (a) identifying the deviations from expected norms, (b) understanding implications of the observed deviations, (c) causes of such deviations, and (d) measures to be adopted for minimizing the associated risks. Devoid of such participatory process, the PAPs, as has been the case in the SSP, would find themselves in a perpetual state of poverty.[13]

In order to plan for integration of oustees into the mainstream economy, it is desirable to distinguish between institutions at the new sites and their access to PAPs. For, the second generation problems of resettlement like access to market and technology, yield risk, access failure to food, pressures on land, leasing out land, seasonal migration etc. need a different treatment than the usual top-down development approach. The basic failure of the existing rehabilitation policy of SSP is the policy makers' overconfidence about its organizational capabilities to respond to rehabilitation problems. The organizational set-up responsible for economic integration in the absence of participation of PAPs, NGOs, agricultural scientists and the community is unable to comprehend the complexity of the process and is rendered unfit to deal with its negative consequences.

For those associated with development planning, the R and R in any guise is soothing for it lends to the philosophy that (a) development is sacrosanct enough to be overtly insensitive to various problems created by itself and (b) the distortions so created can be ironed out by policy interventions. The R and R policy of SSP is also riddled with policy instruments waiting for execution owing to the lack of institutionalization. The foregoing analysis calls for a fresh debate not only on the R and R policy of a development project but also on how the mid-course corrections can be accepted by policy makers. It has also been argued that in the absence of public support, the risk of access failure to food has serious implications. Yield fluctuations in the dry zone are high and it is not uncommon that, though the total food availability is normal, a sizeable section of PAPs may have poor yields. For some, owing to poor quality of agricultural land[14], this could be a perpetual phenomenon. This renders them unfit to cope with their lack of access to food. If the policy makers are serious in minimizing the adverse effects of such access failure, it could be a perplexing task. Otherwise, they could choose to ignore the indications provided by the capability of the allotted agricultural land and availability of alternative employment in the area and remain complacent.

Does it mean that total food production and availability, other things remaining same, have no poverty implication? The situation can be puzzling when despite a substantial improvement in total food production, some households may be facing access failure to food. Sen (1981) has put forward the entitlement approach as an alternative theory of the cauzation of famines. He defines entitlement as a set of different commodities that a person acquires through the use of various legitimate means in his position. In an open economy, his endowment and ownership of productive assets shall in the normal situation provide access to a number of commodities, through economic exchange and production, for his consumption. Abnormal situations like crop failure, severe fluctuations in macroeconomic indicators like total availability of food stock, changes in pattern of normal stock market and hoarding, may result in affecting his endowment -through land alienation, ill health and ability to work or, his exchange entitlement mapping is affected adversely - through wage reduction, increase in food prices, loss of employment and crop failure. Production in relation to ownership pattern, agricultural land with severe problems, access to alternative employment and wages, and more importantly, short-term measures initiated by State provide insights on households' capabilities.

The above argument aims at initiating policy changes. The observation in certain quarters that the relocation package is generous enough to tackle problems relating to resettlement is a misplaced proposition. The relationship between agricultural growth and poverty notwithstanding, depletion of assets, seasonal migration, reduction in current consumption and input use are not unimportant indicators of a process of increasing deprivation. Their inclusion in the analysis would make our understanding richer, and their influence in policy formulation would have far-reaching implications. The inability to command food even if it is available through PDS, is an indicator of want of public action in the form of creating short-term employment. This will not only provide the much needed purchasing power but also improve productivity of land. But in the long run, the land alone should support livelihood. To make this happen, factors constraining technology transfer in agriculture cannot be ignored. The important question is how to institutionalize these processes.

The foregoing analysis indicates that interactions among the State, NGOs as the main organ of civil society and the community on the issue of livelihood adaptation have been insubstantial. Consequently, the State's response to PAPs own coping mechanism has been insensitive. Public actions are reserved for occasions when the whole region is facing access failure to food. The civil society, as an extended arm of public action, has remained superficial in the community's coping mechanism. In the process, the community is forced to take decisions on the consequences of impoverishment risks. This apathy, owing to the lack of participation, resulted in exclusion and marginalization of the affected PAPs in the short run. In the long run, the State and the civil society's actions confirm increasing anxiety to insulate the economy from year to year fluctuations in the rainfall. This indicates some optimism for a process which would lead to a closer interaction among the State, the civil society and the community in the long run.

The absolute failure of the Indian State became visible when the Supreme Court forced the State to accept the Grievance Redressal Authority. The aim of the GRA is to look into every aspect of R and R of Gujarat oustees, including the poor quality of allotted land and the livelihood adaptations. Over nine thousand cases have been addressed by GRA till date. This reflects on the inventory of complaints[15] the State has left for the GRA to resolve.

Shades of Civil Society

Individual researchers (Cullet, 2007) may have taken an emancipated view of civil society involvement in the Sardar Sarovar Project, and may have given due credit to the contribution of Narmada Bachao Andolan. But doing this, Cullet has dwarfed the achievements of Gujarat civil society by not highlighting the role others have played.

'The World Bank loan brought to the Sardar Sarovar Project the whole set of policies that provide the framework for the implementation of bank-funded projects...The involvement and subsequent withdrawal of the World Bank from the project is landmark event... The involvement in SSP was, by all accounts, one of the biggest public disasters for the World Bank. As a result, a number of initiatives were taken to ensure that similar problems would not resurface... After the World Bank withdrawal from the project, the development of SSP took a different turn... From the point of view of *Narmada Bachao*

Andolan, the withdrawal of the World Bank was a boon and a challenge. From March 1993 onwards, much less international pressure could be applied on the Central and State Governments. Eventually, in view of the difficulties faced in making itself heard, NBA decided to have recourse to public interest litigations, which had come to be seen by mid-1990s as one of the best avenues for ensuring justice and securing the realization of human rights' (Cullet, Chapter 1).

The SSP is a product of varied and mixed experiences; good at the level of policy, acceptable in the implementation of relocating PAPs, and poor in case of their rehabilitation. The success of the R and R package at various levels is a product of coming together of many minds. The R and R policy of SSP has evolved over a period of time and after a prolonged struggle by activists in Gujarat. The involvement of NGOs - especially ARCH Vahini, Anand Niketan Ashram and Rajpipla Social Services Society - in R and R in Gujarat can be seen in two phases. The first phase ends by 1987 when these NGOs were able to organize tribals to force the policy-makers to come out with a just R and R policy. The second phase is of post-December 1987 when the R and R package was accepted by the Government of Gujarat and these NGOs decided to become active partners in the relocation process. Notwithstanding the fact that left to the State, the implementation of R and R package would have been as indifferent as has been in other projects in the country. A fair amount of success at the execution of the relocation of PAPs certainly would not have been possible but for the support provided by the non-government organizations, who had earlier fought for a just resettlement and rehabilitation (R and R) policy for the SSP.

It is quite possible that the success of the SSP relocation process will emphasize the inevitability of NGOs' involvement to ensure a fair deal to the PAPs elsewhere. This may be a premature conclusion for, it is possible that what led to the success of a process may end up in its demise when the process is replicated. The working of NGOs reveals a heterogeneous pattern. The NGOs working in rural reconstruction are a mixed lot[4]; some like ARCH Vahini delivered the services keeping their ideology of social reform, but many more are simply participants in what may be termed as 'market of development programmes'. The difference in the actions and ideology of NGOs are built within the character of people running these organizations. Such variations result in indifference in delivering what the organization is supposed to deliver with sensitivity. Importantly, the concept of sensitivity is not static; it varies not only across organizations but also for an organization over time. Thus, it will be a futile exercise to presume consistency in approach. A policy decision to involve NGOs arrived at in good faith that the grassroots level understanding would be helpful In the successful implementation of programmes, may be self-defeating and may not ensure sensitivity as shown by some NGOs in case of SSP.

The post-1988 period saw immense pressures on NGOs. On the one hand, they had to sustain the political will and see that this will was translated into actions. And on the other, the ability of pro-state NGOs to influence and work with the oustees depended solely on fulfilment of promises they had made to them before relocation. These two roles were not congruous. The bureaucracy at the lower level in its turn exploited this contradiction. Allocation of unproductive land, short-changing in land and subsistence allowance were some of the problems, which did not surface for over a decade. Some PAPs who were relocated between 1983 and 1987 when the R and R package was not accepted by the State also faced a problem of discrepancy in the compensation package. They not only got a meagre monetary compensation for their land but their grown-up sons who were recognized as separate PAPs after 1987 had to wait for another five to seven years to receive their package for want of suitable land in the nearby new sites. Fragmentation of family was the tragic outcome in many cases. No matter how hard the affected oustees and the involved NGOs tried to settle these cases, non-availability of land and bureaucratic insensitivity delayed the outcome. The discredit invariably went to the NGOs.

The political will was activated and the bureaucracy did strive for a fast and smooth relocation. The bureaucracy at the grassroots level either did not get the real feedback from the leaders who were the contact points for dealing with PAPs in over 120 locations or preferred to ignore the representations made by NGOs regarding their grievances. This resulted in creating temporary calm, as the real grievances of oustees did not surface immediately. Many of the leaders were also co-opted to voice what the bureaucracy wanted to, that *all is well on the R and R front*. The incentive for such co-optation was the benefit to the leaders in the form of contracts for construction of facilities in the new sites, and the access to closer circles of decision making. As long as the dissatisfaction did not surface especially concerning the quality of land and amenities at the new sites, the NGOs, especially ARCH Vahini, did choose to co-operate with the bureaucracy.

Nonetheless, a group of activists, who in 1989 formed the Narmada Bachao Andolan (NBA), took the stand of *No Dam* on grounds of ecological and human costs, soon after the acceptance of the R and R package in mid-1988. Their struggle, though started around displacement, reopened the question of the project's sustainability. This paradigmatic shift opened a new dimension in the debate on *development*. Sustainability did not remain confined to tribal rights, loss of livelihood and resettlement; it also included ecological and environmental issues associated with the project. Their belief regarding the unsustainability of Sardar Sarovar, strong views about the impossibility of rehabilitation, and the lack of faith in the capabilities of the administration to handle a large involuntary migration—originating from not only Gujarat but also Maharashtra and Madhya Pradesh—brought about a vertical split between the involved NGOs. A group spearheaded by Medha Patkar seriously questioned this development approach. The other group, headed by ARCH Vahini and consisting of majority of NGOs from Gujarat, remained pro-rehabilitation. The latter believed that rehabilitation was possible, provided adequate mechanisms were developed for checks and balances in the resettlement process. 'Tribals', says Vahini, *'have shown clear preference for good quality of land, security of tenure, and much greater access to market and other infrastructural facilities like roads, transport, electricity, schools, and even rudiments of health service. Their access to market, their integration with the market economy is limited'* (Patel, 1997). Making all these happen in the relocation process was, thus, desirable. These views, pragmatic though, are explicitly at variance with the Andolan's ideology. The defence of tribal rights by Vahini took various forms of colloquy - from rhetoric and polemics (ARCH, 1992), to defending the State against the Independent Review (ARCH, 1993). But nowhere ARCH's commitment to serve the interests of the oustees was ever in doubt, neither when it was working closely with the State in the Project nor when it withdrew.

From this pro-rehabilitation position, when ARCH Vahini withdrew itself from the Project in 1995, the question may not have been so much of a failed paradigm. This drastic step more likely would have been taken due to failed processes, which were unable to insulate the PAPs from various problems in their resettlement. ARCH disassociating itself from the R and R almost after a decade of its involvement might also have been because the pro-rehabilitation self of ARCH was in contradiction with its pro-state self. This debate notwithstanding, what should be remembered is that under normal circumstances, the problems faced by PAPs could have been sensed and raised by ARCH much earlier. But their preoccupation with relocation did not allow them to play the facilitating role for such identification; relocation pressures were too intense and too prolonged for them to have either the time or the energy to take up rehabilitation issues.

Though development could have varying meanings, the Indian State used it to achieve a single goal, the goal of capital accumulation for rapid growth. This process demanded sacrifices on the part of the citizens, invariably the poor who have to make the sacrifices for the sake of larger community interests. Development projects, like Sardar Sarovar Project, are the products of this conventional paradigm. At the operational level, more often than not, there are conflicts of interests between the poor and the rich, traditions and development, civil society and State, upstream degradation in Madhya Pradesh and downstream irrigation benefits in Gujarat and between natural resources and its sustainable distribution. This is a process where people with varying capabilities interact for narrow advantages for a particular section of the society. In this debate, the decreasing availability of water has been an important argument for large dams by its proponents. They argue, irrigation is an important input to growth in agricultural production and rural prosperity. Moreover, the increased demand for purchased inputs strengthens the linkages between agriculture and industry. Many do not find this process acceptable. Since this is a conflict between unequals, they resist the process itself. They believe in people-oriented development, which calls for a process where access to natural resources is not adversely affected, and where planning and its implementation improve access to food and services in such a way that social, human and environmental losses are minimized. The resistance to the Indian development strategy, thus, came from many quarters.

An important dissent emanated from those who reject the existing paradigm of development itself. The approach of *Narmada Bachao Andolan* falls in this group. This paradigmatic shift opened a new dimension in the debate on development. Sustainability did not remain confined to tribal rights, loss of livelihood and resettlement; it also included ecological and environmental issues associated with the project. Their belief regarding unsustainability of Sardar Sarovar, strong views about the impossibility of rehabilitation[15], and the lack of faith in capabilities of the administration to handle a large involuntary migration—originating not only from Gujarat but also from Maharashtra and Madhya Pradesh—brought about a vertical split between the involved NGOs of Gujarat. A group spearheaded by Medha Patkar seriously questioned this development approach. The group resisted development on the ground that it had adverse implications. The *Andolan's* approach during early 1990s has changed the very concept of project formulation. No project in the future is likely to go unscrutinised for its assumptions. This is no mean achievement. In the heart of this resistance lies the callous manner the environmental issues were dealt with in the Sardar Sarovar Project. They argued that restricting the natural flow of an irrigation system like Narmada, apart from immediate economic pay-off, has far-reaching consequences. It not only results in submergence of living space and involuntary migration of large population and downstream salinity and waterlogging, but also results in upstream adverse environmental degradation like deforestation, soil erosion, sedimentation, catchment area treatment and biological and zoological degradation. Within this backdrop, the rest of the paper traces the environmental compliance debate of Sardar Sarovar Project.

Environmental Issues

The environment clearance for large dams was introduced only in 1978. The requirement became statutory in 1994 when Environment (Protection) Act, 1986 was modified. Between 1978 and 1980, The Department of Science and Technology was the nodal agency for environmental clearance for development projects. Only after this clearance, the Planning Commission accepted the proposal. The National Committee on Environment Planning and Coordination used to assess the project proposals. With the formation of Department of Environment in 1980, the task of clearance was transferred to the new department. But the Department of Forests and Wildlife had the responsibility to accord forest clearance for the forestland coming under submergence. With the setting up of Ministry of Environment and Forests in 1985, this ministry had the responsibility of conducting an environmental impact assessment and granting environment clearance as well as forest clearance. The Department of Environment and the Department of Forests and Wildlife became part of the new Ministry. It was only from 1994, the environment clearance became mandatory though forest clearance was made mandatory in 1980.

The Environmental Appraisal Committee set up by the Ministry of Environment and Forests performed the function that was originally performed by National Committee on Environment Planning and Coordination. Based on the recommendations of the Environmental Appraisal Committee, the Ministry of Environment and Forests decides whether a project should be cleared unconditionally, or with some conditions or should be rejected. Another committee on forests recommends on clearance of forestland under submergence. The Environment (Protection) Act was amended in 1994 to make public hearings mandatory in the assessment process [6]. Within the Central Water Commission, an Environment Monitoring Committee was constituted in 1990 to oversee the implementation of environmental standards.

The Sardar Sarovar Project came under critical environmental appraisal when Narmada Water Dispute Tribunal made its Award in 1979. For, the location of the project site, flow of water from the catchment area including Narmada Sagar Project, reservoir level, dam height, submergence of forest area, sharing of benefits between Madhya Pradesh, Gujarat and Maharashtra, etc. for the first time became clear. In 1983, both Sardar Sarovar and Narmada Sagar Projects were before the Department of Environment for environmental clearance. The application was supported by benchmark studies conducted by M S University Baroda. However, the environmental clearance was not accorded to the project. The Sardar Sarovar Project authority was informed about the difficulty in the study as well as the additional studies required.

Despite this, in 1985, World Bank approved the credit and loan agreement for Sardar Sarovar Project. Additionaly, in June 1987 the Department of Environment and Forests issued a joint clearance for Sardar Sarovar Project and Narmada Sagar Project. This clearance was accorded with the conditions that more details would be furnished for: (i) catchment area treatment, (ii) command area development, (iii) compensatory afforestation, (iv) resettlement and rehabilitation, (v) flora and fauna study, (vi) carrying capacity of the area, (vii) seismicity, and (viii) health problems. While consideration on Narmada Sagar Project was deferred, the World Bank in 1990 made it clear that the loan for Sardar Sarovar Project would be cleared with the following conditions:

- Progress of R and R and environment would be assessed *as the construction of the dam would progress*; and.
- Satisfactory environmental assessment.

The conditions above are of importance for, they mean that the Narmada Control Authority would ensure that the environmental measures are implemented *pari passu* with the progress of construction of the dam. The interpretations of *pari passu* by the Project Authority, it would seem, were not as the construction progressed but at the end when the dam was ready. The environmental bindings on the project were also to be cleared. This made the Project Authority less vigilant about the emerging environmental issues for, according to their (Project Authority's) interpretation, the compliance became mandatory only with completion of the construction of dam. Consequently, for four years between 1983 and 1987, when the Ministry of Environment and Forests did not clear the project, the Project Authority showed little apprehension and went ahead with the construction without environment clearance. After four years when the clearance was given in June 1987, the Department of Environment and Forests still had questions about the aspects of major environmental issues. This delay and conditional clearance became the issue of debate within as well as outside. The anti-dam movement used these contradictory bits of evidence to prove that Sardar Sarovar Project was a planned environmental disaster. The May 1987 note of Department of Environment and Forests to the Prime Minister of India made detailed analyses for Sardar Sarovar Project and the Narmada Sagar Project separately. Major environmental concerns (from the listed eight concerns above) were unexpectedly found satisfactory except for the Resettlement and Rehabilitation of the oustees. As the environment clearance for the Sardar Sarovar Project was accorded, in October 1988, the Planning Commission also granted approval for the Project.

An analysis of the stand taken by the Department of Environment and Forests whereby in June 1987 it accorded a conditional clearance and its letter to the Prime Minister of India in May 1987 whereby the environment compliance was found satisfactory (except for Relocation and Rehabilitation) was found quite inconsistent. This inconsistency was cashed in on both by the anti-dam activists as well as by the Morse-Berger Independent Review that World Bank instituted in 1991-92. The

Independent Review of Sardar Sarovar Project conducted a detailed analysis of issues such as hydrology, upstream environment, downstream environment, command area environment and health.

Within the context of environmental implications, it may not be out of context to place the hydrology debate that is so very vital for project design. The design of Sardar Sarovar Project is a balance of inflow and rate of discharge from the reservoir. The Narmada Water Dispute Tribunal Award (1979) estimated that on an average 3 out of 4 years (75 per cent dependability), 28 million acre feet (MAF) of water would be available from the project. The Tribunal also allocated this water between 4 states: Madhya Pradesh (65.2 per cent); Gujarat (32.1 per cent); Maharashtra (0.9 per cent) and Rajasthan (1.8 per cent). There are two major implications of the Award. First, what if yields are less; and second its effects on the downstream canal design and irrigation. Both these issues are contentious. For, they influence the availability and hence the design of the project. It has been argued by the critics of Sardar Sarovar Project that the actual yield of 28 MAF is an overestimation and from other sources of Government of India, the critics estimated that the yield could be just 22 to 23 MAF.

Using the data provided by the Central Water Commission, Ram (1993) estimated the variations in actual yields between 22.2 MAF and 22.8 MAF. Ram based his findings on the actual flow of Narmada for 15, 22, 33 and 42 years. This reduction in yield makes the allocation to Gujarat actually 7.3 MAF against 9 MAF designed for the Sardar Sarovar Project. At this stage, the controversy of building Narmada Sagar Project along with Sardar Sarovar Project is irrelevant[8], for even with the Narmada Sagar Project the yield assumed by the Project is suspect. The controversy of yield of Sardar Sarovar Project was also fanned by the May 1987 note to the Prime Minister sent by the Department of Environment and Forests. The note estimated that at 75 per cent dependability, the runoff in Narmada should be only 23 MAF instead of 27.2 MAF as assumed by NWDT. This naturally means less water for irrigation and drinking to Gujarat. Ram (1993) argues, 'As the entire planning for the

Sardar Sarovar Project is based on an assumption of using 9 MAF of water, any decrease in this amount will result in decreased benefits. Indeed, the benefit-cost ratio of project, which at 1.13 is already at a marginal acceptability level according to Government of India and World Bank norms will decrease below acceptable limits if the smaller quantum of assured water is taken into account'.

Following their detailed analysis, the Morse and Berger's Independent Review (1992) of Sardar Sarovar Project recommended to the President of the World Bank that:

> 'We found discrepancies in basic hydrological information related to these works. We therefore examined the stream flow data and did our own analysis. We found that there is good reason to believe that the Projects will not perform as planned. The problems relate to the sequence and timing of stream flow and the capacity of the dam and canal to store and divert water. The effects of Sardar Sarovar upstream, downstream, and in the command area, therefore, will be different from what has been assumed to date whether or not the upstream Narmada Sagar Projects are built as planned. A realistic operational analysis upon which to base an environmental assessment is lacking. This alarmed us and it should alarm others, especially for a mega project with such far-reaching implications as Sardar Sarovar.

For the area upstream of the dam there are piecemeal studies that suggest that the impact on biodiversity will be minimal. But there has been no attempt properly to assess the cumulative effects of the impacts arising from the Narmada Sagar Projects. Although the Narmada Sagar Projects are not within our Terms of Reference, the resulting cumulative impacts will almost certainly be serious. The Bank has placed itself in a difficult position by agreeing to proceed with Sardar Sarovar Projects before the environmental implications of directly related projects upstream are understood.

Programs in the upstream region for compensatory afforestation and catchment area treatment are under way. We believe that these programs, however successful in the short term, are likely to fail because of the lack of participation by local people. It is our view that achieving the necessary cooperation is not likely to be possible within the construction schedule imposed by 'Sardar Sarovar'.

'In spite of non-compliance with Bank resettlement and environmental requirements, the Sardar Sarovar Projects are proceeding—in the words of Chief Minister Patel of Gujarat—as 'an article of faith.' It seems clear that engineering and economic imperatives have driven the Projects to the exclusion of human and environmental concerns. Social and environmental tradeoffs have been made that seem insupportable today.'

'Important assumptions upon which the Projects are based are now questionable or are known to be unfounded. Environmental and social trade-offs have been made, and continue to be made, without a full understanding of the consequences. As a result, benefits tend to be overstated, while social and environmental costs are frequently understated. Assertions have been substituted for analysis.'

'Every decision as to the Sardar Sarovar Projects has always been, and will continue to be, a decision for India and the states involved. Together, they have spent a great deal of money. The foundations of the dam are in, the dam wall is going up, the turbines have been ordered and the canal is completed to the *Mahi* River. No one wants to see this money wasted. But we caution that it may be more wasteful to proceed without full knowledge of the human and environmental costs.

We have decided that it would be irresponsible for us to try to patch together a series of recommendations on implementation when the flaws in the Projects are as obvious as they appear to us. As a result, we think that the wisest course would be for the Bank to step back from the Projects and consider them afresh. The failure of the Bank's incremental strategy should be acknowledged' (Morse and Berger 1992).

The World Bank's withdrawal from Sardar Sarovar Project, following the recommendations of the Independent Review, created a debate that revealed the contradictory interests of various groups. The battle was not alone between pro and anti-Sardar Sarovar agencies but also between (a) submergence in Madhya Pradesh and irrigation beneficiaries of Gujarat, (b) the powerful State and the grassroots activists who understand the R and R problems of the displaced, (c) environmental implications of Sardar Sarovar Project and the past performance of other big projects in India, and (d) sociologist versus economist perspective of development.

How valid is the claim of the Independent Review on Hydrology that 'there is good reason to believe that the project will not perform as planned?' As already mentioned, not everyone involved in the Sardar Sarovar Project has accepted the analysis of Independent Review. For example, ARCH in its response to Independent Review has raised questions on the reliability of data used by the Review; ARCH argues that 'And then very blandly, without giving any evidence and arguments, they (Independent Review) asserts that NWDT's assessment appeared to be unfounded or questionable. A very vague reference is made to an independent hydrologist they had hired. Even his/her name is not given, nor his/her findings and assessment are described or discussed vis-à-vis the findings reported by the country's apex body - the Central Water Commission.' Notwithstanding this and also the fact that hydrology was not in the terms of reference of the Independent Review, there were inconsistent stands taken by different agencies like the Central Water Commission, the Department of Environment and Forests and the Sardar Sarovar Project Authority. Whether or not the Project Authority was overstepping in its role as one who would decide on environmental compliance, the sad part of this incident is the eroding independence of the environmental appraisal agency.

These controversies, and many others, have not only been part of a learning process but also have been documented. But in such documentation (for example, Cullet, 2009), in the zeal to be pro-poor and highlighting such evidence that provides their view-point a stand, injustice has been done to a great deal of evidence, like the stand taken by ARCH. Consequently, such documentation at times sound, mildly put, biased.

NOTES

1. Eventually, these controversies, along with experiences of R and

R of other projects, did become a cause for developing a comprehensive Resettlement and Rehabilitation policy by the Government of India. The draft National R and R Policy (GOI 2007), issued by Department of Land Resources, Ministry of Rural Development, has come out with: (a) appropriate definition of the Project Affected Families; (b) provisions for land for land as well as alternative ways of compensation; (c) creation of Authority of R and R and Plan for R and R; (d) provisions for amenities and facilities in the relocation sites; (e) mandatory Social Impact Assessment; (f) provisions for Grievance Redressal and Monitoring of R and R; and (g) Special provisions for Scheduled Tribes and Scheduled Caste PAPs. Although these provisions, in the draft National R and R policy, are important dimensions towards a just R and R, some of the issues that are missing from the draft R and R policy, are (i) acquiring land for industry by the State; (ii) subjectivity creeping in because of alternative ways of compensation to PAPs; (iii) lack of rigor in Social Impact Assessment; (iv) lack of provisions for mitigating second generation problems of R and R.

2. It is estimated that about 40.7 thousand families from Gujarat, Maharashtra and Madhya Pradesh will be displaced from their living space owing to construction of SSP and out of this, the majority belong to the tribal population. Experiences relating to relocation and rehabilitation (R and R) of SSP displaced people are far from encouraging. A review of the R and R of displaced population of development project reveals that in the absence of a National R and R policy, inadequate legal provisions for land and property acquisition, and the lack of institutional provisions to relocate and rehabilitate, the displaced population faces bureaucratic insensitivity and loss of livelihood. Apart from these, the livelihood adaptation by the community through (i) improving management of commons as envisaged by Jodha (1981), (ii) creating an alternative to top-down approach as envisaged by Susan and Hossain (1997) and scarcity management as envisaged by Desai, Singh and Sah (1979) need to be incorporated in a just policy frame. These provisions are missing from draft National R and R Policy (GOI, 2007).

3. A few *Sarvodaya* activists who took up the cause of the oustees of Ukai Dam in south Gujarat were concerned about the future of the PAPs of SSP. They along with other non-party activists began to work in the area and mobilized tribal population for a 'better deal'. The discriminatory provisions of the 1979 GR were

highlighted. Public demonstrations of the tribal people were organized. A writ petition was filed in the Supreme Court. The Court appointed a commission to inquire into the availability of alternative land for rehabilitation. Media and researchers repeatedly raised issues of proper rehabilitation. As a result of the growing pressures from NGOs world over and their concern for environment and tribal people, the World Bank evolved guidelines for rehabilitation for the projects supported by the Bank. Moreover, by the early eighties the Government of India began to pay attention to the problems of tribal oustees. In 1984, it formed a committee for evolving a policy of rehabilitation for tribal oustees displaced by development projects. The R and R package of SSP is a land for land compensation package which recognized every adult in the submerging village as a PAP and provided five acres of land in resettlement site, along with a house plot and temporary shed plus transportation, plinth construction, village civic amenities, one time upkeep allowance of Rs 4500, and an implements grant. But this package was accepted after a prolonged struggle. This flexibility demonstrated by Government of Gujarat, in liberally defining the PAPs, was forced. To begin with, the Narmada Water Dispute Tribunal Award recognized only legal landowners in submerging villages as PAPs and hence only these were entitled for the compensation package. Pressures from NGOs, social activists and the tribal protests forced the state to recognize encroachers, grown-up sons of the PAPs, and sharecroppers as separate families affected by SSP.

4. ARCH-Vahini was the first NGO in Gujarat to mobilize the tribal community in order to protect their rights to livelihood. Recognizing that the then existing norms did not recognize the landless labourers, sharecroppers and forest encroachers as PAP, ARCH worked relentlessly for forcing a just R and R policy for four years starting 1983. In December 1987, Government of Gujarat was forced by this grassroots movement to announce a new R and R policy. ARCH was joined by other two NGOs, Sarmik Vikas Sansthan and Rangpur Ashram, to help the State in relocating and rehabilitating PAPs after 1987.

5. See the evidence provided by Sah (2006).

6. A total disregard for social implications of relocating PAPs from 19 submerging villages to 120 plus new sites is paradoxical. The relocation process could be seen from two different dimensions; first, the traditional social links and economic institutions at the submerging villages were very important in the life of PAPs. These

arrangements had helped sustaining themselves in the submerging villages. The randomness of relocation in the absence of these arrangements at the new sites has made the PAPs vulnerable to exploitation. The other dimension to the process is the appropriateness of the existing policy. The people associated with resettling the PAPs defend the policy and the process by reiterating that the decision of shifting was an individual decision. The strength of the argument is drawn from the fact that the village is not a homogeneous unit; ; as mentioned earlier, even in a *falia* (hamlet), the people do not always want to shift together. And since the PAPs were shown land in different locations, their moving to the new sites was voluntary, for PAPs preferred the land they are cultivating in the new sites. The argument could have been accepted had there been some method in the randomness of the relocation. It is often argued that the policy provides avenues and instruments of choosing the new site. The fact is PAPs certainly had a choice; to choose the best amongst the worst. Thus, the migration in the absence of social and economic arrangements is not only involuntary but also an outcome of a policy incapable of safeguarding the risk of social disruption. The misery could have been avoided with an adequate policy frame and planning.

7. Displacement from Gujarat is from nineteen villages located in three Zones. Zone I villages were most developed among all the submerging villages. The main tribe living in this zone, Tadvi, being near to the nontribal area, had experience of modern markets and modern agricultural production technology. The villages in Zone II where Tadvi and Dungaree Bhil were the main tribes were underdeveloped. On the other hand, Zone III comprises eight interior villages (with Rathwa, Dungaree Bhil and Nayaka as the main tribes), was the most backward among all the three zones.

8. A large number of problems were cropping up on the field level; there were widespread complaints of shortages in drinking water, frequent breakdowns in handpumps, poor quality of roads and drainage in resettlement sites, water-logging and out-break of disease during monsoon etc. These were communicated by the concerned NGO to the State for necessary actions. But inaction by the State resulted in the deterioration of the well-being of PAPs (Patel, 2001).

9. Apart from poor quality land in the case of about 15 per cent PAPs, 43 new sites are outside command area of the project. In both these regions the livelihood adaptations are only community

induced. The State and the civil society have had no role in this adaptation.

10. Although the pastoral nomads of North Gujarat, Narvies from Saurashtra, road workers from Panchmahals, quarry workers from tribal Bharuch, and tribal workers from South Gujarat are seen in the major industrial towns of Gujarat, the seasonal migrants seldom cross district boundaries and work as farm labour in irrigated areas and casual semi-skilled casual labour in industrial towns. It has been argued that migration could be motivated by the desire to seek skills and leads to development through a process of migration leading to urbanization leading to socio-economic development which ultimately result inside overall development of the area. The other side argues that inclination to migrate is determined by difference in the income between the source and the destination of migration, and may result in achieving the expected income. In Ambavadi and Piparvati, two villages where seasonal migration is relatively higher; about 53 per cent of relocated households have reported outmigration compared to 14 per cent in the sample as a whole. The outmigration in these two locations is owing to the low productivity of land and inability of land to support all the family members. During the summer of 1996, about one out of five members of households in these two locations had migrated for one to four months in search of jobs as masonry helpers, nursery hands and sugarcane cutters in Surat, Ankleshwar, the Dam site and Vadodara.

11. This is one of the major problems faced by PAPs in the new sites. The origin of this problem is the lack of participation of PAPs in the process of land selection.

12. When compared to non-tribal Gujarat, leasing out land in relocated villages is three to four times more prevalent. Preliminary findings of a study on short term land transitions reveal that 75 per cent of such leasing out on sharecropping basis with the tenant bearing all the cost including labour and the produce is shared between landlord and tenant depending upon 50:50 per cent to 67:33 per cent basis. Over 70 per cent of such contracts are because the land owners faced paucity of funds, unavailability of family labour or of bullock power, but 30 per cent of such contracts are owing to land related problems like low productivity. Three new sites Malu, Ambavadi and Piparvati have a large proportion of households who have leased out their land on fixed rent or sharecropping and moved out to submerging villages to cultivate land which

has not yet come under submergence. The bulk of these households perceive that by not opting to move to their submerging villages they are taking an unwarranted risk of yield fluctuations year after year either due to **water logging** or crop failure. All of them would want to come back but would like to relocate to new sites with irrigation facilities (Sah, 1998).

13. In a developing economy like ours, one of the two sectors (agricultural sector) is traditional. It produces wage goods (foodgrains) and has excess supply of labour. The non-agricultural sector is modern and draws capital and labour from the traditional sector. The productive accumulation in the economy can be faster if the agricultural sector performs. This is so because only then (a) strong input-output linkages between the two sectors would be established, (b) terms of trade between sectors would support surplus transfer, and (c) demand for non-agricultural goods in the traditional sector would increase. The overall growth of the economy, in the long run, would be constrained if (i) technology in the traditional sector remains stagnant; (ii) Market links between sectors remain weak or the terms of trade remain unfavourable for resource transfer to non-agricultural sector, and (iii) the contribution of various parts within the agricultural sector is unequal. The above constraints, in the short run, would also increase social and economic inequality. Although, it was observed that high agricultural growth reduces rural poverty and higher consumer price aggravates it, the process may be affected if (a) early growth takes place under extreme inequality and its benefits may not 'trickle down' to large rural masses, and (b) oligopsonic influence of landowners distorts the rural labour market, dampening the on-farm employment opportunities and wage rates. The Indian concept of poverty has moved from identifying a minimum normative absolute living standard in terms of per capita consumer expenditure — may it be the normative food basket or the minimum calorie intake — towards explaining the poverty. It should, however, be noted that any cross-sectional analysis of calorie intake by individuals of PAP households would involve noises despite the fact of a large sample. Moreover, this approach of poverty measurement does not give adequate emphasis to the quality of life: PAPs' access to services, their environment relating to law and order, access to justice, the environment where they live, the air they breathe and water they drink. In absence of these concerns, the measurement of poverty is partial, relating only to food insecurity of PAPs.

14. As for the poor quality land, Sardar Sarovar Punarvasavat Agency (SSPA) reports that to mitigate the problem, necessary measures are under consideration. A technical committee under the chairmanship of Director (Canal) of Sardar Sarovar Narmada Nigam Ltd., (SSNNL) was appointed under the Executive Committee of SSPA. Subsequently, a task force with Director (R and E) and CEO (SSPA) was constituted by GOG to take corrective measures. To begin with, twenty-one sites were jointly inspected by field officers of SSNNL, and SSPA and remedial measures were outlined for each new site. The remedial measures have been taken in forty-three sites, and the work except for the major structure in one or two cases, has been completed. Impact of these measures is yet not clear. Although, the present analysis reveals widespread dissatisfaction amongst the PAPs with respect to land quality, official documents do not show that PAPs have registered their complaints with SSPA. The SSPA received complaints only from seven new sites. As a result, tractorization or partial or entire relocation in these new sites has been in progress. Still this is an issue that needs to be resolved as early as possible. As the progress in identification of poor quality land and corrective measures was too slow, the Supreme Court came in to action.

15. Even the National Policy on R and R has not raised these issues. For a detailed discussion on first and second-generation problems see, Sah (1997; 1998; 1999).

REFERENCES

Acharya, S., S P Punalekar., N K Gourah, and N V V Char. 1992. *Report of Fact-finding Team Appointed by Ministry of Water Resources on Manibeli*. New Delhi: Government of India.

Alvares, C. and R Billorey. 1988. *Damming the Narmada*. Dehradun: Natraj Publishers.

ARCH. 1992. *Letter to Mr. Lewis Preston, President World Bank*. Mangrol: ARCH-Vahini.

ARCH. 1993. *Mouse-Berger Review of Sardar Sarovar Project: A Counterview*. Mangrol: ARCH-Vahini.

Bhatia, Bela. 1997. 'Forced Eviction in Narmada Valley.' In *The Dam and the Nation*, edited by J Dreze., M Samson. and S Singh. Delhi: Oxford University Press.

Cullet, Philippe, ed. 2007. *The Sardar Sarovar Dam Project: Selected Documents*. Hampshire, United Kingdom: Ashgate Publishing Company.

Davies, Susanna. and Naomi Hossain. 1997. 'Livelihood Adaptation, Public Action and Civil Society.' *IDS Working Paper 57*: 1-51.

Desai G M., G Singh. and D C Sah. 1979. *Impact of Scarcity on Farm Economy and Significance of Relief Operations*. Mimeo. Ahmedabad: Indian Institute of Management.

GOI. 2007. *The National Rehabilitation and Resettlement Policy, 2007*. Department of Land Resources, Ministry of Rural Development: Government of India, New Delhi.

Gujarat. 1992. *Human Rights Issues at Manibeli: Fictions and Facts*. Mimeo. Gujarat PUCL: Human Rights Group of Narmada Abhiyan.

Jodha, N S. 1981. 'Role of Credit in Farmers' Adjustment against Risk in Arid and Semiarid Tropical Areas of India.' *Economic and Political Weekly* 26, Nos. 42-43: 1696-1709.

Morse, B. and T Berger. 1992. *Sardar Sarovar: Report of the Independent Review*. Canada: Resource Futures International.

Patel, Anil. 1997. 'What do the Narmada Valley Tribal Want.' In *Towards Sustainable Development*, edited by W F Fisher. Jaipur: Rawat Publications.

Patel, Anil., A Mehta., S Iyengar., T Parekh. and R Mishra. 1992. *Morse-Berger Review: A Search for Truth*. Mangrol: ARCH-Vahini.

Patel, Anil. 2001. 'Resettlement in the Sardar Sarovar Project: A Cause Vitiated.' *International Journal of Water Resources Development* 17, No.3: 315-328.

PUCL. 1993. 'Drowning of Manibeli.' *PUCL Bulletin* 12, No. 7. Report by M Mohanty and C C Kalara. Human Rights Campaign on Manibeli.

Ram, Rahul. 1993. *Muddy Waters*. New Delhi: Kalpavriksh.

Sah, D C. 1995. 'Displacement: National Rehabilitation Policy.' *Economic and Political Weekly* 30, No. 48: 3055-58.

Sah, D C. 1997. 'Second Generation Problems of Involuntary Migration.' *Indian Journal of Agricultural Economics* 52, No. 4: 707-727.

Sah, D C. 1998. 'Avoiding Impoverishment Risks: Towards a Policy Frame of Dam Affected People.' *Review of Development and Change* 3, No. 1: 59-89.

Sah, D C. 1999. 'Pressures on Land, Employment and Migrations.' *Review of Development and Change* 4, No. 2: 237-269.

Sah, D C. 2003. *Involuntary Migration: Evidence from Sardar Sarovare Project*. Jaipur: Rawat Publications.

Sen, A K. 1981. *Poverty and Famines*. Oxford: Oxford University Press.

Shah, G. and Biswaroop Das. 1986. *Voluntary Organization Development*. Mimeo. Surat: Centre for Social Studies.

Shah, G. and Biswaroop Das. 1988. *Voluntary Organization in Gujarat.* Mimeo. Surat: Centre for Social Studies.

Sheth, Pravin. 1995. *Politics of Narmada Project.* Mimeo. Ujjain: Madhya Pradesh Institute of Social Science Research.

Soni, Trupti. and Gautam Appa. 1993. *Sardar Sarovar Project Downstream Impact.* Paper presented in workshop at Narmada Forum, Delhi School of Economics and Institute of Economic Growth.

12

Development at What Cost? A Study of Migration, Loss of Livelihood Security and Development-Induced Displacement in Himachal Pradesh

Richa Minocha

Peoples and communities maintaining the universality of their beliefs and the organizing principles of their specific cultures are challenged in the face of the prevailing development paradigm. Such development has undermined the basis of the equilibrium (ecological and social) which had evolved over generations leading to much loss of indigenous knowledge, effective conservation methods and the language in which local values and cultures are communicated.

In Himachal Pradesh,[1] people established their relationship with common resources on bonds of trust, faith and reverence. The hilltops and valleys have deities' temples with sacred groves around them, enriched by plantations. The symbolic relationship of the people with the commons was strengthened by the deep sensitivity for their protection and conservation. Changes in ownership access and use of common property resources by people, were enforced with greater zeal after independence in 1947. The new forest laws, laws regarding minor forest produce, common lands and water resources, all aided this process.

The demarcation of 'reserved' and 'protected' forests began in most parts in Himachal Pradesh only in 1986. Prior to that only a few areas were demarcated in 1952. In the first round of land classification, since 1947, most land classified as Government land was simply taken over by the Revenue Department. In 1952, many areas belonging to the Revenue Department, especially those with forest cover were 'transferred' on paper, vide a Government notification under Section 4 of the Forest Act to the Forest Department.

This transfer and demarcation was legally incomplete because the subsequent settlement of the rights of the people over these lands and resources under Sections 11 to 16 of the Forest Act was not done for a very long time by the Forest Department. Besides the forest lands, there are large areas of 'ceiling' land all over the State which had in practice become common resources lands. These areas are the excess non-cultivated fallow lands taken over from the erstwhile kings or landlords by the Government under the Urban Land Ceiling Act and Regulation Act 1976. Most of these lands serve a similar purpose as the 'commons', but with the difference that they belong to the Revenue Department and do not fall within the category of land to be transferred to the Forest Department. By and large, these 'ceiling' lands have been fenced by the Revenue Department to control grazing. The other categories of forest and grazing lands, which did not come under the jurisdiction of the Forest Department in Himachal Pradesh, were the *rakhas* and *shamlats*. The *shamlats* are the commons, which came over to Himachal Pradesh from Punjab when the districts and the states were reorganized in 1962. The *rakhas* are the traditional forest preserves (community woodlots) managed totally by the local people. In the non-Punjab districts, the grazing lands are known as *ghasnis*. These *ghasnis* are both privately and commonly owned[2].

It was realized in the early 1990s that in not paying any attention to the traditional community management systems, the administration was evidently not only proclaiming that it had the total scientific expertise in forestry, but also exhibiting gross mistrust in people.[3] Through renewed efforts like the Village Forest Development Societies (VFDS) in the late 1990s there were efforts to involve the people in forest management, recently, political will has been favouring hydropower projects and mining in the State which is resulting in much displacement.

In Himachal Pradesh, the year 2010 has been very illustrative of climate change. This is evidenced in the melting of glaciers, in the occurrence of frequent floods and droughts, the drying of natural water sources and the changing cropping patterns. The people are adapting to changing climate by adopting different cropping patterns[4]. Maize has replaced small millets and buckwheat in upper Shimla district and Kinnaur district. Apple has moved closer to heights where it was not possible earlier (as in Chitkul). Precipitation has been witnessed in the form of rain where it was always snow[5]. Loss of livelihoods and agricultural diversity and the problems faced by women are major issues of concern for civil society organizations in Himachal in general and by an organization Jan Abhiyan Sanstha (JAS), which has been conducting action research in the area, in particular. Civil society organizations have to act as a pressure lobby on the Government to ensure that development projects such as mining, hydropower don't come up where agricultural fields are good and women's livelihoods are likely to be adversely affected. Also public policy has to ensure suitable rehabilitation for women and children where these projects have come up. Displacement has been on the rise in Himachal with Government policy preferring industry and the potential for hydropower projects and cement factories being exploited much. Displacement has adverse effects on children's upbringing as it results in the loss of flourishing agriculture based sub-cultures and livelihoods (Minocha, 2015).

More recently, villagers in the cloud-burst affected Kullu Valley have started maintaining night vigil to guard against flash floods in the wake of widespread news of cloudbursts in Leh, Kullu, Manali and Uttarakhand. Scientists of GB Pant Institute of Himalayan Environment and Development, Himachal unit, say that flash floods will rapidly increase in proportion to the increase in human activities in the hills. A *Times of India* report on September 23, 2010 summarizes that more than 200 people have been killed in incidents of cloudbursts in Kullu, which started from 1994. Studies have indicated that the impact of snow melting in the high Himalayas will lead to flood disasters in Himalayan catchments. Impacts will be more in the western Himalayas where Himachal Pradesh is located as the contribution of snow to the runoff of major rivers on the western side is about 60% compared to 10% on the eastern side (IPCC, 2001).

Review of Literature

Migration

According to Petersen (1966), migration can be classified into four main categories. These are primitive, forced or impelled, free and mass migration. Primitive migration according to him is the result of the ecological push. A primitive migration of an agrarian population takes place when there is a sharp disparity between the produce of the land and the number of people it sustains. In forced migration, the activating agent is the State or some functionally equivalent social institution. It is useful to divide this class into impelled migration, when migrants retain some power to decide whether or not to leave and forced migration, when they do not have this power. In free migration, the will of migrants is the decisive element. And in mass migration, migration becomes a style, an established pattern, an example of collective behaviour. So long as there are people to emigrate, the principal cause of emigration is prior emigration.

Gender

Feminist groups' analysis explores the linkages among unpaid (women's) work, migration policies, plunder of natural resources, unaccountable political elites and globalized capital. Feminists interlink the energy crisis, food crisis, care crisis, climate crisis and economic crisis, and plead for re-embedding the economy in social relations and sustainable relations with nature (Wichterich, 2009: 1).

Just as in other development arenas, women in development-induced displacement and resettlement usually received fewer benefits than men. When women displaced from the Kibale reserve (Uganda) were finally resettled, they still reported increased stress because they no longer had individual gardens to provide food for their families (Feeney 1998: 103). The fertility rate of tribal woman decreased after displacement (Thangaraj, 1996: 230). As compensation payments went to male heads, collective assets of the family became cash- owned by male household heads. Greater dependence on their husbands reduced women's power within the family. Less involvement in decision-making lead to conflict (sometimes violent) (Pandey, 1998: 104). On the Zambian Copper belt, men got housing through their status as workers, and widows had no claim to housing in their own right (Hansungule, Feeney, and Palmer, 1998: 22). In Zambia, when men lost employment and turned to the informal sector, women were displaced from more lucrative informal activities (Hansungule, Feeney, and Palmer, 1998: 30). Indian women faced increasing drudgery after development-induced displacement and resettlement in getting fuel, fodder, and water; they lost earnings from forest, agriculture, common property, and non-farm activities (Pandey, 1998: 93). Indian projects that offered employment as compensation gave few jobs to women.

Patricia Pessar's (1999: 578) study finds that in the 1950s and 60s, neoclassical reasoning about migratory movements were heavily influenced by the role model of 'Western man headed off to the cities where the benefits of modern life could be attained' has not gone out of date. From a post-structuralist perspective, which takes economics seriously as 'a discourse, which actively produces its objects as well as its subjects of knowledge' (Hewitson, 2001: 223) it can be argued that migration models in economics participate in setting a certain type of masculinity as the norm.

Even though today a plethora of empirical studies and theoretical contributions on gender and migration as well as on women and migration exist, gender has still not successfully been integrated into the mainstream of migration studies; 'women' are mostly added or relegated to chapters of 'family and household' and 'gender' is still equated with 'women'. An insightful example is the *International Migration Review* (IMR), the leading journal in the field. In 1984, Mirjana Morokvasic edited a special IMR-volume on 'Women in Migration' in which she made research on female migration visible and criticized most migration theories for offering only very narrow explanations for the movement of women (Morokvasic, 1984). Twenty years later, a special IMR-issue on the 'general' state of the art (Portes and DeWind, 2004) did not even contain a piece on gender and migration, let alone papers which included the gender dimension, except for one anthropological contribution (Levitt and Schiller, 2004). Particular modes of thinking about migration earned the imprimatur of theory, and work by female researchers on women or gender rarely achieved any status (Donato et al., 2006: 8). There are at least five reasons for it: the exclusion of women from academia, the development of hierarchies between research methods and disciplines, gender-biased data and historical sources, the resultant focus on men as sole research subjects and the assessment of women's migration as atheoretical or simply not interesting. To sum up, whereas the existence of gender differences is either not dealt with explicitly or negated, implicit gender knowledge assumes the male migrant as the 'normal migrant'.

Environment, Development Projects and Displacement

While development-induced displacement occurs throughout the world, two countries in particular, China and India are responsible for a large portion of such displacements. Taneja and Thakkar (2000) point out that estimates on displacement in India from dam projects alone range from 21 million to 40 million. The WBED report notes[6] that, in 1993, World Bank projects in China accounted for 24.6 per cent of people displaced in Bank-assisted projects, while Bank-assisted projects in India accounted for 49.6 per cent of the Bank total.

The Narmada Sardar Sarovar Dam Project in India, displacing 127,000 people, has perhaps been the most widely researched and discussed project involving forced resettlement in history. A volume edited by Drèze, Samson, and Singh (1997) provides a comprehensive look at displacement and resettlement in the project. The Morse and Berger report (1992) is the final report of the Morse Commission, the World Bank's internal review of the project, which found systematic violations of Bank policies and loan agreements, particularly those concerning the environment and resettlement. That report eventually led the World Bank to withdraw funding from the project and has been cited as an important factor in pushing the Bank to create its Inspection Panel, a body tasked with investigating claims from citizens in cases where the Bank has failed to enforce its own policies, procedures, and loan agreements. Case studies from different parts of India show that deforestation has exacerbated migration by both men and women. Development policies, whether the building of big dams, taking over of forest and agricultural lands for industrial enterprises or restrictions on the local population regarding the use of forests and common property resources (Minocha, 2005), has meant a loss of control over basic resources for local women and men in Himachal Pradesh.

A significant study was done by Nitya Rao, Kumar Rana in which the case of *santhals* was discussed. With erosion of traditional livelihood and few local options available, *santhals* have been forced to enter the labour market as migrants. Faced with the negative impact on schooling and healthcare, poor living and working conditions, and constant fear of sexual abuse, the entry into the labour market by a large number of *santhals*, is in itself a reflection of a process of development that has displaced large numbers from their traditional livelihoods without providing secure and sustainable options locally. It has brought about an alienation of *santhal* lands primarily through loans and control over capital by a few. Their customary paradigm of community ownership got lost somewhere along the way, and has been replaced by individual progress and fulfilment.

The number of people displaced by programmes promoting national, regional and local development is substantial. The most commonly cited number is approximately 10 million people per year (Cernea, 2000:11). Development projects leading to involuntary displacement include urban relocation and renovation, and water and transport infrastructure. In rural areas, forestry projects, mining, biosphere reserves, and national parks are displacing people. Road and other infrastructure may require urban, suburban, peri-urban, or rural relocation. Scudder (1996: 49) noted four categories of people affected by development-induced displacement and resettlement: the displaced, the hosts among whom they settle, other river-basin residents, and immigrants. While immigrants usually benefit, the other groups risk negative impacts. Attention has been paid to relocatees and more recently to hosts, but the majority of the adversely affected may be in the third category; sometimes at a great distance from the project site, they are rarely included in projects. Spread over wide areas, they are also less likely to mount effective resistance. The non-displaced are affected in many ways. At Sardar Sarovar (India), downstream fisherfolks from Bihar were concerned about the indirect displacement as their families depended on fishing (Appa and Patel, 1996: 145). The Manantali Resettlement Project (Mali) did a fairly good job of resettling the people in the reservoir area, yet no initiative aided the down streamers hundreds of miles away when their agricultural systems were affected by the changing river regime (Salem-Murdock et al. 1994). Hosts have gained more attention in recent years but it is important to remember them. Their interests may be in direct conflict with those of resettlers, even though they have agreed to accept displaced groups. Competition arises due to the added pressure on natural resources, common property, and social services (Pandey, 1998; Koenig and Diarra, 1998).

Many Governments are uneasy about those who use common property or open-access resources. Waterways for instance are considered national or provincial resources whose development should be undertaken in the interest of the public as a whole; Government strategy has often been to convince natives to surrender rights to valuable resources for the common good (Waldram, 1988). Reconstituting common property or open-access resources raises many issues. In some cases, these resources form the main or only resources used by the population, e.g., pastoralists, fisherfolks, foragers (hunters and gatherers), and some farmers. In other cases, the use of common property resources complements income from privately owned farms or wage work. The poorest and women often depend most on these resources (Cernea, 1996). Indian social scientists have argued for the recognition of customary tenure among 'tribals' living in Government forests (Mahapatra, 1999), but have not yet been successful. In many parts of the developing world, urban residents of spontaneous neighbourhoods lack titles to land and are considered squatters. Sometimes, they have the right to compensation; other times, they do not (Meikle and Walker, 1998).

Economic Aspects of Livelihood Restoration and Diversification in Strategies

Economic sustainability, including intergenerational equity, needs to be foregrounded so that stocks of capital assets do not decrease. Consideration of these assets needs to include the stock of skills and knowledge (human capital) and environmental assets (Pearce, 1999: 59). Hayes (1999) suggested looking explicitly at physical, human, social, and natural capital.

Until now, the displaced have been fortunate when a resettlement project reconstituted their major resource. Yet this approach ignores multiple activities undertaken individually or by groups more commonly heterogeneous than homogeneous. In much of the world, rural residents who define themselves primarily as 'farmers' cannot live by farming alone. Lassailly-Jacob (1996: 188) noted that when resettlers became self-sustaining in rural African settlement schemes, it was often due to activities other than farming. Planners have not paid attention to resource diversity in rural areas. In Orissa (India), programmes were planned for viable agricultural fields but ignored homestead plots, leading to a substantial decline in income-earning possibilities for women and variety in the family diet (Pandey, 1998). Viable social systems usually include people with a variety of occupations. While the majority of rural residents may be farmers, there are artisans, traders, and specialized service providers (e.g., health or religious practitioners), often ignored in development-induced displacement and resettlement programmes. Indian resettlement policies often did not recognize residents who did not live from the land as displaced. Craft or service providers who lost their occupations due to displacement were not eligible for rehabilitation and resettlement (Pandey, 1998: 111).

Much literature suggests that development initiatives are now prefaced with calls for 'reversals'—to put the last first, to empower the 'hitherto excluded', to break down the professional and technical barriers that mystify rather than clarify the development process, to put farmers themselves centre stage in the planning and execution of development projects (Chambers, 1985; Chambers and Jiggins, 1987; Chambers et al., 1989). The problems of rural development are no longer seen to reside in the 'traditional' cultures of underdeveloped people, but rather in the partial and biased understandings that have emanated from the unreflexive application of western scientific rationality, and in the results of a rapacious and selfish capitalism that has exacerbated rather than reduced inequalities (Titilola and David Marsden, 1999). Traditional cultures are now being seen as containing the bases of effective development. The development of a 'people's science' draws on a 'populist' tradition within the social sciences while eschewing the gross overgeneralizations of both the modernist and the materialist perspectives in favour of an analysis of the many ways in which sustainability has been enhanced through local experimental responses to changes in both the natural and the cultural environment.

Simmons (1974: 29) advocated that people understand their environment to adapt themselves to it rather than using ecology as a means to adapt the environment to people's industrial concerns. He wrote 'It appears healthier for man to regard the planet less as a set of commodities for use and more as a community of which he forms a part.' He suggested (1974: 33) that non-industrial societies could actually teach sound principles of natural resource management rather than only be converted by them. Referring to the Bushmen of the Kalahari Desert, he wrote that they had adapted to extreme environments in which there was a paucity of resources to the western eye. The recognition of sources of moisture in their arid surroundings is the critical element for the Bushmen. Thus all manner of plants and animals are used as food and some of these probably largely as sources of moisture. The people become adept at spotting the traces of delicacies such as buried ostrich eggs, which add valuable elements to their diet. Simmons extolled the merits of a locally 'preferred limit' to natural resource use. This, he wrote, is the most hopeful way of coming to grips with 'man's most fearsome problems' (Simmons, 1974: 375-376).

Issues and Concerns of Project-affected People in Himachal Pradesh

The scale and the attitude with which new projects are being implemented in the State of Himachal Pradesh leaves little scope for reviewing impacts on local people, local economy and ecology and possible alternatives. This has resulted in project affected people in many places actively resisting the Government's policy. A few ongoing and proposed projects in Himachal Pradesh are discussed below.

1. Renuka Dam Project, Sirmour

On July 1, 2010, Press Trust of India news read, that over 30 prominent environmentalists and intellectuals, had expressed serious reservations about environmental fall out of Renuka Dam project in Sirmaur district of Himachal Pradesh, to meet the water requirements of Delhi. They urged Delhi Chief Minister Sheila Dixit to review her Government's decision of 'poaching' water from far flung areas. In a joint petition addressed to her, the environmentalists pleaded that the Rs. 4,000 crore Renuka Dam project to generate 40 MW power will displace at least 6,000 people from 34 villages. It would lead to, they said, destruction of huge carbon sink and increase in emission of greenhouse gases which was 'complete violation of the declared aim of the National Action Plan on Climate Change and National Green Mission', they added.

The total submergence area was to be 2,000 hectares of which 949 hectares was forest land (reserve forest and Renuka Wildlife Sanctuary) and the rest private land. Of the 400 families in the catchment area to get affected, 100 were to be completely displaced. Downstream areas from Dadahu (dam site) upto Paonta Sahib would be impacted, vis-à-vis irrigation facilities and other river-based livelihoods. Himachal Pradesh Power Corporation Limited (HPPCL) proposed compensation of Rs. 50,000 per *bigha* for uncultivable waste land including grassland, Rs 1.5 lakh for unirrigated agriculture land and Rs. 2.5 lakh for irrigated land whereas the average market rate for the latter in the year 2007 was as high as 20 lakh.

A Renuka Bandh Sangarsh Samiti had been formed in 2007 and the process of mobilizing the affected and downstream populations was started. Although in its August 31, 2010 order the Ministry of Environment and Forests, Government of India declined forest clearance to the dam on the grounds that around 1.5 lakh trees would be submerged by the project, the Delhi Government wanted the project seen through to alleviate the capital's water worries. HPPCL had set in the year 2010, to make a fresh application for diversion of forestland for the Renuka Dam project. In order to represent their case, the project proponents claimed that they will reduce the number of trees to be felled, by making 'alterations' to the 148-metre dam in Himachal Pradesh. While the figure of 1.5 lakh itself is debatable (local people place it at about 13 lakh), the issue is not merely of the 'number of trees' being cut.

The entire affected area, including the 49 hectares of the Renuka Wildlife Sanctuary, has subtropical deciduous forest with species like *sal, khair, shisham, kachnar, toon* and bamboo that adds to the biodiversity of the region and also supports the local economy. Any diversion of 'forest land' for the project would violate the provisions of the Forest Rights Act, 2006, which requires recognition and settlement of the rights of the communities dependent on these forest areas for fuel, fodder and medicinal plants. In a recent report, the National Forest Rights Act Committee has recognized that the Himachal Government has failed to implement the act and that no forests should be diverted for projects like the Renuka Dam until the rights are recognized. Further, as per 2009 Ministry guidelines, getting a 'no objection certificate' from the *Gram Sabha* (village councils) of project-affected villages is necessary before diverting forestlands. This hadn't been done in the case of the Renuka project, which is going to submerge lands owned by over 1,000 families of 37 villages in Sirmaur. The submergence of these lands would not only destroy agriculture but also the socio--cultural fabric of the Giri Valley.

The State Forest Department and project officials are silent on the issue of private and common forests (*shamlat*) that haven't been brought under the ambit of the forest diversion proposal submitted to the central ministry. More than 450 hectares of such forests seem to have escaped the attention of the department, which has recommended the proposal. In a survey of a single revenue village, HPPCL counted 32,640 trees in an area of 445 *bigha* (37 hectares) that need to be acquired. This suggests a density of nearly 1,000 trees per ha[7] of *shamlat* forest, which is much higher than the density of trees in the 775 hectares of reserved forests that is proposed to be diverted for the project. A Supreme Court order, in the 2009 TN Godavraman case states that diversion of forests, not under the jurisdiction of the forest department, should attract the provisions of the Forest Conservation Act, 1980, and that felling of trees and non-forest use of these areas should not be permissible without a forest clearance. Yet trees in *shamlat* forests haven't been included in the survey for the forest clearance for the Renuka Dam. These private forests, along with farmlands, are being forcefully acquired using the 'urgency clause' of the Land Acquisition Act 1894 and the landowners are not being allowed to file any objections with the Government. Evidently, there were many unresolved issues and the Governments in Delhi and Himachal Pradesh had more to answer for before justifying the need for this dam (Asher, 2010). Although Jairam Ramesh affirmed on November 23, 2010 while addressing an all India Sangharsh Media delegation, that the project will be withdrawn, approval was granted by the Union Ministry of Environment and Forests in March 2015, and the decision conveyed to the State Government. Even though an appeal was pending before the National Green Tribunal against the coming up of the project, forest clearance for the diversion of forestland which has 1,41,944 trees has been granted. It was on August 26, 2014, that the Himachal Government sought permission to divert forestland for the project. Himachal Pradesh Power Corporation Limited

(HPPCL) claims that they have already paid Rs 144 crore as compensation to those whose land has been acquired out of the Rs. 200 crore given by the Delhi Government. Further Rs. 1,983.35 crore has been sought from the Central Government for the relief and rehabilitation of villagers who will be displaced[8].

The residents of Chulli Dadahu Panchayat refused to give no-objection certificate to the project, stating that blasting for tunnels and other works will cause irreparable loss to ecology. According to the Panchayat Pradhan's statement to the Tribune, the project envisaged construction of 2 km diversion tunnel from Renuka Dam to the Jalal River through Dadahu and blasting in the area would trigger landslides, develop cracks in houses and make the area prone to natural disasters. The dumping site which is to be 500 metres away from Dadahu Village, would according to the residents, convert it into a highly polluted village, affecting tourism in the Renukaji Wildlife Sanctuary as well as health of the people. Other residents felt that with felling of lakh of trees and plants, the threat of cloudbursts and soil erosion would aggravate and frequency of earthquakes will increase.

2. Baddi Barotiwala Nalagarh Development Area (BBNDA), Nalagarh, Solan

The Government of Himachal Pradesh first extended the Town and Country Planning (TCP) Act, 1977 to Barotiwala in late 1980s to urbanize the peripheries around the industrial areas of Baddi and Barotiwala in Solan District. The TCP was extended in 2006-07 to a larger area of 231 revenue villages and the Baddi-Barotiwala-Nalagarh Development Authority (BBNDA) was formed. The authority in mid 2008 proposed a draft master plan for the area which met with severe resistance from the residents of the region. The master plan intends to earmark areas in the BBNDA region for housing, industries, entertainment and commercial purposes. This has met with opposition as the existing livelihoods of the people have been completely overlooked in the master plan which the locals claim has randomly designated sites for industries. Another reason is the expansion of roads for which lands are being acquired compulsorily. The local people are also agitated because of several bureaucratic requirements of being a part of the special area which requires them to approach the BBNDA for all day to day needs like water, power and other basic facilities. The agitation which gained momentum in September, 2008 under the banner of BBNDA Kisan Sangarsh Samiti, is demanding a complete withdrawal of the master plan, on the grounds that it will mean acquisition of agriculture lands for roads, shopping malls and industries.

Depletion of ground water due to heavy extraction, increasing river pollution, toxic air pollution, flyash, and illegal dumping of hazardous waste, illegal river bed mining are some of the key problems identified in the area. Discharge of contaminated waste from the industrial units into the local water bodies have gravely polluted 6 to 7 small streams flowing into the Sarsa River, a tributary of the Satluj. It is an already well-established fact that industrial development drastically impacts local environment, causes damage to agriculture, livestock, impacts health and sanitation among other several issues. In context of Baddi Barotiwala Nalagarh industrial area, a study published in 2011 by Punjab University has indicated high concentration of heavy metals in groundwater due to excessive contamination by industrial units, and stated that the water had been rendered unsuitable for drinking purposes. Another IIT (Indian Institute of Technology) Kanpur study submitted to the Himachal Pradesh Pollution Control Board (HPPCB) in 2012 too revealed high levels of particulate matter, lead and arsenic in the ambient air; thus violating standards prescribed by the Ministry of Environment and Forests (MoEF). Volatile organic compounds have been found beyond permissible limits in air samples based on a community monitoring sampling done by Himparivesh, a local environment group.

Even, Central Pollution Control Board's own findings in 2011 have confirmed the presence of Volatile organic compounds (VOCs) and cancer causing carcinogens in the air in Baddi Barotiwala Nalagarh (BBN). The Government stresses that the extension of TCP and the master plan are essential for planned industrialization and development of the area. The people of the area argue that for the last three decades there has been a haphazard growth of severely polluting industries in Baddi and Nalagarh and the government has not paid any attention. The policy implications of the Town and Country Planning Act and the Special Area Development Authority need to be understood. Apart from this the issue of stone quarrying has affected this area leading to floods and other problems. Despite the locals having raised issues of air, water, and noise pollution in their respective areas, there was little action from the factory authorities and Pollution Control Board. With the locals even having resorted to protests, like in the case of Sara textiles at Bhatiyan, the effluents continue to be released day and night impacting health and agriculture in the area. Ironically, the pharmaceutical units producing life saving drugs have become a nuisance for the farming communities. As a result of the contaminated water seeping into the fields, the land productivity is according to locals rapidly declining. The fields close to the pharma units stand virtually destroyed due to the effluents. Irrigation systems have been worst affected by industrial pollution and the farmers are left with no option but to irrigate with polluted water. Local women from Bhatiyan reported that working on fields was increasingly difficult and had to be done at the risk of developing several skin allergies. The factory management responded by stopping release of effluents during the day. It was only much later, the locals realised that the effluents were now being discharged at night. With the pharma and cosmetic units at Jhar Majri and Bhatoli Kalan, the units were mixing fresh water with toxic effluents to dilute the impact. People living close to the units are worried that they suffer constant exposure to toxics- while working in the fields, while bathing, washing clothes.

3. Bhakra Affected Communities

The Bhakra multipurpose project and dam was the first project of India and was commissioned in the early 1950s. Before the construction of the dam, an agreement was signed between the ruler of erstwhile Bilaspur princely State and the Government of Punjab on July 7, 1948. The agreement spoke of rehabilitation measures for the displaced people[9]. In 1971, the Himachal Pradesh Government evolved a rehabilitation and resettlement policy that provided for 'land for land' (agriculture as well as homestead). The rules for such allotments were made in 1972 but even the delayed effort has not been implemented till today.

However, neither the Central Government nor the implementing agency Bhakra Beas Management Board (BBMB) then had any clear cut idea of the Research and Rehabilitation (R and R) problems. Therefore the issues of R and R could not be addressed in a proper manner. The successive Governments did not accept this truth boldly and the problems of proper resettlement of the oustees and the unfulfilled promises are still looming large. One can feel the gravity of the issue from the very fact that the oustees were asked to settle in the nearby forest lands without proper allotments. The rural farmers were displaced by paying a few hundred ruppes per *bigha* as compensation. People here are struggling to get their occupations on Government land regularized. There are two cases pending in the Supreme Court on the issue of inadequate settlement of the Bhakra oustees.

According to a Times of India coverage on October 22, 2013 titled '50 years on, Bhakra Dam oustees wait for rehabilitation' 36,000 families had lost their homes and land to the project. The President of Gramin Bhakra Visthapit Sudhar Samiti[10] said that about 371 villages—256 from former Bilaspur province, 110 from erstwhile Kangra province and five from Mandi—were submerged in the Bhakra dam catchment area. About 10,000 acres of agricultural land and 20,000 acres of forest land were submerged. Some of the displaced people were rehabilitated in Sarsa, Hisar and Fatehbad districts of Haryana. Several others were settled in Ropar (Punjab) and Bilaspur, Nalagrah and Una in Himachal Pradesh. Apart from this, some of the displaced have also been resettled along the forested slopes on both sides of the reservoir from Bhakra to Slaapad and Lathyaani. After acquisition of land the government provided them 2.5 *bigha* land as part of the displaced people's share. Since then life has been a struggle for them, since surviving on this small piece of land is difficult. 3,600 families were promised, that land will be granted to them in Haryana, but about 740 of them returned since they could not be accommodated there. Of the remaining 2,860 families, only 800 could get ownership of land in Haryana. Oustees were promised plots in new Bilaspur town but very few could get it while others were forced to rehabilitate in the nearby forests. Many people were forced to settle in the forest and sanctuary areas and, to date, have not been given ownership rights. While the landed received some compensation at rates varying from Rs 1,000 per acre for agricultural land to Rs 250 for uncultivable land, the landless received merely Rs 200 as an overall compensation. There is no official figure for agricultural labourers, landless persons, potters and many others who were displaced by the dam. The official records only show 11,000 as project displaced people.

As per the Punjab State Reorganization Act of 1966, Himachal Pradesh has 7.19 per cent share in projects under BBMB (Dehar, Pong Dam and Bhakra projects) from where power and water is supplied to other States. After the Himachal Pradesh Government moved Supreme Court, the Apex court in September 2011 directed the Union Government to intervene to ensure that other States pay the due amount to the hill State. Following Supreme Court directions, Himachal Pradesh has started getting 7.19 per cent share from the Hydro-Power Projects, but it is yet to get the revenue share as other States has lowered the amount from Rs. 4,250 crore to around Rs. 3,400 crore[11].

Researched by a team led by Shripad Dharmadhikary, the recently published *Unravelling Bhakra: Assessing the Temple of Resurgent India* provides disturbing evidence of the hype around Bhakra, which has been used to justify hydropower development. Increase in irrigation has been little. The total area under Bhakra's command has been 20 per cent of all cultivable area in Punjab. In real terms, it meant that 372,000 hectares land got covered under irrigation from the Bhakra canal network in the State. However, an analysis of the command area reveals that much of the command area in Punjab was already irrigated, or was in areas well endowed with water. On top of it, the dam helped only 12 per cent of the State's agriculture growth.

Carved out of Punjab in 1966 three years after Bhakra was commissioned, Haryana seems to have gained more from the project. A total area of 1.16 million hectares has been irrigated in the neighbouring State that contributes 15 per cent to its total crop production. Often these are the statistics that are used to not only justify Bhakra but other large dam projects too. The question is: what would have Punjab and Haryana looked like if the Bhakra dam had not been built? *Unravelling Bhakra* contends that the twin States would have definitely looked different without 449,000 hectares of waterlogged land and 687,000 hectares of salt-affected area. Curiously, the permanent degradation of cultivable area due to (over) irrigation has been deflected with 'that is the cost of doing it!' Groundwater irrigation through diesel pumpsets and tubewells has taken a quantum jump following the Bhakra project. From at around 20,000 tubewells in each of the two States during 1965-66, the figure now for Punjab is 910,000 whereas Haryana is not far behind with 583,705 tubewells. Researchers argue that 43-46 per cent of all agricultural production in Punjab is based on unsustainably mined groundwater. For Haryana, the figure is 35 per cent. Proponents of the Bhakra dam often argue that much of this has been possible due to groundwater recharge through canal seepage. Conversely, however, that does not seem to be the case as only 17 per cent of the groundwater recharge can be attributed to canal irrigation in Punjab and the figure is 24 per cent for Haryana. Researchers further contend that canal irrigation is on the decline in both the States.

Hence, there is much hype over big dams as the case study of the Bhakra Nangal brings forth. While Himachal suffered much submergence and displacement, Punjab and Haryana didn't gain as projected.

4. Kinnaur District longs for Development without Destruction

Mega hydro-electric projects have been coming up in Kinnaur district that are encroaching upon vast tracts of forest land besides diverting the natural course of rivers and water systems. Various hydro-power projects such as Nathpa Jhakri,

Bhabhanagar and Karcham Wangtoo in Kinnaur district have indulged in intensive mining and construction activities resulting in much loss of vegetation and changes in land use. Numerous other hydropower projects are coming up in Kinnaur including Tidong, Shongtong Karcham and Integrated Kashang hydro-electric project. The ecology of the district is under immense pressure from these projects. Kinnaur has been ripped, of many of its *chilgoza*[12] pine and *chuli*[13] forests.

The focus seems to be merely on expropriating commercial gains and there is little concern about repercussions on the environment and damage caused to local inhabitants in the surrounding vicinity. In order to identify the affected population, stress is merely being laid on 'submergence' criteria. But locals are also affected by blasting of tunnels which is an essential element of these 'run-of-the-river' based technologies. Villagers have been complaining that incisions made to the mountain facade are drying up water springs vital for their livelihood. Dynamite blasting causes noise and vibrations and is a potential threat to land and property. Further, it weakens the sloped mountainous terrain, making the affected region prone to landslides. Unfortunately, geologists engaged to assess the nature of damage pass such disasters off as 'natural calamities' unrelated to project construction activities and no compensation is sanctioned.

Rainfall used to be very scanty in Kinnaur during summer. But over the last two decades, erratic and heavy rainfall in summer and less snowfall in winter has been witnessed. When the sloped mountain terrain is fragile and loose, excessive rainfall of this magnitude invariably causes landslides. The setting up of hydro-electric projects has aggravated the situation by making the soil structure loose and more susceptible to landslides, both directly and indirectly- directly, because of dynamite blasting, and indirectly, due to felling of trees that hold the soil together.

The main issues that the locals are fighting for (as regards the Karcham-Wangtoo project in particular) are that though submergence problems have been taken care of, no cognizance is being taken of those villages that are susceptible to damage on account of tunnel-blasting. Further, the proposed compensation does not take care of damage that affects livelihoods of the people. It is limited to the nearest time horizon. Environmental impacts being the major issue, other issues that the locals have been raising are that the State's share in the electricity generated be increased from 12 per cent to 25 per cent, so that some of this electricity can be channeled to the local area, free of cost.

4a. Pangi Village in Kinnaur District: Revisited as Site for Kashang Hydro-Power Project

The village Pangi is located 9 kms from Kinnaur District's headquarters in Reckong Peo and is in Kalpa Block. The village has been cited for the phase I of the integrated Kashang project. Common property resources area in the village, commonly referred to as *Kanda* is where the dam is coming up. The channels being constructed underneath for the project have turned the land into a sliding zone as some households have had to shift residence base as the houses were falling down as a result of the construction.

There are nine hamlets in Pangi and four primary schools in four of them including one each in lower Pangi, Khonta, Then Pangi, and Pangi Khas and also a secondary school in Pangi. There is also an Ayurvedic hospital and a Veterinary hospital in Pangi near the senior secondary school. There is a Co-operative bank near the local bus stand and also a branch post office housed in a private building. An IPH drinking water scheme operates in the village as also natural water sources (springs) exist, the water of which is used both for humans and cattle. The road between Pangi and Reckong Peo is metalled. The Public Distribution Scheme and the Antodya Scheme are also functional in Pangi.

The programme run by the State Government include the *Indira Awas Yojana* under which 35 houses have been constructed; the *Swarn Jayanti Rojgar Yojana* under which thirty people have been benefited; the National Rural Employment Guarantee Programme under which 381 job cards have been created so far and also five *kuhls*[14] and five roads have been constructed; and the weaving/tailoring scheme under which two self help groups have been financed and one partially revolving fund has been constructed. Of the 569 total households, 158 (28 per cent) are scheduled caste households and 411 (72 per cent) are scheduled tribe households. 77 households (13.5 per cent) are below poverty line (BPL) all of who are identified as IRDP households. Of the BPL households, 27 are only BPL and 50 are also Antodya households. 29 SC families are BPL households of which 3 are only BPL and 26 are also Antodya. 48 ST households are BPL including 24 that are only BPL and 24 who are also Antodya. The total SC population is 684 including 367 males and 317 females and the total ST population is 2109 including 1080 males and 1029 females. The total population of the village is 2793, the male population is 1450 and the female population is 1343. The female to male ratio is 0.93:1. 1528 of the total population is employed (including 801 males and 727 females) and 1265 of the total population is unemployed (including 649 men and 616 females). The average family size in the study area is 5.3. Most of the people are dependent on agriculture and only a very few are in private or government jobs. While a significant proportion of the elderly are illiterate, the new generation is receiving education and some of them have been sent to Shimla and Solan and other parts of Himachal to live with relatives and study[15].

There are two co-operative societies in the village, one called the Dev Sabha Samiti and the other called the Gram Vikas Samiti. There is a Panchayat Centre Bhavan, a Mahila Mandal Bhavan and a Sports Club in the village. There is also a Forest Nursery near the bus stand and five *Anganwari* centres, one each in Khonta, Rantendan, Then Pangi, Ragben, and main Pangi.

Impact of Kashang I Project

A significant number of people have lost land to the Kashang I project at Pangi Khas and Kashang Gram. The *patwarkhana* records revealed that cropping pattern has changed much in all the nine hamlets over the last ten years. While earlier buckwheat including *ogla* and *phafra* were cultivated to a large extent, the main crops cultivated now are *rajmah* and apple, there by reflecting the trend towards commercialization of agriculture and a reduction in crop diversity. A few families have also suffered loss of *chilgoza* and *chuli* trees, with one particular family having lost a whole jungle of both *chilgoza* and chuli to the Kashang I HEP.

Although most of the land acquired/in the process of being acquired for the project has been entered as either *Banjar* (barren land) or *Bakhal* (unirrigated land) most of the people asserted that the land they lost to the project was banjar only to the extent that they could only practice mono-cropping earlier at the dam site due to the extreme cold. They also said that water was not a problem and the barley, buckwheat and pulses they grew on the Kanda land (dam site) were all irrigated crops. Only some families reported that as there were a lot of households dependent on water from a single *kuhl* or water channel, the water was closed for them very fast and they got it only for a couple of days per six months. Others also said that various groups had been formulated, the Vikas Committee in the village had also taken keen interest and the groups had constructed *kuhls* in collaboration with the Department of Irrigation and Public health after collecting money from each member in the group. Some families complained that the compensation they received in lieu of the land was too little, especially given the fact that their land they got compensation for was undivided and the money had to be divided amongst a significant number of individuals. Others said that the division of their joint family households took place only because of the project and now some of them are coping with living in a single room with their divided families and trying to organize funds to reconstruct their houses.

Impact on Culture and Ecology

A number of people said that there were strong interlinkages between culture, ecology and agriculture/horticulture in their village Pangi which were likely to get impacted by the project as the traditional livelihood bases will be disrupted with the coming of the project. Also there were other reasons as the younger generation was getting western education and getting computer trained etc they were not interested in agriculture and were looking for regular government jobs or other private sector jobs. The most important deities in the village are Shishiring and Nagis, both of who are worshipped together. Also Shishiring's mother and Buddhist deities have temples dedicated to them in the Village Pangi. An interesting conversation, took place among the locals rendering their free labour for construction in the main Shishiring-Nagis temple, when I and my group members were taking pictures of the carvings on the exteriors of the village. Some of the people tried to stop us saying that in any case we will be embarrassed as the pictures will not come and our camera rolls will turn blank. The others started laughing at those who said this and conveyed to them in the local language that they are the ones who are likely to get embarrassed because all previous experiences with tourists have revealed that pictures with the deities do come.

However the co-existence between the Hindu and the Buddhist Gods and the strong community bonds that existed in the village as people worked together for the re-construction of the temple, and there were others who cooked for them (tea and food), was exemplary. While some people said that respect, love and fear of the deities will not allow radical change, there were others who were sceptical and said already the scenario had changed and it could be observed in that although there were a few young girls offering free labour at the temples, there were no young men.

There are three temples involving the deity *Sheshering*, including one dedicated to his mother; one that he shares with *Nagis*[16] and one that is dedicated to *Sheshering* alone. There are also two Buddhist temples including one for *Jhumos* (Buddhist nuns). The most important festival was *Dakhren* which revealed strong bonds that continued between the living and the dead. The people pointed to a place on a peak where they had dug flags and said that both men and women went there every year and carried things which their dead ancestors liked in terms of food and wine. Some women said that they dressed in clothes and jewels which their mothers, grandmothers liked when they were alive. A fair is held in Pangi from the 15th to the 17th of July every year in the memory of the dead. Pictures of the dead are adorned in garlands made of *chilgoza* and *chuli* seeds.

During occasions such as marriage and birth as well wearing garlands made of *chilgoza* and *chuli* seeds are considered auspicious. *chilgoza* and *chuli* are used also in the worship of the deities. The first garland when the *chilgoza* is in fruit and the first bottle of wine made locally from *chuli* is offered to the deity. However some residents said that the ecology of the area was changing and the availability of *chilgoza* and *chuli* was declining both as *chilgoza* forests had either been replaced with apple or axed because of the power projects. Some *chuli* forests have also been acquired by the HEP for clearing the land for their colony. People complained that no compensation is enough for *chilgoza* forests as a *chilgoza* tree planted today starts giving fruit after fifty years. Others said that in any case there is hardly any *chilgoza* and even before the project some areas had been uprooted of *chilgoza* to clear for apple plantations. Hence while earlier the conservation of *chilgoza* forests was considered important so that the area received good snow, the ecological and cultural contexts are changing. Commercialization and development projects have all taken their toll and the belief systems of the people are changing.

Cropping Patterns

Cropping patterns in the village have changed. Earlier though there was mono-cropping in the *Kanda*[17] areas (where land has been acquired by the project for construction of dam) all of barley, buckwheat and local varieties of *rajmah* (pulses) were being cultivated. However now only *rajmah* is being cultivated in the *kanda* area and some people have apple orchards. People said that glaciers originating from the *Kanda* often spoilt produce in the Khonta and Pangi *mohals* but earlier people always had incentive for hard work in agriculture. In Pangi, Khonta, and Kashang Gatinge *mohals* where land has been mainly acquired for the project apart from the Kanda area, also earlier barley, buckwheat (*ogla, phafra*), *chuli* and *chilgoza* were significant crops but now the main crops are *rajmah* and apple.

Social Exclusion

Although caste barriers exist and are manifested in that people don't share the same water sources with the scheduled castes, it emerged that the traditional system gave due acknowledgement to the scheduled castes and included them in the worship of the deities. Singing and playing of instruments by them is considered auspicious. While 28 per cent of the households in Pangi are scheduled caste very few could be found for survey, revealing that some of them have jobs outside and are maintaining second homes. However it appears that although jobs and economic security among scheduled caste had emerged, caste barriers are reiterated at other levels such as exclusionary patterns in children being able to attend *Anganwaris* and exclusion from social ceremonies and temple interiors, not being able to entre upper castes kitchens etc.

Conclusions

In Himachal Pradesh, development which is not inclusive is resulting in caste and gender differences being reiterated. Caste and gender differences which were to an extent obliterated in the State are being reiterated where these projects are coming up at a fast pace. The reiteration takes place in a very symbolic context in the worship of the deity, while the real essence of the deity culture is getting lost. The deity culture and traditional knowledge related to ecological conservation and folk medicine are/were an integrated whole in most parts of the State. This culture had been for centuries connecting people and conserving ecology, and language. However these deities who were the spirits of the sacred groves and sanctuaries are losing out to the development projects and so are the common bonds of reverence that united communities.

The juvenile sex ratio in the State is declining rapidly and the growth rate of incidences of violence against women has been high over the last few years. In terms of the many dimensions of village life a lot seems to be changing in rural culture. On the economic front, even prosperous landowners seek a future outside their village or in non-farm enterprises. While the poorer villagers have urban aspirations, the rural rich engage with the outside world from a position of relative strength. However more than the former, they and especially their youth see their future outside the village. Agriculture is reducing in the villages to an economic residue that generously accommodates non-achievers resigned to a life of enforced satisfaction. It is no longer profitable to cultivate land and real estate appears to be a viable option. Policy and policy-makers need to address these issues along with questions such as – 'Whose development and at what cost?' Issues related to the dilemma of the people as change is catching on at a fast pace are not only issues of academic interest for students of anthropology, political ecology, gender studies and social philosophy, but also issues deserving immediate interventions based on a people-centric/sensitive development policy. It is emerging that women and children are the victims of this negative scenario for agriculture.

People engaged in movements in Himachal Pradesh have identified their needs as policy interventions for rehabilitation and determination of compensation, lobbying against land acquisition process and exemptions in compulsory land acquisition under Section 118. State level networking and advocacy for bringing together communities in project affected or project proposed areas to build an alliance to influence the Government is also considered important. Apart from mobilizing communities to understand the politics for development and displacement and building capacity in them to understand various legislations and protective provisions in law, the need for highlighting issues in the media has also been identified.

Research in different parts and districts in Himachal Pradesh reveals that the scenario is much the same. Communities mentioned lack of political will in agriculture promotion and extension, lack of irrigation facilities, preference for real estate as agriculture was no longer profitable, land acquisition, the youth having lost interest in agriculture and wanting alternate livelihoods, as the main reasons for the decline in agriculture. On the other hand political will prefers Corporate and International Agencies investments in hydro power and mining.

From 1981 to 2012, as per the Forest Department's own data, more than 10,000 hectares of forest land, on which people had user rights, have been diverted for hydropower, mining, roads and other projects. This does not include the thousands of hectares of forest lands diverted for projects like Bhakra dams before 1980. As in many parts of the country, agriculture and the agriculture communities suffer. Much ecological and environmental loss results, also lost in the process are the rich cultures and the indigenous knowledge regarding conservation, traditional medicine, cuisine and much more that is based on the Ecology.

Acknowledgement

The project on which this research article is based was funded by the Indian Council of Social Science Research (ICSSR). However, the responsibility for the facts stated, opinions expressed, and conclusions reached is entirely that of the project director/author and not of the Indian Council of Social Science Research.

NOTES

1. Himachal Pradesh, a State located in the North Western Himalayas, covers an area of about 56 thousand square kms and has a population of almost 6.9 million according to the 2011 census. Administratively, the State is organized into 12 districts, 75 tehsil and as many development blocks. Himachal Pradesh, though envied for its water resources as a source of power, however hydel power generation makes a huge demand on investment, carries immense rehabilitation and ecological costs and requires a long gestation period (*Himachal Pradesh Development Report, 2014,* Planning Commission). Forest land constitutes about two-thirds of the total geographical area of the State, however it is also being diverted for various state-sponsored developmental activities and infrastructure building. The major share of this diversion is on account of hydro electric projects and related activities including laying of transmission lines. Development of communication network including construction of roads and setting up of industry, particularly limestone based, is causing other areas to shift land use from forests.

2. Minocha, Richa (2008).
3. Report of the National Social Forestry Project, USAID/IDA, New Delhi, 1993.
4. Survey conducted under ICSSR project 'Development at what Cost? A Study of Migration, Loss of Livelihood Security and Development-induced Resettlement in Himachal Pradesh'
5. Survey conducted by an organization Jan Abhiyan Sanstha (JAS) in Himachal Pradesh
6. http://www.forcedmigration.org/research-resources/expert-guides/development-induced-displacement-and-resettlement/global-overview
7. hectare
8. Pratibha Chauhan (2015). *The Tribune*, March 2. Retrieved 10 March, 2015 from http://www.tribuneindia.com/news/himachal/renuka-dam-project-gets-moef-approval/48913.html
9. The Bhakra dam across the river Satluj was proposed in the year 1944 in the Bilaspur State. The construction of Bhakra dam was to result in submergence of a large territory of the Bilaspur State but would benefit the Province of Punjab. Hence, the Raja of Bilaspur agreed to the proposal only on certain terms and conditions detailed in a draft agreement which was to be executed on behalf of the Raja of Bilaspur and the Province of Punjab. These terms and conditions included payment of royalties for generation of power from the water of the reservoir of the Bhakra dam. The formal agreement between the Raja of Bilaspur and the province of Punjab, could not be executed as the Bilaspur State ceded to the Dominion of India in 1948. When the Constitution of India was adopted in the year 1950, Bilaspur and Himachal Pradesh were specified as Part-C States in the First Schedule to the Constitution. In 1954, Bilaspur and Himachal Pradesh were united to form a new State of Himachal Pradesh under the Himachal Pradesh and Bilaspur (New States) Act, 1954. The new State, however, continued to be a Part-C State until it became a Union Territory by the Constitution (7th Amendment) Act, 1956. In 1966, Parliament enacted the Punjab Reorganization Act, 1966 which bifurcated the erstwhile State of Punjab to two States, Punjab and Haryana, and transferred some of the territories of the erstwhile State of Punjab to the Union Territory of Himachal Pradesh. With effect from 25.01.1971, this Union Territory of Himachal Pradesh became a full-fledged State by the State of Himachal Pradesh Act, 1970. The new State of Himachal Pradesh thus constitutes (i) the erstwhile Part-C State of Bilaspur; (ii) the erstwhile Part-C State

of Himachal Pradesh and (iii) the transferred territories of State of Punjab.

10. A movement for the proper settlement of Bhakra dam oustees since the majority of people who gave their land for the 'new temple of resurgent India', in Jawaharlal Nehru's words, have not got their dues in the past 50 years.
11. Anand Bodh (2016). CMs' meet to settle HP's share deferred, *Times of India*, June 21.
12. Nuts
13. Apricot
14. Water channel
15. Survey of Pangi revenue village conducted in 2012 under ICSSR project
16. Snake Gods and Goddesses
17. Common property resources used as grasslands

REFERENCES

Appa, G. and G Patel. 1996. 'Unrecognised, Unnecessary and Unjust Displacement: Case studies from Gujarat, India.' In Understanding Impoverishment: The Consequences of Development-induced Displacement, edited by C McDowell. Providence, RI and Oxford: Berghahn. Pp. 139-150.

Asher, Manshi. 2010. 'Diverting the Real Issues.' *Hindustan Times*, OPED, December 3, 2010. Retrieved October 2011 from http://www.hindustantimes.com/editorial-views-on/chunk-ht-ui-viewseditorialsectionpage-oped/Diverting-the-real-issues/Article1-633659.aspx.

Cernea, M M. 2000. 'Risks, Safeguards and Reconstruction: A Model for Population Displacement and Resettlement.' In *Risks and Reconstruction: Experiences of Resettlers and Refugees*, edited by M M Cernea and C McDowell. Washington, DC: The World Bank. Pp. 11-55.

Cernea, M M. 1996. *Eight Main Risks: Impoverishment and Social Justice in Resettlement*. Washington, DC: The World Bank, Environment Department.

Chambers, R. 1985. *Rural Development: Putting the Last First*. London: Longman.

Chambers, R. and J Jiggins. 1987. 'Agricultural Research for Resource-Poor Farmers, Part II: A Parsimonious Paradigm.' *Agricultural Administration and Extension* 27: 109-128.

Chambers, R., A Pacey. and L A Thrupp, eds. 1989. *Farmer First: Farmer*

Innovation and Agricultural Research. London: Intermediate Technology Publications and New York: Bootstrap.

Donato, K M., Donna Gabaccia., Jennifer Holdaway., Manalansan IV., Martin. and P R Pessar. 2006. 'A Glass Half Full? Gender in Migration Studies. Introduction to the Special Issue on Gender and Migration.' *International Migration Review* 40, No. 1: 3-26.

Drèze, J M., Samson. and S Singh, eds. 1997. *The Dam and the Nation: Displacement and Resettlement in the Narmada Valley*. Delhi: Oxford University Press.

Feeney, P. 1998. *Accountable Aid: Local Participation in Major Projects*. Oxford: Oxfam Publications.

Hansungule, Michelo., Patricia Feeney. and Robin, Palmer. 1998. *Report on Land Tenure Insecurity on the Zambian Copperbelt*. Oxford: Oxfam GB in Zambia.

Hayes, Juliette. 1999. *Participatory Development: Militating against Impoverishment in Involuntary Resettlement*. MSc Dissertation, London School of Economics and Political Science, London University.

Hewitson, G J. 2001. 'The Disavowal of the Sexed Body in Neoclassical Economics.' In *Postmodernism, Economics and Knowledge*, edited by S Cullenberg., J Amariglio. and D F Ruccio. London/New York: Routledge.

Inter Governmental Panel on Climate Change (IPCC). 2001. *Third Assessment Report on Climate Change* – The Scientific Basis.

Koenig, D. and T Diarra. 1998. 'Les enjeux de la politique locale dans la réinstallation: Stratégies foncières des populations réinstallées et hôtes dans la zone du barrage de Manantali.' *Autrepart: Cahiers des Sciences Humaines nouvelle série numéro* 5:29-44.

Lassailly-Jacob, Véronique.1996. 'Land-based Strategies in Dam-related Resettlement Programmemes in Africa. In *Understanding Impoverishment: The Consequences of Development-induced Displacement*, edited by C McDowell. Providence, RI and Oxford: Berghahn.

Levitt, Peggy. and N G Schiller. 2004. 'Conceptualizing Simultaneity: A Transnational Social Field Perspective on Society.' *International Migration Review* 38, No. 3: 1002-1039.

Mahapatra, L K. 1999. *Resettlement, Impoverishment and Reconstruction in India: Development for the Deprived*. New Delhi: Vikas Publishing House.

Meikle, Sheilah. and Julian Walker. 1998. *Resettlement Policy and Practice in China and the Philippines*. Escor Research Scheme Number R6802. London: Development Planning Unit, University College.

Minocha, Richa. 2005. 'A Case for Nature Based Tourism in Himachal Pradesh—The Great Himalayan National Park.' *The Green Portal Tourism Journal 2*, No. 2: 35-62.

————. 2008. *Environment, Agriculture and Community in Himachal Pradesh*. Mumbai: Himalaya Publishing House.

————. 2009. 'Ecological and Cultural Dimensions in Development - A Case of Selected Villages in Shimla District.' Draft Working paper, Asia Research Centre, London School of Economics and Political Science. Unpublished Document.

————. 2015. 'Gender, Environment and Social Transformation: A Case of Selected Villages in Himachal Pradesh.' *Indian Journal of Gender Studies 22*, No. 3: 1 23.

Morokvasic, Mirjana. 1984. 'Birds of Passage are also Women.' *International Migration Review 18*, No. 4: 886-907.

Pandey, Balaji. 1998. *Depriving the Underprivileged for Development*. Bhubaneswar: Institute for Socio-economic Development.

Pearce, D W. 1999. 'Methodological Issues in the Economic Analysis for Involuntary Resettlement Operations.' In *The Economics of Involuntary Resettlement: Questions and Challenges*, edited by M M Cernea. Washington, DC: The World Bank.

Pessar, P R. 1999. 'The Role of Gender, Households and Social Networks in the Migration Process: A Review and Appraisal.' In *The Handbook of International Migration: The American Experience* edited by C Hirschman., P Kasinitz. and J DeWind. New York: Russel Sage Foundation.

Peterson W. 1966. 'A General Typology of Migration.' In *Readings in the Sociology of Migration*, edited by C J Jansen. Great Britain: Pergamon Press.

Portes, A., and De Wind, Josh. 2004. 'A Cross-Atlantic Dialogue: The Progress of Research and Theory in the Study of International Migration.' *International Migration Review 38*, No. 3: 828-851.

Rao, Nitya. and R Kumar. 1997a. 'Land Rights and Women: Case of Santhals.' *Economic and Political Weekly 32*, No. 23: 1307-09.

Rao, Nitya. and R Kumar. 1997b. 'Women's Labour and Migration: The Case of the Santhals.' *Economic and Political Weekly 32*, No. 50: 3187-3189.

Salem-Murdock, M., M Niasse., J Magistro., C Nuttall., M Horowitz M. and O Kane. 1994. *Les Barrages de la Controverse: Le cas de la Vallée du Fleuve Sénégal*. Paris: Harmattan.

Scudder, T. 1996. 'Development-induced Impoverishment, Resistance and River-basin Development.' In *Understanding Impoverishment: The Consequences of Development-induced Displacement*, edited by C

McDowell. Oxford: Berghahn Books.

Simmons, I G. 1974. *The Ecology of Natural Resources*. London: Edward Arnold Ltd.

Taneja, Bansuri. and Thakkar Himanshu. 2000. *Large Dams and Displacement in India*. Cape Town, South Africa: Submission No. SOC166 to the World Commission on Dams. Retrieved September 5, 2012 from http://www.dams.org/kbase/submissions/showsub.php?rec=SOC166.

Thangaraj, S.1996. 'Impoverishment Risks Analysis: A Methodological Tool for Participatory Resettlement Planning.' In *Understanding Impoverishment: The Consequences of Development-induced Displacement*, edited by C McDowell. Oxford: Berghahn Books.

Titilola, S O. and David Marsden. 1999. 'Indigenous Knowledge as Reflected in Agriculture and Rural Development.' In *The Cultural Dimension of Development: Indigenous Knowledge Systems*, edited by D M Warren., L J Slikkerveer. and D Brokensha. London: Intermediate Technology Publications Ltd.

Waldram, James. 1988. *As long as the Rivers Run: Hydroelectric Development and Native Communities in Western Canada*. Winnipeg: University of Manitoba Press.

Wichterich, Christa. 2009. 'Free Trade Policies and Impact on Sustainable Development, Social and Gender Justice: A Case Study of the EU-India Trade Relations.' Workshop on Focus on the Global South, India and WIDE (Brussels) organized by Heinrich Boell Foundation (India), Centad (New Delhi), ICR (New Delhi).

World Bank Environment Department Report (1996). Retrieved March 10, 2013 from

http://www.forcedmigration.org/research-resources/expert-guides/development-induced-displacement-and-resettlement/global-overview.

13

Emergence of Megacity: Impact on Poor – An Analysis Based on the Field Study in the Peri-Urban Areas of Hyderabad

B Suresh Reddy

I Introduction

Last two decades witnessed changes in the land use from agricultural to residential and industrial in the peri-urban areas of Hyderabad. Simultaneously, changes in livelihoods of different groups have taken place. Many changes were seen in relation to access to land. In this scenario, mechanisms which regulate access to and management of such resources are essential. These include land tenure systems and the role of local Government in negotiating the priorities of different users and in providing a regulatory framework which safeguards the needs of the most vulnerable groups while at the same time, making provision for the requirements of economic and population growth. Such mechanisms continue to call for attention, to make it possible for more vulnerable groups to successfully plot a course through this increasingly complex 'landscape'. If we do not conceive the synergies between urban and rural areas, both the urban and rural poor may get left behind (Garret and Chowdhary, 2005). In this context, a study was conducted during the year 2005-06 for looking at the land tenure issues in the peri-urban areas and then to put forth policy recommendations on how to strengthen the hands of the poor during these changes. The objective of this paper has been to bring out the changes in land use that are taking place in the peri-urban areas of the emerging megacity Hyderabad and also to analyze its impact on people' life with a focus on the poor.

This paper has been organized into eight sections including this introduction. Section two is on study area, data and methodology of the study. Basic features of the study area are discussed in section three. Changes in land prices have been discussed in the fourth section. Issues in land transactions have been presented in section five. Impact of real estate and development activities have been discussed in the sixth section. In the seventh section impact of development on the poor and Dalits is discussed. In the last section, some conclusions are made based on the empirical evidence.

II. Study Area, Data collection and Methodology

To probe the land tenure issues in the peri-urban areas and its impact on people, a few emerging peri-urban areas have been identified for field research. Three areas of the Ranga Reddy District which surrounds Hyderabad have been taken up. Ranga Reddy district is located in the rocky Deccan landscape adjacent to Hyderabad, the capital of Telangana. Today, it is the fastest growing district in the State and perhaps in the country. Several companies, SEZs and institutions of international stature are located there. The research locales include Maheswaram Village (Maheswaram Mandal) which has an internationally well-known watershed and the development has just started. The new international airport is a few kms away from this village. Kondapur (Sherilingampally Municipality) is the second research locale and is quite near to the city and the development has taken place with conversion of village into a part of the city. The transformation has already occurred in this site. The third area is Shameerpet village (Shameerpet Mandal) where the development has started but has not yet got completed.

Secondary and primary data were collected during the study. Focused group discussions and PRAs were conducted with different sections of people who are dependent on land. To gain an in-depth understanding of the issues related to land tenure and its impact on the people, individual case studies were done with the poor, women, small and marginal farmers, large farmers, shepherds, the landless, realtors, brokers of real estate business, local politicians and members of the civil society. The case studies were guided by a checklist. Women, single women, landless and agricultural labour were given due priority while identifying the case study farmers as they constitute the poor.

Over the last two decades there has been a gradual shift away from externally determined, product-based development, to participatory systems of research and decision-making which allow categories of people hitherto excluded to become more powerful (Chambers, 1990). In this study, we used the participatory rural appraisal (PRA), which is a useful methodology to focus attention on people, their livelihoods, and their interrelationships with socio-economic factors. Timeline and trend analysis were done to get a grasp of the basic issues related to land tenure.

III. Basic Features of Study Area

Study sites Kondapur, Maheswaram and Shameerpet were subjected to changes due to the real estate and other developmental activities within their surroundings. Among them, Kondapur, which presently comes under the Sherilingampally Municipality has been completely transformed into a city and is almost one of the prominent places in Hyderabad surrounded by reputed institutes like Hitech city, National Academy of Construction (NAC), Indian Institute of Information technology (IIIT), Indian School of Business (ISB), Satyam Computers and Tata Consultancy Services. Earlier it used to be called as Masjid Banda.

Shameerpet, still presents a village environment with some crops and livestock. Interestingly when compared to Kondapur and Maheswaram, the activity of real estate/economic development has been gradual and was not overnight. The big companies which have come up in Shameerpet are Biotech Park, BITS Pilani, Nalsar College of Law, Surya Vamshi Spinning Mills, Apparel Park and ICICI Knowledge Park.

Maheswaram is an interesting area where the things have changed at a much faster speed due to real estate activity.

Table 1: Basic information/characteristics of the study villages (2004-05)

Particulars/Village	Kondapur	Shameerpet	Maheswaram
Distance from Hyderabad	21 kms	32 Kms	28Kms
No of Households	1472	1280	3500
Total population	5985	7769	25000
a) Male	3154	4171	12856
b) Female	2831	3598	12114
c) SC	320	1428	520
d) ST	60	64	5346
Major institutions/ companies coming up	Hitech City, National Academy of Construction, IIIT, NIFT, Indian School of Business, Satyam computers, Tata Consultancy Services, Jayabheri towers and Shilpa Residency, etc.	Biotech Park, BITS Pilani, NALSAR College of Law, Surya Vamshi Spinning Mills, Apparel park and ICICI Knowledge Park.	International airport, Fab city and real estate ventures.
Land value/acre (lands having access to roads)	Rs. 12-15 crore	Rs. 1crore to 1.20 crore	Rs. 80 lakhs to 1.10 crore
Land value of housing plots	Rs. 35,000 to 60,000/yard	Rs. 2000 to 5000/yard	Rs. 8,000-22,000/-yard
Decline in agriculture area started from	1985	1995	2005
Wage rate			
a) Agriculture labour			
1) Women	Rs. 120-130/day	Rs. 35-50	Rs. 50-60
2) Men	Rs. 150/day	Rs. 80	Rs. 80
b) Skilled workers	Rs. 250/day	130-150	Rs. 150-180
c) Wage labour			
1) Women	Rs. 120-130/day	70	Rs. 100
2) Men	Rs. 150/day	100	Rs. 120
d) Housemaids	700-800/month	300-400/month	300-400

Source: Field survey

Table 2: Land use pattern in research locales

Particulars/Village	Kondapur	Shameerpet	Mahesvaram
Total Geographical area	1942.16 acres	5770.1acres	5001 acres
Forests	-	-	300
Barren & Uncultivated lands	-	1900.02	1600
Land put to Non-agriculture Use	1083.29 acres	364.11	There has been drastic change from 2005 and the latest official data regarding the land put to non-agriculture was not available. However, physical observation of the village suggest that already 25 per cent of the land has been converted to housing plots and some building construction was also seen.
Pastures and grazing land	-	200.11	196
Cultivable waste	863 acres	2249	2000
Other fallow lands	27 acres	572	200
Net area sown	15 acres (officially) Another 25 acres of assigned land is cultivated by SCs	529	500
Crops grown	Jowar, vegetables, paddy, leafy vegetables, green fodder and Mango garden	Paddy, Maize, Jowar, Chickpea, Chillies, Onion and Vegetables	Paddy, Vegetables, Maize, Jowar Castor, Floriculture.
Total Livestock	30	2230	6172

Source: Field survey

However, it still looks like a village. Negligible farming is seen with a drastic reduction in the livestock population. Villagers were caught unawares of what was happening to their village during the year 2006. The change has been due to the upcoming international airport and the proposed Fab city in proximity to the village. Maheswaram is located from the airport, the proposed Fab city and Outer Ring Road distances of 18, 6 and 8 Kms respectively.

The real estate activity almost reached a saturation stage in Kondapur with no more land left except by reselling. Contrary to this, there was heavy flow of money and high real estate transactions in Maheswaram, whereas in Shameerpet the real estate business is moderate and the flow of money is comparatively lesser than Maheswaram and Kondapur. There is still a lot of land under the control of locals. The local residents have negligible land under their control in Kondapur and in Maheswaram the land from villagers is moving into the hands outsiders at a much faster rate. Table 2 gives us an idea about the land use in the three study villages.

Decline in Net Sown Area

Due to factors such as economic development, real estate business, expansion of city, growing population and reduction in returns from farming and lack of interest of present generation in farming, farming in the peri-urban areas of Ranga Reddy district has been adversely affected. There has been a decline in the net area sown by 1,25,586 acres during the period from 1996 to 2006. As a result of this, livelihoods dependent on these lands have also got affected. Figure 1 gives us an idea of the decline in net area sown in Ranga Reddy district during the period 1985-86 to 2005-06.

Figure 1: Status of Net Area Sown in Ranga Reddy District

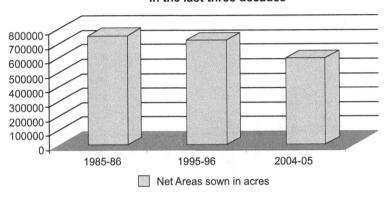

Decline in Net area sown in the Rang Reddy district in the last three decades

Net Areas sown in acres

Similarly an effort has also been made to have closer look at what is happening to land use in the Mandals of peri-urban areas of Ranga Reddy district where the influence of development and real estate activity is the maximum. For this purpose, twenty Mandals of Ranga Reddy where the influence is high have been analyzed. Figure 2 shows us that area under current fallows is increasing from the past one decade and the net area sown is decreasing. Similarly the area under the permanent pastures and other grazing lands is coming down. This has a bearing on livestock population which is also coming down. However, as per the data it can be said that land put to non-agriculture use has increased slightly. But in reality, this seems to be much higher. During the private conversation with the revenue officials, it was conveyed to us that as most of these lands have been converted into housing plots and no construction has yet taken place, and that these lands are being shown than the head other than fallow land. If the area is shown under land put to non-agricultural use, there may not be the necessity of a Mandal Revenue Office in the area.

Figure 2: Land Use Pattern in Ranga Reddy District

**Comparison of Land use (acres) in 1994-95 and 2004-05
in 20 mandals of Ranga Reddy**

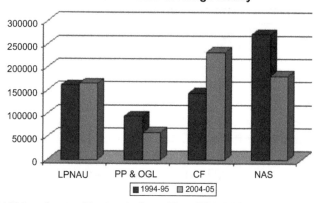

LPNAU: Land put to Non-agriculture Uses, PP&OGL: Permanent pastures and other grazing lands
CF: Current fallows, NAS: Net area sown

Livelihoods

The increasing activities of real estate business, economic development and proposed new projects have led to major changes in the livelihoods of the people in the study areas (Table 3). Previously, farming and agricultural labour used to be the main occupation of the villagers. Now farming takes a back seat in Shameerpet and Maheswaram. Negligible farming is seen in Kondapur. Livestock rearing, vegetable cultivation and dairying still find a liking with many families in Shameerpet. A few pairs of bullocks and some buffaloes can be found in Kondapur.

In Maheswaram, the livestock population has come down with several lands being fenced due to purchase by outsiders, resulting in the lack of grazing land. People who used to depend on the agricultural labour work have moved to other livelihoods such as daily wage labourers and construction workers. The local people in the study sites are facing tough competition from the migrant labour from Andhra. Real estate brokering and masonry have become prominent means of livelihood for a

Table 3: Livelihoods of the Study Villages

Village	Earlier in 1985	In 2006
Kondapur	Farming, vegetable cultivation, livestock rearing, lorry and tractor hiring, grocery shop, dairy, agricultural labour, potters, barbers, washermen, goldsmith, blacksmiths, fuel wood selling, sale of milk and curds.	Construction contractors, realtors, business, vegetable vending, grocery shop, goldsmiths, Barbers (own shops), agriculture labour, stone-cutters, labourers in earth workers, housemaids, software employees, hiring of houses for outsiders, real estate brokers, farming, dairying, whitewashing of houses, municipality workers and auto drivers splitting of fuel wood and job holders.
Shameerpet	Agriculture, livestock rearing Agricultural labour, small petty business shops, grocery, barbers, washermen, potters, goldsmiths and blacksmiths.	Agriculture, Agricultural labour, petty business, vegetable vending, hotel business, tailoring, saree selling, grocery shops, masonry work, earthworks, earthworks under Employment Guarantee Scheme, labour work in companies, All community serving skills are intact in the village (they have moved from houses to shops) and to real estate broking business.
Maheswaram	Farming, livestock rearing, dairy, vegetable cultivation, community serving skills, provision stores, meat shops, shop and migration for wage labour, fuel wood selling, as piece-workers in various places in Hyderabad.	Farming, agricultural labour, wage labour in construction, hotels, meat shops, fruit and vegetable vending, jewellery shops, automobile showrooms, electronic shops, textile showrooms, mechanic shops, dairy, livestock rearing, real estate business, real estate brokering, all petty business, community serving skills.

Source: Field Survey

substantial number of families in all study locations. In a place like Maheswaram all kinds of livelihoods have come up. Until, three years back there was a not even a proper bicycle repair shop. Now one can see jewellery shops and showrooms of major automobile companies.

Transformation in Livelihoods

There has been a change in livelihoods of various people since past two decades due to various developmental activities in the peri-urban areas of Ranga Reddy District. Some households have totally moved out of their previous livelihoods and the others have upgraded their livelihoods according to the demands of the area and opportunity. Table 4 gives us an idea about how the livelihoods have been influenced in one of the study sites.

Table 4: Impacts of Development on Livelihoods of Kondapur

Category of people	25 years back	In 2006
Washerman	Provided services to the villagers	Work from small shops
Potters	Made pots and provided them to villagers	Not making on own, but selling them by bringing from outside
Blacksmith	Provided services to people in the village and surrounding villages	Does not exist now
Goldsmith	Worked at the village level	Now continues work from shops
Barbers	Used to provide services to villagers and police constables in the APSP battalions	Now operate from own shops.
Vysyas	Petty grocery shops	Maintain big provision stores
Agricultural labour	Worked in agricultural fields	Now majority work under masons, do earthworks, work on tractors, stone cutting, private companies etc.
Stone cutters	Stone cutting	Stone cutting

Vegetable vendors	Used to sell by carrying the vegetables in baskets on their heads and roaming in the village	This is now taken over by outsiders from Andhra regions. They have established vegetable shops.
Housemaids	Continuing	This number has increased with outsiders joining the stream
Farmers	Cultivated crops like paddy, jowar, vegetables, ragi, etc.	Now the area is under cultivation has reduced. Mostly Scheduled Caste people of Bikshapathi Nagar cultivate the land given to them by the Government under Lavanya Patta. Cultivating vegetables and jowar.
Dairy farmers	Supplied milk to city	Now a negligible number of people keep buffaloes for livelihoods.

Source: Field survey

Changes in the Livelihoods of Poor and Dalits

Along with the other households in the village, the livelihoods of Dalits and poor too were also affected. Especially, Dalits were more affected due to their small landholdings and their dependency on agricultural labour. When the SCs in Kondapur were asked whether there was any improvement in their living conditions, Gandaiah, a Dalit says *'Ippudaithe, roopaila charana manchigane bathukuthunnaru'* (Now 25 per cent of SC households are leading a good life). Some of the people who got good money by selling out their patta lands (lands with clear titles) also have good houses. Some youths from SC colony work in housekeeping sections and also in security wings. They earn Rs. 2,500 and Rs. 3,500 per month respectively. For other people the daily wage earnings are the main source. In spite of being so near to city there are hardly any degree holders or Government employers in the families of SCs living in the area. The change in the livelihoods of Dalits of Kondapur is presented in Table 5.

Table 5: Changes in Livelihoods of Schedule Caste Households

1985	In 2006
• Stone cutters. • Fuel wood collection and selling. • Worked as monthly contract labourers with farmers having wells. • Agriculture wage labour	• Farming (nearly more than 20 families have 25 acres of assigned land which they used to grow vegetables). • Vegetable cultivation and selling. • Go for whitewashing of houses. • Work as assistants to masons. • Housemaids. • Tailoring. • Splitting of fuel wood. • Painting of houses. • Piece-workers in the nearby firms. • Municipality workers and auto drivers.

Source: Field Survey

From Table 5 it is very clear that the Dalits were forced to diversify into various livelihoods. Earlier they were primarily dependent on farming directly and indirectly. With the total disappearance of agriculture in Kondapur, they entered into a range of livelihoods, even doing not so respectable jobs like municipal workers and housemaids. Slowly similar trends could also been seen in Shameerpet and Maheswaram.

Laxmi of Kondapur points out that all the good agricultural lands are being used for the construction of houses and establishment of big companies. Hence, the women like her who used to depend on agricultural labour, now are left to the mercy of these companies for wage work. She feels that had there been cultivation of crops on such lands the scenario would have been different. Rajamma of Kondapur says *Maku pani companeelalo, canteenlo chippalu kadugudu lekapothe uppari pani, diniki minchi inkoka paniledhu.* (Now we the women have to wash utensils in the companies or canteens or else go to masonary work, there is no other go. *'Musali vallaku panulu levu, kalupulu thesu koni bathukutuntimi. Ippudu aa panulu levu'*says Akkamma an old woman from Kondapur (The old women do not have much work to do; earlier we used to survive doing weeding operations in agriculture, now there are no such jobs). Variations in the nature and scale of rural-urban interactions and livelihood patterns both between and within different locations underline the necessity to tailor policies to local circumstances and to the specific needs and priorities of different groups, especially the poor and vulnerable ones (Taccoli, 2002).

However, according to Laxmi of Kondapur there are quite a few number of SC families who made money due to increasing land prices. Money earned by these sections of people is being lent to the poorer people at a monthly interest of 3 per cent. Even to access these loans, one has to keep gold as collateral security. The women of these families stay at home and are doing such lending business. Lacking formal education and awareness related to other investment options, this seems be the easiest and a safe way of multiplying money for them.

IV Drastic Change in Land Value

The changes in land prices have been mind-boggling. The three study villages present a different and interesting scenario (Table 6). The prices in Kondapur have been on the rise since the announcement of establishment of Hitech City in early 1990. Kondapur is comparatively a peaceful place without much land grabbing. By the time realtors understood the boom in Kondapur, all the lands were sold out.

During 2006, the land price near the Kothaguda circle where Kondapur and Kothaguda Village boundaries meet, was between Rs. 35,000-40,000/square yard. At prime places it has reached up to Rs. 60,000/yard in Kondapur. The per acre land price is ranging between 120 million-150 million/acre. This entire price hike has happened due to software employees' preference to stay close to Hitech city for easy mobility even during night shifts. So, naturally, to meet this demand more and more apartments are coming up in the locality.

On the other hand, in a span of 2-3 years, the increase in prices at Maheswaram village has been very steep and astonishing. The villagers themselves are not able to believe the sudden increase which they did not even dream of. Within a span of two years from 2004 Sept to 2006 September, the land prices have moved from 1 lakh/acre to 1.30 crores per acre. This has been attributed to the upcoming international airport in the vicinity and more so due to the proposed Fab City by the Government of Andhra Pradesh.

It was sad to know that most of the villagers in Maheswaram sold out their major portion of land when the price was around Rs. 6 Lakh/acre. 'Renduveyila nalugulo, thinadaniki thindi lekunde, bassulo daily ayidhu vandala mandi poyyedhi nirudyogulu' says Prakash 'In 2004 people were not even having proper food to eat, 500 people used to go to city in buses in search of employment'. Now, everything has changed. Now the same people who used to go to city have become construction contractors, managing finance companies, real estate brokering and own business, etc.

The activity of plotting the lands for residential purposes has increased in a big way in Maheswaram from the year 2005. This has been due to influence of International Airport and Fab City. Now the sq. yard rate is Rs. 9,000-10,000 in well-developed road side ventures with all facilities. In the interior real estate ventures it is Rs. 5,000-6,000/yard. It was mentioned that a few people (both local and others) made enormous amounts of money in the last one year by acting as middlemen, paying the advance for the agreement and before it was registered on their names they were selling the land to someone else for phenomenal profits. In the year 2006, Maheswaram was having nearly 150 people who were either middlemen or brokers or realtors in the village itself. *'Okappudu kilo biyyam kone satta lenodu, nedu karlo thiruguthunnadu'* 'A person who could not afford to buy a Kg rice is owning a car now' says, Yadaiah of Maheswaram.

An incident narrated by the villagers tells us how the real estate business is flourishing in the Maheswaram. In the year 2005, a person has purchased 5 acres of land from the villager for Rs. 4 Lakh/acre. He has in turn sold it out after a couple of months back to a realtor for Rs. 1.10 crore/acre. The realtor in turn is selling the same by plotting it for Rs. 9,000/yard. For an acre he is making 20 plots of 200 Sq.Yds size. In this way he earned Rs. 3 crores 60 lakhs. Significant is the fact that all this is happening in a short period of 12-18 months. Ten per cent of the land in the Maheswaram village is in the control of farmers and is yet to be sold. They are waiting for the further hike in the land rates.

In Shameerpet, until 1990 the land price per acre was ranging between Rs. 40,000-50,000 (on the main road). It was 10-15 thousand less for the interior lands. Major jumps were seen only after 1995. A huge jump was seen after 2000. In the last six to seven years, the land rates increased 50 to 60 times on the main roads. People of Shameerpet village say that when compared to the other parts of the city surroundings, the increase in land prices in their village was gradual and stable. They feel that, in future too, the prices are not going to collapse due to any negative development in the real estate market. The housing plots are sold at the rate of Rs. 4,000-5,000 per sq. yard on the main road and Rs. 2,000-3,000 in the interiors of the village.

In addition to the increase in land values and housing plots there was also increase in the advance amount as well as monthly rent for commercial shops in places like Kondapur. Earlier a decade ago in Kondapur, there was not much *pagdi* (advance for renting the shops for business) for shops. Hitherto, it used to be 15,000/year. Now the *pagdi* is Rs. 2,00,000/shop of normal size. Monthly rent for a normal shop space is Rs. 1,500 and near the circle it is Rs. 6,000/shop. In general, there has been a sudden spurt in the land prices after the municipal election in 2004. A summary of table showing the comparison of increase in land prices in three study areas is given below:

Table 6: Comparison of Changing Land Prices in the Research Locales

Year	Kondapur (per Sq. yards)	Shameerpet (per acre)	Maheswaram (per acre)
1980	Rs. 5	Up to this period	Rs. 25,000 to
1985	Rs.15	Rs. 40,000 to Rs. 50,000/acre	50,000/acre
1995	Rs. 75-100		
2000	Rs.300-500	Rs. 1 to2 lakh on main roads. Rs. 80,000 to Rs. 1 lakh for paddy fields.	

2001	Rs. 1,000	Rs. 20 lakh on main roads. For the paddy fields it was still Rs.1.5 to 2.5 lakhs.	
2002	Rs. 2,000-2,500	Rs. 30-35 lakh on main roads. For the paddy fields it was still Rs. 1.5 to 2.5 lakhs.	
2003	Rs. 2,500-3,000	Rs. 30-35 lakh on main roads (From here onwards the price for the paddy fields also increased considerably and was less just by 20-30 per cent than that of the cost of lands on main roads.	
2004	Rs. 5,000-7,000	60-70 lakh	Rs. 50,000 to 1 Lakh
2005	Rs. 20,000-25,000	70-80 lakh	Rs. 50 lakh/acre
2006	Rs. 35,000- Rs. 50,000	1.10 crore to 1.30 crore	Rs. 1 crore 10 lakhs to 1.30 crore

* As Kondapur has been transformed into a residential area, people felt it convenient in expressing land rates in yards.

At present, hardly few acres (10-15) of agricultural land is left.

Source: Field Survey.

The changes in land prices have been shown graphically in Figure 3. It could be clearly seen that as compared to the land prices in 2000, there were phenomenal increases in all the study areas in the peri-urban areas in the year 2006.

Figure 3: Land Prices of Peri- Urban Areas

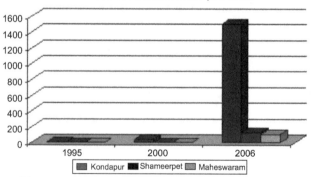

Comparison of Changing Land Prices (lakhs) of Peri-Urban Areas per acre

Source: Field Survey

Early Land Sale by Villagers

In Kondapur village, 75 per cent of the agricultural land was sold out by people before 1990 when the land price was around Rs. 90,000-1.5 Lakh. *'Appudu agvala ammukunnaru'*, says Nagesh goud of Kondapur. Remaining 25 per cent was sold out between 1990 and 2000. The rate obtained by them was Rs. 8-10 lakh/ acre in early 90s and 20-25 lakh/acre in the year 2000. All these lands were purchased by the private people for the purpose of plotting and construction of offices and apartments. Now hardly 6-8 local people still hold on to an area of 15-20 acres. In 2006 the market value of the land in Kondapur has reached up to Rs.12 to15 crore/acre and sq. yd. cost in normal places is 20,000-25,000/yard and in prime places it is around 60,000/yard.

Table 7: Details of Land Sale by Approximate Number of Households at Different Rates

Village	Price	Category of farmers(per cent)				
		Small	Medium	Large	SC	ST
Maheswa-ram	Rs. 2-3 lakh	5	15	2	25	-
	5- 6 lakh	90-92	80	88-90	75	25
	Rs. 1 crore to Rs. 1.10 Crore	2	5	10	-	75
	Nearly 300 acres of land is still left with more than 200 Households					
Kondapur	Rs. 90,000-Rs. 1.5 Lakh	85	75	75	90	-
	Rs. 8 Lakhs to Rs. 10 Lakh	10	20	15	10	-
	Rs.20 Lakh- Rs. 25 Lakh	5	5	8	-	-
	Rs. 3 crore to 5 crore	-	-	1	-	-
	Rs.10 Crore to 12 Crore	-	-	-	1	-
	Only 10-15 acres of land is left with local villageRs.					
Shameerpet	Rs. 40,000 to Rs.. 50,000	2-4	3	5	-	-
	Rs. 3 Lakh to Rs. 5 Lakh	95	75	70	60	-
	Rs. 70 Lakh to 1Crore	1	12	25	-	-
	Nearly 60-70per cent of the HHs of the village, still own a minimum of 1-2acres of lands					

Source: Field Survey

According to some local people, given the land rates there are no poor people in the Kondapur village. But when we make a comparison between the rich and the other people, like that of SC community of the Kondapur itself, there is a drastic difference and in fact they have relatively become much poorer now. Similar is the opinion of Narsamma, a Dalit woman from Maheswaram village. A couple of years back, she sold a piece of her land for Rs. 3,00,000/acre. But the same land rate at present is Rs. 1 crore. Despite earning money earlier, seeing the present situation, she says, *'Daridram ma venuke undi'* (the bad luck is after us). She adds further, saying, 'Original land-owners like us have become poorer and the people who purchased lands from us have become much richer'. Efforts have to be made to understand, how people having lost their lands have eventually been co-opted into the new economic order and how many have remained victims of the development (Sharma, 2002).

Just like in Kondapur, even in the Shameerpet, some of the villagers sold out land when the price was around Rs. 6 lakh/acre. Fortunately, not many sold their total lands in the initial stages. Only those few people who had to perform marriages of their daughters and those who had huge debts sold out their lands. The real estate activity was seen mostly from the year 2005 in Maheswaram. By the year 2006, almost all the patta lands with clear title were sold out by the villagers. *'Kali Golla kurmolla daggara unna'* (only a few little shepherd families have a few acres), says, Sreenu of Maheswaram. These people had livestock and were depending on them for their livelihood. So naturally to meet the fodder needs they retained the land without selling in the early period. This has become a very good fetching point for these families which helped them to get enormous prices for their lands when compared to what their peers obtained.

V. Issues in Land Transactions

Nexus between various actors

According to a source, in an area of nearly 20-30 acres of Government land, illegal plotting for housing was done in various places in Kondapur by realtors. In spite of many agitations by a few pro-poor local politicians, not much could be done due to the strong informal nexus between revenue officials, politicians and realtors. Police Department also seems to have turned a blind eye to these connections. The people who were fighting the cause had to give up after some time. Realtors also bribed and lured some of the people agitating to weaken the agitations. The people leading the agitations were made to go through all sorts of harassments like filing cases against them, sending some people to jail in some cases, creating rifts in their families and making roads through their lands deliberately. *'Peda vaniki Nyayam leneledhu'* ('There is no justice to the poor in this development') says a local leader.

The realtors buy the land for agricultural purpose. This will reduce registration charges for them. They manage the MRO. Then they take up plotting. In this way, they transfer heavy registration charges to the clients who in turn buy plots from them.

Land Acquisition Notices: Realtors Take Advantage

These notices are being served on farmers whenever the Government wants to take up any activity for the public purpose. Whenever such notices are coming to the farmers, they are taking hasty decisions to sell their land to get a far better price than the Government compensation. In spite of issuing notices, the realtors are knowingly purchasing such lands. People allege that at later stage may be due to genuine reasons/ political influence/realtors' influence, these notices are withdrawn by the Government saying that the proposed project cannot be taken up due to some reasons. By this time, land prices in the area will be increasing by 10-20 times in a span of 1-2 years. All those farmers who sold out their lands for fear of losing their lands get shocked at the turnaround of the events. Being voiceless and powerless they are not able to do much except weep. Many such incidents have happened over the past few years in the peri-urban areas of Hyderabad putting landholders to irreparable loss. These days, realtors are easily spreading rumours in the peri-urban areas, saying that lands in a particular place will be acquired by the Government for the proposed new projects. Losing of housing area by Dalits of

Kondapur is an excellent example to understand how these forces operate. They are doing this to convert the situation to their convenience. This is creating great confusion among the people holding land in the peri-urban areas.

Outer Ring Road (ORR) Proposal hiked Land Prices

After the conceptualization of ORR, the land values in more than 80 villages of Ranga Reddy through which the ORR passed increased suddenly between the years 2004 and 2006. It was learnt that many NRIs, realtors, software professionals, politicians and film stars have together spent thousands of crores to purchase lands along the ORR. The prices skyrocketed from Rs. 40,00,000/acre to even 5 crore/acre in some villages after the ORR was proposed. The highest price was Rs. 14 crore/acre in Kokapet. The registration department has earned high revenues due to these transactions.

Middlemen and Commission

With the proposed new developmental projects and increased activity of real estate, the local households who were new to this kind of business also ventured into it. Local politicians and their disciples, opinion makers, youth without permanent jobs and other people capable of dictating terms at the village level are into this business. The situation is such that even a person who is not literate and cannot even sign is doing this brokering business. Illiteracy is in no way preventing people from doing brokering. Being local they have a fair bit of understanding of the lands, their clear titles and any complications involved with lands. Being from the same village they have good human relations with their own villagers who repose confidence and trust in them. They themselves had a few acres of land holdings which some of them used effectively to sell and obtain money. This money was properly invested by the intelligent people of the village back in the real estate business with calculated risks. Farmers living in the area might find non-agricultural income sources to be more profitable and may go in for land speculations (Renaud, 1979). As the market has seen only the upside over the past one decade, especially with the steep rise in last two to three years, almost everybody who invested in one form or the other has benefited enormously. It has been expressed in a single voice by all categories of people from the three research locales that the middlemen and people who were involved in the real estate business have made huge amounts of money.

According to a source, in 2006, three middlemen who played a role in the sale of one acre of land in Raghavendra Colony of Kondapur area got a commission of Rs. 50 lakh each. There would be around 100 real estate brokers in Kondapur out of which 50 per cent are local. Big realtors are only two or three people.

Box 1: Radical Change in an ordinary person's life

During the year 1979-80 Mr. Rajesh (not the real name) a person from Cuddapah district came to Kondapur. His brother was working as a Reserve Sub Inspector. Rajesh used to give VCRs on rent by taking it to each and every household hiring it. That was his main livelihood. Later on, he started showing interest in the real estate business. Taking advantage of the innocence of local people, he did a good business in real estate and today he is one of the leading realtors in the Kondapur area. He has earned more than 50 crore in a span of just 10-15 years. Local people find it difficult to digest the turnaround in his life. There are numerous such examples of middlemen making money in Kondapur using their brains, knowledge, power and capacity to mesmerize the customers without having to spend much initial capital in business. In this process, many a time they exploited the illiterate, resourceless and voiceless people.

Source: Field survey

Laxmi of Shameerpet is of the opinion that brokers have benefited a lot in real estate business. The middlemen are generally paid 2 per cent commission on the total transaction value. If the deal amount crosses 50 lakh the commission will be around 1 per cent. If the deal runs into crores, the percentage comes down to 0.50 per cent and even less. Sometimes the middlemen are paid by both buyers and sellers. At times, only one party pays. In this way, some have earned even lakhs of rupees. With the money earned, they are constructing houses and are renting them out.

Box 2 : Provoked and misguided by real estate brokers

55 year old Narsamma belongs to Shameerpet village. Hitherto, she owned 2 acres of land. Her husband took a unilateral decision and sold it for Rs. 3,00,000/acre in 2005. He did not listen to the advice of any person in the family. He believed more in the real estate brokers. The money obtained was used to perform the marriage of three daughters. Still, youngest daughter is doing her graduation. Part of the money was used for the construction of their house. Narsamma recollects that the land sold by her husband had very fertile soil, which produced good crops. He was hoodwinked by the real estate brokers and he succumbed to the temptation in spite of other family members' objection. She is very unhappy about the provocative role played by the brokers.

At present, the land rate is too high reaching nearly Rs. 70 lakh/acre. Till one year after the land sale, the prices were the same and later on they suddenly peaked. Our land was brought by some people from Hyderabad. We requested them to return our land. But they disagreed. At the time of registration the buyer was intelligent enough and took the signatures of all the four daughters as a precautionary measure. 'If I think of that land, I become very depressed for selling at such a low price, I had the same land now, would my life not have been entirely different? Those who have brought the land have benefited heavily. We, the actual owners who cultivated it for so long, have lost badly'. Today, even her husband repents about his decision to sell the land. The only solace to him is that he could perform the marriage of three daughters.

Narsamma complains about her husband saying that even today, he does not allow her to go out and work. 'He runs the family and we do not have freedom to go out. He takes all decisions according to his wishes and I am not consulted or given preference in any decision'. Just like Narsamma, nearly 10 per cent of the villagers have sold out their lands at a much lower price. 'They too feel bad like us', says, Narsamma. Out of these people, some have cleared their debts and others mismanaged money by getting habituated to alcohol, etc., and have lost badly.

Source: Field survey

Unexpected Money for Some Families

An old GO of the Government is fetching a few households, some extra and unexpected money. The people of Maheswaram revealed that, in early 1950's a GO was issued by the Government saying that whoever is cultivating the land becomes the owner of it. *'Chesinollake PT antondhi GO'* ('Those who cultivated the land will have pattedar tenancy right' says the GO) says Prakash of Maheswaram. So some people who used to give their lands to others for cultivation due to various reasons had to give up those lands. So the people who were cultivating land have become Pattadar tenants. These Pattadar tenants got rights over the land due to the GO in 1950s; when they tried to sell such land they had to take the signatures of the old pattadars (legal title holders) on whose name the land was before the GO transpose was issued. This was a blessing in disguise for some households. It was revealed by the villagers that some people who sold their own land early for lesser prices, got some more money when someone else in the village sold land at later stages and their signatures were needed for them to clear the process of registration. Nearly Rs. 2-3 lakh were paid/acre for signatures during the registration (at this time land was being sold for more than 50 lakh/acre). These people are called in the village as PT tenants. *'PT ante sagam kabjadar'* (PT means 50 per cent land ownership right), says, Lingaiah of Maheswaram. According to a conservative estimate nearly 25 per cent of the land in Maheswaram is with P.T tenancy rights. This means that these lands belonged to somebody else and due to GO in early 1950s the farmers who are cultivating them got the Pattadar tenancy right. Till now more than 80 farmers were paid money by the PT tenants when they needed the signatures of these people.

According to the villagers of Maheswaram, throughout the Mandal, the land price is around 50 lakh/acre. However in Maheswaram it has crossed more than 1 crore/acre. In the whole process of land transactions, middlemen are making a huge amount of money. There is a minimum of 2 per cent of commission on land price/acre.

When the villagers were asked the reason for selling total

land without holding back a few acres, they replied saying, '*Current ledhu, water ledhu ani visigi poyi ammuthunnaru, manaku bhoomi unnantha kalamu kastame undhani, ammithenanna bagupaduthamani ammuthunnaru*' ('No proper electricity, no water, got fed up with farming. Hope to better their condition at least by selling and hence started selling'). So when they got a few lakhs a couple years back, they started selling their lands, otherwise now they could have made huge money with the same land. '*Vyvasayam koddigananna labamunte, intha thondaraga ammakuntimi*' ('Had the farming been a bit profitable, we would not have sold our land so early') says Kishan of Maheswaram.

Revenue System and People's Agony

As per the farmers, the revenue system which maintains the land records is not farmer-friendly. Especially for the poor, if there is any genuine problem with the land records, it would be a nightmare. Narsa Reddy of Shameerpet, says, '*Revenue vyvasthalo beeda prajalaku yedaina samasyalosthe cheppularigedaka thipputundru*' ('If any problem arises with regard to land records, the poor are made to make umpteen trips to Mandal revenue office till their slippers wear out'). This statement of a farmer clearly tells the kind of problems they go through whenever there is an issue with land records. For problems like '*patta marpidi*' (change in land ownership) it is announced that if a farmer pays 500 rupees fees, it will be done. But in realty, the story is different. The Mandal Revenue Office gives the concerned farmer memos unnecessarily to make him scared. Unless Village Secretaries are bribed, the change in land ownership cannot be done. The whole revenue system has a firm grip over the farmers, their land records and thereby indirectly get benefit during title transfers and registrations.

Role of Patwari/Village Secretary

Across all the study areas, the people, especially the illiterates, backward communities and SCs have strongly criticized the role of Patwaris (this patwari system was abolished in the early 1980s). People complained that they manipulated the land records and whoever was in their favour, their lands were deliberately changed putting other people to loss or disadvantage. Sayanna of Maheswaram says *'Valla daggarane pennu, valle rasedhi, valle kattedhi'* ('Patwaris only used to write and pay the tax on behalf of us, we are totally in the dark'). For the mistakes committed by these patwaris long back, the farmers in the peri-urban areas are paying a heavy price, not being able to cash in on the boom in real estate. All those lands with complicated titles could not be sold easily. People also allege that the lands which they have been cultivating since three generations have been entered as assigned lands in the basic documents. Even today many educated and experienced people are not well versed with the land records. The deeper we go into this subject, tougher will it be for the common man to understand the rules related to land records. With the increasing land prices, the knowledge about the various kinds of lands and procedures becomes very important. People also blamed the role being played by the revenue officials at the local level for the discrepancies in land records.

Role of Surveyors

The details of land and their whereabouts have to be explained by surveyor. They would be aware of almost each piece of land in the Mandal. Generally, the MROs get transferred frequently and the new person depends on the surveyor for land details. Unfortunately, the surveyors sometimes help land-grabbers. During the real estate boom, they do play a key role.

VI Impact of Real Estate and Developmental Activities

Families Became Rich Overnight

Some households have become richer overnight due to the steep increase in land prices. A few households have become richer by selling their own land and some by getting into real estate business and real estate brokering business. 'The one who has not seen a hundred rupee note is seeing crores of rupees (*'Rupai notuchoodanodu, kotlu choodabatte'*) says Ramulu', a farmer from Shameerpet. Vijayama of Maheswaram says, that, 'Now people do not listen to you if you talk in lakhs, they will care for you only if you talk in crores'. This statement shows how the things have changed. However, it was observed that the majority of the households did not benefit as much as they should have. Most of them sold when the prices were just peaking and the people to whom they sold made huge profits when compared to original landowners who cultivated the lands for long. A few households who had large areas of land, earned more, even if they did sell at lower prices and those households who waited until 2005 end and the middle of 2006 made huge profits. Table 7 gives us an idea of land sale by different categories of people in the study areas at various prices.

Self-Help Groups Become Defunct

The real estate activity has a solid blow on the women's groups encouraged by the Government in a big way. The damage was greater in Maheswaram with sudden money entering into the area and people becoming rich overnight. In Maheswaram there used to be more than 50 Self Help Groups (SHGs) which were functioning from 1996. They were among the successful SHGs of the State. Until 2004, there was not much progress related to the international airport and other developmental activities in the area, and the groups were intact. The families of the women depended on these groups for loans. They availed loans for purposes like agricultural inputs, consumption needs, marriages, festivals, petty business and for all other purposes. Some of these DWCRA groups got LPG gas connections as a part of the 'Deepam' Scheme of the Government. After the formation of SHGs, the women became economically stronger, active and clever. Groups helped them to cultivate the habit of savings. They started visiting Government offices and banks regularly. In places like Shameerpet, women from communities like Reddys and Muslims never used to go out. But then came a stage where women from all these communities could be seen visiting Government offices. Errolla Ramalaxmi of Shameerpet says, that, 'Before becoming a member of an SHG, the money used to be under the control of husband or the mother-in-law. Now these women have their own bank accounts and manage the finances'.

Until the year 2004, men used to request the women to get

loans from their SHGs. 'They used to depend on women for their financial needs, and used to accompany us, till the banks.' (*'Rendusamvathsarala kinda maku aasha paddaru, sangham poyi thepondi, bankula loan adugundi, an ma venukala vacchevallu'*), says, Rajamma of Kondapur.. This was the case in all the study areas. Now after this real estate boom in the peri-urban areas, these groups are slowly becoming defunct and the men don't care for women so much as they are getting money from this real estate business. *'Okappudu memu panichesi isthe, karchulaku paisaluntunde'* ('Once upon a time, these men used to depend on us for their pocket money, which we used to give them from the wages earned'), says, Bhagyamma of Maheswaram.

As advised by their husbands, most of the women in Maheswaram and Kondapur are trying to take their savings back and cancel their membership from these groups so as to say goodbye to them. Unlike other areas, the women's groups of Shameerpet are intact. This is due to the sustainable increase in the land prices. The groups were formed in the year 2000. The interest charged by these groups is similar to the bank interest.

All the groups are functioning well in Shameerpet Village irrespective of real estate activity, whereas in Maheswaram and Kondapur, this social capital and united strength of women have been greatly damaged. Some of the women who were moving out freely due to their involvement in the SHGs have been restricted by their husbands to stay back at home. The reason, men say is that 'We have enough money and you need not attend these groups meetings any more'.

Due to the economic development activities and real estate business, the human and financial resources pumped in by the Government in the peri-urban areas of Hyderabad and other towns are likely to be not so productive. Alternately, in future, focus may have to be on the landless, resourceless and vulnerable sections in these areas so that Government efforts are not wasted.

Changes in Lifestyles

There has been a dramatic change in the lifestyle of people living in the study villages in the peri-urban areas due to the boom in the real estate market and initiation of developmental activities by Government. People did not visualize these turnarounds even in dreams. They felt that such changes could be seen only in movies. Everything happened in a few months. Agricultural fields disappeared, and in place of huts, huge buildings have come up. One who could not afford to buy a cycle is now driving around in a car. The land that was not producing even a handful of grains is fetching crores of rupees. Certain sections of households did benefit from the real estate activity. The major changes noticed in the three study locales can be summarized as follows:

- Cars and two wheelers have become prominent.
- People are wearing costly clothes. Each man has a gold ring, chain around the neck, and wears costly dresses. There are separate cell phones for wives and husbands.
- Earlier there was not much money flow; it was difficult to see even a single 100 rupee note. The one who has not seen a rupee note is now seeing crores of rupees.
- People have demolished their tiled houses and have constructed RCC buildings in their place.
- Some people are leading a lavish life celebrating with more and more parties.
- Now all households have steel utensils. Earlier they used to be of aluminium.
- Now the people get up at 8 o'clock to cook food on the gas stoves. Earlier they lived in huts and cooked food using fuel wood.
- Mismanagement of Money: The sudden money in their hands has made some men spend lavishly. They have got addicted to various bad habits which will have lasting effects on their health.
- There are 15-20 such households in Kondapur who have not managed the money properly and are leading poor lives now.
- Hitherto there used to be lots of food reserves in the house which used to be stored in traditional storage bins like Donthulu, Gullalu and Golyalu. Now everything

is being brought with polythene wraps before a few hours/days of cooking. Now nearly all the villagers in Maheswaram together buy 1000 Bibo water bottles. Earlier most of the households used to get meat once in a month, but now they eat thrice a week.

- Human relations are becoming weak; people have become busy. Hitherto relatives were happily hosted for even ten days. Now that kind of affection is not seen. Now the families are showing disinterest in the visit of relatives (expecting that they may ask for money). Earlier, till a couple of years back, when anybody asked for the address of a person, they used to accompany the person till the house which he was looking for. Now the people do not bother even to talk to the person enquiring.
- The prices of lands were different hitherto and the kind of affection shown towards people was also different ('*Appati daralu, premalu kooda verenude*'). The situation was good earlier. 'We used to be very cooperative with each other', says Yadamma of Maheswaram. Now the comforts have increased and correspondingly the diseases have increased.
- The older generation members who were uneducated have become millionaires. Now they have admitted their children and grandsons in international schools.
- The women who did not possess even one tenth gram of gold earlier, are now wearing at least 50 grams of gold.
- People have started going to tourist sites which are far away. Earlier they used to go to places within a radius of 50 kms. Now they go to Tirupati, Srisailam, etc.
- The women are not going out for work now. They are not even bothered to know what is happening in the neighbour's house. They are coming out just to buy vegetables, visit relatives, and to go to parties.
- Now people do not listen to you if you talk in lakhs; they will care for you if you talk in crores.
- The present generation is selling the lands inherited by

them from ancestors and are trying to lead a lavish life. They don't show interest to work hard so as to earn and perform the marriages of their children.

- The olden period was like that of Lord Rama's rule, now it is the Devil's rule. This statement is not aimed at the Government as such but at the prevailing conditions. *'Appati rajyamu ramarajyamu, ippati rajyamu yeminolla rajyamu'.*

Development and Women's Concerns

Though men have been eager to sell the land they inherited from ancestors, women have been more careful and thoughtful regarding land sale. Errolla Laxmi of Shameerpet was one of those women who was not interested to sell her land in the early stages of real estate boom. There were lots of requests to her to sell one acre of land her family possessed. She firmly replies to them saying that, 'If I see temporary benefit, I will suffer in future'. She also says, that there is no dearth of wage work and hence I can manage my life without any financial problems. She expects that ten years down the line, her land rate may reach Rs. 2.5-3 crores/acre. 'The cars, gold and money will not last long', says Laxmi. Tempted by the real estate market and looking at others, if I sell our one acre land, our family will face problems in the future'. Sammava of the same village, says that, 'The land rates are increasing without any control. It is difficult to talk about it'. All the good lands where crops used to grow well are being used for construction of houses. Laxmi of Maheswaram also has the same opinion. She says, *'Bhoomi unte padi untadhi, paisalu untaya maku, yemi kasthamu vacchina kani bhoomi ammamu'* ('The land will stay with us, if we sell it money will not stay for long with us. At any cost I don't want to sell the land'). 'She firmly says, *'Bhoomulu konudu Ammudu maku ishtamu ledhu'* (We are not interested to either sell or buy the lands). *'Once we sell our land where should we go'?* is the question being asked by women. Ultimately, we have to come back to our own village. 'Money will come and go, whereas the land once sold, you cannot buy it again. The farmers who have sold their lands a year back have lost very much', says Laxmi.

It was only middlemen who made these deals possible and the actual buyers from outside got benefited a lot.

Women, especially those from the poorer households in Maheswaram were concerned about the future of the few thrift and credit groups which are still functioning. With money coming in, dependency on groups for financial matters has reduced and hence in places like Maheswaram, more than 70 per cent households, men are not allowing/encouraging the women to participate in group meetings. All those women who used to work in the agricultural fields alongside of the women from the poor and landless are confined to their houses now.

Lack of Social Respect, Peace of Mind and Breaking Relationships

Though a few people have earned huge amounts of money, they are not happy with the kind of social respect they are getting now. Sreenu of Maheswaram says '*Appudu samthrupthikaramga untunde adayam, appudu vandal unte santosham, ippudu laksha unna spotlo ayipothunnai* (Hitherto we derived satisfaction from our earnings. Earlier if we had a 100 rupee note we used to be happy, now even if we have one lakh it is getting finished at one go'). Yadaiah says '*Appudu prashantanga untunde, ippudu urukulu parugulu theesthundru*' (Earlier people used to be peaceful whereas now they are running around and have become quite busy)'. Though a person has become rich, people are not giving respect as it was money quickly earn without real effort. Earlier when one was doing well in farming and earned a small amount of money he was respected a lot for his hard work. '*Ippudu paisalu unna, bhoumammukundu, thintundu antunaru* (Now though we have lots of money and have become rich, people are saying that just because he sold his land, he is getting on well with that money)', says Laxman. Earlier they used to say '*kastapadi vyvasayam chestaru, manchiga panta pandichi bathukuthunnarani gouravamisthundri* (People used to say that they are working hard, growing crops well and hence are respecting us)'.

For some families, access to money has become a big problem. They do not know where to store it. They do not have sound sleep due to this. Money is also creating rifts within the family members like between father and son, between brothers, between sisters, father and daughters, etc. Daughters are asking for their share in the property. Daughters are filing cases against fathers. If parents are not willing to sell the land, children are fighting against them.

VII. Development—Devoid of Basic Amenities

All the study areas, especially the Kondapur and Shameerpet are called developed places. Particularly, Kondapur is generally considered as a highly developed place with huge buildings. But when probed deeper, these places are found lacking minimum basic facilities, in spite of crores of rupees flowing into the economy of these places. The development clearly tells us that it was not planned in places like Kondapur with no proper drainage facility and so on. Land use planning and the pattern of development such as urban sprawl, relationship between residential and industrial, commercial and office complexes do also have a considerable impact on the environments (Singh and Steinberg, 1996). Government also failed to provide the necessary basic amenities to these fast developing locations in the peri-urban areas. With the lack of basic amenities, it would be difficult to call these places as really developed. The following table gives us an idea of the basic amenities present in the study areas.

In all the three areas, there is no single good shop of electronic goods, utensil shops, fruit shops and sweet shops. The weekly markets were completely unhygienic. However, all the three areas had good access to public transport.

What is happening to Poor and Dalit in this Development?

The interactions with the people, especially the poor and Dalit revealed that they have not made much profits due to land sale when compared to others. These people generally had small holdings of land which were having clear land titles. These lands have been sold quite early. Gunduswamy of Kondapur, says that, all SCs patta lands (lands with clear titles and own) were sold prior to the year 1985. They were very small patches,

Table 8: Basic amenities in study villages (2005-06)

Facility	Kondapur	Shameerpet	Maheswaram
Drinking water	No tap water supply. Only community posts.	No tap water supply. Have to fetch from 2 kms./or from water tanker supplies which come to the village	No regular tap water supply. Normal water is supplied by the Panchayat through their taps.
Sewerage system	No proper underground sewerage system	Under construction	No proper drainage
Ground water	Problem in summer	Good availability	Good availability
Individual latrines	Present	Lacking in some old houses. Lack of open place for defecation for the women	Lacking in old houses
Electricity supply	Not so problematic	Irregular supply	Irregular supply
Fogging for mosquitoes / Sprinkling of Bleaching powder	Done only when VIPs visit	Done only when VIPs visit	Not done
Junior college	Not there	Not there	Not there
Government Hospital	Present	Present	PHC [Primary Health Centre]
Good private Hospital	No	No	No
Supermarket	No (likely to come up in the near future)	No	No

Source: Field survey

Box 3 : Road Widening: *How Dalits*
(Scheduled Castes) Have Lost

Dalits of Kondapur had houses near the Kothaguda Circle to which the road from Hitech city and Shilparamam leads. Nearly 20 families had houses on the circle on one side and the door numbers were allotted to them. This land was given to them long back as a part of **'Gramakantam'** (On this land given by Panchayat, one can just construct houses). Unfortunately there was road widening a couple of years back and majority of them lost their houses in that process. They were given Rs. 10,000-15,000 of cash and a plot of 60 Sq. yds behind the Bikshapathi Nagar near to their assigned lands with Lavanyapatta. Given the location of place where the land price is Rs. 30,000-40,000/yard, the compensation amount seems to be meagre.

On the other hand, it was interesting to note that 3-4 families did not lose their houses in road widening. Now the real estate brokers entered the scene. The families were fed with the false information that another round of road widening would be done for the international airport at Shamshabad and the remaining few houses would also be affected. All sorts of techniques were employed to create fear in them. This was happening silently and internally without giving much clue to others in the village. The illiterate, poor and powerless Dalits were not sure of what was going to happen in the future. Comparing the compensation given by the Government to families who had already lost their houses, they decided to sell their houses to realtors. A family having 60-80 sq yds was paid Rs. 10-12 Lakh by the realtors. Four families who did not get disturbed at all in the road widening together sold out an area of 300 sq yds at such a prime place. Presently the value is Rs. 40,000 per sq yd in this area and the value of 300 sq yds would amount to Rs. 1,20,00,000 whereas the 4 families might have been at the most paid Rs. 50 lakhs. If the second road widening does not take place Dalits would lose heavily which they slowly started understanding. Thonta Mallesha, a Dalit farmer says 'Migilindante vain adrushtam, poyindante vadu munigipoyinatte (if the person who purchased the land does not lose it in case if further road widening does not take place, he would be very lucky, otherwise he would lose heavily)'. Only time has to prove it. In the old colony all the facilities were there to them including the drinking water whereas in the relocated place all sorts of problems are present. The only consolation for them is that it is near to the assigned agricultural land given by the Government to them for cultivation.

Thonta Mallesha, 48 years, was one such person who sold out his land to realtors with the fear of future road widening. He got an amount of Rs. 12 lakh for 60 square yard. Out of this he has spent Rs. 8 lakh to purchase a 120 square yard house of a Muslim, quite near to the other people who were relocated in Bikshapathi Nagar. As it was not so good he demolished and reconstructed it spending Rs. 2.75 lakh. When asked the reason for demolishing the house which was not so bad he says *'vallu muslimulu, valla vasthu mana vasthu saripodhu* (they are Muslims and our vasthu rules and their rules of designing a house do not match). 'In this way, he has almost spent the amount' got due to the sale of his house in a prime place. In addition to that he is totally unhappy with the facilities in the Bikshapathi Nagar. *'Akkada anni soulath unde* says Mallesha (In the old colony all facilities like drinking water, drainage, etc., were there and was convenient in many ways)'. His wife Poshamma says *'Ikkada thanalakunte battalaku levu, Battalakunte thanalaku levu* (In the new colony, if we take bath there will be scarcity of water for washing clothes and vice-versa)'. The Mallesha along with his wife Poshamma and four children lead the same life as earlier doing labour work and cultivating vegetables in the land given by the Government.

In the new colony, there is no drinking water and drainage. Recently they have pooled some amounts to get electricity to their colony. Dalits were resourceless, lacked proper guidance and opted for safer option of selling their houses to realtors. They felt it was a far better proposition than the situation of getting a meagre compensation from the Government in the event of the second road widening.

Source: Field survey

whereas most of the BCs sold out before 2000. Households of Scheduled Communities (SCs) also still possess assigned lands which were given by the Government. But the Dalits are not entitled to sell these lands as per the law nor is anyone allowed to buy.

SCs in Maheswaram had lands which were given to them as 'Inam'. Government also gave patta to these people. *'Besthola dantlo, SC's lalo thondaraga ammi loss ayyindru* (Mostly, farmers from fishermen BC community and SCs sold out early and got low prices when compared to others)' says Sreenu of the village. However Scheduled Tribe (STs) people living in the Nagulthanda, Kothvalcheruvu Thanda and Dayalkunda Thanda, hamlets surrounding Masehwaram, still have some lands. These people had livestock and were depending on them for their livelihood. So, naturally to meet the fodder needs they retained the land without selling in the early period. They sold some of their land a bit late in 2006 and got good prices for their lands. These families were keen on agriculture and did not rush to sell their lands. Overall in the village, in 2006 nearly 300 households still have 1-2 acres of land to sell. The remaining land is with realtors.

More importantly, the poor and Dalits in the study villages

Box 4: Dalit Family Repents Early Sale of Agricultural Land

Rajamani, aged 45 years belongs to the Dalit community of Shameerpet village. She owns a kutcha house. She goes for earthworks and her husband Sattayya works on a lorry as a labourer. 'I have one son and two daughters', says Rajamani. The elder daughter works in a vineyard and gets Rs. 30/day as a wage labour. Two and a half years back they have half an acre of land for Rs. 1.75 lakh. 'As soon as we agreed to sell and took the advance amount, someone else came and offered a price of Rs. 5 lakh. As I had already taken the advance I could not go back on my word. She had a loan of Rs. 70,000 on her name in the SHG and she used the money obtained by selling land for clearing that loan in the SHG. Now she is left without any land. The present land value is ranging from 40-70 lakh/acre. Rajamani says '*Ma mama sampadinchina bhoomi ammina, konnodu bagupade memu loss ayithimi* (We sold the land brought by my mother, the one who purchased it has benefited, and we lost heavily)'. The remaining one lakh rupees is being rotated for monthly interest at the rate of 3 per cent. This is being done keeping in view the children's future. In land transactions it is the brokers who are benefiting most; we too have paid Rs. 25,000 to the brokers, says, Rajamani. With such money, brokers have constructed huge houses and are giving them for rents. As many people are migrating to this place these brokers are making good money with the rented houses.

Source: Field Survey

were not having access to any kind of advance information related to the proposed new developmental projects by the Government. They could not resist the temptations of the real estate brokers. They were influenced by the decision of landlords who were selling their small portions of lands from their bigger holdings. Illiteracy was another obstacle for the poor to understand the developments taking place in their surroundings. More importantly, there was no body to take their side and guide them during this crucial time of development in the peri-urban areas. Rajesh, a youth of Kondapur, says, 'most of the SCs are leading the same life as they used to earlier'.

Can Dalits Protect their Assigned Lands in Prime Places?

Gundu Swamy, aged 50 years, is one of those Dalits who had assigned lands adjacent to huge apartments in the prime locality of Kondapur. He is working as a piece-worker in a nearby hotel. Swamy's family was one those who lost houses in the road widening. He lost his house with 100 sq yards and was allotted a house in 50 sq. yards. He has 2.5 acres of land with Lavanya Patta (Box 1) given 30-35 years back during the regime of the Late Smt. Indira Gandhi. His patch of land along with other SCs lands lies in a crucial location right in the middle of residential areas. It was revealed during the fieldwork that some realtors tried to grab it from them, but could not as they were united and alert. Surrounding these huge apartments, National Academy of Construction (NAC) and famous Vignan College have come up. For the past few years, Dalits left the land fallow for want of rains. Now, with the availability of drainage water from apartments and water from their own colony being diverted into small pockets within these lands. Vegetables are being cultivated. Swamy says *'Idi kooda theesukuntarani bayapettindru* (Recently, we were threatened that these lands too would be pulled out from us)'. Kharif season 'when they started ploughing the land, the Revenue Development Officer (RDO) came and prevented us from cultivating' says Swamy. RDO was of the opinion that, if the SCs start cultivating and take possession of the land, they may not be ready to vacate in future. However, Dalits confronted him saying that these lands belonged to them and there was a gap in cultivation due to the unfavourable climatic situation. RDO had to leave the place, after listening to their argument. Thonta Gandiah, another Dalit of the same colony says, *'Operation chesukoni, kashtam Pani Cheyaleka pareshan ayyindru, cheyyakunte thindi ledhu, addam doddam chesthe naralu debbathine aarogyam karab ayyindhi'* ('These lands were given to our fathers in return for accepting to undergo family planning operation)'. After the operation, these men were unable to do heavy jobs. If they did not do, they were unable to feed themselves and their families. So the nervous system of those people who were forced to lift heavy things and do hard work has suffered. 'As our fathers have passed through so much pain, we filed a case asking for the registration of these lands on our names', says, Gandaiah. Now in Kondapur, 25-30 households eke out their livelihood mainly working on these lands. *'Pedda manushulaithe deenimedhane aadharam'* says Thonta Poshamma ('Specially aged people depend on these lands for their bread and butter)'. She adds saying *'vayasollu latest panulu chestahru, pedda manushulu yada chestharu'* ('The youths do all the latest jobs how can the old generation people do all those things)'. Hence, we mainly depend on these lands for our survival.

According to Swamy, he earns at the most daily rupees 40-50 by selling the leafy vegetables and other vegetables being grown in his lands with the drainage water. Swamy says *'Neelu yekkanidaniki jonna alkinam, poyinadikku kooragayalu pettinam* (Wherever water could flow due to the lie of the land, we cultivated vegetables and in higher elevations we sowed jowar. Swamy is the only farmer among SCs who has a pair of bullocks. Other farmers hired the tractors or used spades to overturn the soil for cultivating the vegetables. Swamy grows jowar, hibiscus, chillies, ridge-gourd, amaranthus, coriander etc. Others farmers cultivate crops like spinach, horsegram, cluster beans, ragi, fenugreek, brinjal and okra. As there are many people staying in the apartments, there is a good market for these vegetables. *'Kooragayalakaithe saavu ledhu, kausu neelo givusuneelo posi pandistham* ('There is tremendous demand for vegetables'). 'By using either drainage water or some other waste water we can cultivate vegetables from these lands', says, Gundu Swamy.

Efforts to Change Proposed Housing Site due to Increased Land Prices

Another classic example of what is happening to the poor in this development can be understood by listening to the voice of the poor in Shameerpet. Two years back, for the poor in the Shameerpet village, it was decided to give housing plots in an area of 50 acres near NALSAR Chinta which is quite close to the village. 2,300 plots were allotted to the poor. Now after the drastic changes in the real estate market and increased land rates, efforts are being made to shift the location of the housing area to a 2 kms away site called Jawaharnagar which is the dumping ground of waste. Satyanarayana of Shameerpet says *'Puttina oorla ivvaka, yekkadano isthe yetla* (The villagers have to be given plots near to the village where they were born; what is the use of allotting a plot at faraway place?). After allotting the plots why should one try to change the location questions Ramaraju of the same village. The final decision has not yet been taken. But if the site change happens, the poor will lose badly and they have to live near the garbage dumping ground with poor environmental conditions.

Problems in Relocated SC Colony in Kondapur

As discussed earlier, Dalits (SCs) have lost their houses in the road widening in Kondapur. They have been relocated to another place in the Kondapur and the colony was named as Bikshapathinagar. The place where they lived earlier was convenient on all counts. But the new colony has several problems making life difficult for the poor Dalits.

The old people find it difficult to fetch water from distance place in the new colony places. In the earlier colony, there was piped water supply right in front of the house.

- We lost 120 sq yards there but we were allotted only 60 sq yards in the relocated colony. Authorities are trying to forcibly put down our requests for equal areas of land. BCs and people associated with political leaders are being given bigger size plots by making false measurements of the lost land in road widening.

- Hitherto, the community water taps used to very near to the houses. Water was available twice a day between 6-12 pm in the morning and 4-8 pm in the evening.
- Here in the new colony, there is drinking water scarcity. In this new colony we are hesitating even to offer a glass of water to the visitors. Such is the scarcity.
- Recently a bore has been drilled but pipes have to be laid out and connections are to be given.
- Lack of latrines.

Dalits find it hard to cope with the new environment and have to run around influential people to improve the facilities in their

---

Box 5: Story of Konda Babu: Being a Dalit, Could not Protect his Land

Konda Babu is a Dalit of Kondapur. Just like others in the community, long back during the regime of Mrs. Indira Gandhi he had undergone the family planning operation. As a reward for it he was given 2 acres of land in the village which happens to be behind Bikshapathi Nagar colony. This colony is by the side of road from Miyapur to Kondapur. His brother-in-law was a sub inspector of police and due to this he managed to safeguard this land for a long time in spite of active real estate business in the area.

But the road widening indirectly affected him severely. As the State itself was against him this time, he could not do much to resist it. After the road widening, all those families (nearly 40-50 people) who lost lands near the Kothaguda Circle were allotted a few sq yards per family in his land. As his land was given by the Government and it was near to the road Government decided to allot this land to the people who lost houses in road widening. *'Polisollanu petti bediriyya vattiri, yemi cheyaleka poyindu, migilina bhoomulanni vidichi petti pedhoni bhoomi icchindru* ('The police force was used while allotting the plots to people and he could not do much. Leaving aside all other lands in the village, Government distributed the land belonging to a poor Dalit') says Ramaiah (not real name). All families belonging to the same Dalit community who lost lands in road widening were on one side and Konda Babu on the other side. Finally he had to give up.

Source: Field survey

---

colony. In the Peri-urban areas like Kondapur where only money speaks, who is going to pay immediate required attention to these poor, disadvantaged voiceless people? Is it the officials or the politicians?

VIII Conclusion

Land transaction has been an important area of rural urban linkage in the present economic development. The findings from the peri-urban research locales point to significant increases in land prices due to developmental projects of the Government and real estate activity. Land is changing hands very fast. It could be clearly seen that there was a major transformation in the livelihoods of the people in the fully developed peri-urban areas and in other study locales. This had an adverse influence on the livelihoods of poor, Dalits, agricultural labour and the landless too. Most of the Dalits with negligible acreage and those households who sold their lands early have become relatively poorer when compared to others.

Though a small percentage of families in the study villages have made good money, it was mainly the outsiders who benefited more due to their financial strength and access to information related to the possible future developmental activities and significance of these projects for the development of these peri-urban areas. All those households which could delay the sale of their land due to various reasons for a year or two after the initial real estate boom have gained highly. A few innocent farmers were lured and duped by the real estate brokers to sell their land in the very initial stages of the economic development and the real estate boom. Today they have realized that the decision is proving too costly. Villagers could not visualize the steep increase in the land prices. With better access to all kinds of information, the realtors took calculated risks, which paid off for them. It was alleged by people that a few staff members of the revenue department have also helped the cause of realtors both directly and indirectly. The farmers of all the study locales have heavily criticized the revenue department as such and more specifically the role played by Patwaris/village secretaries who assist in the revenue system at the village level. They are not people-friendly, especially the poor and the illiterate. In this whole process of development, the poor and Dalits were affected badly.

The Government has to focus on livelihoods of those poor, Dalits, landless and vulnerable households who have become relatively much poorer and are being burdened by the high cost of living in the emerging scenario. Similarly, the revenue department has to be made farmer-friendly and procedures have to be made transparent. The following strategies need attention for the betterment of the poor and Dalit communities in the peri-urban areas.

> ➢ Dalits, landless and the poor of the peri-urban areas have to be made partners in the decision making of developmental programmes aimed at them so that their real basic needs are met. The basket of livelihood options for the poor and women should be qualitatively improved. Participation of people is another important aspect of urban development (Ramana, 1989).

> ➢ The revenue system has to be more farmer-friendly, uniformity in all ensuring revenue records related to farmers' land holdings and transparency in work.

> ➢ Protection of assigned lands of the Scheduled Caste communities.

> ➢ It must be ensured that the land acquisition policies/ notifications do not harm the interests of the poor and Dalit farmers of peri-urban areas.

> ➢ In the event of any land acquisition, landowners should be provided good compensation packages which would more or less match the benefits one could get in the open market.

> ➢ Proper planning of the peri-urban areas must be done for the provision of basic amenities to Dalits in the newly relocated areas.

> ➢ Efforts must be made to protect the innocent and illiterate farmers from the influence of realtors. The information related to proposed developmental projects by Governments and their significance should be conveyed to poor farmers and Dalits of the peri-urban

region earlier than the realtors.
- ➢ Illiterate and innocent people of peri-urban areas who got money due to land sale must be made aware of better investment options, so that the funds are gainfully utilized.

REFERENCES

Allen, Adriana. 1999. *Environment Problems and Opportunities of the Peri-Urban area Interface and their Impact upon the Poor.* Endleigh, London: Development Planning Unit, University College London.

Allen, Adriana. 2003. 'Environmental Planning and Management of the Peri-Urban Interface: Perspectives on an Emerging Field.' Environment and Urbanization 15, 135-147.

Banerjee, B. 1996. 'Urban Land: Is there Hope for the Poor.' In *Urban India in Crisis*, edited by K Singh and Steinberg. New Delhi: New Age International Limited.

Bidwai Praful. 2006. *SEZ Articles: Special Economic Zones, Path to Massive Land Grab.* Rome: Inter Press Service News Agency.

Brennan, Ellen. 1999. 'Population, Urbanization, Environment, and Security: A Summary of the Issues. Washington.' *Comparative Urban studies Occasional Papers Series 22.* DC: Woodrow Wilson International Centre for Scholars.

Burton, T. and M Lilli. 1996. 'Urban Foot Prints: Making Best Use of Urban Land and Resources- A Rural Perspective.' In *The Compact City: A Sustainable Urban Farm?* edited by Mike Jenks., E Burton. and K Williams. London: Oxford Brooks University, Oxford and Spon Press.

Chambers, R. 1990. *A Workshop on Participatory Learning Method.* MYRADA, PRA-PALM Series # 1, Bangalore, India.

Chennamaneni, R. 1998. 'Watershed Management and Sustainable Land Use in Semi-Arid Tropics of India: Impact of the Farming Community.' In *Towards sustainable Land use- Furthering Cooperation Between People and Institutions*, edited by H P Blume., H Eger., E Fleischhauer., A Hebel., C Reji. and K G Steiner. Reiskirchen: Catena.

Deshingkar, P. 2004. 'Rural-Urban links in India: New Policy Challenges for increasingly Mobile Populations.' Paper Presented at World Bank Rural Week in the Session on *Ditching the Dichotomy: Planning and Development based on Understanding Continuous Rural and Urban Space*, Commissioned by the Urban and Rural Change PD Team, DFID.

Garret, J. and S Chowdhary. 2005. *Rural Links and Transformation in Bangladesh: A Review of the Issues.* Washington: IFPRI.

Iyer, G K. 2004. 'Status of Land Reforms in Andhra Pradesh and the Need to Implement Radical Land Reforms.' Summary Paper at Hyderabad Convention on Land Reforms and State Repression, Hyderabad.

Oliver, Spingate-Baginski., V R Reddy., M G Reddy. and S Galab. 2001. 'Watershed Development in Andhra Pradesh- A Policy Review, Livelihood-Policy Relationships in South Asia.' *Working Paper 5,* UK: DFID.

Ramana, K V. 1989. 'Institutional Approach to Inner City Development: A Case study of Hyderabad.' In Urban *Renewal: The Indian Experience,* edited by R Prasad, pp. 199-210. Hyderabad: Regional Centre for Urban and Environmental Studies, Osmania University.

Sheng, Y K. 2004. *Poverty Alleviation through Rural-Urban Linkages: Policy implications.* Poverty Reduction Section, Economic and Social Commission for Asia and the Pacific.

Sharma S. 2002. Social Transformation in Urban India. New Delhi: Dominant Publishers and Distributors.

Singh, K. and F Steinberg. 1996. *Urban India in Crisis.* New Delhi: New Age International Ltd.

Sinha S. nd. 'The Conditions for Collective Action: Land Tenure and Farmers' Groups in the Rajasthan Canal Project.' Gatekeeper Series No SA 57. UK: IIED.

Tacoli C. nd. 'Bridging the Divide: Rural-Urban Interactions and Livelihood Strategies.' Gate Keeper Series No SA 76. UK: IIED.

Tacoli, C. 2002. 'Changing Rural Urban Interactions in Sub-Saharan Africa and their Impact on Livelihoods: A Summary.' *Working Paper Series No. 7* (Rural-Urban Interactions and Livelihood Strategies). UK: IIED.

Tacoli. C, ed. 2006. *The Earthscan Reader in Rural Urban Linkages.* London: Earthscan Publishers.

List of Contributors

B. Suresh Reddy, Associate Professor, Centre for Economic and Social Studies, Begumpet, Hyderabad 500 016, Email: srihithasuresh@yahoo.com

Bhaskar Majumder, Professor in Economics, G.B. Pant Social Science Institute, Jhusi, Allahabad 211 019, Email: majumderb@rediffmail.com

Charu Singh, Independent Researcher (New Delhi), Formerly with Council for Social Development, New Delhi, Email: 2005charusingh@gmail.com

D C Sah, Formerly Professor and Director, Madhya Pradesh Institute of Social Science Research, 6, Ramsakha Gautam Marg Administrative Zone, Bharatpuri Dewas Road, Ujjain 456 010, Email: dc_sah@yahoo.co.uk

Felix Padel, Research Associate, Centre for World Environment History, University of Sussex, Sussex House, Falmer, Brighton, BN1 9RH, United Kingdom, Email: felixorisa@yahoo.com. Also Visiting Professor, Jawaharlal Nehru University, New Delhi

K Anil Kumar, Assistant Professor, Discipline of Anthropology, School of Social Sciences, Indira Gandhi National Open University (IGNOU), Maidan Garhi, New Delhi 110 068, Email: anilkumaranthro@gmail.com

K B Saxena, Distinguished Professor, Council for Social Development, Sangha Rachna, 53, Lodi Estate, New Delhi 110 003, Email: dev@csdindia.org

Pratyusna Patnaik, Assistant Professor, National Institute of Rural Development and Panchayati Raj, Rajendranagar Mandal, Hyderabad 500 030, Email: rinkusp@gmail.com

R Siva Prasad, Professor, Department of Anthropology, University of Hyderabad, Hyderabad 500 046, Email: sivaprasad53@gmail.com

Richa Minocha, Independent Researcher and Former C R Parekh Fellow, London School of Economics & Political Science, Email: richaminocha@jasindia.org

Rudra Prasad Sahoo, Assistant Professor, Centre for Inclusive and Exclusion Policy, Babasaheb Bhimrao Ambedkar University, Lucknow 226 025, Email: Lucknowrudrasahoo27@gmail.com

Sanatan Nayak, Professor, Department of Economics, Babasaheb Bhimrao Ambedkar University, Lucknow 226 025, Email: sanatan5@yahoo.com

Satyapriya Rout, Assistant Professor, Department of Sociology, University of Hyderabad, Hyderabad 500 046, Email: routspr@gmail.com

Shubhra Singh Tomar, Researcher, Madhya Pradesh Institute of Social Science Research, 6, Ramsakha Gautam Marg, Administrative Zone, Bharatpuri Dewas Road, Ujjain 456 010

Sujit Kumar Mishra, Associate Professor, Council for Social Development, 5-6-151, Rajendranagar, Hyderabad 500 030, Email: sujitkumar72@gmail.com

Vasudha Dhagamwar, Legal Activist, 101 Asara Apartments, 12th Lane, Prabhat Road, Pune 411 004, Email: vasudhagam2007@airtel mail.in